Mircea
ELIADE

After Spirituality

Studies in Mystical Traditions

Philip Wexler and Jonathan Garb
Series Editors

Vol. 3

ADVISORY BOARD
Professor Jeffrey J. Kripal and
Professor William B. Parsons, Rice University

The After Spirituality series is part of the Peter Lang Education list.
Every volume is peer reviewed and meets
the highest quality standards for content and production.

PETER LANG
New York • Washington, D.C./Baltimore • Bern
Frankfurt • Berlin • Brussels • Vienna • Oxford

MOSHE IDEL

Mircea ELIADE

FROM MAGIC TO MYTH

PETER LANG
New York • Washington, D.C./Baltimore • Bern
Frankfurt • Berlin • Brussels • Vienna • Oxford

Library of Congress Cataloging-in-Publication Data
Idel, Moshe.
Mircea Eliade: from magic to myth / Moshe Idel.
pages cm. — (After spirituality: studies in mystical traditions; v. 3)
Includes bibliographical references and index.
1. Eliade, Mircea, 1907–1986. I. Title.
BL43.E4I34   200.92 —dc23   2013021085
ISBN 978-1-4331-2013-8 (hardcover)
ISBN 978-1-4331-2012-1 (paperback)
ISBN 978-1-4539-1181-5 (e-book)
ISSN 2167-8448

Bibliographic information published by **Die Deutsche Nationalbibliothek.**
Die Deutsche Nationalbibliothek lists this publication in the "Deutsche
Nationalbibliografie"; detailed bibliographic data is available
on the Internet at http://dnb.d-nb.de/.

The series editors and the author wish to thank the
JULES AND GWEN KNAPP CHARITABLE FOUNDATION
for their generous support towards the publication of this volume and the entire series.

The paper in this book meets the guidelines for permanence and durability
of the Committee on Production Guidelines for Book Longevity
of the Council of Library Resources.

© 2014 Peter Lang Publishing, Inc., New York
29 Broadway, 18th floor, New York, NY 10006
www.peterlang.com

Printed in the United States of America

In the Memory of Leon Volovici

J'ai la clé des événements, un système d'interprétation infaillible.

—EUGÈNE IONESCO, *RHINOCEROS*

Whoever believes that the past is dead is an idiot. Behold, it is here, beside us, alive and reproachful.

—MIRCEA ELIADE, "A 14-YEAR-OLD PICTURE"

My brain is thirsty for mystery, for occult correspondences, for cosmic senses.

—MIRCEA ELIADE, "ŞANTIER"

CONTENTS

PREFACE

$\mathcal{M}$y first encounter with Mircea Eliade's books was sometime in 1964 or 1965, when I attempted to improve my English by reading books written in an easy style that also had some interest for me. Strangely enough, it had nothing to do with the obviously Romanian name of the author. However, the interest in Jewish thought took me in another direction, and I returned to read Eliade again only later in the mid-seventies, when preparing my Ph.D. thesis. However, it was only much later that I discovered that Eliade was actually the friend of Mihail Sebastian, my favorite Romanian playwright, about whose life I did not know anything while in Romania. Toward the end of the seventies, I heard some rumors about the possible affiliations of Eliade with the extreme right, and spoke briefly with Gershom Scholem about them in 1979. However, it was only a month after the death of Eliade, in a conversation with Prof. Wendy Doniger in Jerusalem, that I repeated these rumors, which she vehemently denied. I decided then to read much more systematically and investigate the problem. For this reason I met with Sebastian's younger brother Benjamin Andrei (Beno, Benu/Bimbirică) in the summer of 1986 in Boulogne, and he confirmed Eliade's affiliation with the Iron Guard, though he had a rather reconciling attitude toward what he nevertheless described as an affiliation. Some months later I became acquainted with Leon Volovici's plan to write a book on interwar nationalism in Romania, and it was obvious that he was much better prepared to engage the problem. Nevertheless, I continued reading about Eliade, and received copies of material relevant to my interest from a variety of sources, but especially from Volovici. My meeting with Ioan P. Culianu and additional discussions with Prof. Doniger sustained my interest in the topic in the late eighties and early nineties.

Meanwhile, the story took me to much more research of many of the Jewish authors in interwar Romania, especially Benjamin Fondane, Sebastian, Ion Călugăru, Ury Benador, and I. Peltz, as part of my interest in the Jewish past in Romania. This interest was considerably facilitated by the fall of the Communist regime in Romania in 1989 and the much easier access to material that was earlier accessible only with difficulty. The explosion of the Eliade scandal, prompted by the publication of Volovici's book on Romanian nationalism in the interwar period, by Norman Manea's article on Eliade, and especially by the publication of Mihail Sebastian's *Journal* in 1996, and then my participation in different conferences related to Eliade, Culianu, and Sebastian held in Bucharest, Jerusalem, Paris, and Chicago, generated some publications of mine, mostly in Romanian journals and newspapers.[1]

The immense amount of literature by Eliade himself that was printed in Romania after 1989, especially by Mircea Handoca, and the long series of studies that elucidated many important topics related to interwar Bucharest and Romania in general, helped immensely in getting a picture of the background of both Eliade and Sebastian, which also includes other major personalities: Eugène Ionesco,[2] Constantin Noica, Emile Cioran, Mircea Vulcănescu, and especially Eliade's "Professor," Nae Ionescu, and Eliade's older contemporary, Lucian Blaga. Also reading more modest figures from the point of view of literary heritage, such as Marcel/Mihail Avramescu, Arşavir Acterian, and Petre Pandrea, provided some insights. Due to the major contributions of scholars such as Liviu Bordaş, Ioan P. Culianu, Alexandra Laignel-Lavastine, Andrei Oişteanu, Zigu Ornea, Marta Petreu, Mac Linscott Ricketts, Marcel Tolcea, Florin Țurcanu, and last but not least, the late Leon Volovici, it became easier for an amateur in the field to engage really complex topics, when informed by these studies. When attempting to situate Eliade's theory of religion mainly in the context of the Eranos encounters in Ascona, Steven Wasserstrom's monograph *Religion after Religion* was very helpful.

During the nineties of the last century and first decade of the present one, I had the opportunity to discuss problems related to Eliade with a variety of scholars in Romania and elsewhere, including Sorin Alexandrescu, Sorin Antohi, Matei Călinescu, Eugen Ciurtin, Michael Finkenthal, Maurice Olender, Zigu Ornea, Dan Petrescu, Marta Petreu, Liviu Rotman, Tilo Schabert, and last but not least, the late Dr. R. Alexander Safran, as well as some others whose names were mentioned above, but none of these discussions were as productive from my point of view as those with Leon Volovici, to whose memory this book is dedicated. The final draft of the book has been read by Sorin Antohi, whose remarks corrected and improved it. From many sources I received material which otherwise would not have been available to me, and I would like to mention here the kind assistance of Madeea Axinciuc, Eugen Ciurtin, Dan Dana, Dan Petrescu, Marta Petreu, Mac Linscott Ricketts, Mihaela Timuş, Marcel Tolcea, and especially Liviu Bordaş and Volovici. In the final stage of writing the book I used the library of the Center for the Study of the History of Romanian Jewry at the Hebrew University in Jerusalem, and I would like to thank Dr. Miriam Caloianu for her help and for adding the Romanian diacritics. I would like to acknowledge the help of the Jules and Gwen Knapp Charitable Foundation in the publication of the book.

Most of the scholarship on Eliade as a historian of religion that was written in the West, both before and after the fall of Communism in Romania in 1989, is based on his later writings, without taking into consideration, in the vast majority of the cases, the earlier Romanian studies. Such an approach is prone to draw conclusions based on historically loose assumptions that create a linkage between his allegiance to the Iron Guard and the content of his scholarly claims. I attempted to take into consideration also the Romanian writings, not just to allow a more historical picture, but also to achieve another balance between the various aspects of his *academica, biographica.* and *literaria.* Though the gist of the book deals with some themes that I consider to be crucial for his theory of religion, toward the end I had to address aspects of his political involvement, which, though known earlier, nevertheless require, in my opinion, a more elaborated inspection.

My analyses below are based much more on the earlier stages in Eliade's writings, as found in his Romanian writings, literature, and correspondence, which have been known to scholars in the West in quite a fragmentary manner until recent decades. Even the most heroic and comprehensive effort to deal with Eliade's Romanian roots, by a Western scholar during the end of the Communist era, Mac Linscott Ricketts, which was done under great restrictions of access to material, could take into consideration only part of the pertinent literature. So, for example, Eliade's correspondence was unpublished at that time and in fact unavailable, as was his *Portugal Journal,* which he much later translated into English, not to mention Sebastian's *Journal.*

However, due to the efforts of Mircea Handoca and more recently of Liviu Bordaş, unknown material of Eliade's has been published, allowing a much wider perspective on the adolescent and young Eliade. For the time being, all those interesting materials are available only in Romanian. Their importance consists in making it possible to build a picture of his earlier *Bildung,* as a precocious reader with extraordinarily wide interests on the one hand, and to understand the emergence of the more mature phases of his thought on the other hand, in a much better manner.

Moreover, my leading assumption is that without a significant acquaintance with the historical circumstances of Eliade's activities in Romania in the twenties and the thirties, beyond the perusal of literary sources, it is hard to understand the main triggers for his activities. This is not a matter of understanding only the tortuous Romanian politics of the interwar period, but also the literary corpora of his teachers and friends, both in the high school period and in the university years, and afterwards during the thirties, especially Nae Ionescu's writings and those of the members of the Criterion group, which, again, are available almost in their entirety, only in Romanian. I attempted to peruse as much as possible of those documents in their original and translate what I found necessary, but I rely as little as possible on building theories on secondhand analyses, which have been duly referenced.

An amazing part of this initiation into the culture and politics of the thirties was the perusal of the literature related to the Iron Guard, or the Legion of the Archangel Michael, the anti-Semitic and ultranationalistic movement that attracted first Eliade's main mentor, Nae Ionescu, and a short time later on, also Eliade and some of his closest friends. This reading was necessary in order to prevent repetitions of unchecked clichés and anachronisms. Ionescu and Eliade, and some of the young intellectuals from their entourage, became substantially involved in the propaganda of the movement, and perhaps indirectly, also in the formulation of some aspects of its ideology. The pertinent material is itself a vast literature, which includes many books and booklets printed in the thirties, some of them certainly read by Eliade, which are now relatively more easily available, even on the Internet; all this is in addition to the scholarly debates about the nature of this movement, and the diverging accounts of the histories of the movement by various factions of the legionnaires themselves. As I shall try to show, especially in chs. 3 and 7, it is hard to understand the Eliade of the thirties as operating outside the major political and cultural turbulences of this temporal and conceptual framework, and also some later aspects of his thought are opaque since Eliade himself decided to obscure his attitudes of the earlier period, and their possible relevance for his development.

Nevertheless, my assumption is that we should be cautious not to reduce his thought to an adoption of extreme right clichés, or describe him as "fascist" or "anti-Semite," but to understand him and his sources as belonging to a much greater variety of cultural and religious trends, some of them predating his rapprochement to the Iron Guard in late 1935. This is a hard intellectual exercise, especially for a scholar whose main academic interests are far from Eliade's main backgrounds. No less noteworthy is the emotional pressure for a Romanian Jew, and an Israeli, as well as for just a human being, to learn in detail about the ideologies and delirium that instigated the persecutions, discriminations, and on many occasions, the extermination of hundreds of thousands of Romanian Jews that took place in those times and places. Reading several histories of the Iron Guard, written by independent scholars and by its adherents, and learning details of the association of intellectuals to it in the mid-thirties, provided a special perspective for understanding some aspects of Eliade's thought, which needs further clarification.

Notes

1. See, e.g., M. Idel, "*Camuflarea sacrului* în memorialistica, beletristica și literatura științifică a lui Mircea Eliade," tr. Bogdan Aldea, *Apostrof*, XIX, 1–2 (2008), p. 212; my 2002 lecture in Bucharest printed in Oișteanu, *Religion, Politics, and Myth*, pp. 191–196, 210–211; my 2006 lecture at the New European College in 2006, summarized in Alexandru Matei, *Observator Cultural*, 310 (March 2006); "Mircea Eliade and the *Zohar*: Moving Sands," *Kabbalah*, 23 (2010), pp. 9–28, translated into Romanian by Matei Pleșu in *Dilemateca*, VI, 63 (2011), pp. 13–28; and my *Ascensions on High*, pp. 216–231, and "O 'umbră' printre rinoceri: Mihail Sebastian și scandalul unei duble identități," tr. Bogdan Aldea, in *The Dilemmas of Identity*, ed. Volovici, pp. 35–75; as well as Antohi-Idel, *What Unites Us*, pp. 123–167. Most of the material in these studies has been integrated into various chapters in this book.

2. Hereafter I shall use *Ionesco* to refer to Eugène Ionesco, and *Ionescu* to refer to Nae Ionescu.

INTRODUCTION

Eliade's Life

$\mathcal{M}$ ircea Eliade's life[1] can be divided into two major parts from the temporal point of view: the Romanian part, 1907–1944, and the extra-Romanian one, the "exile" years 1944–1986. Most of the former period was spent in Romania—with the exception of three years in India—and then in London and Lisbon between late 1940 and late 1944. During this period most of what he wrote, quite precociously—literature, journalistic and scholarly—was done in Romanian and intended for a Romanian audience, though he aspired to a much more international audience. It is a vast literature, which started in the prodigious high school years, and it includes several novels, hundreds of feuilletons printed in daily newspapers, monographs, and collections of studies. A few of his writings in this period were done in other languages; especially noteworthy was his book on Yoga, based on his Ph.D. thesis submitted in 1933 at the University of Bucharest, which was translated and published in French in 1936, and some feuilletons in Italian and Portuguese. Eliade was then a famous and prolific Romanian author of several novels and innumerable journalistic feuilletons, and an emerging and promising scholar of religion, but he was also thought of quite widely as the leader of the 1927 generation, namely, of the young Romanians who were destined, according to their self-perception, to create a vibrant and vital new Romanian culture, related to the new geographical-political situation generated by the emergence of Greater Romania after WWI. This prominent status, the result of being a successful writer of novels, a scholar of religion who was slowly starting to be recognized internationally, and a frequent contributor of many hundreds of feuilletons to a long series of Romanian periodicals, was unparalleled by anyone in the history of Romania in his generation.

This very promising situation as an academician, a writer, and a leading intellectual, which was evident until 1938, deteriorated in the Romanian political elite because of his adherence, spiritually and to a certain extent also politically, to the views of the legionnaire movement, known also as the Iron Guard, an extreme right, ultranationalist, and anti-Semitic organization. His adherence caused his arrest and detention for four months, together with some of the Iron Guard leaders, in the camp of Miercurea Ciuc in 1938. Following his liberation from the camp, his situation turned precarious, both financially and socially.[2] This is the reason why he preferred to leave Romania in late 1940 as a representative of his country in London and then Lisbon.

With the beginning of the "exile" in Paris in 1945, most of his academic writings were written in French and then in English, and the intended audience was international. This was part of his activity first in France, at the Eranos meetings in Ascona, and then at the University of Chicago beginning in 1956. He continued to write prose in Romanian, and his greatest novel, *Forbidden Forest*, was expressly intended to garner a Nobel Prize in literature. Given the fame he achieved especially in his period in the USA, he was understood and discussed largely for what he did after 1945; he was translated and printed in European languages, but to a much lesser extent, taking into consideration the voluminous Romanian material, which was barely available because of the language barrier, but also because of the restrictions of the Communist regime in Romania, which did not allow easy access to interwar material.

When he embarked on his American adventure in 1956 after a decade of sojourn in Paris, he left behind him not only the Old Continent, to which he preferred to return rather regularly and for long holidays, but also a personal history, the Romanian one, some of which he preferred to forget. However, the geographical shift could not and did not change the chapters of his biography he preferred to relegate to oblivion. Rumors about a rather shameful past started to surface, even in his lifetime, and reached the ears of even his closest admirers among the academicians. This is the case for persons like one of his translators in French and a close friend, Henri Pernet, and Arnaldo Momigliano, Gershom Scholem, and Ioan P. Culianu. It was a difficult experience to become acquainted with these details, and Pernet, for example, preferred not to ask Eliade about them,[3] while Scholem[4] and Culianu[5] tried to inquire, but the answers they received were quite evasive and in any case incomplete. It is not the place to engage his reactions to these questions here, and I hope to do it elsewhere, though some aspects of their historical background will be addressed in ch. 7.

Scholarship on Eliade

Eliade's prodigious, prolific, and innovative writings attracted a lot of attention. The lead was taken by American scholars in the late seventies, mainly dealing with his post–WWII scholarly writings, which were available in European languages, mainly French and English. However, the studies of his pre–WWII period done by Ioan P. Culianu, Mac Linscot Ricketts's heroic monograph on the Romanian roots of Eliade, and Leon Volovici's on the early period of Eliade's political background, were done in much harder conditions, since much of the pertinent material on the interwar period in Romanian was hardly available. Concerning the image of Romania in a difficult and rather shameful period of its extreme right-wing history, the salient material was "protected" even by the Communist party. This is the reason why the analyses of Eliade's thought against the richer and much more variegated documentation was a hard task.

After the fall of Communism in Romania most of the material became accessible, but its sheer amount turned out to be another great problem. A slow but obvious change started after 1989, when both the quantity and sometimes also the very high quality of the studies of Eliade shifted from the non-Romanian scholars in the direction of Romanian scholars. The amount of material that has been printed and reprinted, both his earlier writings, some of which were published for the first time, and reprintings of the old editions, making available material that was hardly accessible, is staggering, and there is good reason to assume that more will be done in this direction in the near future. Here, the many contributions of Mircea Handoca, the devoted collector and editor of Eliade's works since his publications in the eighties during the Communist regime, are quite obvious and extremely helpful, though they are to a great extent technical. It is sometimes also intellectually biased, creating a feeling that criticism of Eliade might necessarily stem from unfair approaches.[6] A very decisive contribution has been made by the recent full publication and the detailed exegesis of Eliade's *Portugal Journal* and other works written in Portugal, undertaken by his nephew Sorin Alexandrescu with the cooperation of some other scholars. The publication of Eliade's extensive correspondence with many scholars that burgeoned in the last two decades, especially by Handoca, added new dimensions to our knowledge of details of his life and thought. So, in addition to the much discussed two letters to Scholem, the correspondence with Constantin Noica, Henri Pernet, Stig Wikander, Raffaele Pettazzoni, Károly Kerényi, and Ioan P. Culianu, to give only some examples, has been edited and sometimes even translated, and briefly analyzed.[7]

However, in addition to this recent *avalanche de richesses* of extremely important material, no less decisive is a dramatic change in the tone and the quality of what can be discerned from the perusal of the analyses published by the young generation of Romanian scholars since 2000. If the first generation of publications starting with the fall of Ceaușescu's regime in 1989 was in many cases apologetic, or attempting to rescue the image of Eliade from accusations leveled at his involvement in the Iron Guard propaganda, the more recent scholars display a much more objective and critical attitude. First and foremost, Florin Țurcanu's massive and outstanding monograph on Eliade in French, describing him, sarcastically, as a "prisoner of history," is balanced, extremely well informed, and replete with incisive analyses about Eliade's life and some of his conceptual developments.[8] A contribution on Eliade's political views can be found also in Alexandra Laignel-Lavastine's critical *L'oubli du fascisme*. More specific topics have been investigated more recently in great detail and in a careful manner in the insightful and indispensable studies of Marta Petreu, Liviu Bordaș, Andrei Oișteanu, Mihaela Gligor, and Dan Dana, to mention only some of the main scholars. Especially, Petreu's erudite and courageous analyses have been a source of information and inspiration, at the same time, for understanding the interwar figures. Most of these contributions are found in only Romanian, though a part of Dana's study on Zalmoxis is available now in French.[9] In my opinion, the Romanian scholars took the leadership both quantitatively and qualitatively, and without being intimately acquainted with it, it is hard to speak about serious treatments of Eliade.

Below I shall deal with some specific topics in Eliade's thought, each of them important though relatively neglected as subject matter. My intention is not to offer a comprehensive or systematic picture of his thought, an issue that is hardly achievable given what I call the incoherence and incompatibilities, which I address immediately below. However, there are also other important topics that are important for understanding his thought, and I would like to deal with them in the next paragraphs, though I am not going to offer in this Introduction an exhaustive treatment. They constitute the framework of Eliade's thought no less than the other topics that will enjoy a more comprehensive treatment in this book.

The Magical Universe

I would like to delineate here what seems to me a major development in Eliade's thought concerning the nature of religion, which escaped the scholarly analyses of his approaches. This can be articulated as the shift from an earlier, more magical universe to a more mythical one later on. In the first writings, especially the Romanian ones, Eliade operated in the framework of what he called a magical universe. This is an important topic in his scholarship but also of his own experiences and aspirations. In his autobiography, Eliade confesses that, unlike what his colleagues think, "I did not have a mystical vocation. In a way, I was closer to 'magic' than to mysticism.[10] Even in adolescence, I have tried to suppress normal behavior, had dreamed of a radical transmutation of my mode of being. My enthusiasm for Yoga and Tantra was due to some Faustian nostalgias."[11]

This is a very precious confession since it reflects the predilection of events taking place in the cosmos, and the harmonization between the human acts and the cosmic processes, over changes within the human psyche. Eliade mentions a piece entitled "The Magical Deed" that he wrote in 1928, but that was lost. However, from the context we may guess that it had to do with "presenting the structure of magical philosophies and of showing to what extent magic constitutes one of the temptations of the spirit."[12] Indeed, discussions concerning the magical understanding of the universe permeate Eliade's early writings, and they constitute one of the most productive assumptions that inform many of his other conceptualizations in matters of religion. The centrality of this early concept of the universe has escaped the scholarship of Eliade's thought,[13] and I shall try to delineate some of its occurrences in his writings. The earlier significant discussion is found in his high school piece entitled "Science and Occultism," written as a polemic with a Jewish colleague, Solomon Israilovici. The latter criticized the interest in spiritism, which certainly Eliade pursued in the later years of his high school, as we know from other sources, and he reacted to Israelovici's "enlightened" critique. Eliade claims that ancient esotericism developed parallel to the more rational faculties, as did

> faculties that remain "occult" since they were not put in use, as it was with for example the permanent intuition, *la clairvoyance*, telepathic communication, and others that we cannot dwell upon here. If by the *rationalist means* we cannot grasp but the external formal aspect of things—since those means stems from the *senses*—by the occult features the "I" takes the direct contact with reality, without the mediation of the senses and without being duped by the *forms* of nature....In one word, they[14] were liberated of the heavy yoke of the rationalist presumptions, developing his pure rationality and also the other occult means.[15]

Later on in this essay, after quoting the "Hebrew magical book of the Zohar" as a very ancient text, anteceding the heliocentric vision of the world,[16] he writes that "I hope that I proved now how the ancient esoteric science knew things of importance more than our science, since it proceeded on a more secure path."[17] In fact, the entire essay is a sustained effort to validate the contribution of occultism to a wider understanding of reality, beyond the positivist type of science. In 1927, he wrote a feuilleton entitled "Magic and Metapsychism" where he proposes a combination of the study of history of religion with some form of parapsychological and telekinetic phenomena he would refer to as metapsychism.[18] In the same year he wrote an extremely interesting short story that helps in illustrating my point as to the emphasis on the more ergetic aspects of the early Eliade, "The Man Who Wanted to be Silent," where the assumption is that by dint of silence, one can become God and create a variety of androidic beings out of one's thought.[19] The extraordinary powers of the taciturn man are denied by the civilized people, a doctor and persons resorting to technology; in fact it is a critique of modernity and its skepticism as to the possibilities found in forms of ascetic techniques, a point that will be amplified later on, as we shall see below.

In 1928, we find an important discussion where the sort of the religious universe and techniques are described as follows:

> We mentioned the magical potency of the word. This is explained by the dynamic, energetic concept of the cosmos. The universe is in continuous movement. There is no immobility. In each movement there is a sound…by mastering those sounds you master the things. An ancient concept of the "names" we can find, from the primitives to the Kabbalists.[20]

Nota bene: The view of the Kabbalists is described as similar to that of the primitives; all this is in the context of magic and power of spoken language, basically some form of vibration. Probably this is also an impact of the Neoplatonic and Hermetic views found in the Italian Renaissance concerning the concept of *vis verbis*, which should also be taken into account.[21]

In a rather ambiguous statement he also suggests that magic should be checked.[22] In his *Solilocvii*, a booklet that comprises in an embryonic manner some of the ideas that are going to become important in his later works, he reiterates the concept of magic several times.[23]

It seems that 1936 and 1937 are the years when magic looms in a sharper manner than earlier in Eliade's writings. It is found in many places in the Yoga book, and in his analyses of the Babylonian cosmology,[24] as well as in his understandings of the folklore. There can be no doubt that this fascination with magic is reflected in the reiteration of the praises Eliade bestowed on Bogdan Petriceicu Hașdeu, one of his cultural heroes, some of whose writings he edited in two volumes, as someone who put a magical net upon the material he studies and upon the universe.[25] Mac Linscott Ricketts has duly recognized the importance of this figure for Eliade, and he surveyed the latter's anthology of Hașdeu.[26] Later on in his life Eliade himself recognized that his early approach to Hașdeu was hagiographic.[27]

In the introduction to his anthology of his writings Eliade argues in 1937 that his predecessor:

> has a huge romantic thirst for synthesis and encyclopedic, of brave rapprochements between facts that are remote from each other. The distances are lost in this romantic vision,

a vision that concentrates space, creating a Universe of unseen harmonies and symbols. The young eye of Haşdeu sees unexpected resemblances between all the orders of existence. It is as if a magical net linked one thing to another, one genius to another, one episode to another. By grasping a thread from this unseen net that unifies and organizes the entire universe of facts and signs—Haşdeu believes that he finds out[28] or reconstitutes any reality, seen, unseen or even "lost." His romantic instinct is, in fact, a magical conception which he found, otherwise, in a good part of his great European contemporaries.[29]

Elsewhere in the same introduction he speaks about Haşdeu's "magical conception of existence"[30] and about him as someone who "accomplished a magical Romanian vision."[31] Immediately afterwards, he describes Haşdeu as someone who "restored the romantic vision on its true axis—the magic."[32] In my opinion, Haşdeu's views should be counted among the most formative sources of Eliade's vision of religion, including his privileging of Romania in the worldview, an approach I shall refer as megaloromanism.[33]

Needless to say, this characterization of Haşdeu has something to do with his spiritualist attempts to communicate with his young daughter Iulia, who died prematurely, which turned into some form of obsession, a well-known tragic episode in Haşdeu's later years that Eliade does not mention in this specific context. It is as part of his desperate effort to remain in touch with his beloved daughter that Haşdeu wrote in April 16, 1888: "I want to untie the secrets of the Universe."

In several instances written at the end of his stay in Portugal, in January 1945, Eliade reiterated his conviction that the magical universe, namely, the unusual, supernatural achievements of the few persons in history, like those of the yogins and fakirs, are neglected in the positivistic approach to the human being—especially the Heideggerian one—and to religion, founded on the basis of the experience of what he calls "the decayed European of today."[34] He mentions his intention to counteract Hegel, as part of his projected book that became *The Myth of the Eternal Return*.[35] Some days later he assesses that his passion for the history of religion betrays

my interest in a world of freedom, lost by modern man long ago. This explanation is valuable also for my propensity (since high school) for occult sciences and magic: the freedom achieved by man by means of certain techniques. Even now I am not confident whether the occult sciences are "real." But at least its world is comfortable: there man is free, is powerful, and the spirit is creative.[36]

This is quite a revealing passage since it betrays some form of hesitation as to the validity of his earlier conviction in the power of magic. This magical approach to the universe did not remain the patrimony of the Romanian stage of Eliade's writings, but was reiterated in some other instances later on. In a review of works of the

Italian scholar of religion Ernesto de Martino printed in 1948, he refers to similar attitudes found not just in de Martino's studies, but also earlier in Andrew Lang and especially in Julius Evola's approach.[37] In this review Eliade refers to some of his earlier expressions of this view in his Romanian essays, as well as to the importance of the Hindu examples for the extraordinary powers that can be acquired by human efforts.[38] It also crept sometimes into his most well-known book, *The Myth of the Eternal Return*, where he writes rather cryptically about the "possibilities of 'magical creation,' which exist in traditional societies, and which are real."[39]

Eliade emphasizes the importance of magic in a variety of other discussions in this influential book,[40] as well as in the later and most elaborated book on Yoga, where he writes:

> Although the magical conception of the world is more accentuated among the Indo-Europeans, we may hesitate to make them the source of the magical tendency present in the yoga complex and to give the entire credit for the mystical tendency to the aborigines. In our view, it seems more in agreement with the facts to find the Indo-European contribution in the considerable importance of ritualism and the speculations to which it gave rise, and to leave to the aborigines the tendency toward the concrete in religious experience, the need for a mystical devotion to personal or local divinities (Ishtadevata, Gramadevata).[41]

We may understand Eliade better by conceiving the nature of his universe as a confluence of approaches found in diverse literatures, like theosophy,[42] occultism, yoga, magic, and folklore.[43] In some cases the amalgam, which is very difficult to describe, has been understood as a corrective to the more positivist approach of science and study of religion, as practiced in the 19th century. All of them informed the very young Eliade, and corroborated with each other in generating a type of universe in which he believed, and which was conceived of as a matter of ontology, not just culturally articulated worldviews. It is possible to call Eliade's approach ergetic, which means that understanding of a certain universe is a matter of doing, performance, techniques, and rituals, and not only a matter of cognition of the nature of reality.[44] This ergetic approach is coupled by an assumption that may be called, following Eric Voegelin, metastatic; namely, the possibility to change the structure of reality.[45] The ergetic aspect is related to the vision of archaic religion as centered on circulation of energy that is triggered by sacrifices, including human ones, and by orgies.[46]

I propose to understand this fluidity as related to the concept of the divinity as power, found again in the early writings of Eliade.[47] This vision of fluid universe allowed, in his opinion, some sort of performances that are contradicting the positivist understanding of the world based on the irreversible and thus final nature of many processes, especially death, as we shall see in ch. 3. Eliade's assumption is a matter of his confidence in the validity of reports in parapsychology, in folklore, or in private experiences, and despite my different assumptions, I do not see the reason to argue with an approach that may, in principle, become valid, at least in small part, because of new developments in science of which we are not yet aware. My concern in this presentation is to do justice to the cosmological framework that was adopted by Eliade not only as part of the representation of a closed past, but also as a worldview that served as background to additional approaches in matters of religion in the present, and also inspired much of his literary writings, though it did not attract the same attention of the many exponents of his religious thought.

This magical and fluid universe is sometimes described as reflecting an archaic ontology that was understood by an archaic mentality, which changed over the centuries and obscured what Eliade calls the practical affinities that seem to us to be unrelated to the positivist form of causality. Eliade's picture of ancient religion as predominantly cosmic is the major background of his concept of Cosmic Christianity, found especially in his opinion on the Romanian space in ancient and modern times, as we shall see below in ch. 8.

It should be pointed out that there is a resemblance between Eliade's early vision of the universe and that of Carl G. Jung, who spoke about synchronicities. Eliade pointed to the affinities between his own vision of correspondences and Jung's,[48] and in my opinion these affinities are the result of drawing on common sources in Western occultism. Moreover, the interest in magic as an aspect of ancient and medieval European culture has its parallel in the somewhat earlier studies done by the members of Warburg Institute in Hamburg, and then in London, but the early Eliade—who visited Germany several times—does not mention the findings of the Warburg school. The Warburg school, however, is much more philological and historical than Eliade, and concerned less with a comprehensive vision of religion or reality than with an analysis of neglected cultural dimensions. Unlike Eliade, they did not attempt to marginalize the "center" because they were part and parcel of it, despite having been rejected by German academe because of their Jewish extraction.

A Universe of Multiple Correspondences

Several trends in the ancient and medieval periods operated with the assumption of strong correspondences between man and the universe. The best known of them in the West are the micro-macrocosmos theories. Eliade's magical universe is the matrix of innumerable correspondences between its different planes, which are discovered by mankind with the passage of time. This is a basic assumption of his thought, and one of the most outspoken expressions of this view is found in a book published in

1937, *Cosmology and Babylonian Alchemy:*

> In a *Weltanschauung* grounded in the perfect homology between heaven and earth, and in
> magic, all the things participate in the archetypes,[49] all have certain magical virtues, by
> themselves or by participation. It suffices that a soulless object will have a certain form or
> a certain color—that innumerable latencies with magical virtues will arouse in it.[50]

Nota bene: the recurrence of the term "magic" in this passage. This view is known as part of the Hermetic magic, or talismanic magic, and indeed, the literature on these phenomena of magical sympathy were known very well in medieval Europe and the Renaissance.[51] Eliade was concerned mostly with the sexual polarity that permeated the universe, and he adduces an example from R. Bahya ben Asher, a late 13th- and early 14th-century Kabbalist and exegete in Spain, in order to show that those correspondences survived to quite a late date.[52] Indeed, Eliade insists on the importance of polarities on different levels and the correspondence between them.[53] However, the alchemical affinities between metals and their combinations are conceived of as a degradation of the earlier, more organic, affinities within the universe, a process that will become well established in the Renaissance vision of inorganic universe.[54]

In this context, Eliade elaborated a general principle about the development of the human mentality: each stage in the development of human consciousness, like the discovery of agriculture or of metallurgy, allows a specific type of experience and the discovery of new sorts of homologies in the universe. "Each fundamental stage in the history of mankind"—writes Eliade—"facilitated the 'fathoming' of man of other cosmic levels"[55] and the "discovery of analogies between the levels of reality which are quite different from each other."[56] The noncorrespondences are, according to ancient texts, conceived to be reasons for maladies.[57]

At the same time, the new type of consciousness generates a certain obfuscation of the earlier type of consciousness, since an entire previous structure of experiences and symbols becomes opaque.[58] Thus, he refuses to assume a historical development that is necessarily a sort of progress, writing that these stages in the mental history of mankind are not always an evolution.[59] It seems that according to such a view, mankind cannot transcend this form of dynamics, which means new discoveries but also new forms of opacities. Here we may see an anti-Hegelian approach that operates with concepts that are Hegelian, like totality, dichotomous poles that should be reconciled, *coincidentia oppositorum*, but emphasizes the archaic rather than the utopian, the material rather than the spiritual, and credits the fundamental importance of dramatic changes.

In the same year, 1937, in the introduction to Haşdeu's writings (quoted in the previous section) Eliade claims that Haşdeu has seen "unexpected resemblances between all the levels of existence" and that he "created a universe of unseen harmonies and symbols."[60] And, again, elsewhere in the same piece he writes that Haşdeu "wanted to know the secret of harmony and of the celestial 'correspondences,'"[61] and for this sake he applied "'the magical method': that of restoring, or reconstituting, of guessing of abyssal realities by means of simple human 'documents.'"[62] Indeed, the "magical method" consists in "the certitude that between all the orders of existence there are certain correspondences, seen and unseen, which, by understanding or 'untying' them, man can fathom with his mind everywhere, and may see the beginning…as well as the end (post-mortem life)."[63] It is in the context of Haşdeu that Eliade mentions for the first time the syntagma "magical time,"[64] which will occur also later on in one of his own books.[65]

Let me ponder the possible significance of the above evaluation of Haşdeu's opus. He is described in terms reminiscent of the traditional mind, someone who is on the one hand a scholar and on the other, some form of magician. Haşdeu is a great mind capable not only of reconstructing lost worldviews on the basis of documents, but also of entering some form of universes accessible only to rare spirits. In other words, it is not just an academic performance that Eliade attributes to Haşdeu, but much more: fathoming the very mystery of reality ontologically. Eliade's predecessor was living at the end of the 19th and early 20th centuries, and died in 1907, the year Eliade was born in the same city, Bucharest. As such, Haşdeu is envisioned as having access to dimensions of reality which were lost to what Eliade calls the positivistic sets of mind, especially by decoding the correspondences allegedly found in the objectively existing worlds. In similar terms we read about the Hindu mysticism. In Eliade's book on Yoga we find the following passage:

> In general, symbolism brings about a universal "porousness," "opening" beings and things to trans-objective meanings. But in tantrism "intentional language" becomes a mental exercise, forms an integral part of sadhana. The disciple must constantly experience the mysterious process of homologization[66] and convergence that is at the root of cosmic manifestation, for he himself has now become a microcosm and, by "awakening" them, he must become conscious of all the forces that, on various planes, periodically create and absorb the universes.[67]

The concept of porosity, sometimes described as the opening,[68] is central for Eliade's vision of the different planes of the universe, and it occurs in several of his other discussions.[69] Reference to it avoids the use of terms such as "transcendent" or "immanent" insofar as the sacred is concerned, and this porosity is expressed from time to time by Eliade's concept of the rupture of levels, namely, some form of intervention of one level of reality in another. In 1939, Eliade speaks about magical correspondences that are parts of reality and not a metaphorical language.[70] The emphasis on correspondences between levels of reality is found also later on.[71] However, the above speculations are not just efforts to characterize mental universes of the part; they are relevant for the personal worldview. So, for example, while in India, contemplating the embrace of a young couple in darkness, Eliade describes himself as follows:"My mind is replete of a thirst for mystery, for occult correspondences, for cosmic senses."[72] Almost a decade later, in late 1940, we find a fascinating reflection on his fate after the death of his admired mentor Nae Ionescu:"I was asking myself…after the death of Nae Ionescu…whether my own end is not coming soon. I was asking myself whether our fates are not solidary in a mysterious manner, whose meaning I do not understand."[73]

Immediately afterwards, he draws a parallel between Ionescu's cardiac malady and his own pneumonia in 1938, when both were interned in the detention camp of the leading legionnaires at Miercurea Ciuc. In the same context, he again fears death during his presence in London as the result of the German bombardments, together with many other people:"I felt that the image of the imminent'collective death' tries to reveal to me a secret, but I did not succeed in understanding it."[74] Also, his assumption that the *maya* repeatedly uses various women in order to tempt him, as part of a much greater scheme intended to guide him to greatness, is based on a correspondence between events—first temptation and then liberation from a certain type of activity, in order to prepare him to fulfill his mission—linkages whose affinity an ordinary eye cannot discern, some form of private mythology.[75] Also in his Portugal period Eliade was looking for signs, as his interpretations of the separations from Maitreyi and Nina are understood, providentially or soteriologically.[76] His confidence that his destiny was governed by some providence is found also in one of his last interviews.[77]

We can easily understand this effort to guess the future on the basis of the past by finding correspondences if we assume that it is Eliade's worldview that such a universe operates not only in the past but also in the present, and he tries, like the people in the past, to decipher messages related to him. Ancient Babylonians, Hindu yogins and Tantra practitioners, a Romanian scholar Eliade admired who lived not too many years earlier, and also presumably Eliade himself, all share the same intuition into a hidden access to reality, which may in principle survive even in contemporary minds. This is the matrix of the early Eliade's thought: the world is miraculous since we do not know reality, and sometimes we may recognize the hidden reality by what Eliade called"contact," namely, putting together two events.[78]

Techniques of Ecstasy

Closely related to this fluid magical universe is the other topic that preoccupied Eliade very much in his earlier studies: the existence and efficacy of techniques to achieve some forms of extraordinary experiences or techniques for redemption.[79] In my opinion, his two most important studies, the book on Yoga and that on Shamanism, are based on the ontological assumptions related to the existence of a magical/fluid universe, and represent expositions of paths to integrate in a meaningful manner in such a universe and thus to transcend the ordinary type of existence. In general, Eliade's vision of religion is much more that of teaching a way to inhabit the world, namely, an experiential lore, and the emphasis on techniques is part of such an approach.

As Eliade mentioned in the citation from his *Autobiography*, adduced above, his interest in Yoga is related to an attempt to achieve a transmutation of his own being. However, despite the ontology which served Eliade's interest in techniques, a sort of ontology that personally I do not share, his contribution in putting into relief the importance of the techniques in religion is, in my opinion, tremendous. If we assume either some form of psychosomatics as the reason for the efficacy of the techniques, as I assume, or some form of integration within a cosmic order, as Eliade believes, there can be no doubt that techniques existed and held a great attraction for mystics, not to mention magicians, and we may assume that they used them. In 1931, he collected material for a book that was supposed to show the way for the primordial union, though without resorting to mystical texts.[80]

It seems that Eliade was attracted to Yoga because of his own concern with transcending the normal human situation, and his doctoral thesis was written by someone acquainted with Yoga as a practitioner.[81] However, we may find early in his career a concern with techniques not necessarily related to it. In his 1932 volume of essays entitled *Solilocvii* he presents as one of the reasons for the divine embodiments—the plural here is indeed quite important—the guidance to show to men "the path, the technique, the secret of becoming divine."[82] Similarly, he writes that the divinity offers the divine grace not to the individual but to mankind, and the divine "has embodied and will embody in order to disclose to us the technique of becoming divine."[83] Interestingly enough, though using the rather ecclesiastic Romanian term for becoming divine, *indumnezeire*, he avoids resorting to the even more technical term *theosis*, which is regarded as one of the main aims of humans, according to the Christian Orthodox religion.

His emphasis on the magical-technical aspects of some phenomena like alchemy is obvious already in the 1934 piece *Asiatic Alchemy*, where he mentions the "magicomystical techniques" in alchemy intended to attain "integration."[84] Such an approach is found in the book on Yoga, printed for the first time in 1936:

> Although the latter [Yoga] is neither magic nor shamanism, many magical marvels are accepted among the siddhis and a number of shamanic techniques are successfully homologized with yogic exercises. From all this we can divine the pressure exerted by the immemorial magico-religious substratum that preceded the constitution of Yoga in the strict sense,

a pressure that, from a particular moment on, succeeded in sending to the surface, and incorporating into Yoga, certain elements of the extremely ancient, aboriginal spirituality.[85]

This passage contains much of the seeds of Eliade's thought, including his theory of the archaic substratum, understood as both magical and spiritual, that resists later religious developments—an adoption of the theory of the revolt, here understood as pressure, of the pre-Latin forms of the Geto-Dacian religion of the Romanian scholars Lucian Blaga and Vasile Párvan, that contributed to Eliade's theory of cosmic Christianity—, the centrality of magic understood as part of spirituality, the theory of homologies, and finally the affinity between Yoga and Shamanism. This is a cosmic mentality based on natural correspondences and not on a personal approach to the divinity, as we learn also from the following passage:

> According to Patanjali [*Yoga-sutras*, II, 45], this divine aid is not the effect of a "desire" or a "feeling" for God can have neither desires nor emotions but of a "metaphysical sympathy" between Ishvara and the purusha, a sympathy explained by their structural correspondence. Ishvara is a purusha that has been free since all eternity, never touched by the kleshas [*Yoga-sutras*, I, 24].[86]

Perhaps the strongest expression of the centrality of the magical desires of the yogins was formulated in the following passage:

> We always find some form of Yoga whenever the goal is experience of the sacred or the attainment of a perfect self-mastery, which is itself the first step toward magical mastery of the world. It is a fact of considerable significance that the noblest mystical experiences, as well as the most daring magical desires, are realized through yogic technique, or, more precisely, that Yoga can equally well adapt itself to either path.[87]

Mysticism and magic are therefore not two exclusive moments, but goals that may be achieved by the very same techniques.

Symbolism and Hermeneutics

Closely related to the search for correspondences and their meaning is Eliade's emphasis on symbolism and hermeneutics. According to one of his formulations, the world is understood as if speaking to a person with "words" that should be deciphered.[88] However, it was a preoccupation not so much with textual understanding, since original texts are only rarely analyzed, as with what he called history, or cosmic events whose meaning should be decoded, or just interpreted by the hermeneutist, even if those events may originally be meaningless. These two alternatives are quite different, and even contradictory. If the universe and history are permeated with

meaning, as Eliade's texts adduced above alleged, then decoding such a cosmic meaning is in itself a salvific activity.

The literary production of Eliade is predicated to a substantial extent on the
irruptions of the sacred within the fabric of profane reality, and these irruptions, or
hierophanies, ontophanies, or kratophanies, should be decoded. However, if these
irruptions do not occur, as Eliade seems to assume in the later phase of his life, it is
hard to understand how such an interpretation would be helpful. Eliade claims that
interpretation will generate a more meaningful framework for life, instead of the
insipid chains of meaningless events, which may be called the "terror of history." In
this latter case, Eliade recommends inventing a meaning that interprets one's life so
that it becomes more supportable:

> Every exile is a Ulysses traveling toward Ithaca. Every real existence reproduces the Odyssey.
> The path toward Ithaca, toward the center. I had known all that for a long time. What I
> have just discovered is that the chance to become a new Ulysses is given to *any* exile *what-
> soever*....But to realize this the exile must be capable of penetrating the hidden meaning
> of his wandering, and of understanding them as a long series of initiation trials....That
> means: seeing signs,[89] hidden meanings, symbols, in the sufferings, the depressions, the
> dry periods in everyday life. Seeing them and reading them even *if they aren't there*; if one
> sees them, one can build a structure and read a message in the formless flow of things and
> the monotonous flux of historical events.[90]

The frequent resort to the word "every" is characteristic of Eliade's style, and creates too homogenous a vision of religious life.[91] Elsewhere, he resorts also to
"always."[92] This seminal passage reflects a strong totalizing tendency characteristic
of Eliade. If all the events are understood by individuals in an idiosyncratic manner,
then the interpretation of history will become a matter of sharp division between people—hardly a humanistic enterprise. If not, as seems to be implied in the first part
of the passage, we may speak about what I propose to call a "hermeneutic of indistinction," namely, the reduction of the diversity of events that happens in reality to
a small series of archetypal myths, in our case, that of Ulysses's adventures. By means
of such a hermeneutics, one integrates himself within an already existing paradigmatic
myth, explaining his specific experience by means of an assimilation to something
conceived of as much wider, sometimes understood as a totality or as the coincidence
of the oppositions.[93]

Moreover, as seen above, Eliade believes in the existence of correspondences and
homologies between various planes of the universe, which is another type of creating indistinction by imitation and repetition. Moreover, the theory of the camouflage
of the sacred in the profane or in the banal, to be discussed in detail in ch. 1, creates
again some form of indistinction.[94]

Indeed, in two short characterizations of Eliade's thought, Ioan P. Culianu proposed a quite daring description of Eliade's literary writings. In one of them, intended as a question to be addressed to Eliade himself—an event that never happened—he wrote:

> My interpretation of your [Eliade's] literary opus is that of Eliade as a great mystagogue, who creates myths while aware that they are based on nothing, but he is convinced of their existential and pedagogical value. The aim that is sought is, in a certain sense, soteriological. He wants to help man to retrieve the lost significance of his existence, of his fate on this earth....Is this description convenient to you?[95]

Culianu explicitly restricted his formulation to Eliade's *literaria*. Similarly, another literary critic, Eugen Simion proposes an interesting term to describe Eliade's understanding of the role of his literature: "literature should assume the engagement of the camouflaged sacred in history."[96] It maybe said, however, that the mystagogic function of the literary opus is also not alien to many of his academic writings, which turned more and more prescriptive rather than descriptive with the passage of time.[97] Once he said: "the historian of religion ultimately envisages the modification of man."[98] However, in both cases, the mystagogic role was, in my opinion, the result of Eliade's strong confidence in the unique role he was destined to play in the world, as adumbrated in some of the quotes that follow in ch. 1.[99]

Here we are, far away from the early ontological understanding of the sacred as camouflaged in the world. In fact, this term is absent, and the center of gravitation shifts from the deciphering of messages inherent in an objective manifestation of the divine, to the projection of a narrative that creates certain significance to the meaningless sequence of events in a private or historical series of events. In this case, it is much less the need of recognition, or the decoding, that allows discerning of a message from beyond, than the ingenuity of an exegete that is capable to insert, because of its creative imagination, meanings, even if they do not constitute an adequate understanding of personal life or of history. Let me emphasize that symbols in Eliade are mainly natural entities, like stones, and much less words, reflecting the archaic layer, or epoch in Heideggerian terms, that fascinated him.

I see an affinity between the shift from magic to myth, that was described above, and that of exegesis/eisegesis of Culianu's. If in the first stage the porous ontology is the main preoccupation of Eliade as a scholar, since he can operate in reality by changing the status of the person using techniques, in the second stage he does not change reality itself, but only its meanings.

It is quite obvious that the three different planes of discourse, the personal, the literary, and the religious, do not differ in a significant manner: All events or texts are raw material for an insightful interpretation. We witness here a shift from a phenomenon that David Tracy called "the hermeneutic of retrieval"[100] to what I would describe as a creative process of arcanization, which infuses new meanings in texts or events which may not have been intended at all.[101] I assume that also in this latter case the inventive creativity, or creative imagination, may be nourished by the awareness of the religious narratives found already in the store. This shift is especially evident in a passage from a letter to one of his high school friends that will be quoted in ch. 1.[102]

Eliade's recommendation for creative hermeneutics is hardly acceptable without the existence of an explicit and elaborated hermeneutical grid. If "everyone" and "always" are the dominant tone, how can one distinguish between good and bad? And how is one to interpret events he experienced, like the rise and decline of the Iron Guard, whose members he believed were "spirituals," or the meaning of the Holocaust, if everyone is always doing the same, for pretty similar reasons? Were indeed the Nazis in a search for a racially pure paradise, just one of the innumerable pursuits for the lost perfection Eliade attributes to the nature of man? And why should a historian of religion avoid speaking about and interpreting the most shocking events in his life, and in the history of mankind in general so far, in terms that he conceived of as generating a meaningful historical or intellectual scheme? If the learned proponent shunned doing it, why does he believe that a much more modest and inexperienced person in matters of religion would be able to do so? Thus, if a scholar would like to become a guide and create a "new humanist," in my eyes not a necessary part of the academic task, it would be more constructive to engage the great problems in much more detail, or, at least, to serve as a model of behavior. By refraining from inquiries of both detailed textual analyses and the specific historical contexts, there is not too much substance in a recommendation to invent interpretations in order to feel better if he is depressed, an application of a Freudian complex in a different way. This is more a therapeutic than a critical approach, intended, as he said in one of the passages cited above, to create a "comfortable" situation.

The Decline of Magic and the Ascent of the Myth in the Prescriptive Eliade

I expatiated on the four interrelated points dealt with above in order to put into relief a major component of Eliade's thought that is rather neglected in the current scholarship on his thought. While he was called the "magician of his generation" by a contemporary in the late twenties,[103] in the West he was thought of much more as the discoverer of the myth. This is the case, for example, in Ionesco's eulogy after Eliade's death in 1986.[104] When dealing with the sacred, Eliade himself says that "symbol and myth will give a clear view of the modalities that a rite can never do more than suggest."[105] Nevertheless, in this book magic plays a certain role.[106]

In a way, this is a transition from the stronger emphasis on rituals and techniques in the first period of his life to symbol and myth in the second period. In other words, we may discern here a transition from a descriptive type of discourse to a prescriptive one in the last decades of his life, when he was not practicing Yoga or Tantra or any other religious discipline, or living with two women at the same time in order to reach some form of extraordinary experience, as we shall see in chs. 2 and 3 below, but was teaching in the university and delivering lectures at conferences. This transition started in 1944, as we learn from a passage from his *Portugal Journal*, where he writes that he tries to return to the path of 1928:

> I look for new tools for the problems and the techniques [addressed] then. Magic, eroticism, chastity etc., are insufficient. I try to give coherence to the recent discoveries: any human experience to be considered as a paradox; redemption by integration; the symbol, [as] the only path to contact with all the ontic domains, remaining nevertheless in the concrete, without refusing the experience.[107]

The shift from techniques to symbol is quite explicit. The transition is most obvious in his *The Myth of the Eternal Return*, but it is apparent also in his later studies, which are collected in the books entitled *Myth and Reality*, *Myth, Dreams, and Mysteries*, and *Aspects du mythe*. Also, books about Eliade's theories emphasize the later aspects of his view, like Allen's *Myth and Religion*, marginalizing the magical aspects in his early thought and in his book *Yoga*. This transition is clear in the phrase "connaitre le mythe," which recurs in one of his books, as "essential" for the archaic man.[108]

It is easier to preach the importance of myths in Paris, Ascona, or Chicago than to convince academicians in urban milieus as to the actual efficacy of archaic rituals and techniques and their relevance for their own lives. Though he never gave up the emphasis on originality and the ontological efficacy of the cosmic religion, he tacitly presented its relevant aspects for the modern man in the retrieval of the mythical dimensions and its camouflaged existence in history, or alternatively in the possibility of imagining it as if it existed. In his later writings, especially the literary ones, he preaches the possibility of the intrusion of the sacred, basically unexpected, and much less the initiative of the person in inducing such experiences by means of rituals and techniques.

The magical universe is concerned with the possibility of man transcending his condition and reaching some form of deeper change, bringing him closer to the sacred. On the other hand, the concept of camouflage is related to the mythical aspect of religion that assumes the possibility of the sacred intruding in the profane realm. While the religious man attempts to exit normal life and, according to Eliade, out of time, the sacred penetrates time as what he called hierophanies, which are much more locatively situated. The avatars of these forms of negotiations between the two realms are the core of Eliade's vision of the nature of religion. Though the two ways of crossing borders are not exclusive, the different accents put on them differ in the various stages of his academic activity, and I propose not to offer a unified vision of his religious thought but to distinguish between two different stages.

Let me point out that the magical-technical stage is dominant in the first part of his academic activity, roughly coinciding with the Romanian years, while the mythical one flowered while he was active abroad. While the former is much more concerned with power, the latter is concerned much more with deciphering and understanding. Interestingly enough, while the mythical material is much more Romanian, the technical analyses drew on non-Romanian sources: ancient magic and Yoga. In a way, Eliade became more "Romanian" after he left Romania. This shift is related both to his strong nationalist shift since 1936, on the one hand, and to the feeling of an exile who attempts to keep his identity, on the other.[109]

From Incoherence to the Absence of Incompatibilities

The first part of the book will deal with three major themes in Eliade's writings: the camouflage of the sacred in the profane, the concept of the androgyne, and Eliade's thanatology, each being analyzed in a separate chapter. To my best knowledge, no special study has been dedicated to any of them, though each of these themes has been mentioned in many studies. I attempted to collect the earliest and the more significant occurrences of these themes, analyze their specificity, and check the sources and their wider role in Eliade's thought. My assumption is not that there was a necessary process of development, from the earlier to the later, but much more an enrichment of earlier themes that were articulated in Eliade's youth. Divergences I discern between the various treatments of these themes will not be harmonized, but left as they are, or at least as I perceive them. My assumption is that these themes are not just neglected issues but actually quite major topics in his thought, both because Eliade himself has claimed so, and because of the statistical density of these discussions in his writings. The second part of the book, chs. 4–6, deals also with topics I consider of importance in Eliade's thought, namely, a variety of discussions on Judaism, Kabbalah, and Jews. Again, though these topics are addressed sporadically in some earlier studies, I believe that the treatments below add not only more details, but also a wider and different perspective than reflected in the available studies on Eliade. Last but not least, in ch. 7 I shall deal with the connections between Eliade and the Iron Guard, and in ch. 8 I deal with Eliade as a Romanian thinker.

Despite the fact that my expertise in the political dimensions of Eliade's activities in the late 1930s is certainly my weakest part in understanding his background, I decided not to overlook it, given the need to address questions raised by many scholars as to the affinities that exist between the scholar's thought and his political proclivities in formative years of his life. Moreover, when perusing some of the historical material in the last stages of preparation of this study, issues that were left aside in scholarship emerged, and I felt compelled to address them, especially since some details of the Romanian background were not necessarily explicated in scholarship available in English.

A basic assumption that underlies the present study, as well as many of my studies in the domain of Jewish mysticism in general,[110] is that traditional thinkers as well as scholars are often times incoherent. This is not a critique addressed to them or in this specific case to Eliade, but an inherent part of a problem of epistemology or cognition in humanities in general. In other words, it is not just a matter of hiding, camouflaging, or changing views, but also of inconsistency related to conscious and unconscious shifts in one's thought. Those inconsistencies are generated by a series of different causes: conscious changes of opinion due to the development of one's thought, unconscious shifts, and in more substantial manner, the impossibility of reducing large amounts of texts, concepts, and contexts to categories that will do justice to many of their details. In traditional cases, the need to take into account tradition, with all its strata, and authorities of texts, which are not always homogenous, impedes the coherent emergence of systematic schemes. In the case of Eliade, we have an explicit early statement saying that "only the madmen and the saints do not contradict themselves."[111] The same assumption of incoherence is inherent also in the case of Sebastian, as we shall see below in ch. 6. Such incoherence differs from changes in style over years in Eliade, which Matei Calinescu has noticed, [112] or the theory of multiple personalities and a Prometheus complex, as claimed by Marta Petreu.[113] This assumption prevents simplistic and reductionist labels of Eliade as concentrating on one topic or another, of having one single view on a certain topic, or of being fascist or anti-Semite or not. Singular answers are often too simple, and the emphasis on the existence of different approaches, synchronically or diachronically, does better justice than the other approach. This does not mean that some topics are not more important than others, or that one is not responsible for one of his views, even if he also had another one.

However, beyond incoherence there is also another question that should be addressed, namely that of incompatibilities. I take this term from a passage from Mihail Sebastian's *Journal* in which he describes the cultural attitude in Bucharest in 1933: "there is nothing that is serious, nothing grave, nothing is true in this culture of smiling lampooners. Especially, there is nothing that is incompatible....See we are just friends. No one commits himself to anything."[114] Sebastian was appalled by what he saw in his immediate entourage, including Romanian and Jews together, some sort of special "Bucharest psychology." This noncommitment, the result of an unserious approach, is the result of the easy publication of newspaper pieces and nonacademic writings, always under the pressure of time and sometimes of financial problems, and often during controversies where the personal dimensions were very significant. This is in my opinion also the problem with Eliade's many hundreds of feuilletons, printed in the span of 15 years in numerous newspapers. Also, friendship did not mean too much, as it can be seen from Nicolae Iorga's rather negative eulogy of Nae Ionescu: "Friendships have no value,"[115] or the indifferent attitude of Eliade to Sebastian during the years of WWII.[116] As the latter remarked, Eliade's involvement in the Iron Guard—unlike Constantin Noica's—does not "oblige too much" where his personal well-being was concerned.[117] He served the regime of King Carol II, whom he detested because he killed the leaders of the Iron Guard in 1939, and then the regime of Ion Antonescu, who repressed the Iron Guard in 1941. But this incompatibility is also present in the behavior of Eugène Ionesco toward two of his Romanian acquaintances whom he described in 1945 as legionnaires, though some few months later he befriended them again.[118] This is also true of Sebastian himself, who remained attached to both Nae Ionescu and Eliade, even after he was acutely conscious that they adhered to the anti-Semite Iron Guard.[119] This absence of incompatibility is found also in the behavior of some of the protagonists of Eliade's novels in the mid-thirties, as we shall see in some detail in ch. 3.[120]

Eliade's Three Main Literary Corpora

There is hardly a modern scholar in the last generation in the field of humanities who wrote so much and in so many literary genres as Mircea Eliade did. Academic studies of many types: monographs, editions, commentaries, numerous detailed and specific studies, a history of religious ideas, and, finally, he edited an encyclopedia; he also founded three journals dedicated to matters of religion. Let me designate all these activities as *academica*. Eliade published several novels, a great number of short stories, as well as a few plays; let me refer to these writings as his *literaria*. Before WWII he had an extensive journalistic career, which includes the publication of a huge variety of political and cultural feuilletons. Several books include interviews he gave, and one consists of lectures he delivered on Romanian radio in the late thirties. On a more personal level, he left a huge correspondence, kept memoirs, and wrote an autobiography, and these writings may be designated as *personalia*. Three voluminous books compiled recently by Mircea Handoca constitute what is called his bio-bibliography, namely the enumeration of his writings and reviews on them.

Indubitably, Eliade's oeuvre as a whole is both an extraordinary and audacious literary and academic enterprise. It seems as if he tried to compete with an idol of his youth and then one of his protectors (and later, his sharp critic), the prolific historian Nicolae Iorga, about whom Eliade asserted that he was "the man who wrote more than anyone else."[121] The recent publication of several important volumes that contain unedited materials by Eliade, and the reprinting of many of his interwar feuilletons—several hundred, maybe more than a thousand—that were neglected or unknown previously by scholars, add very much to his literary corpus and allow fresh perspectives on his life and thought.

Moreover, as we see in the citation from the *Portugal Journal*, sometimes the personal, the literary, and the academic overlap and are discussed in the very same passage. In such a case, a separation of the three planes of discussions is hardly reasonable. I shall attempt, therefore, to point out the need to be aware of this intertwined relation of the three, rather than only the two—the *literaria* and the *academica*—as mentioned in scholarship. In fact, his *literaria* is, in many cases, quite autobiographic on the one hand, and replete with discussions about the nature of religion on the other, so it is hard to excise either the *personalia* or the *academica* from its interpretation.[122] This is also the nature of Eliade's *personalia*: It is replete with references to both his *literaria* and his *academica*. At least in one case, Eliade confesses that his own experiences practicing Yoga exercises are reflected in his book on Yoga,[123] and his tantra experiences in the ashram are also part of his *literaria*. Moreover, it should be mentioned that important sources for understanding his thought are his numerous reviews of books, a wealth of material that has been only marginally used by scholars.[124]

However, what is even more salient for our discussions below is an important remark by Eliade in his *Portugal Journal*, where he asks rhetorically, "Should I be ashamed of the autobiographical substance of my entire opus?"[125] which is both an interesting and a crucial lead for my approach in this study.[126] Though all literary writings and even scholarship depends, to a certain extent, on events in the life of the writer or the scholar, it is only rarely, as we shall see below, that a hermeneutics of one's life may inspire patterns that characterize basic subject matters in scholarship. The strong structural affinities between the experiences of his youth and the manner in which he understood them on the one hand, and Eliade's literature and academic works on the other, seem to me major factors in Eliade's development that have not been taken into consideration sufficiently. An attempt is made here to illustrate some of the possibilities inherent in a study based upon such a presupposition.

However, there are also other good reasons to do so: His *personalia* contain invaluable details for understanding the genesis of his literary writings and even some important commentaries on them by their author. His vast correspondence includes innumerable relevant details about his academic relations with several major scholars of religion, and can contribute much to the understanding of his career and plans. Last but not least: Eliade should be understood not only on the basis of what he wrote, but also taking into consideration what he did, and the question of the possible affinities between his life and politics; and his thought should be addressed, though again in a cautious manner, without attempting to build too coherent a picture and subordinating one type of sources to others.

The problem presented by such an integrative approach is, however, the sheer amount of material, in several languages, which can only hardly be mastered by a single scholar. The extensive scholarship written on Eliade in the last generation complicates the problem even more, especially because more and more polarized opinions about his past and its impact on his scholarship are continuously and vertiginously growing. Since I am concerned here mainly with the religious outlook of Eliade, I shall deal much less with the historical aspects, to which I shall refer by pointing to the major studies found in the field. Especially important is a comprehensive, brilliant, and balanced contribution to understanding Eliade's biography and his diverse cultural backgrounds that has been recently made by Țurcanu; it is extremely helpful, both in its details and its general approach, and I hope that it will nourish much of the further serious research in the field.[127] I shall not survey the various critiques of Eliade's scholarship, as this has been done in a balanced manner in some studies,[128] but I refer to them in the salient notes.

Notes

1. For the best accounts of Eliade's life, see Țurcanu, *Mircea Eliade*, Culianu, *Mircea Eliade*, and Ricketts, *Romanian Roots*.
2. See, e.g., the 1938 letters he sent asking his friend to give his family money in order to survive, printed in *Eliade File*, II, pp. 161–165. On some aspects of this chapter in Eliade's life, see ch. 7.
3. See *Mircea Eliade—Henry Pernet, Corespondență 1961–1986. Dragul meu prieten*, ed. Mihaela Gligor (Casa Cărții de Știință,Cluj-Napoca 2011), pp. 28–29.
4. This issue will be the topic of a more detailed study.
5. See *Interrupted Dialogues*, pp. 125–135, and the letter to his friend Gianpaolo Romanato, "Amintirea unui prieten: Ioan Petru Culianu," in ed. Sorin Antohi, *Ioan Petru Culianu*, p. 135.

6. See, however, his introduction to *Eliade File*, II, pp. 5–11. In his footnote to *"Capricorn,"* *"Memoirs of Mircea Eliade,"* p. 198, note b., he wrote: "Mircea Eliade let himself be duped by the external aspects of the demagogy of the Legionnaire movement."

7. See especially the three volumes compiled by Handoca, *Correspondence*.

8. As the subtitle of his *Mircea Eliade—Le prisonnier de l'histoire*—shows.

9. See his *Métamorphoses*.

10. On the magical Christianity of Eliade, see Bordaș, "Nae Ionescu, India, and Mircea Eliade," p. 49. Compare, however, Dancă, "The Origin of the Concept of Mysticism in the Thought of Mircea Eliade," in *The International Eliade*, ed., Brian Rennie (Albany, 2007), p. 222, who claims that Eliade identifies magic and mysticism. In fact, Eliade was wary of the interiorizing developments in religion, which he attributes to Judaism. See *Myths, Dreams, and Mysteries*, p. 143.

11. *Autobiography*, I, p. 256. A similar passage is found at ibid., p. 110, where he mentions also the "magical pragmatism" of one of his other heroes, Giovanni Papini. On this passage, see also below, ch. 2. See also Handoca, *The Life of Mircea Eliade*, p. 266.

12. *Autobiography*, I, p. 149. On the possible content of this article, see the interesting discussion of Liviu Bordaș in his unpublished thesis *Eliade Secret: India și "metafizica" în construcția filosofiei religiei lui Mircea Eliade* (Bucharest, 2010), pp. 203–262, of which I have seen only the abstract.

13. See, e.g., Allen, *Myth and Religion*, Dancă, *Definitio Sacri*, or Rennie, *Reconstructing Eliade*.

14. Namely, the neophytes of the ancient esotericism.

15. Reprinted in *How I Found the Philosopher's Stone*, pp. 244–245. Emphases in the original. Thus, Eliade was concerned with the topic of extraordinary powers quite early in his life. See also Ricketts, "Eliade's Religious Beliefs," p. 34 n. 34. Compare Wasserstrom, "The Dream of Mankind," pp. 194–195.

16. On this issue see below, ch. 5.

17. *How I Found the Philosopher's Stone*, p. 246.

18. Printed originally in *Cuvântul*, III, 786, pp. 1–2, reprinted in ed. Mircea Handoca, *Itinerariu spiritual, Scrieri din tinerețe, 1927* (Bucharest, 2003), pp. 206–207.

19. Printed in *Maddalena*, pp. 121–130.

20. "Varnamala or the Garland of the Letters," printed in *Virility and Askesis*, p. 196. On the magic of the sound, see also Ioan P. Culianu, influenced by Al-Kindi. See "Stăpânul Sunetelui," *Pergamentul Diafan, Ultimele Povestiri*, (Bucharest, 1996), pp. 37–45.

21. On this topic in Pico and in the Renaissance in general, see Antonella Ansani, "Giovanni Pico della Mirandola's Language of Magic," in *L'Hebreu au Temps de la Renaissance*, ed. I. Zinguer (Leiden, 1992), pp. 89–114; D. P. Walker, *Spiritual and Demonic Magic from Ficino to Campanella* (London, 1958); Yates, *Giordano Bruno and the Hermetic Tradition*, pp. 62–116; Wirszubski, *Pico della Mirandola*, passim; Charles Zika, "Reuchlin's *De Verbo Mirifico* and the Magical Debate of the Late Fifteenth Century," *Journal of the Warburg and Courtauld Institutes*, 39 (1976), pp. 104–138; Allison Coudert, "Some Theories of a Natural Language from the Renaissance to the Seventeenth Century," *Magia Naturalis und die Entstehung des modernen Naturwisseschaften: Studia Leibnitiana*, Sonderhelf (Wiesbaden, 1978), pp. 56–118; Brian Vickers, "Analogy versus Identity: The Rejection of Occult Symbolism, 1580–1680," in *Occult & Scientific Mentalities in the Renaissance*, ed. Brian Vickers (Cambridge, 1986), pp. 95–163; id., "On the Function of Analogy in the Occult," in *Hermeticism and the Renaissance*, ed. I. Merkel–A. Debus (Cranbury, 1988), pp. 265–292.

22. See *Virility and Askesis*, p. 100.

23. pp. 48, 50, 52, 55, 60, 68, 72.

24. See his "Cosmos şi magie în Mesopotamia," *Vremea*, X (martie 7, 1937), p. 11, and (martie 14, 1937), p. 10, as well as his "Metale, Plante, Sex şi Magie," *Vremea*, X (martie 21, 1937), p. 10.

25. See his earlier short piece, "Haşdeu şi cultura românească," *Vremea*, V, 253 (4 septembrie 1932), p. 7; and Bordaş, "The Conflict of Generations," pp. 6–8.

26. *Romanian Roots*, II, pp. 931–952.

27. See in the 1977 letter to Culianu, printed in Culianu, *Interrupted Dialogues*, p. 96.

28. In Romanian *surprinde*.

29. *Haşdeu*, pp. xlii–xliii. On Eliade and Haşdeu, see Gligor, *The Troublous Years*, pp. 193–194. On the perception that Eliade wanted to be the Haşdeu of his generation, see the view of Ionesco, *NO*, p. 132, printed in 1934.

30. Ibid., p. lxxx.

31. Ibid.

32. Ibid.

33. See *Autobiography*, I, pp. 70–71, 94, 107, 110, 116, 203, 245, 270, 298, 299, and his *The Fate of Romanian Culture*, p. 43.

34. See *Portugal Journal*, I, pp. 282, 283. See also below, ch. 8, for another earlier critique of European culture, in a vein reminiscent of both Guènon and Evola.

35. Ibid., I, p. 283. For the repeated resort to magic as explaining the manner in which a writer creates his characters, see ibid., p. 173.

36. Ibid., pp. 285–286. See also Ricketts, "Eliade's Religious Beliefs," p. 35. Compare also to Pettazzonni, Spineto, *Eliade-Pettazzoni*, pp. 70–71.

37. See Mircea Eliade, "Science, Idéalisme et phenomemes paranormaux," *Critique*, 3. 23 (avril 1948), pp. 315–323. See also *Ordeal of the Labyrinth*, p. 146; Ricketts, *Romanian Roots*, II, pp. 869–872; and Culianu, *Mircea Eliade*, pp. 220–222.

38. Eliade, "Science, Idéalisme et phenomemes paranormaux," p. 322. See also Culianu, *Romanian Studies*, I, pp. 244–245.

39. p. 158, n. 14.

40. Ibid., pp. 96–98. On magic and mysticism in Eliade's *Yoga*, see Ricketts, *Romanian Roots*, I, pp. 501–521.

41. *Yoga*, pp. 360–361.

42. See Spineto, "Mircea Eliade and Traditionalism."

43. See especially his 1937 piece "Folklore as an Instrument of Cognition," to be discussed in ch. 3 below, or his 1939 piece entitled "Superstitions" printed in *Master Manole*, pp. 189–190, as well as his footnote, ibid., p. 139, n. 6.

44. On the term *ergetic* see M. Idel, *Golem: Jewish Magical and Mystical Traditions on the Artificial Anthropoid* (Albany, 1990), pp. XXVI–XXVII.

45. See Idel, *Old Worlds, New Mirrors*, pp. 37–40.

46. See, e.g., *Myths, Dreams, and Mysteries*, pp. 142–143. See also *The Myth of the Eternal Return*, p. 110, and *The Forge and the Crucible*, p. 31.

47. See *The Myth of Reintegration*, p. 382; id., *Patterns in Comparative Religion*, p. 31; id., *Myths, Dreams, and Mysteries*, pp. 143–154; and Dancă, *Definitio Sacri*, pp. 134–135. For a connection between between the microcosm-macrocosm and the circuit of fluids, see Emilio Giuseppe

Rosato, *L'uomo microcosmo e la circulazione dei fluidi in Shabbatai Donnolo* (Cassano delle Murge, 2012).

48. See *No Souvenirs*, p. 49.

49. The connection between participation in the archetype and magic is found also in *The Myth of Eternal Return*, p. 30.

50. *The Way to the Center*, p. 534. See also in an earlier piece, *Asiatic Alchemy*, ibid., pp. 580–581; id., *The Myth of Eternal Return*, p. 4. On homologization, see also in *Aspects du mythe*, pp. 102–104, 124. Eliade's *Patterns in Comparative Religion* is replete with homologies like female, soil, moon.

51. *The Way to the Center*, pp. 534–535.

52. Ibid., p. 535.

53. *The Quest*, pp. 173–174.

54. *The Way to the Center*, p. 535.

55. Ibid., p. 536.

56. Ibid. For homologization and Kabbalah, see below, ch. 2.

57. Ibid., p. 538.

58. Ibid., p. 536. See also Eliade's *No Souvenirs*, p. 268, to be discussed in ch. 1.

59. *The Way to the Center*, p. 536. On the same page, Eliade describes the Renaissance as a "sterile conception of the universe," because of its mechanistic and positivist derivates.

60. *Haşdeu*, p. xlii.

61. Ibid., p. xliii.

62. Ibid., pp. xliii–xliv.

63. Ibid., p. xliv. See also below ch. 3, end of section 8.

64. Ibid., p. xlvii.

65. See *Patterns in Comparative Religion*, p. 388: "magico-religious time."

66. For examples of homologizations, see also, e.g., Eliade, *Yoga*, pp. 233–235, 254–255.

67. *Yoga*, pp. 250–251.

68. On opening, see also *Myth and Reality*, pp. 139–143; id., *The Sacred and the Profane*, pp. 26, 34.

69. See, e.g., his *Images and Symbols*, p. 178.

70. See *Fragmentarium*, reprinted in *The Way to the Center*, p. 139.

71. *Patterns in Comparative Religion*, p. 391.

72. *Şantier*, in Eliade, *Prose*, p. 282.

73. Ed. Handoca, *Eliade File, II*, pp. 149–150.

74. Ibid., p. 150. See also Ricketts, *Romanian Roots*, II, p. 1093.

75. For more on this issue see below, ch. 1, and Petreu, *From Junimea to Noica*, pp. 348–350.

76. *Portugal Journal*, I, pp. 270–271. See also ibid., p. 303, and Ricketts, "Glimpses into Eliade's Religious Beliefs," pp. 35–38.

77. Given to Petru Cârdu and printed in Liviu Bordas, "Ultimul interviu a lui Mircea Eliade şi *felix culpa*," *România literară*, XLIII, 50 (December 16, 2011), p. 13.

78. See *Oceanography*, p. 70, translated in ch. 2.

79. On this topic, see Culianu, *Mircea Eliade*, pp. 60–74, and his "Mircea Eliade et l'ideal de l'homme universel," in Schwarz, ed., *Dialogues avec le sacré*, pp. 11–12.

80. See *Şantier*, in *Prose*, p. 422.

81. See his *Autobiography I*, pp. 189–190.

82. *Solilocvii*, p. 60.

83. Ibid., p. 61.

84. In *The Way to the Center*, p. 588. See also ibid., pp. 594, 599, 603, 604, n. 1.

85. *Yoga*, p. 341.

86. Ibid., p. 74.

87. Ibid., p. 360. See also ibid., p. 90.

88. "Methodological Remarks on the Study of Religious Symbolism," pp. 98–99, rpt. in *The Two and the One*, pp. 201–202, *Aspects du mythe*, p. 177, and his "Dimensions religieues," p. 274. See also Dudley, *Religion on Trial*, pp. 149–150. Compare also to Eliade's much earlier *Journal of Vacation*, p. 117.

89. See also his *Images and Symbols*, p. 170. On Eliade's demand of seeing signs, see more below, at the end of ch. 6.

90. *No Souvenirs*, pp. 84–85 (January 1, 1960), emphases in the original. See also Călinescu, "Introduction," pp. xiv–xv; id., *About Culianu and Eliade*, pp. 35–37, 139–140; and Petrescu, "Ioan Petru Culianu and Mircea Eliade," pp. 410–412. Paraphrasing this quote, though—interestingly enough—without mentioning Eliade's name, Culianu said in a feuilleton in *The Sin against the Spirit*, p. 133, that every exile should identify with Elie Wiesel. I would just say that every exile should find his/her own way independently of any model, without imitating anyone. Compare to Eliade's *Journal*, III, p. 277. For a more conservative reading of Eliade's hermeneutics, see Allen, *Myth and Religion*, pp. 299–300.

91. See, e.g., *The Sacred & the Profane*, pp. 63–64.

92. See his *Myths, Dreams, and Mysteries*, p. 126.

93. For more on these issues, see below, chs. 2, 4, and 7.

94. Indistinction is also creating a confusion between the descriptive and the prescriptive Eliade, or between the scholar and the reformer, or between the two different meanings of mystagogue, as we shall see below.

95. *Mircea Eliade*, p. 270. See also ibid., p. 256. Culianu refers to Eliade as mystagogue several times in his characterization of Eliade as a writer. See ibid., pp. 247, 250, his "Mircea Eliade et la Tortue Borgne," in Arcade, Manea, Stamatescu, eds., *Homo Religiosus*, pp. 83–84, and his "Mircea Eliade et l'ideal de l'homme universel," in Schwarz, ed., *Dialogues avec le sacré*, pp. 15–16; and Glodeanu, *Coordinates of the Imaginary*, pp. 58–59. See also Matei Călinescu, "The Professor," in Bădiliță, ed., *Eliadiana*, p. 10. This aspect of Eliade is much closer to Pettazzoni, who understood Eliade solely in the first sense of mystagogue. See Spineto, *Eliade-Pettazzoni*, pp. 72–74.

96. *Mircea Eliade*, p. 219. On the issue of "humanitarian engagement," see Culianu, *Mircea Eliade*, p. 97.

97. See also Dubuisson, *Mythologies*, pp. 192, 280, 304. It should be pointed out that some mystagogic or "prophetic" components are to be found also in the perceptions of the works of Jung, Corbin, Scholem, and Leo Strauss, especially by their followers. However, these four thinkers only rarely went as far in their prescriptive tone as Eliade did.

98. *The Quest*, p. 67.

99. Let me point out that Eliade distinguishes between mystics, whom he sees in a positive light, and the mystagogues, described negatively and related to the theosophy of Madame Blavatsky. See his feuilleton "A Simple Intermezzo" (1935), reprinted in *Romanian Prophetism*, II, p. 102.

100. *Plurality and Ambiguity, Hermeneutics, Religion, Hope* (San Francisco, 1987), p. 100, and *The*

Analogical Imagination, Christian Theology and the Culture of Pluralism (New York, 1981), pp. 156, 205.

101. See, e.g., Idel, *Absorbing Perfection*, pp. 9–10, 253–254, 280–283.

102. See *Correspondence*, I, p. 112.

103. See Victor Stoe, "The Magician of a Generation," *România Literară*, 1930, reprinted in Handoca, ed., *Eliade Files, I*, pp. 37–40.

104. See the addenda to *Memoirs*, p. 212.

105. *Patterns in Comparative Religion*, p. 9.

106. Ibid., pp. 9–10.

107. *Portugal Journal*, I, p. 232.

108. *Aspects du mythe*, p. 24.

109. For more on this issue, see chs. 7–8.

110. See, e.g., Idel, "On the Identity of the Authors of Two Ashkenazi Commentaries to the Poem 'ha-'Aderet ve-ha-'Emunah' and the Concepts of Theurgy and Glory in R. Eleazar of Worms," *Kabbalah*, 29 (2013), pp. 67–208 (Hebrew); id., "*Adonai Sefatai Tiftah*: Models of Understanding Prayer in Early Hasidism," *Kabbalah*, 18 (2008), pp. 7–111; id., "Prayer, Ecstasy, and Alien Thoughts in the Besht's Religious Worldview," in *Let the Old Make Way for the New: Studies in the Social and Cultural History of Eastern European Jewry, Presented to Immanuel Etkes*, vol. I: *Hasidism and the Musar Movement*, ed. D. Assaf–A. Rapoport-Albert (Jerusalem, 2009), pp. 57–120 (Hebrew); and id., "Mystical Redemption and Messianism in R. Israel Baal Shem Tov's Teachings," *Kabbalah*, 24 (2011), pp. 7–121.

111. *Solilocvii*, p. 61. For Ionesco's view of Eliade as espousing different, though not necessarily contradictory, views in the same statement, see Ionesco, *NO*, p. 133. See also Cioran's claim in a letter to Arşavir Acterian, *Cioran, Eliade, Ionesco*, p. 130: "I live by contradictions."

112. See his small Romanian piece "The Professor," in ed. Bădiliţă, *Eliadiana*, p. 108.

113. *From Junimea to Noica*, pp. 345–346.

114. Sebastian, *How Did I Become a Hooligan*, pp. 243–244; Manea, "The Incompatibilities," p. 34; Călinescu, "The 1927 Generation in Romania: Ideological Options and Personal Relations," tr. in Sebastian, *Under Times*, p. 11; Petreu, *The Devil and His Apprentice*, p. 133. Compare also to Eliade, *Autobiography*, I, p. 293.

115. Rpr. in ed. Râpeanu, *Nicolae Iorga, Mircea Eliade, Nae Ionescu*, p. 295.

116. See Petreu, *The Devil and His Apprentice*, pp. 242–243.

117. *Journal*, p. 236.

118. See Laignel-Lavastine, *L'oubli du fascisme*.

119. For more on this issue, see below, chs. 6 and 7.

120. Petreu, *The Devil and His Apprentice*, pp. 239–240.

121. See the essay of the same title written in Portuguese in 1944, and translated into Romanian in *Portugal Journal*, II, pp. 359–368. Though Iorga wrote even more than Eliade did, the latter uses a much greater variety of genres in his writings and is incomparably more studied by scholars than Iorga was.

122. See, e.g., the passage about Vishnu and Narada, dealing with the concept of maya, found in *Forbidden Forest*, p. 399, but dealt with academically in *Images and Symbols*, pp. 70–71.

123. *Autobiography*, I, pp. 189–190.

124. For the use of reviews, see below, in the Introduction and in ch. 4.

125. *Portugal Journal*, I, p. 297.

126. In other instances, too, Eliade calls for an interpretation of his oeuvre as a totality. See his *Ordeal by Labyrinth*, pp. 186–187, as well as the discussion of this issue in Marino, *The Hermeneutics of Mircea Eliade*, p. 439 and n. 34–36; Tolcea, *Eliade, The Esotericist*, p. 14; and Glodeanu, *The Coordinates of the Imagery*, pp. 96–97. This approached has been adopted also by Doniger, "Time, Sleep, and Death," pp. 1–21; and Cave, *New Humanism*, and Reschika, *Mircea Eliade*.

127. *Mircea Eliade.*

128. See Allen, *Myth and Religion*, and Olson, *The Theology and Philosophy*, pp. 7–13.

· 1 ·

CAMOUFLAGED SACRED IN ELIADE'S SELF-PERCEPTION, LITERATURE, AND SCHOLARSHIP

This theme constitutes the key to all the writings of my maturity.
—ELIADE, AUTOBIOGRAPHY

*T*he present chapter deals with a major aspect of Eliade's opus, the camouflage of the sacred, a principle that informs his creative imagination as it emerges from many of his written documents. Our discussions below will have little to do with him as a person or as a political man, despite the content of some of the quotes adduced below. Though this topic was dealt with in his disparate types of writings—religious, political, historical, literary, and personal—there is a shared assumption that appears early and underlies some of them: the sacred camouflages itself within the profane, and as such, it is largely unrecognizable. In order to reach a higher form of existence, one should be able to recognize those hidden revelations, which are sometimes expressed by signs. When this recognition takes place, because of the initiative of either the human person or the sacred, Eliade speaks about hierophany, kratophany, and ontophany, and less about the more theologically oriented theophany. This is the main religious ethos of Eliade himself and of some of the protagonists of his literature, and finally of religion as a spiritual phenomenon, as envisaged by him as a scholar. Penetrating beneath the surface of "banal" existence in order to encounter the "real," understanding one's destiny, and teaching this imperative to decode to others are, according to him, the noblest of human enterprises. The worldview of the scholar coincides, therefore, with the manner in which he understands his life, his vision of the academic field he studies, and also the deep structure of his literary writings. Though the unrecognizability of the sacred and its camouflage are tightly connected, this is basically one aspect of the latter topic, the camouflage, especially in banal things, that will concern us more in this chapter.[1] I am concerned with the history of this aspect of Eliade's theory of the sacred, and its occurrence on three planes related to him, rather than with a conceptual exposition or a critique of it.

Let me start with a methodological observation: I shall use material found in diverse types of literatures, as mentioned in the Introduction. One may well object to mixing together journal articles, correspondence, fantastic literature, and academic analysis in order to draw any conclusion. In principle, this is quite a plausible argument. However, it runs against the manner in which Eliade himself wanted to be understood, since he explicitly and repeatedly required an understanding of his opus as a unified corpus, as seen in the Introduction.

Three Intertwined Domains of Camouflage

Let me point out from the very beginning that the importance of the role played by the theory of "the camouflage of the sacred" in Eliade's opus has been addressed, though succinctly, by many scholars. In terms of the literary works, several literary critiques have drawn attention to the importance of this approach: Matei Călinescu,[2] Virgil Ierunca,[3] Gheorghe Glodeanu,[4] and to a certain extent, Eugen Simion.[5] In matters of religion, the series of scholars who touched on or dealt with this concept is quite long, and I adduce here only some of the names in the field: Adrian Marino,[6] Sergiu Al-George,[7] Ioan Petru Culianu,[8] Mac Linscott Ricketts,[9] Douglas Allen,[10] Jean-Jacques Wunenburger,[11] Carl Olson,[12] Bryan S. Rennie,[13] Daniel Dubuisson,[14] Wilhelm Dancă,[15] Steven M. Wasserstrom,[16] Robert Lazu,[17] Marcel Tolcea,[18] and more recently and quite extensively in the context of the camouflage of sacred time, Elvira Groza.[19] Especially interesting is a small article by Cornel Mihai Ionescu printed in *Viaţa Românească*.[20] Nevertheless, those learned analyses deal with a relatively small selection of pertinent texts, and they engage only one of the two fields of Eliade's oeuvre, the *literaria* or the *academica*, but pay scarce, if any, attention to the importance of the *personalia*—and even less to the possible contribution of Eliade's self-understanding—for a better understanding of the first two literary corpora.

Eliade claimed that he was concerned with the unrecognizability of the miracle, the unrecognizability of the transcendental "that is camouflaged in history," and the intervention of the sacred in history, in the period 1929–1932, his Indian period.[21]

He describes different paths in his writings that stem from this problematic, both in his literary writings and in his theory of religion.[22] In my opinion, this passage presents one aspect of Eliade's fluid universe in which the sacred and the profane are mixed, as discussed in the Introduction.

It seems that the first substantial discussion of unrecognizability is found in Eliade's *Solilocvii,* where he wrote:

> Concerning "the unseen God."
>
> Jesus said: "No one has seen Him."[23] It is not His invisibility that is mentioned but the unrecognizability. God is so that He cannot be recognized anywhere, because He said:[24] "I am what I am." This is a metaphysical sense. Insofar as the metaphysical sense is concerned, He is the God of Israel.[25]

Eliade distinguishes between the Christian theology based on unrecognizability and the Jewish one that is depicted as metaphysical. As to the latter interpretation, it fits the Christian understanding of the biblical verse from Exodus, as found in the books of Etienne Gilson, but it has nothing to do with its classical Jewish interpretations.[26] As to Eliade's interpretation of the claim of invisibility in the Greek Bible as unrecognizability, it is a conjecture that is not explicated, and I can hardly see its philological validity. However, what Eliade did not mention explicitly is the presence of the divine in banality, namely, the hidden aspect of the divine within Jesus himself as an ordinary person, within which divinity has been incarnated, as Eliade will say later on.[27] What is interesting in this passage is the attempt to anchor his theological intuition in two segments of verses, but without any analysis.

Let me turn to the most extensive and compact formulation of the theory of the comprehensive camouflage in banal, and adduce first a compact passage that seems to have been quite neglected in the analyses of the topic. In the memoirs that he redacted in the sixties, Eliade comments upon his marriage with his first wife, Nina Mareş, in January 1934:

> So far as I was concerned, banal existences attracted me. I said to myself that if the fantastic or the supernatural or the supra-historical is somehow accessible to us, we cannot encounter it except camouflaged in the banal.[28] Just as I believed in the unrecognizability of miracle, so I also believed in the necessity (of the dialectic order) of the camouflage of the "exceptional" in the banal, and of the transhistoric in historic events. These ideas, which I was to formulate later in *The Snake* (published in 1937), *The Forbidden Forest* (written between 1949 and 1954),[29] and in several works of history and philosophy of religions, sustained me in the experiment that I had begun. Actually, when instead of returning to India I accepted a situation that inevitably led to marriage, I was consenting to do in Bucharest that which I knew I should be forced to do in Calcutta or Benares: namely, to

camouflage my "secret life" in an existence apparently dedicated to scientific research. But with this difference—that at this point a somewhat tragic element was introduced—my certainty that I understood my destiny, precisely because my marriage to Nina seemed, *apparently*, to be a disaster, it must, if I believed in the dialectics and mystery of camouflage, mean exactly the opposite.[30]

Two words serve as the leitmotif of this passage, and of some of our discussions below: "camouflage" and "banal." According to Eliade's views, the sacred, or the miraculous, needs a camouflage that will hide it. This reference to camouflage, a military term that had been introduced during WWI, is interesting, since it differs from the more standard theory of accommodation of the divine to lower planes of existence, or theories about the contraction of the unlimited divinity when revealing itself, or of the concept of *deus otiosus*. "Camouflage" as used by Eliade here is meant to emphasize the fact that there is a case of disguise involved, and thus the need to fathom what is disguised. It is only one who is already acquainted, in some form or another, with the disguised form that may recognize it. The "banal" is therefore hiding something that is dramatically different from it, by containing it within itself, in the case of both Nina and Mircea.

Three distinct matters converge here: the personal, the literary, and the academic. Different as they are, they correspond since in all these cases there is an expression of a more comprehensive, ontological situation. The specific incident of his decision to marry Nina serves as the starting point of a reflection that encompasses immediately a much broader range of topics. The private case attracts a reflection on the general situation; the particular event is seen as integrated into a much larger series of individual events, and into a more comprehensive understanding of reality.

The personal constitutes the answer Eliade provides, to the surprise of his family and friends, as to his decision to leave one of his two girlfriends, the demanding actress Sorana Țopa, and marry the more modest Nina Mareş.[31] What for others was hardly understandable was for Eliade a wise decision, taken because of his belief in the pervasiveness of camouflage. I assume that the brighter and more prominent Sorana was thought a more appropriate consort for the already famous Eliade than Nina. It is not my concern here to elaborate upon the ways in which Eliade reflected upon the choice he made in this case: He claimed that he promised to himself and to Nina to recompense her for all the vicissitudes that happened to her before they met, and twice in this context he refers to the formula *restitutio ad integrum*.[32] However, ironically enough, in two instances in his writings he confesses that he asked her to abort pregnancies because he did not want children at that stage,[33] and he had the impression that this surgery might have been the reason for her later illness that caused her death.[34]

Therefore, Eliade contemplated his involvement with Nina according to the theory of camouflage, and thus it seems that he relied on some form of the camouflage theory quite early in his life, at the age of 26, or even earlier, judging by his remark about what might have happened in Calcutta or Benares. Much more important, however, is the reference to another form of camouflage mentioned in the passage: that of the "secret life" probably hidden "in an existence apparently dedicated to scientific research."[35] The camouflage is strengthened by the second occurrence of the adverb "apparently." In other words, the academic activity camouflages another activity, the secret life, whose purpose is higher, and to a certain extent it is disguised by it. Just as the marriage to Nina is part of the *restitutio ad integrum* that transcends the ordinary forms of marriage (traditionally intended to lead to procreation), so also the scientific research serves as pretext, occasion, or camouflage for a more sublime and presumably different form of life. Expressed in the early sixties, when Eliade's academic life was already a definite choice, this formulation about the status of academic research is quite exciting. If indeed the feeling he had about his marriage and his way of involvement in academia extended as far back as the early thirties, then we have a long-standing confession about the way in which he envisioned all his most important activities: He enters a certain institution, marriage or academia, considered to be banal, in order to search there for something much more sublime.

What is the nature of this more sublime, or "secret life"? According to another passage, Eliade confesses that his love for Nina and his adventure in the Iron Guard were a matter of his search for the Absolute.[36] This means that, again, Nina, namely human love, and the Iron Guard, presumably representing for Eliade some form of spiritual religion, are conceived as paths for reaching the Absolute.[37] Or, to formulate the entire problem in a different manner: The manifestation of the transcendental needs the power of discernment of the human. The miracle is recognizable only to one who believes, expects, or longs for that miracle. The attentive openness of the spiritual man is therefore conceived as strictly necessary, since the sacred does not reveal itself in a manner that is uniformly manifest to everyone.

Let me draw attention to what is the most interesting aspect of the above passage: Eliade's confidence that he himself is in a privileged position of discerning the uncommon nature of his future wife, in comparison to the other different reactions. Neither his family nor his friends—with the exception of Mihail Sebastian[38]—is sensitive to the special character of his choice. This privileged status assumes some form of special providence that one is guided to make the right choices, which are hardly understood by others, and we shall return to this point later on. Since the "others" belong to the banal life and judge events accordingly, the inverse of their opinion "must" be true, and Eliade stands therefore on the opposite side of their understanding of the world. The use of the word "must" is quite revealing. He assumes that by understanding the ordinary attitude, one may extrapolate the inverse and thus reach some form of special insight. The hermeneutics of a certain situation is therefore a matter of the special individual, and it is therefore hardly a matter of consensus.

However, it should be emphasized that the above aptitude is not only a matter of understanding Eliade's private life or his literature, but it also became, according to a sentence in the above passage, the bases of what is found "in several works of history and philosophy of religions" by Eliade. This claim is the main reason for my dwelling upon the importance of this text; it provides Eliade's self-awareness that a common denominator unifies the three main levels of his life—the private, the literary and the academic. The underlying assumption can be formulated as follows: The principle that it holds for understanding his literature is also salient for understanding his "history and philosophy" in the academic field of religion, and also for fathoming the meaning of at least some events of his life.

The above passage describes deliberations concerning events that took place in late 1933 or very early 1934 (January), the date when Eliade married Nina. However, the autobiography was written many decades after the event, and it may be, for a skeptical reader, too hazardous to attribute to those years the emergence of the theory of the sacred as camouflaged. However, in my opinion, the early date for Eliade's embracing this vision of the sacred is quite plausible, for two different reasons. In an interview he gave in October 1981 to Mircea Handoca, he mentions a play he did not finish, entitled "The Death Comedy" (*Comedia Morții*), which he started to write in 1931 in India. Eliade reminiscences that

> what seems to me interesting now, half a century later, is the fact that in that play I have anticipated the technique of the fantastic novels which I wrote in the last thirty years, and even the concept of "the camouflage of the sacred within the profane," which guided my research in the study of religions.[39]

Thus, the Hindu background for the emergence of the theory of the camouflage of the sacred is quite evident, as we shall see further. Here the assumption that the camouflage theory guided his academic studies of religion occurs again. In other words, the clue for understanding what Eliade depicts as a guiding concept of his study of religion, "the camouflage," was forged already at the early age of 24 in the context of a literary work, the unfinished play. More evidence is found in a discussion in a collection of essays published in 1934 under the title *Oceanography*. There the theory of camouflage is not found explicitly, but that of "the unrecognizability of the sacred" is quite recognizable: "Unrecognizability is the perfect form for a divine revelation, since the divinity does not manifest itself by the way of contrast,[40] but operates directly in humanity by the way of contact, by the coming together."[41] Conspicuous in this passage is the presupposition that the unrecognizability is a matter of an ontological manifestation. The change is in the manner in which the sacred manifests itself, which may be related also to its being recognized by the religious person, but it has an objective status. In this context, Eliade mentions the fact that the perception or the conception of the mystery does not coincide with the mystery itself.[42] We may indeed regard Eliade's approach as a "mystery" without theology.[43]

Let me turn now to a somewhat later reverberation of the ideas found in the first passage quoted above, found, again, in the first volume of Eliade's *Autobiography*:

> When I received the galley proofs,[44] I could scarcely believe my eyes....*Şarpele* was written as I had "seen" it from the beginning: a story with banal characters....It is as if the everyday world camouflages a secret dimension which, once man knows it, reveals to him simultaneously the profound significance of the Cosmos and his authentic mode of being: a mode of perfect, beatific spontaneity, but which is neither the irresponsibility of the animal existence nor angelic beatitude. Unconsciously and unintentionally, I succeeded in "showing" in *Şarpele* something I was to develop later in my works of philosophy and history of religions: namely that the "sacred" *apparently* is not different from the "profane," that the "fantastic" is camouflaged in the "real," that the world is what it shows itself to be, and is at the same time a cipher.[45]...The same dialectic...also sustains *The Forbidden Forest*...with the difference that at this time no longer was it a question of the profound meaning of the Cosmos, but of the "cipher" of historical events. The theme of the "fantastic" camouflaged in the everyday occurrences is found again in several of my novellas written still more recently, for example *La Ţigănci*...and *Podul*. In a certain sense, one could say that this theme constitutes the key to all the writings of my maturity.[46]

In the context where this passage occurs, Eliade describes his finding out, as a surprise, the meaning of the story where the camouflaged message is encoded, apparently without being aware of his intending to do so. As he confesses in the passage immediately preceding the above quote, the short story was written during nights. This is part of what Eliade called his nocturnal mode, which differs from the diurnal, scientific, and critical ones.[47]

A similar surprise is evident also in the above-mentioned interview with Mircea Handoca. This is also the case in another similar instance, when he writes: "Dumbfounded over the 'discoveries' that I am making about my novels: *Isabelle* and *La Lumière qui s'éteint*."[48] Those astonishing "discoveries" have to do both with the religious conceptual content of his novels, which were not so clear beforehand to the author himself, and with the autobiographical meaning they contain.[49] In general, let me point out that the concept of cipher and deciphering, as applied to what has been called the "mystery" of Eliade's life and destiny, occurs also in another important instance in the early stages of his life.[50] From this point of view, there is no difference between his interpreting the various mysterious stages of his life and the hidden messages unintentionally harbored by his novels, and his deciphering religious documents written by another person in his scholarship. Something secret is found there that requires a special type of hermeneutics. However, unlike the tone of the passage in *Oceanography*, where the ontological sort of camouflage is evident, in the last quote Eliade uses the expression "as if," which demands a less ontological understanding.

Perhaps the strongest expression of Eliade's preoccupation with the theory of the camouflaged sacred is found in his *Journal*, in two consecutive notes in March 1976 about his rereading of his earlier autobiographical notes:

> While rereading what I wrote, I go from discovery to discovery. Why did I stress—but differently, and with extreme passion—the subjects that I had, however, dealt with abundantly both in my journal and in other writings? The mystery of the dialectic of the camouflaging of the sacred in the profane, for example. One would think that this is a subject that preoccupies me to the point of obsession. Not content to confront the issue in my works on the history of religions and in my literary writings of the last few years, I must still grapple with it in what I note for myself alone!…The fervor with which I rework to better develop reflections inspired by the camouflaging of the sacred in the profane must have a deeper meaning, and I'm just beginning to have an inkling of it. This dialectic of camouflaging is infinitely more vast and goes much farther than all that I've been able to say about it up until now. The "mystery of the camouflage"[51] is fundamental to an entire metaphysics, for it is the very mystery of the human condition. If it obsesses me so much, it is because I don't decide to go into it in more depth, to make a systematic presentation of it, to study it from its own unique perspective, that of philosophical meditation.[52]

I wonder if there is a more powerful recognition of the centrality of the camouflage theory than these two passages and the term "obsession," which Eliade uses twice. Not only did this theme occur as a guiding theory since Eliade's youth, it became an obsession for him in his later years. In any case, Ioan P. Culianu summarized nicely the importance of the camouflage theme when he wrote: "For Eliade the world was a camouflage through which more profound signs transpired."[53] Also important is Eliade's admission that he did not elaborate in a systematic manner on what obsessed him.

The Camouflage: A Hindu-Christian Synthesis

In an excellent analysis of some of Eliade's discussions of the camouflage of the sacred, the Romanian indologist Sergiu Al-George has pointed out the affinities between it and the Hindu concept of maya.[54] Indeed, this proposal is quite plausible; we mentioned above one more reason for such a connection, the unfinished play commenced in India, and we shall see in the next section in a quote from the short story "The Bridge" a clear connection between the two, made by Eliade himself in an explicit manner. A reading of most of Eliade's texts about camouflage may leave the impression that we deal with either a personal or trans-historical situation of camouflage. However, in another passage, Eliade claims that the camouflage of the divine has a history in religion. In his *No Souvenirs*, we read about a discussion he had with a reader of one of his short stories, again in the context of "The Snake":

> . . . my theory of "the incognizability of miracles"—or in my theory that, after the Incarnation, the transcendent is camouflaged in the world or in history and thus become "incognizable." In "The Snake" a banal atmosphere and mediocre characters are gradually transfigured. But what came from "beyond," as well as all the paradisiac images of the end of the story, were already there from the beginning, but camouflaged by the banality of everyday life and, as such, unrecognizable.[55]

Here the reference to the concept of camouflage in literature is again put in direct relation to a theory in history of religion. Eliade does not assume that his theory holds in the cases of all religions as such, but only for post-Incarnational religious events. The Christian tenet of incarnation deals not with a specific event in the story of a certain religion, but with a sharp ontological shift, after which only smaller manifestations are possible. This historical event seems to be less a Hindu than a Christian vision of the development of religion, as we also learn from this passage:

> The history of religions—from the most primitive to the most highly developed—is constituted by a great number of hierophanies, by manifestations of sacred realities. From the most elementary hierophany—e.g., manifestation of the sacred in some ordinary object, a stone or a tree—to the supreme hierophany (which, for a Christian, is the incarnation of God in Jesus Christ), there is no solution of continuity. In each case we are confronted by the same mysterious act—the manifestation of something of a wholly different order, a reality that does not belong to our world, in objects that are an integral part of our natural "profane" world.[56]

Here is a conflation of the Hindu theory of maya as manifestation with the Christian vision of the special status of Incarnation as revelation,[57] which follows a certain pattern found already in *Oceanography*.[58] Interestingly enough, Eliade distinguishes between "primitive" and "supreme" manifestations of the sacred. The more diffuse forms of hierophanies before Incarnation, the gods, were restricted to a hierophany camouflaged in a human person. It should be pointed out that in *Oceanography*, as in the last quote—though more emphatically—the Christian type of miracle that is unrecognizable is conceived to be higher than anything beforehand.[59] A further stage of camouflage happens in what Eliade calls the Judeo-Christian tradition:

It is only through the discovery of History—more precisely, by the awakening of the historical consciousness in Judaeo-Christianity and its propagation by Hegel and his successors—it is only through the radical assimilation of the new mode of being represented by human existence in the world that myth could be left behind. But we hesitate to say that mythical thought has been abolished. As we shall soon see, it managed to survive, though radically changed (if not perfectly camouflaged). And the astonishing fact is that, more than anywhere else, it survives in historiography.[60]

An interesting formulation of this theory, which includes a term that is important in our context, is found in a parallel to this quote in his *No Souvenirs*: "I came to understand that modern science would not have been possible without the Judeo-Christian tradition, which emptied the cosmos of the sacred, and thus neutralized and banalized it."[61] Here, "banal," a term used several times in the context of camouflage, is used in a more comprehensive context.

In a way, Eliade sees himself as retrieving the situation before the emergence of the vacuum allegedly created by the Judeo-Christian tradition, which "banalized" the world.[62] Just as he was able to understand the unique and sacred hidden in Nina, he was also capable of creating heroes who search for and sometimes meet the camouflaged sacred, and so too was he able to restore the sacred, which allegedly has been abandoned in the West.[63]

Camouflage, Maya, and Women

The most outstanding discussion of the camouflage, which sheds some light on the origins of this theory, is found in the short and quite enigmatic short story "Podul" (The Bridge), which includes some themes relevant for our discussion. It includes a rather lengthy reflection that, to my best knowledge, did not attract the due attention of most scholars who dealt with this topic:

Sometimes, in the case of some persons, the profound structures of reality are revealed under the aspect of the most stringent banality. Structures that otherwise, to speak rationally, are inaccessible to us.[64]…However, ultimate reality cannot be grasped in concepts nor expressed in language. For our mind, the ultimate reality, being, is a mystery, and I define mystery: that which we cannot recognize, what is unrecognizable. This may mean, however, two things: either that we cannot ever know ultimate reality, or that we can know it anytime, on the condition that we learn to recognize it under its infinite *camouflages in appearances*, what we call immediate reality,[65] within what the Hindu call *maya*, a term that I would translate as the immediate *unreality*. You understand what I allude to: incidents, events, fortuitous encounters that apparently may have no significance. I say apparently. But what if reality is only a pit created by maya, the cosmic witch, matter in its becoming? This is the reason why we speak about *coincidentia oppositorum*,[66] about that mystery in which being may coincide with non-being. I repeat: *may* coincide. But they do not always coincide, since if they coincide it would be no more a mystery....When I understood that *atman* is identical to *brahman*, the lieutenant understood that he died for the world, that he awaked suddenly detached of everything, and though this death means his freedom, he was what the Hindu call "a dead in life,"[67] and that—as it happens in such limit-cases—sometimes one feels life, sometimes you feel instead death.[68]

First, it is not only events but also banal persons that may sometimes be portents of the mysterious presence of the sacred. Just as in the case of his description of Nina Mareş adduced above, also here an apparently banal person is potentially a host of a higher mystery. This seems to be also the case with a much earlier literary figure, the librarian Cesare, the main protagonist of *The Light that Fails*, one of Eliade's earliest novels, conceived and written in 1930 while he was in India, and with the later Ştefan, the protagonist of his most important novel, *Forbidden Forest*.[69] In both cases, it is easy to find some parallels between the literary protagonist and the life of Eliade himself, though neither Cesare nor Ştefan were only complete representatives of the author. Later on, in his novel *Youth without Youth*, Eliade refers to camouflage in several instances.[70] The existence of a banal individual who incarnates a mystery is, therefore, the most common way of self-revelation of the sacred. Unlike the "heroic" nature of the founders of the world religions, for Eliade it is the more discreet, modest, barely recognizable hidden nature of the person that transforms him into a candidate for hosting mystery.[71] Also, trivial events and encounters may be harbingers of sublime messages. Thus, the trivial and the sublime sometimes coincide, and the act of pinpointing these instances constitutes the discovery of the mystery.

What is conspicuous in this seminal passage is the strong claim that the camouflage theory is related to the Hindu concept of maya, understood as both revealing and concealing something deep in the structure of reality. What in some other cases is presented as his theory, unrelated to any specific religion but dealing with the nature of sacred as such, is here explicitly traced to three major concepts in Hinduism. Interesting in this context is the expression "camouflaged optimism," which Eliade attributes to Indian spirituality.[72]

Let me turn to another discussion of maya, this time directly related to Eliade's early life. In his *Autobiography*, and in another form, in his *No Souvenirs*, he describes his reaction to the warning of a hermit in connection with his affair with Jenny Isaac in the ashram in Rishikesh:

For a second time in less than a year I had let myself be deceived by my own imagination— in Indian terms, by illusions created by maya. Just now, when it seemed to me that I had "awakened," I have fallen prey to the first magical temptation that an unresting maya had produced in my path....Once again a young woman had embodied a secret that I had not known how to decipher....I could not know it then, but eternal maya, in her blind wisdom, had set those two girls on my path in order to help me find my true destiny. Neither the life of an "adopted Bengalese" nor that of a Himalayan hermit would have allowed me to fulfill the possibilities with which I had come into the world.[73]

Therefore, Jenny, a South African Jewess in search of Hindu spirituality, and the sexual relations he had with her, just as was the case with his beloved Maitreyi Dasgupta some few months earlier, allegedly embody a secret that Eliade, according to his self-understanding, was supposed to be able to decode, but he failed to do so. This is an interesting confession of failure, but it is nevertheless an instance of a *felix culpa*. According to other discussions, his failure to decode the message is part of a much bigger scheme concerning Eliade's mission, namely, to cause him to leave the ashram, or the trans-historical India, just as his erotic involvement with Maitreyi was intended by the same maya to cause him to disentangle himself from historical India, the Bengalese society. Fascinatingly enough, the magical power of maya is concerned more with the destiny of Romanian culture than with the Hindu one, as we shall see immediately below.

The question may be asked, when exactly did Eliade "understand" or decipher these events in his life as having a special meaning? Is it only much later in his life, as claimed by one of the greatest experts on Eliade, Mac Linscott Ricketts, in a review of an earlier version of this chapter,[74] that Eliade's mentioning of maya is to be understood not as a reaction to events on the spot, but as an interpretation forged much later in his life, when Eliade reflected on his experiences in retrospect. Alternatively, as proposed already, it was close in time to the events, as I think. In favor of this view, there is a passage in the *Autobiography* where Eliade says: "I could not know it then, but eternal maya, in her blind wisdom, had set those two girls on my path."[75] However, it is not clear when he understood the role of maya—much later, when he redacted the memoirs, as Ricketts claims, or much sooner, as I propose. Let me adduce for this purpose what Eliade himself wrote, in the translation prepared by Ricketts himself:

> After a few weeks I realized that I was beginning to be in better spirits. At the same time, I was beginning to understand the reason for the events that had provoked my breakup with Dasgupta. If "historical" India were forbidden to me, the road was opened to "eternal" India. I realized also that I had to know passion, drama and suffering before renouncing the "historical" dimension of my existence and making my way toward a trans-historical, atemporal paradigmatic dimension....Later on I understood that my drama itself followed a traditional model...I told myself that I was now in the phase of "trial."[76]

When did Eliade understand that his life was running in a providential manner, and that events in it had a special meaning? My answer to this question is that it happened close in time to the events, namely in India, while one of the greatest experts on Eliade, Mac Linscott Ricketts, argued that it happened much later, and thus was a retrospective understanding of his life.[77] If this claim is true, it invalidates some of my arguments as to the quite early occurrence of the idea of camouflage. However, Eliade's references to the expression "few weeks," namely some time in 1930, and the phrases "at the same time I was beginning to understand" and "It is now," do not support Ricketts' speculation on retrospectives. What Eliade understood later he mentions explicitly, writing, "Later on I understood."[78]

However, even more immediate is his account of his search for signs and camouflage in connection to another woman, Nina Mareș. In a passage reporting an event in late 1933, Eliade wrote: "In a flash, I knew that all I had said to her was a last, demonic attempt of maya to destroy me."[79] "In a flash" is the most dramatic way to describe the manner in which Eliade used maya in order to understand his experiences with women. Moreover, the reference to the term "last" shows that already in 1933 he regarded the actions of maya as appropriate also for earlier experiences; in my opinion, those in India related to two other women. Despite the claim of Ricketts to the contrary,[80] the Hindu aspect of his understanding of events in his life is obvious also immediately after his return from India, when he writes in another remarkable passage, once again in the context of his involvement with women:

> After all I thought I learned from my experiences in India, less than two years after my return I was wandering once again in the labyrinth. I believed I'd learned at least not to be deceived by the mirages and snares that I well knew *she* was producing continually—"the Mother of us all"—maya.[81]

So Eliade was confident that he had learned something in India about the hidden meaning of his life, but he was not cautious enough, and became involved again in an erotic complex affair. He "knew" in 1933 that maya was haunting him. Ricketts' attempt to postpone the Hindu-oriented reflections on Eliade's life to a quite late phase is contradicted by Eliade's formulations, but also—in my opinion—by the understanding of his evolution: Earlier in his life he used the terminology that influenced him more, the Hindu one of maya, and consequently the feminine forms,[82] while later on, when he converted back to some form of Orthodox Christianity after 1937,[83] he used much more Christian terminologies, as we shall see immediately below. My interpretation is corroborated by an expression Eliade attributes in 1933 to Nae Ionescu as to the necessity that one writing in a newspaper interpret on the spot: "the decipherment of events in the source of their unfolding."[84]

The feeling that he has been privileged even when apparently he failed has to do with Eliade's self-understanding that he had a mission to accomplish. This mission involves, in another case, the need of a separation from another woman, Nina.

Reflecting about her death, which he regretted terribly, he nevertheless writes in his *Portugal Journal*:

> Nina did not leave me out of her will, since God took her in order to cause me to think in a creative manner, namely in order to facilitate my redemption. Nina's depart will have for the rest of my life a soteriological sense. My separation from Maitreyi nineteen years ago had too a sense: I escaped India, I abandoned Yoga and Hindu philosophy for Romanian culture and for my literature.[85]

God, or "Dumnezeu," the Christian Romanian term, now plays the role previously played by maya; however, it should be stressed that in both cases, separation from a woman is conceived of as ultimately providential, and painful as the experience may be in a certain moment, it had an ultimate positive value: to guide Eliade to his mission.[86] The Hindu terminology disappeared, and in lieu he used monotheistic terminology, which is part of a greater shift toward a more Christian religiosity characteristic of his period in Portugal, when he turned to perusing the Bible and Leo Shestov's writings. Some years later, in his *No Souvenirs*, he considers his separation from Romanian culture part of his journey toward a universal approach.[87] It seems that in Eliade's view, his destiny is a series of escapes from limited universes that confine his spiritual and intellectual aspirations, and those universes have been represented by the various women with whom he was close, and the final journey toward a more universal perspective and destiny.[88] Eliade assumes that he was predestined to become what he imagined he became, and also that the women were milestones in his personal journey to glory. Let me point out that despite this plausible reading of the above sources, I hardly believe that this was always the manner in which he initiated his behavior, but rather that this is a late reflection of the possible meaning of events in his life.[89] Nevertheless, the emergence of such a narrative is important in itself, even more so when it informs some of his literary creations, the most representative in this context being *The Hooligans*, and to a certain extent, *The Forbidden Forest*.

To return to the passage from "The Bridge" cited at the beginning of this section: In this story the lieutenant, that is, the privileged spiritual individual, encounters every evening as part of a mysterious ritual several women—girls, widows and married young ladies—in order to try to find out who, in a certain given evening, embodies, if at all, the goddess. So, for example, we read: "This is the problem of the lieutenant: how to identify the great Goddess among those five or ten young and beautiful women who are around him every evening?"[90] The answer to the problem of how to discern the daily embodiment of the Goddess, which is not clear to me, is based in principle upon the existence of a concrete affinity between the naked body of the great Goddess and the stalk of grapes and the cluster of grapes that emanate from that body.

The awareness of the concreteness of the affinity is, according to the writer, the answer to the question as to the manner in which "the lieutenant identifies every evening the great Goddess that is camouflaged in one of those ladies, widows, or mademoiselles."[91] Elsewhere, the mystery of which of those ladies embodies the Goddess in a certain evening is mentioned.[92] Again, a woman is the embodiment, in a camouflaged manner, of a higher principle, and the male constitutes the privileged person who understands this coded though concrete message. In this context, it should be mentioned that the mystery related to the naked body of Melania exposed in the context of an unspecified ritual lies at the core of Eliade's *The Light that Fails*—though I did not detect a reference to the term "camouflage" in this early novel. In any case, it is interesting to point out that Eliade confessed that he understood the hidden meaning of this novel only later on, in 1963: "The 'mystery' of *La Lumière*…was really only the mystery of my existence in Dasgupta's house."[93] Again we witness a vision of Eliade's life as mystery, and an important piece of evidence that the author himself considered his *literaria* as a helpful source for his self-understanding of his *personalia*. Moreover, this novel was written while Eliade was immersing himself in the practices of Yoga.[94] Since, as Eliade recognizes, some of the experiences he had were at the basis of techniques as described in his book on Yoga, he could not describe them otherwise because only a new language could allow it.[95] This novel, alongside the other later novel *The Secret of Dr. Honigberger*, may also have a possible contribution in this context. In short, some of the personal experiences related to the Yoga exercises found their expressions in the academic book on Yoga, some others in Eliade's literary work.

Eliade's Attitude to the Science of Religion and the Problem of Decoding

At a certain advanced level of studying the oeuvre of a scholar, when his major claims are understood, the doubts that scholar had, if not incorporated in his studies, may become as helpful for understanding him as his positive arguments. After all, the emergence of serious scholarship is a long and often tortuous process whose details and rejected alternatives may teach an advanced scholar as much as the conclusion one reached in a certain moment. In most scholarship, this stage of indecision and then of selection is not given an explicit expression. This is the reason why a perusal of Eliade's *personalia* may contribute much to a better understanding of his attitude to his field of investigation. From a perusal of confessions found there we may see that Eliade was aware of two weaknesses related to his academic oeuvre: that it deals with a field that is hardly understandable in too an erudite manner, and that he himself did not indeed prove his major theoretical claim about the camouflaged sacred.

The sources of Eliade's camouflage theory in Hindu views of maya and the theory of cosmic correspondences have their important cognitive repercussions. Operating after the Kantian revolution—though not so much after the Copernican one—Eliade is well aware that a scholar can hardly exhaust the meaning of such a subtle, cryptic, and fluid event as a hierophany in the way he understood it. That the science of religion is haunted by this cognitive problem, we learn from some interesting expressions we may detect in his more personal writings and much less in his academic ones. Indeed, if religion is so strongly gravitating around "dialectics and mystery of camouflage," as mentioned in one of the citations above, the deciphering is rarely something that can be done with a great amount of certainty. This is why, in a critique of Eliade's method, Hans H. Penner penetratingly wrote on his approach: "a science of religion based upon a mystery remains a mysterious science."[96]

The cryptic nature of Eliade's sacred is emphasized elsewhere as part of, in my opinion, the logic of camouflage:

> When something sacred manifests itself (hierophany), at the same time something "occults" itself, becomes cryptic. Therein is the true dialectic of the sacred: by the mere fact of *showing* itself, the sacred *hides itself*. We can never claim that we definitively understand a religious phenomenon: something—perhaps even essential—will be understood by us later, or by others, immediately.[97]

However, what this surface is, and how one is certain that there is real sign intended for him, are important questions that did not enjoy any detailed answers from Eliade.

In fact, we may discern a shift between the more experiential period in his youth, especially in India, when the manifestation was more "impressive," and a later one, in which the human imposing of meaning is less a matter of deciphering than one of building a narrative to be imposed upon the formless flux. This later phase can be described as more "expressive" of the human spirit, or more humanistic. The former is something more like a Platonic recognition, a disclosure of the hidden and closer to manifestation of the objective, while the later one is closer to a sort of proclamation related to the specific ingenuity of the individual. As pointed out by Ioan P. Culianu, the "first" Eliade deals with the real irruption of the miraculous in the world, while the "second" Eliade assumes that meaning is established by the hermeneutical process itself, as part of Eliade's much stronger emphasis during this period on the power of imagination.[98] In both cases, however, the *homo religiosus* can learn from the history of religion patterns that may help them to see through the camouflage. Though I accept this distinction in principle, it should be pointed out that his short story "Under the Shadow of the Lily," written late in his life, in 1982, reflects the approach of the early Eliade.

However, the vagueness of Eliade's hermeneutics has much to do with the vagueness of his vision of the sacred, an issue that will be dealt with below. The vagueness in both fields is hardly helpful for scholars, but much more inspiring and creative for religious persons in search of an encounter with the sacred. However, in both instances, it is harder to speak about an articulated hermeneutic of Eliade comparable to those of Paul Ricoeur or Georg Gadamer than about a hermeneutic orientation, which draws from the past ideals with which *homo religiosus* should identify. Thus, the question can be asked, to what extent do the categorizations found in his *Patterns* help more in the existential search to identify or to decipher something meaningful in reality, or to interpret it creatively, than the approach of a scholar concerned more with comprehensive religious systems that are fragmented into unrelated themes, when their elements are dealt with in an isolated manner?[99]

Eliade's "Camouflage of the Sacred" and Contemporary Types of Scholarly Esotericism

Understanding has much to do with comparison: it implies perceiving both similarities and also differences. Eliade, like Jung, was more concerned with the former. From time to time, however, close analysis of details may disclose that dissimilarities may teach as much as perceived resemblances. The two Jewish scholars Leo Strauss and Gershom Scholem, who were somewhat senior to Eliade, but whose roads crossed often, were deeply interested in esotericism. A comparison between the ways in which esotericism functioned in their studies may illumine Eliade's own reference to "camouflage."

Strauss engaged a theory concerning the history of philosophy, according to which esotericism is a special manner of writing intended to preserve secrets from the multitude and to defend the philosophical elite from misunderstandings from both the multitude and rulers. Starting with Plato, a series of Western thinkers, Muslims, Jews, and Christians, adopted this approach, to which Strauss devoted a long series of monographs. This type of philosophical esotericism is political in essence, but it entails a vision of religion as a special type of knowledge; in fact, a fiction invented by philosophers in order to regulate the behavior of the multitude. From this point of view, Strauss claimed that many philosophers masked their views, and plausibly Strauss himself did so, at least in some cases. In one case at least, Eliade mentions the need of "means of camouflage" in order to survive the terror of history, namely the possible occupation of Romania by Soviet Russia.[100] This is an obvious case of political camouflage.

In a manner similar to Strauss, though openly, Gershom Scholem recognized that he himself used some form of camouflage. In an interview he gave in 1974, in a passage that has been ignored in scholarship, he said explicitly:

> Beyond all the camouflages, the masks, and the philological games in which I excel, something hidden is also inspiring me. I can understand that something of this kind is kindled in the hearts of my listeners—among the secular ones—just as it kindled in me.[101]

The something "hidden" is an aspect of Kabbalah that is capable of inspiring people in different periods, and Scholem confesses that he also is inspired. The Hebrew term I translated as "camouflages" is *haswwa'ot*, which is the single parallel term in Hebrew for camouflage. Scholem describes the academic games he accepts as camouflage, and there is something external that is implied here, namely, a certain Kabbalistic matter that would inspire him, just as other Kabbalistic aspects inspired other persons over the centuries. In any case, the camouflage is not a form taken over by the sacred, but a cover Scholem himself adopts as part of his scientific enterprise. As Steven M. Wasserstrom has pointed out, Joseph Weiss, a close student of Scholem's, described him already in 1948 in quite similar terms, using the Hebrew term for "camouflage" in order to claim that Scholem has disguised as a scholar his quality as a metaphysical thinker.[102] Unlike Eliade's "banal" persons, who are the camouflage of the sacred and the mysterious, in the cases of Scholem and Strauss, we are dealing with exceptional individuals who choose masks in order to operate in their academic environments. Their esotericism or camouflage is related not so much to ontological manifestations of the sacred, but to some dimensions of texts, or their understanding of those texts. Unlike Scholem and Strauss (and to a great extent, also Henry Corbin), Eliade's esotericism and camouflage is much less concerned with texts. The single instance in Eliade where the camouflage has to do with hiding ideas is found in his *Forbidden Forest*, mainly in the context of disguising one's ideas under the Communist regime.[103]

However, different as the three scholars are, and divergent as their understandings of esotericism are, they nevertheless share interesting features in common. All three are part of what I would call "the generation of discontent," namely, interwar scholars for whom religion was not only a scholarly enterprise, but also part of their protest against the intellectual and religious establishment. They attempted to "recover" or retrieve an alleged forgotten, repressed type of spirituality by finding new clues to traditions that had been understood differently in their cultural entourage. However, their efforts were much more extensive than putting into relief some forgotten texts; they forged much more comprehensive schemes, dealing with phenomena that took place during millennia, and in different continents. This is the way in which Scholem sees the history of Jewish mysticism as a repressed dimension of Judaism, and Strauss sees the esoteric dimension of philosophy from Plato to Al-Farabi, Maimonides, until Spinoza. The three are "protestant" thinkers, attempting to reform the domineering understanding of humanities, and keys-seekers, or, better, universal keys-seekers.[104] Only by their claims for comprehensive clues were they capable of reforming the respective fields in such a dramatic manner.

Some Conclusions

In one of the passages quoted above, the outstanding phrase "the mystery of the dialectic of the camouflaging of the sacred in the profane" occurs. In different combinations, the elements found in this phrase recur also in other passages, eminently in a letter to Eliade's friend Barbu Brezianu, cited below. The explanatory power of clusters of terms where mystery accompanies camouflage, dialectic is coupled with mystery, when they describe the sacred disguised within the profane, the emphasis on the "dialectics of hierophany,"[105] or when camouflage is used in a paradoxical manner,[106] is not self-evident, nor is it a perfect recipe for clarity. Often times, Eliade refers also to ambivalence, ambiguity and paradox in the context of his treatments of the sacred.[107] It is hard to add more vague terms, and I cannot but wonder how such clusters could help convey a theory that may inspire poor scholars like me who deal with religious texts in a detailed and articulated analyses of primary materials. It is possible that Eliade's effort to integrate the oral and material forms of religious expression, in a scholarly culture based so dramatically on analyses of texts, invited a more vague type of definitions of both the topics and of the hermeneutical tools.

Eliade expressed himself on the theory of camouflage of the sacred without always indicating on what terms precisely he does so. No one is entitled to argue with a personal conviction about the way in which someone understands his life, or even makes important decisions following some theories. In principle, adopting a certain theory of the divinity or reality, or a certain anthropology, in order to write novels, is a practice no one would object to in a novelist, particularly when some of those novels and short stories are understood to be fantastic. For an expert on Eliade's literary opus like Eugen Simion, the theoretical assumptions of Eliade as narrator were rather vague.[108]

However, insofar as a scholar of religion is concerned, Eliade's general claims about the nature of religion or the sacred, in itself or in its camouflaged forms, must be fostered by as many primary material expressions or texts as possible and by their detailed analysis, in order to allow the acceptance of such a general and comprehensive understanding of religion or the sacred. Surprisingly enough, unlike Heidegger, whom he read,[109] Eliade did not do so in a systematic manner anywhere in his academic writings I am acquainted with.[110] The two short mentions of camouflage in the first volume of *A History of Religious Ideas* do not analyze even a single text, but instead refer to Greek religion in general terms,[111] or to the camouflage of the sacred in the radical desacralization of physical love, "such as is found in so many other creations of the Greek genius."[112] In both cases, he hints at what he will write in volume III, a book that was never written.

Eliade probably was aware of this major lacuna in his treatment, as we learn from another important passage written as late as 1976: "I'd have to develop considerably what I understand by 'dialectic of the camouflaging of the sacred,' and that would take sixty pages. . . ."[113] However, this promise to himself and to others[114] never materialized during the last decade of his life. Nevertheless, scholars dealing with his theory of the camouflaged sacred had to speculate about or attempt to reconstruct his precise intention on such a crucial concept.[115] However, fascinating as those reconstructions are for the history of the scholarship of religion, or in themselves as ingenuous intellectual exercises, in my opinion the fundamental problem for the more mundane history of religion should be formulated as follows: What are the underlying primary sources that justify the very formulation of the theory of camouflage as part of a general theory of the sacred, in addition to the Hindu theories of maya? Are there substantial additional understandings of the sacred as camouflage that are independent of the Hindu ones that would justify an extension of a basically Hindu theory, with some Christian additions in some cases,[116] to a general theory of the sacred? Personal convictions or insights reached by the imaginative or oneiric processes related to writing fantastic literary writings, or "philosophical meditations," may serve as starting points that may inspire a process of collecting primary material in various religions, but they cannot replace a critical presentation of such a material. The fact that the most articulated and elaborated discussions on this topic occur in personal notes and in literary writings rather than in academic ones is quite problematic from a critical point of view. Indeed, in a very important passage for our argument here, Eliade describes in some detail how his academic writings emerged from intuitions found first in his literary ones.[117]

It seems that even Eliade was somehow aware of this situation when in 1978 he remarked to Claude-Henri Rocquet, in the context of the camouflage of the profane in the sacred in modern times: "But all that is still a problem, and I very much hope that someone will go into it properly, really set about deciphering *the camouflage adopted by the sacred in a desacralized world.*"[118]

However, more interesting is one of the last articulated remarks on camouflage, in a letter in 1979 addressed to his high-school friend Barbu Brezianu, a historian of art, which restates his call for a hermeneutical move of deciphering, which is tantamount to projecting mythical elements onto events that perhaps have nothing to do with them—what I call, in the context of Jewish interpretation, "arcanization":[119]

> Condemned as we are to decipher the "mysteries" and "to discover the way to redemption"
> via culture, namely through *books* (not via oral traditions transmitted from a master to a dis-
> ciple), we have nothing better to do than to deepen the dialectics of the mysterious *coinci-
> dentia oppositorum*, which allows us to discover "the sacred" camouflaged in the "profane"
> but also to *resacralize in a creative manner* the historical moment, in other words to trans-
> figure it, by attributing to it [*acordindu-i*] a transcendental dimension (or "an intention").[120]

This view sustains Culianu's claim, adduced above in the Introduction, as to the mystagogical nature of Eliade's project, namely, his intention to guide people more than to study religion. Some years later, he suggested in an interview for a movie that the sacred is camouflaged in "crime," in the case of Abraham's sacrifice of Isaac,[121] and in an optimistic description of the wonderful camouflaged worlds.[122] The scant discussions of primary sources that may foster an academic theory of camouflage may be compared to the much more documented manner in which Eliade made his other central points in the phenomenology of religion like Shamanism, and in his analyses of Yoga or the importance of the center and of *axis mundi*. In these cases, a huge variety of religious sources have been quoted, referred to, sometimes analyzed in a rather detailed manner, and they may serve as starting points of fruitful schol-arly discussions or, when necessary, critiques.[123]

From another point of view, the theory of the existence of a camouflage of the sacred within the profane and even in the banal represents the vastest scholarly effort in modern times to re-enchant reality in a world that opted dramatically for disenchantment. The re-enchantment is based on older religious examples related to extraordinary events and magical assumptions as to how the universe operates, which means a strongly pre-Copernican worldview, and though it opts for a cosmic form of life, it hardly takes into consideration the new worldviews that have been increasingly adopted by larger audiences in the last two generations. There is noth-ing wrong with attempting to understand the worldview of pre-Copernican societies, but their worldview is hardly an apt proposal for reforming the religious life of mod-ern persons who live, knowingly or not, in an Einsteinian universe. Neither is the importance of the creation myths as paradigmatic, so evident in Eliade,[124] easily digestible by a modern audience, in a period when the modern cosmogonic theories differ so much from the traditional creation myths. If one follows the path proposed by Eliade, one should pursue detection of mysterious signs not only in history but also in science.

Let me attempt to summarize my discussions above from the point of view of how to understand the thought of Eliade. I propose to see in the two most significant parts of his life, the Romanian inter-war period and the much shorter Hindu experience, and his acquaintance with these two cultures, the determinant factors in his thought and literature, as well as in his self-awareness. A third major source of inspiration for Eliade's approach to religion is the Italian Renaissance, a topic to which he dedicated his masters thesis in 1928, and in his writings he returns many times to the paradigmatic nature of the intercultural encounters of the Florentine Renaissance and its reverberations in the European occultist movement, like René Guènon and Julius Evola.[125]

In fact, Eliade called forth "a second Renaissance," which should be much more comprehensive than the Italian one, and this approach is fundamental for him.[126] This call for a new, expanded humanism that is inclusive of many cultures unknown to the Italian Renaissance thinkers is definitely reminiscent of the Italian new concept of humanism.[127] This emphasis on these three topics as formative for Eliade's worldviews means that two other intellectual factors in Eliade's life, his more formal adherence to the Iron Guard at the end of 1935, to be dealt with below in ch. 7, and his prolonged participation in the Eranos encounters at Ascona from 1950,[128] should be seen as less formative from the intellectual point of view, as their impact on Eliade's writings can only be established by resorting to strict historical and philological tools. The first event was early but relatively short, while the second one was a long one, but relatively late in his intellectual development. In both cases, it is difficult to pinpoint precise sources and ideas that altered Eliade's earlier views, and the issue of the interference of the Iron Guard and Eliade's writings will be discussed in ch. 7. In the case of the three other sources the impact is, however, quite obvious and profound. This does not mean that the latter two events should be ignored or neglected in scholarship, but that only a careful inspection of the possible impact of more concrete literary sources should determine the relevance or the depth of the impact of those events.[129]

To be sure: Eliade's actual biography did not serve as a major blueprint for his literary works or for the theories about the camouflaged sacred that he introduced in his academic writings. However, the way in which Eliade imagined the meaning of his life plausibly did so.[130] This type of *imaginaire* regarding one's life no doubt has much to do with real events, but also with theories one learned or inherited before real events happened, or afterwards. Though one may live his life without resorting to too many profound theories and belief in mysteries about it, one may remember more the way that he imagined it post-factum. If there is a pattern for this remembering events of one's life as a meaningful and mysterious narrative, one can hardly wonder if an entire fantastic literature was not written under the impact of such a blueprint.

However, what concerns me more is the extent to which one's academic activity is also affected by it.[131] After all, the significance of the academic discourse consists in its being a discourse that can be shared with others in as transparent a manner as possible, and in its being verifiable by other scholars who do not share the life experiences of a certain scholar.

Theosis

Eliade's strong and early experiences related to Yoga and Tantra exercises were a major source of his confidence in his special destiny, namely to build a special narrative concerning his life based on the "providence" implemented in a camouflaged manner by maya, or on what he called his "personal mythology" related to mystery.[132] For him, his own literary works constitute sometimes a form of hierophany, which operates with an oneiric state of mind, and this is the reason why he is surprised by the content he discovers in them, especially when they deal with the camouflage of the sacred. Sometimes intuitions that found their first expressions in Eliade's *literaria* contributed then to his *academica*. This means that for him, the creative literary process was conceived of as an occasion or perhaps even a technique for triggering some sort of revelation of the sacred.

Did Eliade also believe—one may ask—that he himself was in a way a divine manifestation, camouflaged in an "apparently banal" human being? Or, alternatively, did he imagine that he reached a special or extraordinary human status by means of his Yoga exercises?[133] In one case, he says that "nostalgia for the 'divine condition' conquered by force, magically, has never ceased to obsess ascetics and yogins."[134] However, it seems that already in 1927 he assumed that it is possible to become God by employing the technique of absolute silence, though the person that acquires special powers may be regarded as crazy.[135] Becoming God is described as the real purpose of Jesus's incarnation, since it exemplified the peak of human experience.[136] In this context, Eliade uses the phrase "the technique of becoming divine."[137] Thus, the two religious traditions Eliade admired more than any other—and practiced, at least for some period of time—are conceived of as conducive to theosis. His novel *Youth without Youth* describes a mutant that is presented as the future man.

However, in 1931 Eliade speaks about being fond of his weaknesses, and of his fear of becoming an angel.[138] I would say that if indeed Eliade nourished such unusual self-perceptions in his youth, they diminished in his mature years, as part of what I claimed was a more moderate belief in magic.

Notes

1. Let me specify from the very beginning that my analysis in this chapter refers to the term "camouflage" only as it occurs explicitly in Eliade's own writings, not to the metaphorical uses of some scholars who attribute to him the covering of his past, as found in the writings of Adriana Berger or Daniel Dubuisson. From my perspective here, such a metaphorical use of *camouflage* may confuse arguments made below. See the latter's *Mythologies*, pp. 213, 285, 293 n. 105.

2. See, e.g., his "Introduction: The Fantastic and Its Interpretation in Mircea Eliade's Later Novellas," in *Mircea Eliade, Youth Without Youth and Other Novellas*, tr. Mac Linscott Ricketts (Columbus, 1988), pp. XVI–XVII.

3. "L'oeuvre litteraire," *Cahier de l'Herne, Mircea Eliade*, p. 222.

4. *The Coordinates of the Imaginary*, pp. 42–43, 45, 48–49, 51, 53–54, 235.

5. *Knots and Signs of Prose*, pp. 209–210, 216–218.

6. *The Hermeneutics of Mircea Eliade*, pp. 158–159.

7. *Archaic and Universal*, pp. 160–165. An English version of the pertinent discussion is found in "India in the Cultural Destiny of Mircea Eliade," *Mankind Quarterly*, v25, 1/2 (1984), pp. 115–135.

8. *Mircea Eliade*, pp. 39–40, 252–253.

9. *Romanian Roots*, II, pp. 878, 1209, and in his review of the first version of this chapter in "Politics, Etcetera," pp. 277–282.

10. *Myth and Religion*, pp. 87–92.

11. *Le Sacré* (Paris, 1990), cf. the Romanian translation of Mihaela Calus, *Sacrul* (Cluj-Napoca, 2000), p. 89, and the translator's introduction, p. 31.

12. *The Theology and Philosophy of Eliade*, pp. 38–39, 52–53, 59, 95, 162, 164, 169.

13. *Reconstructing Eliade*, pp. 215–218.

14. *Mythologies*, pp. 203, 233, 293 n. 105, 276, 296.

15. *Definitio Sacri*, pp. 209–223. This monograph is a very valuable analysis of Eliade's theory of the sacred, and contributes to a broader understanding of his sources, which cannot be summarized in this context.

16. *Religion after Religion*, pp. 33–34, 42, 270–271 n. 32.

17. "Dialectica Sacrului între teologie şi metafizică," in eds. Corneliu Mircea–Robert Lazu, *Orizontul Sacru* (Iaşi, 1998), pp. 111–112.

18. *Eliade the Esotericist*, pp. 266–267.

19. *The Phenomenolization of Time*, pp. 191–217, 250–255.

20. "'Ascundere' şi 'Camuflare,'" *Viaţa Românească*, LXXXVII (martie–aprilie 1992), pp. 138–142.

21. According to a survey of his thought and literary writings he sent in 1953 to his friend Virgil Ierunca, another expatriated Romanian in Paris, and printed in the Romanian journal *Caete de Dor*, reprinted in *Memoirs*, pp. 229–230. On this passage, see also Monica Lovinescu, "Mircea Eliade and Time," in Bădiliţă, ed., *Eliadiana*, p. 126.

22. *Memoirs*, p. 230.

23. Cf. John 1:18: "No man has seen God at any time; the only begotten God, who is in the bosom of the Father, He has explained Him."

24. Exodus 3:14.

25. *Solilocvii*, p. 59. For this text as predating the texts I adduced in the published version of this chapter, see Ricketts, "Politics, Etcetera," p. 279, and independently in a personal communication by Dan Petrescu.

26. See Idel, *Old Worlds, New Mirrors*, pp. 40–47.

27. See especially the passage from *Portugal Journal*, I, p. 1, and Ricketts, "Glimpses into Eliade's Religious Beliefs," p. 34. See also Eliade, "Puissance et sacralité," pp. 42–43.

28. See, especially, the resort to the past tense, here and immediately below, as reflecting what probably he already thought in 1934, not when he redacted his memories decades later. We shall return to it immediately below.

29. Indeed, in this novel the concept of camouflage occurs many times, but the best parallel to our passage here is on p. 193.

30. *Autobiography*, I, pp. 274–275 (emphases in the original). There is overlapping between some parts of this passage and what Eliade says later on in the same book (see p. 322), and I shall return to some formulations not found in the quote above in my discussion below.

31. Ibid., I, pp. 271–275.

32. Ibid., I, pp. 272, 277.

33. Ibid., I, p. 277, and *Portugal Journal*, I, p. 274. See also Alexandrescu, *Mircea Eliade from Portugal*, pp. 210–211.

34. *Portugal Journal*, I, p. 274.

35. An issue that deserves a special investigation is the possibility that in a lost letter addressed by Eliade to Julius Evola, he might have implied that he intends to serve as "a Trojan horse" in the academy. This possibility has been mentioned to me by the late Dr. Leon Volovici. However, given the fact that this is an implication from a formulation found in Evola's letter written at the end of 1951, which answers Eliade's lost letter, caution is important. See Marin Mincu–Roberto Scagno, *Mircea Eliade e l'Italia* (Milan, 1987), p. 253.

36. *Portugal Journal*, I, p. 293.

37. For the affinity between Nina and the Iron Guard, and her possible influence on Eliade, see Ţurcanu, *Mircea Eliade*, p. 264.

38. *Autobiography*, I, p. 275. Sebastian was probably well acquainted with Nina before Eliade fell in love with her, and he maintained fond feelings for her until her death. See the passages in Sebastian's journal dealing with her death and the reminiscences he had since he knew her, in Sebastian, *Journal*, p. 572, and see also Eliade, *Autobiography*, I, pp. 175, 241, as well as below, end of ch. 6.

39. *Interviews with and about Mircea Eliade*, pp. 11–12.

40. From the context, this form of revelation is characteristic of ancient religions, while the contact represents the Christian type of revelation. See also his *Images and Symbols*, p. 171.

41. *Oceanography*, p. 70. For an English translation of the context of this quote, see Girardot–Ricketts, eds., *Imagination and Meaning*, p. 182. This is quite a triumphalist vision of Christianity. The first to point out the importance of this passage for the history of Eliade's theory of unrecognizability are Culianu, *Mircea Eliade*, pp. 210–211, and Dancă, *Definitio Sacri*, p. 217. On the superiority of the Christian theophany according to Eliade, see Groza, *The Phenomenolization of Time*, pp. 154–155, and Paul M. McKowen, "The Christology of Mircea Eliade," in Arcade–Manea–Stamatescu, eds., *Homo Religiosus*, pp. 184–191.

42. *Oceanography*, pp. 69–70, trans. in *Imagination and Meaning*, pp. 181–183.

43. I adopt this phrase, used in another context by Bruno Pinchard, *Meditations mytho-logiques* (Paris, 2002), pp. 91–96.

44. Of his short story "The Snake," which was written in hurry, without even consulting the earlier parts that had already been sent to the typist.

45. Compare, however, Eliade's quite different assumption where another short story of his is concerned, "With the Gipsy Girls," which he recommended reading not as a cipher but as containing a message about a different reality that is created in the literary work itself. See *No Souvenirs*, pp. 307–308. It has to do with a certain type of death, an issue that will be dealt with in ch. 3.

46. *Autobiography*, I, pp. 321–322. On this passage, see also Allen, *Myth and Religion*, p. 88. See also the interesting parallel found in an autobiographical fragment of 1953, translated in Girardot–Ricketts, eds., *Imagination and Meaning*, pp. 123–124. It should be mentioned that in one of his latest short stories, "Under the Shadow of a Lily," the issues of "banal" and "camouflage" play a major role. See *Inedited Short Stories*, pp. 122, 124, 135.

47. See *Waiting for the Dawn*, pp. 19–20. See also Eliade's confession as to his attraction to night and darkness in *Portugal Journal*, I, pp. 257–258. Eliade believed in the affinities between the sacred, myths, art and literature, and oneiric states of mind. See Allen, *Myth and Religion*, pp. 181, 272, 278, 281. In an interesting instance found in his *Journal*, on November 3, 1949, he explicitly connects the composition of his literature to an oneiric state of mind, which cannot coexist with a critical one. See Mac Linscott Ricketts, "Mircea Eliade and the Writing of the Forbidden Forest," in *Imagination and Meaning*, pp. 105–106. For the separation between the literary and the scientific, see also Eliade's essay written in 1953, reprinted in *Memoirs*, p. 229, where he describes his work on "The Snake." For the discovery of night by romantic authors, see *No Souvenirs*, p. 326.

48. *No Souvenirs*, p. 184.

49. See below for another quote from this page.

50. See *Autobiography*, I, p. 153. For more on Eliade's spiritual journey, see Rodney L. Taylor, "Mircea Eliade: the Self and the Journey," in *Waiting for the Dawn*, pp. 131–133.

51. The English translation has here "mask," but the Romanian original has here "misterul camuflajului." See *Jurnalul*, II, ed. Mircea Handoca (Bucharest, 1993), p. 222.

52. *Journal*, III, pp. 220–221. See also ibid., pp. 135–136, 227–228. Eliade did not leave a sustained reflection on the topic in the last decade of his life.

53. Culianu, *The Sin against the Spirit*, p. 131. On "signs," see more below at the end of ch. 6.

54. *Archaic and Universal*, pp. 160–165. For other important references to Eliade's Hindu background, see also Dancă, *Definitio Sacri*, pp. 193–198, 209–216; Dudley, *Religion on Trial*, pp. 105–118; and Aldo Natale Terrin, "L'Ame orientale dans la methodologie et dans la pensée historique de Mircea Eliade," in *Deux explorateurs de la pensée humaine, George Dumézil et Mircea Eliade*, eds. Jules Ries–Natale Spineto (Turnhout, 2003), pp. 263–288. See also the more general observation of Eliade himself in his *Autobiography*, I, p. 203.

55. *No Souvenirs*, p. 191.

56. Eliade, *The Sacred & the Profane*, p. 11. The marginal role played by the concept of camouflage in this book should be pointed out. See pp. 186, 187, for short discussions of the camouflage of myths in literature. In this passage, the assumption is that hierophanies are objective events, and not a matter of hermeneutics. See also ibid., p. 12. For another instance of interpreting Jesus the historical person as a concealment of the divine nature, see Eliade, *Images and Symbols*, pp.

170–171.

57. See also Eliade, *Patterns in Comparative Religion*, p. 30 n. 1. It is surprising that in this first substantial survey by Eliade of the morphology of the sacred, the concept of camouflage of the sacred is absent.

58. *Oceanography*, p. 70.

59. Ibid. This is also the case in the formulation found much later in Eliade, *Myths, Dreams, and Mysteries*, p. 124.

60. *Myth and Reality*, p. 113, and see also *The Sacred & the Profane*, p. 112.

61. *No Souvenirs*, p. 71. For an interesting parallel to this view, that Eliade claims there that "I came to understand," see the view of Julius Evola, with whom Eliade was in close contact, as adduced by Dubuisson, *Mythologies*, p. 292, n. 81. See also in that volume p. 293, n. 98.

62. I find the entire scholarly tradition that refers to the syntagm "Judeo-Christian" as a homogenous entity over two millennia quite problematic, especially because Eliade is so eager to distinguish within Christianity a separate entity he designates as cosmic Christianity, which allegedly survived in the same Carpathians. See also his *Images and Symbols*, pp. 164, 168–170. See also below, Final Remarks.

63. The vision of a homogenous West is barely understandable, because of his strong reading of the Judeo-Christian tradition. In a way, Eliade was a Hegelian thinker, since he attributes to some developments, like the Jewish discovery of meaning in history and the exclusive adoption of the linear time, the Christian Incarnation, or the impact of Hegel, too great an impact on large-scale groups. Those dramatic shifts added new theories to old ones that continued to have their impacts later on.

64. I skip here a very important discussion dealing with the negative role of language in Western thought, to which I hope to return elsewhere.

65. On the concept of "immediate realities," see also Eliade, *Images and Symbols*, p. 177.

66. On this pattern, which is very important in Eliade's phenomenology of religion, see, e.g., his *Patterns in Comparative Religions*, pp. 419–420; Wasserstrom, *Religion after Religion*, pp. 67–82; and the next chapter.

67. On this concept, see his short survey in his *Fragmentarium*, published in 1939 and reprinted in *The Way to the Center*, pp. 126–127.

68. "Podul," in *In Dionysius's Court*, pp. 197–198. See also Eliade, *No Souvenirs*, p. 205, and Glodeanu, *Coordinates of the Imaginary*, pp. 102–103.

69. See below at the end of ch. 6.

70. Printed in *In the Court of Dionysius*, pp. 566, 572, 577, 593.

71. See especially Eliade's totally unheroic description of Jesus in the *Portugal Journal*, I, pp. 273–274, and its less provocative reverberation in his *Images and Symbols*, p. 170. Eliade ignores the entire scholarly literature and primary texts dealing with the extraordinary biography of the founders of religion, e.g., Lord Raglan, *The Hero: A Study in Tradition, Myth and Drama* (Mineola, 2003).

72. *Autobiography*, I, p. 190.

73. Ibid., I, p. 199. See also *No Souvenirs*, pp. 188–189, where again the work of maya is invoked in the context of Eliade's two girlfriends.

74. Cf. his "Politics, Etcetera," p. 278.

75. *Autobiography*, I, p. 199.

76. Ibid., p. 189.

77. "Politics, Etcetera," p. 278.

78. See also *Autobiography*, I, pp. 256–257.

79. Ibid., I, p. 264.

80. His "Politics, Etcetera," p. 280.

81. *Autobiography*, I, p. 256. Emphasis in the original.

82. On Hindu influence in early Eliade, see, more recently, Ţurcanu, "Southeast Europe," p. 242.

83. See Ţurcanu, ibid., p. 246.

84. *Autobiography*, I, p. 246.

85. *Portugal Journal*, I, pp. 270–271. See also Alexandrescu, *Mircea Eliade from Portugal*, pp. 215–216.

86. This mission is described in the same journal as the discovery of the pre-Socratics—namely, the primitive men—and bringing them back to life. See ibid., I, p. 284.

87. *No Souvenirs*, p. 189.

88. See Eliade's remark about another girlfriend he had in 1928, Rica: "I knew that I shall leave her behind, and that I shall go ahead, alone" ("Şantier," in *Prose*, p. 362). Compare to the descriptions of the protagonist's relationship with his girlfriends in his early novel *Gaudeamus*. This lady was identified as Rica Botez, who recalled her relationship with Eliade in an interview with Handoca, *Interviews with and about Mircea Eliade*, pp. 82–93.

89. See also Alexandrescu, *Mircea Eliade from Portugal*, pp. 215–216, who mentions Eliade's modelation of his life.

90. "Podul," in *In Curtea lui Dionis*, p. 202.

91. Ibid.

92. Ibid., p. 199.

93. *No Souvenirs*, p. 184. Compare also to his *Autobiography*, I, p. 153.

94. See *Autobiography*, I, p. 191.

95. Ibid., pp. 189–190. See also Eliade, *Ordeal by Labyrinth*, p. 47.

96. "Creating a Brahman: A Structural Approach to Religion," in *Methodological Issues in Religious Studies*, ed. Robert B., Baird (Chico, 1975), p. 55; and Dubuisson, *Mythologies*, p. 193.

97. *No Souvenirs*, p. 268. For this dynamic, see also the discussions in *Cosmology and Babylonian Alchemy*, adduced above in the Introduction.

98. Culianu, *Mircea Eliade*, p. 256, and his "Mircea Eliade et la Tortue Borgne," in Arcade–Manea–Stamatescu, eds., *Homo Religiosus*, pp. 83–84; and see also Eliade, *Images and Symbols*, pp. 20–21.

99. See also Allen, *Myth and Religion*, pp. 268–269. Eliade was indubitably aware of this problem, but he chose another methodological approach. See, e.g., Eliade, *Images and Symbols*, p. 163; id., *Myths, Dreams, and Mysteries*, p. 118.

100. "Capricorn," p. 211.

101. *Devarim be-Go, Explications and Implications* (Tel Aviv, 1976), p. 52 (Hebrew). Thanks to the late Leon Volovici who drew my attention to this passage.

102. *Religion after Religion*, p. 59.

103. pp. 141, 476–477.

104. For Scholem's search for keys for understanding Kabbalah, see Idel, *Old Worlds, New Mirrors*, pp. 109–131.

105. See *Images and Symbols*, p. 178.

106. See Eliade's introduction to his *Two Strange Tales*, p. x.

107. See Allen, *Structure and Creativity*, pp. 130–133; id., *Myth and Religion*, pp. 96–97, 110–113; and Dubuisson, *Mythologies*, p. 305. For maya and Varuna as ambiguous and ambivalent, see Eliade, *History of Religious Ideas*, I, pp. 202–203.

108. Simion, *Knots and Signs of Prose*, p. 217.

109. On Eliade's interpretation of Heidegger as if dealing with camouflage, see ch. 3.

110. His article "Survivances et camouflages des mythes," included in his *Aspects du Mythe*, pp. 197–231, deals with the camouflage of myths, but only briefly with the camouflage of the sacred, while elsewhere he deals with the camouflage in modern artists; the sole brief discussion of camouflage, on pp. 174–175, does not, again, refer to any specific source. See Allen, *Myth and Religion*, pp. 269–290. My concern here, however, is with the pertinence of the theory of the camouflage of the sacred in the banal in religion, not in modern life in a more diffuse manner, which is another topic.

111. *History of Religious Ideas*, I, p. 263: "sacrality is in a sense camouflaged in the immediate, in the natural, in the everyday....The sacralization of human finitude and of the banality of the ordinary existence is a comparatively frequent phenomenon in the history of religion." This statement is reminiscent of what he wrote in his *personalia* and *literaria* adduced above. Here we have a tangible example for a transition of earlier views expressed in non-academic contexts, in an academic text. See also the next footnote.

112. Ibid., p. 283, no one single reference to those cases was given. It should also be mentioned that in Eliade's reader *From Primitives to Zen*, pp. 155–175, in the section entitled "Man and the Sacred," no one single text or remark dealing with the theory of camouflage can be found. This does not mean that more diligent scholars of Eliade's work than I will not discover somewhere some more references to camouflage of the sacred in his *academica*, and I very much look forward to reading them.

113. *Journal III*, p. 228. See also, above, the quote from ibid., pp. 220–221. He returned, however, to the topic of camouflage once again in 1982, in his "Under the Shadow of a Lily." For other recurrences of this theme, see *No Souvenirs*, pp. 31, 205.

114. See *History of Religious Ideas*, I, p. XVI.

115. See Rennie, *Reconstructing Eliade*, pp. 215–230, and Dancă, *Definitio Sacri*, p. 219.

116. The combination of the Hindu and the Christian elements in Eliade's theory of camouflage has been pointed out by Lazu, "Dialectica Sacrului," pp. 110–116.

117. See the autobiographical fragment of 1953, translated in *Imagination and Meaning*, pp. 123–124. For the Romanian original see the appendix to the *Memoirs*.

118. *The Quest*, p. 139, emphasis in the original. See also Eliade, *Ordeal by Labyrinth*, pp. 151, 155, 177.

119. See e.g, *Absorbing Perfections*, pp. 8–14, 184–185, 263–265, 280–283.

120. *Correspondence*, I, p. 112, emphases in the original. See also Acterian, *Cioran, Eliade, Ionesco*, pp. 50–51.

121. *Journal IV, 1979–1985*, tr. Mac Linscott Ricketts (Chicago–London, 1990), pp. 111–112; compare to his *History of Religious Ideas*, I, p. 176.

122. See Paul Barbăneagră, *Arhitectura și geografia sacră, Mircea Eliade și descoperirea sacrului* (Iași, 2000), p. 199. Here Guènon's theory accompanies that of Eliade's.

123. See Smith, *Map Is Not Territory*, pp. 88–103, 128.

124. See, especially, Eliade, *Patterns in Comparative Religion*, pp. 410–419; his *Master Manole*, pp. 104–110; id., *Zalmoxis*, pp. 183–187. See also Martin Buber, *The Origin and Meaning of Hasidism*, tr. Maurice Freedman (Atlantic Highlands, 1988), p. 121; and the many myths analyzed by Bruce Lincoln, *Myth, Cosmos and Society* (Cambridge, 1986), and Idel, *Absorbing Perfections*, p. 99.

125. See Eliade, *Contributions à la philosophie de la Renaissance*, pp. 9–59; id., *History of Religious Ideas*, III, pp. 251–255; id., *The Sacred & the Profane*, p. 227; id., *The Quest*, pp. 37–39; id., *Ordeal by Labyrinth*, p. 20; id., *Journal*, III, p. 280. See also Culianu, *Mircea Eliade*, pp. 138–140; Țurcanu, *Mircea Eliade*, pp. 39–42, 112–115; Dudley, *Religion on Trial*, pp. 43–44; Dancă, *Definitio Sacri*, pp. 47–54; Faivre, *Access to Western Esotericism*, p. 44; Dubuisson, *Mythologies*, pp. 275, 279, 294, 297–299, 310 n. 25; Wasserstrom, *Religion after Religion*, pp. 42–47. It should be mentioned that a strong proclivity to occultism is evident in a quite early piece written at the end of his high school period, "Science and Occultism," reprinted in *How I Found the Philosopher's Stone*, pp. 246–247, which has been dealt with in the Introduction and which we shall return to in chs. 2 and 5.

126. See *The Quest*, pp. 55–57. There were, nevertheless, earlier European calls for integration of India in Europe, such as Schopenhauer's. See also below, ch. 5.

127. See ibid., pp. 1–11; Faivre, *Access to Western Esotericism*, p. 108; Țurcanu, *Mircea Eliade*, pp. 443–446.

128. See Wasserstrom, *Religion after Religion*.

129. See my *Ascensions on High*, pp. 216–228, and ch. 7 below. Let me point out that I do not recommend extrapolating from my analyses of the vicissitudes of the academic inquiry of the camouflaged sacred to any other topic in Eliade's works.

130. See, especially, what he wrote in his *Journal*, III, p. 277.

131. Compare to Sorin Alexandrescu's distinction between the literary as imaginative and the academic as retrieving and critical, in "Mircea Eliade, la narrazione contra il significato," in Mincu–Scagno, *Mircea Eliade e l'Italia*, p. 311.

132. See his *Journal*, III, p. 277. See also above, Introduction.

133. On the possibility of transcending human condition by resorting to Yoga techniques, see Eliade, *Yoga*, pp. 85–90, 313–318, 339–341, and some remarks throughout his memorialistic literature. In some instances in his novel *Bengali Nights*, Eliade reports that Maitreyi was looking at him as at a god. On the centrality of the concept of theosis in Orthodox Christianity, see his *History of Religious Ideas*, III, p. 217.

134. *Yoga*, p. 90.

135. "The Man Who Wanted to be Silent," in *Maddalena*, p. 130.

136. *Solilocvii*, pp. 60–61.

137. Ibid., p. 61.

138. "Șantier," in *Prose*, p. 409.

· 2 ·

ANDROGYNE, TOTALITY,
AND REINTEGRATION

Androgyne as a Symbol for
Wholeness and Perfection

*T*here are few themes in the history of religion that have fascinated so many
scholars of religion as the androgyne. Though some studies regard it as an
archetype, others do not.[1] In two important cases, the androgyne is understood as
representing, schematically, the concept or state of wholeness. This is the case, in an
accentuated manner, in Eliade's writings, and in those of Carl G. Jung[2] and many of
their followers. As towering intellectual figures, both thinkers extended their interests beyond the classical forms of the Judeo-Christian tradition and integrated into
their writings and thought the contents of literatures and modes of thought that were
marginal in European culture. Jung had progressively developed his theory of archetypes, and as part of it, the androgyne—or the hermaphrodite, as he preferred to designate it—which was understood as referring to the union of opposites, or what he
called the conjunction, taking place within the psyche of the individual.[3] As part of
this understanding of the concept of individual wholeness as the union between the
contraries, based most substantially on Chinese philosophy and alchemical texts, later
he also adduced several Kabbalistic texts basically extracted from Latin translations, and in a way an interpretation of Kabbalistic texts done by Christian

Kabbalists and published in the late 17th century as the voluminous collection of different texts known as *Kabbala Denudata* produced by Knorr von Rosenroth, who was also an alchemist.[4] Also, Jung's heavy reliance on Arthur Waite's writings concerning Kabbalah does not add to accurate information, as he was a kind of modern esoteric figure who offered synthetic views based on different sorts of knowledge.

For Jung, the hermaphroditic expressions are reflections of inner developments, signs of a spiritual progress, rather than a symbol for a form of behavior, as we shall see below in the case of Kabbalah. The Swiss psychoanalyst conceived of the androgynous Adam as expressing a form of totality.[5] The Platonic origin of Jung's vision of the hermaphrodite as perfection is obvious, as he used the image of the sphere for the self. As he put it in the context of the Anthropos, or the hermaphrodite: "The self wants to be made manifest in the work, and for this reason the opus is a process of individuation, a becoming of the self. The self is the total, timeless man and as such corresponds to the original spherical, bisexual being."[6] In fact, when dealing with an earlier stage of the spiritual process, Jung says: "Our pictures of the *coniunctio* are to be understood in this sense: union on the biological level is a symbol of the *unio oppositorum* at its highest."[7] Needless to say, Jung conceived his understanding of the meaning of androgyny to be universal,[8] and in general, his theory as a science.[9]

Independently of Jung's theory of the archetypes, and in quite similar terms, we learn from Eliade in his *Myths, Dreams and Mysteries* that androgyny is "an archaic and universal formula for the expression of wholeness, the coexistence of the contraries, or *coincidentia oppositorum*...symboliz[ing]...perfection...[and] ultimate being."[10] The basic assumption is that androgyny points to an integrated human being, regarded as perfect.[11] In a way, this approach is basically a Platonic view, since the initial androgyny is supposed to be recuperated by the union between the two parts of the divided sphere. The mythical Adam of Genesis 1 before bisection, and Plato's spherical androgyne, are both conceived by Eliade as ideal figures, symbols of a state that should be retrieved by a spiritual development that will annihilate the present separation and blur the differences between the sexes. Crucial for understanding my analysis below is the occurrence of the term "universal." This universal nature is related to what I refer to as an assumption of stability, namely the existence of basic meaning that underlies the different versions of theme in the various cultures. Moreover, according to Eliade, it is also an archaic symbol.

The question may be asked: Why was this imposition of Plato's interpretation of androgyny as explaining the original perfect unity, and thus the later erotic attraction between the two sexes, so successful? I would like to offer two answers, which are interrelated: First, unlike in other cases where androgyny is discussed, Plato offered an explicit and rather elaborate meaning for the myth he told, and second, the basic situation found in the Platonic myth, the divided human, has been associated with the dominant religious theology, Christianity, with its tenet of the fallen humanity, and implicitly with anthropology. In both cases, there is a divinity which punishes man, and division is conceived of as being part of the human plight, namely, of the fall. Implicitly, Plato was understood as offering an answer to the question that preoccupies some spiritually oriented modern minds discontent with solutions offered by historical religions: What can be done in the present situation of the fall, that is, how is it possible to achieve perfection by [re-]integration? Moreover, the repetition of Plato's myth in Western culture in a variety of forms created the feeling that androgyne has only one specific meaning. This is the case with some Gnostic, Neoplatonic, and Hermetic thinkers, with Christian mystics like John Scotus Eurigena, Jacob Boehme, Emanuel Swedenborg (and under his influence, William Blake and Balzac), Franz von Baader, and the Shakers, and more recently with Schleiermacher and Nietzsche, and the Russians mystical thinkers who adopted and developed sophiological-mystical approaches, like Vladimir S. Soloviov and Nicolai Berdiaev, and theosophists like Rudolf Steiner, to give only a few outstanding examples.

Moreover, it is plausible that some of the Kabbalistic discussions contributed to the emergence of the discussions of the sexually distinct poles in each of the two sexes, as found in the 17th- and 18th-century European occultists who have been discussed at length, especially in the studies of Antoine Faivre.[12] However, all of them belong to what can be called the Platonic-Christian tradition, which can be described as Eurocentric, which has been understood as dealing with spiritual issues that are independent of circumstances, so that a specific Platonico-Christian concern was imagined as representing a universal meaning. The very reference to the concept of archetype is of Platonic extraction, assuming both a vision of reality in general and a common source and meaning for all the human expressions of bodily duality. It should be mentioned that although it also deals with the archetype of the androgyne, Elemire Zolla's later essay on the topic was much less inclined to adopt a uniform and clear-cut vision of its meaning, opting instead to refer to it as conveying elusiveness and sexual indeterminacy.[13]

The Androgyne in Eliade's Academica: A Tentative Inventory

Since 1938, Eliade returned in many of his writings about religion to the significance he discerned in the various myths of the androgyne, a theme that encapsulates, according to his interpretations, some of his most important ideals of archaic religions. Also, scholarship in the field started to address this theme,[14] which is central to Eliade's vision of religion, and that scholarship significantly reverberated in theories of other scholars who did not deal with Eliade's thought per se.[15] In fact, Eliade reiterates some discussions found in writings by a series of 17th- and 18th-century theosophists and occultists that were influential on some late 19th- and 20th-century figures whose writings he was acquainted with.

I shall try below to deal with the subject of androgyny in a much more detailed manner than has been done previously. On the one hand, taking into consideration the centrality of some early Romanian treatments of Eliade's, I compare them with the different later versions of his treatments and survey the changes; on the other hand, I shall analyze some of the sources he adduced and his interpretations of some of them in order to articulate his understanding of the androgyne as an archetype. My claim will be that in important discussions of the theme in the early Eliade, he was influenced by some Kabbalistic themes that later on were eliminated from his presentations, for reasons I shall suggest below. Methodologically, I shall adopt the approach that was stipulated by Eliade himself, and used also by other scholars, which assumes that in order to understand him better, we should consider the three major types of his literary works, the academic, the literary, and the biographical, which I mentioned in the Introduction. Let me start with mapping the major steps of his academic discussions of the theme, then turn to the pertinent literary expressions, and finally to some of the salient biographical data. I shall try to exhaust the first and last short discussions [A] and [F] immediately below, while the longer essays in Romanian, the variants [B] and [C], the French [D], and the French/English [E] will be dealt with in the following two sections.

[A] In March 1938, Eliade published in Romanian a short essay entitled "Allegory or 'Secret Language,'" which dealt in its first part with the mystical nature of the content of the biblical Song of Songs.[16] The possible contribution of this essay (which actually has a much earlier version that is less relevant for our discussions below) for understanding some of Eliade's earliest sources and the manner in which he dealt with them has not been recognized yet by scholars, and for this reason I shall start my survey with a more detailed description of some of its contents. Eliade quotes a Zoharic statement to the effect that (I translate from his Romanian text) "It is necessary that man should sanctify himself before the conjugal union, so that the infant that will be born will have a complete figure....The human form corresponds to the celestial forms."[17] The Zoharic text is drawn from Paul Vulliaud's book *La Cantique des Cantiques d'après la tradition juive*.[18] The French author, who belongs to a tradition of French occultists, fascinated Eliade for many years, and, as pointed out by Wasserstrom, Eliade visited Vulliaud's house in France and even wrote a preface to one of his books.[19] In fact, the extent of his influence on Eliade insofar as other topics is concerned still needs special inquiry.[20] In the footnote to the Zoharic passage quoted above, Eliade wrote:

> The expression "so that the infant will have a complete figure" refers, indubitably to "an entire[21] man," the androgyne, the ideal of all the metaphysical and religious traditions. The references to the "original man" in the Zohar are innumerable,[22] and that [the generic] man comprises the female and the male that are melted perfectly in one body and which have a single soul (like Adam, before Eve was created from his rib).

The term "androgyne," like the assumption of the melting of the male and female into one body and one soul, are not found in the Zoharic text, and in my opinion, they do not reflect a plausible reading of the Zoharic thought. However, Vulliaud's claim of total union comes from a passage found in a book by an occultist author, the Lyonnese author Antoine Blanc de Saint-Bonnet, a follower of Swedenborg, adduced again verbatim by Vulliaud one page before the above passage from the Zohar, where it is written at the end of the citation: "L'homme male et l'homme femelle sont constitutes de telles sorte que'ils doivent devenir un seul homme, ou plutot une seule ame: et quand ils sont devenue un, il sont l'homme complet."[23] This is part of a lengthy exposition of a Christian understanding of the relations between male and female, quoted by Vulliaud, which culminates in a passage that is not quoted by Vulliaud, but follows the French citation adduced above: "Car ni « l'homme n'est point sans la femme », ni « la femme n'est point sans l'homme » dit S. Paul.[24] Sans cette union, ils sont deux; chacun se sent comme un être divisé."[25] Thus, the passage adduced by Vulliaud from his older Lyonnese compatriot has nothing to do with Kabbalah, at least not explicitly, but it is a nice Catholic mystical interpretation of a view that is attributed, problematically, I must say, to St. Paul, combined with a vision of reintegration of the lost unity, stemming most probably from an earlier occultist tradition.[26] However, immediately after the quotation he cited from de Saint-Bonnet,[27] as adduced above (without, however, mentioning St. Paul), Vulliaud writes: "La citation serait interminable. On se rappelle les textes identiques de la Kabbalah."[28] Indeed, Vulliaud presents immediately afterwards a series of Zoharic texts that actually discuss the conjugal union between male and female, without referring to the loss of their sexes.

When reading Vulliaud, the quite young Eliade was impressed by the French occultist's claims that the Kabbalah agrees with the passage of de Saint-Bonnet, and, in turn, he presented the Zohar in such a manner, dealing with the strong union of the two sexes, culminating in becoming one body. Then, on the basis of the misunderstanding created by Vulliaud's claim, Eliade introduced the concept of the melting of the two bodies (in Romanian, contopire[29]), which subsequently attracted a strong

androgynous reading of the Zoharic source. To be sure, such an androgynous reading is not found explicitly in either the interpretation of de Saint-Bonnet or in that
of Vulliaud, who did not use this term, at least not in this context, and even less in
the Zoharic source. In this context, the important observation by Wasserstrom as to
the contribution of Christian Kabbalah to understanding the concept of reintegration of all beings should be highlighted.[30] He pointed out the common reference by
both Scholem and Eliade to the concept of the reintegration of all beings, which stems
from the mid-18th-century occultist Martines de Pasqually (c. 1725–1774), who was
perhaps of Marrano origin. About his views, Eliade writes that "it suffices to say that
for him the goal of initiation was to reintegrate man with his lost 'Adamic privileges,'
i.e., to recover the primeval condition of 'men-gods created in the image of God.'"[31]
However, in Eliade's idiosyncratic interpretation, the Zoharic passages dealing with
marriage have become a pursuit of a reintegration into androgyny. Immediately
before the passage dealing with the Zohar, Eliade wrote: "Love and marriage are even
today, in some extra-European human societies, rituals and metaphysical valorifica-
tions of existence....Even the physics of love has a ceremonial character, by means of
which man integrates himself in cosmic rhythms."[32]

Thus, the alleged Zoharic "androgynous" state is invoked in order to exemplify
the experience of integration within the cosmic rhythms by love or marriage. Eliade's
assumption is that according to the Zohar, marriage is described as a return to the
Adamic state, and thus to androgyny. I do not know why Eliade implies that the
Zoharic texts refer to the integration in cosmic rhythms, though a reading of the
Zohar allows the assumption that human sexual love imitates and also has an impact
on divine sexual intercourses. This brief discussion contains the first available nexus
between the state of androgyny and the integration into a wider situation that is the
core of Eliade's later discussions of the androgyne. If I am correct, it seems that
Eliade's reading of the Zohar, mediated, as seen above, by occultists and esotericists,
contains the first textual document that illustrates Eliade's valorification of androgyny as a main symbol for a transformation that is related to reintegration.[33]

To summarize the importance of this short discussion found in Eliade's 1938
essay: For the first time I am aware of in his writings he references the concept of the
androgyne as "the ideal of all the metaphysical and religious traditions," and this is done
on the basis of what he understood to be a Zoharic passage. This approach, which
looks for one unifying persistent tradition, becomes a blueprint of Eliade's later discussions of the androgyne, even when the book of the Zohar is not mentioned again.

[B] In January 1940 Eliade published in the periodical *Universul Literar* a small
piece entitled "In Search of Adam." Written in Romanian for a larger audience, there
are only few footnotes.[34] This short treatment is part of a longer series dealing with

related issues such as "Adam and Eve," "Adam and Golgotha," and the androgyne in Balzac's short story "Seraphita," which were published before and after this piece in the same periodical. This is a series of essays that was not necessarily unified, and reading them, one does not have the feeling that one cannot understand one piece without reading the others. Though some of the essays deal with dualities regarding gods and men, this duality is not necessarily a matter of a sexual polarity. The content of this piece, as well as the elaboration in [C], will be discussed below in section 3.

[C] In the second part of 1942 the entire series of articles mentioned above was reprinted as a booklet entitled *Mitul reintegrării* (*The Myth of Reintegration*) in Romanian in Bucharest.[35] In it the material is presented in a relatively more unified manner, and is accompanied by more footnotes, and some few short passages have been added to version [B]. In this variant, the essays published earlier become part of a more accentuated vision dealing with what Eliade described now emphatically as "the myth of reintegration." This is a loose title, which represents only some parts of the essays, but it creates the impression that there is one overarching theme unifying the booklet. This myth seems to be constituted by the totalization of good and evil, or the sacred and profane, which is a parallel of the totalization related to the androgyne, namely of male and female, and confers some form of unity, as reflected in the title which emphasizes "the myth." Thus, androgyny, or androgynization, is part of a wider mythical complex, that of reintegration of things that were split into polarities and are reunited in order to reconstruct the primordial perfection. This time, the piece on the search for Adam is entitled "The Androgyne Archetype." The work of re-editing the material that strives to transform the separate essays into a more integrated volume was done mainly in Lisbon, as Eliade was a cultural attaché of Romania in Portugal. Eliade describes it as just a "simple essay."[36]

[D] Eliade delivered a lecture at the Eranos conference in Ascona, Switzerland, which was published in French in the *Eranos Jarbuch* of 1958 as "La *coincidentia oppositorum* et le mystère de la totalité." It covers some of the topics discussed in the essays collected in the *Myth of Reintegration*.[37] Its content will be discussed in section 3.

[E] The Eranos lecture was slightly amplified, both in text and footnotes, and published again in French in 1962 as part of the collection *Méphistophélès et l'androgyne*.[38] The duality of the content reflected in the title better reflects the content of the essays, since his discussions of Faust and Mephistopheles do not assume an androgyny. This French version has been translated into English in the collection of articles *The Two and the One*, published in 1965.[39] This variant is the best known, and many of the descriptions of Eliade's view on the androgyne are based on it.

[F] In Eliade's *Encyclopedia of Religion* the entry on the *androgyne* was signed by

Eliade himself, together with Wendy Doniger O'Flaherty.[40] This is a more sophisticated piece from the conceptual point of view, based on a new distinction between the splitting and fused androgyny found in some years beforehand in Doniger O'Flaherty's book,[41] but the broader content does not fall under my concerns here, except for the repetition of some of his earlier views, especially those in *The Two and the One*.[42] So, for example, we learn that

> In the mythology of mysticism, however, chaos is positive; the desire to merge back into chaos is the goal of human existence, the supreme integration toward which one strives. In many rituals, too, androgyny is "a symbolic restoration of 'Chaos,' of the undifferentiated unity that that preceded the Creation, and this return to the homogeneous takes the form of a supreme regeneration, a prodigious increase of power."[43]

In the *Encyclopedia*, the androgyny of Adam according to the Bible and the Midrash are succinctly mentioned, but again, neither the Zohar nor the Kabbalah in its Jewish forms, the most important literature, with the rich repository of different concepts and approaches to the androgyne, are mentioned.[44] It should be mentioned that despite the existence of this encyclopedia entry, for a long period in his career, namely between 1958 and 1986, Eliade did not return in a significant manner to the topic of androgyny that had fascinated him so much in the earlier phase of his life. It seems that the variant [E] represents the longest and most representative treatment of the theme under scrutiny here.

The first five versions are part of a growth of a small nucleus that was articulated already in 1938, but, as we shall see below, this is not just a matter of adding more material to the later versions, but also of subtracting from the French-English versions some of the sources used in the two earlier Romanian versions. In addition to these treatments, the issue has been dealt with in a more succinct manner in his other writings.[45] Thus, despite the very significant textual fluidity, due to both the expanded size and the translation from language to language, conceptual fluidity is relatively small.

Early Conceptualizations of the Androgyne in Two Romanian Essays

Let me elaborate now on the two Romanian versions [B] and [C], which are less known in Western studies that capitalize much more on [D] and [F]. What are Eliade's major claims in the earlier nucleus as formulated in these two Romanian versions? Let me summarize the claims in versions [B] and [C]:

1. The myth of the androgyne is found in the three mystical traditions of
    the monotheistic religions, as a secret tradition expressed in allegories
    and symbols, and in such a manner, alchemy also should be understood.

2. Secrecy is connected to the "fact" that those mystical traditions have been
    conceived of as heretical, and also because this myth stems from the
    Greco-Christian Gnosticism, which inherited this view from much
    earlier sources that predate the later monotheistic religions by a millen-
    nium. Gnosticism itself was a secret-occult movement based on rituals
    of initiation. According to Eliade, the myth of the androgyne occupies
    a central place in Gnosticism, and he adduces three examples from
    Gnostic texts as preserved by the Fathers of the Church: from the
    Evangelium of the Egyptians, quoted in Clement of Alexandria; from
    Simon the Magus, as preserved in St. Hypolitus; and from the Naasean
    Gnostic school. Eliade quotes briefly from the three Gnostic sources.
    Though the Gnostic traditions are fragmentary, they are understood as
    preserving much earlier traditions.

3. Eliade claims that the androgyne is a symbol for human perfection, and
    that the achievement of such perfection is predicated upon the transcen-
    dence of the sexual polarity and the return to the primordial state, to
    an amorphous and indeterminate situation, which he refers to explic-
    itly as a reintegration, or "totalization."

4. This return is compared to the mystics' loss within or their absorption
    into the divinity, or the Hindu ascetics' state of impassibility and detach-
    ment, "like stones." This is the result of the thirst for abolishing the
    human condition, a claim that runs through Eliade's oeuvre in general.

5. This understanding of the androgyne is conceived of as being shared by
    persons over millennia and in different religions, and conceived of as an
    "archetype."

6. In some Jewish traditions Adam was conceived of as bisexual and thus
    an undetermined being, and the reintegration is predicated upon a
    return to an Adamic state.[46]

7. Eliade mentions explicitly the interest in the topic of androgyny by Jacob
    Boehme, E. Swedenborg, and F. von Baader, thus inscribing himself in
    the series of occultist thinkers.[47]

In the enlarged Romanian version [C], Eliade added some notes and footnotes
and a few paragraphs, which do not transform the earlier version in a dramatic man-

ner. Nevertheless, among the most significant changes we may mention is the reference to Philo and early Christianity as expressing an androgynous vision in the figure of the Logos. Now the reintegration is depicted as taking place within the "pre-existent totality of the Logos," as part of a scheme that includes three stages:

1. The pre-existent Logos as the total, universal or divine, reality.
2. The fall, or the fragmentation, and its corollary, suffering.
3. The Redeemer reintegrates in his totality the entire existence, differentiated in individual lives.[48]

Interestingly enough, this threefold drama, which combines cosmic and individual events, does not recur in the later variants of Eliade's discussion of reintegration.

Those additions are creating a tension between the claims in version [B] as to the subversive dimensions of the secret traditions and the claim in [C] that Philo and Paul adopted androgynous approaches. It is hard to see in those two figures hidden Gnostics and marginal figures in the history of the monotheistic traditions.

This regression to the amorphous totality is described now as having a "deep metaphysical" sense. The spiritual reintegration has been formulated, according to Eliade, "sometimes in mythical terms, sometimes in theological terms."[49]

In the two later Romanian versions, Eliade refers to the Jewish mystical tradition, and made some observations in this context. In comparison to both the Christian and the Muslim mysticisms, he gives more space to the Jewish material, and following the assessments in variant [B], he writes:

> The myth of the androgyne was likewise active in Kabbalah, though those texts, which are extremely difficult, circulated in very restrained circles of learned persons and Jewish mystics. The Zohar (III, 5a, 18b etc.) preserves even a "marital" interpretation. Of the myth of the androgyne: man does not become a real person (namely an original man), but when he achieves on earth the conjugal union. This is an echo of an ancient mystical function of the marriage: the perfection of the individual by totalization. In fact, the entire Kabbalah is based upon the homologization of man/God, and the human marriage is not, for the Jewish mysticism (which in its majority is occult commentaries on the Song of Songs),[50] but a pale image of the union of Israel with God. On another occasion we shall see how the myth of the androgyne is clearer at the beginning of Judaism, since Adam was conceived of as an androgyne.[51]

Indeed, as he promised, he returned to the question of Adam's androgyny in another essay published in the same month, January 1940, in the same journal, entitled "Adam and Eve."[52] Here, on the bases of some studies concerning the interpretation of Genesis 1:27 and of Midrashic interpretations of the verse, he describes

Adam as an androgynous being. His claim is that the primordial men in many cultures were always described in such a manner, and he minimizes the importance of the claim of one of the scholars[53] who proposed to see an Indo-European impact on the Semitic versions of this myth, arguing that the theme of the androgynous first man is too widespread to adopt such a solution.[54] Eliade adopts the proposal of another scholar who suggested amending the Hebrew text of Genesis 1:27 from the traditional version 'otam, that is, them, to 'oto, that is, him, thus assuming that the creation in the verse refers to the male alone, and not to the male and female together.[55] This is done in order to elicit from the biblical verse a clear androgynous interpretation.[56] As to "homologization," this term stands for the universe of correspondences that Eliade believes the *homo religiosus* discovers between the various planes of reality.[57]

In the earlier versions of the essay on the androgyne, Eliade introduces the importance of ritualistic orgy as one of the means of achieving the state of totalization, or androgynization, an issue that will often preoccupy him in scholarship later.[58] Though this is not the only path toward reintegration—the other one would be Yoga[59]—Eliade assumes that by means of the orgy, the intention was to attain a

> totalization of the good and bad, the same coincidence of the sacred and the profane, the definitive melting of the contraries, the annihilation of the human condition, by a regression toward the nondifferentiated, in the amorphous. The "shift of the garments" is framed perfectly in the orgiastic experience, since also the androgyne is the melting of the contraries in the same individual.[60]

He regards the type of religiosity that pursues reintegration as some form of constant in religion, and writes: "The ideal type of humanity which has been dreamt also by Plato and the Gnostics, and the mystics in the Middle Ages, and the German romantics—is dreamt and realized, by rudimentary ritual means, by 'the wild people now-a-days.'"[61] In *The Myth of Reintegration* he repeats the view found in the earlier essay on the secret language as to the ritual dimension of love.[62] Also here [C], he employs the concept of melting.[63]

Thus, Eliade adopts an approach that conceives of androgyny as both a very ancient tradition and one that inspires the centuries-long search for perfection in the form of androgyny. This perfection is presented by him not just as a myth or an ideal, but as a major topic that is accompanied by rituals of androgynization.[64] Eliade assumes that perfection was envisioned as including the ideal of androgyny and deeds intended to enact it, in both hoary antiquity and during the Middle Ages, as well as much earlier, in archaic traditions. We may therefore discern, in the manner in which the androgyne theme is addressed, that we have here the first meaningful example of the method that is going to inspire Eliade's entire project in the years to come: the importance of a primordial religion, and the repetition of the ancient acts or rituals in order to retrieve the lost perfection.

To summarize the Romanian versions: They are predicated on the assumption that the traditions about the androgyne are very old, were transmitted orally, and reached some Gnostic sources that influenced the three main secret traditions, and from those medieval traditions, modern thinkers like Swedenborg and, under his influence, also Goethe and Balzac, drew their inspiration for their literary compositions. According to the second piece, entitled "Adam and Eve," an ideal vision of Adam, as if he comprises an androgynous structure, reverberated in Midrashic sources. In at least in two places in those essays Eliade refers in a clear manner to the coincidence of the opposites, though this concept does not play a central role in the Romanian essays.[65]

But what is new in the later versions of the earlier Romanian variants? First and foremost, it is the sharper emphasis on the *coincidentia oppositorum* as one of the most significant parts of the totality, and to a certain extent, the emergence of a claim as to the affinities between orgiastic practices and the attainment of the reintegration. However, Eliade is much less interested in integrating religion in the history of Western philosophy than in a prehistorical archaic moment that is reverberating in philosophy.

The Eranos Lecture and Its Later Version

Eliade's paper delivered at the Eranos conference in Ascona on the androgyne was published in French in 1958 as "La *coincidentia oppositorum* et le mystère de la totalité." It seems that the plan to publish in French a more elaborate version of the second Romanian version can be dated as early as February 1943, as we learn from a letter Eliade addressed to his friend in Romania the philosopher Constantin Noica, who took care of publishing his books in Bucharest.[66] In this much later French variant he presented most of the topics found already in the series of publications reprinted in *The Myth of Reintegration*, but the manner in which the material was represented, and the decisions about what parts of the material adduced earlier should be eliminated, generated a dramatically different exposition, though the original message remained basically the same. Eliade excluded the theory of the secret transmission, the references to the three mystical traditions, and any discussion of Adam as androgyne, while adducing other materials never mentioned beforehand in the Romanian essays.[67] A comparison of the third Romanian variant [C] with the Eranos lecture shows that it is from such a text that Eliade prepared his French lecture, since he included in the later variant almost all the new material found in the 1942 text but not in the variant of 1940. In any case, the 1958 exposition reflects developments in Eliade's scholarship in the early fifties, which include, especially, references to the androgyny of shamans and Yogins. Thus, a totally different balance between the identity of the sources that fostered Eliade's earlier claim about the meaning of androgyne is conspicuous in the Eranos lecture and its later elaboration: It is now grounded in the most recent material he dealt with rather than in what was cited in the Romanian versions, as the occurrence of Shamanism shows.

The exclusion from the new variant of some important parts of the Jewish material, biblical and Kabbalistic, has nothing to do with an effort to repress it, since he introduced a discussion of a Jewish author whom he did not mention earlier in this context, Leone Ebreo, and he still refers to the Midrashic discussion of Adam.[68] There must be one or more reasons for the shift in the nature of the material now considered appropriate to illustrate his theory of reintegration within the totality. It is not the problem of the specific interpretation that Eliade offered, based on the centrality of reintegration, that deterred Eliade from referring to the Zohar at the Eranos meeting, as he did in his earlier versions, but rather, in my opinion, the very situation of engaging the Zohar. One of the reasons for such a reluctance seems to be the daunting and perhaps also haunting presence of Gershom Scholem, who lectured at the Eranos conferences for several years beforehand; I can imagine that Eliade was reluctant to make claims about the nature and history of Jewish mysticism, or what is the meaning of the passage of the Zohar, in Scholem's presence. Scholem, like Eliade, refers to the notion of reintegration.[69] In fact, in the short presentation of the topic of androgyny and wholeness in another lecture delivered at Eranos in 1953, Eliade singled out only the Midrashic passage as relevant for his claim.[70]

However, this explanation holds much less for the removal of the biblical Adam as an archetype or as an androgynous figure. The two Jewish references do indeed deal with the instances where the Greek term "androgyne" has been explicitly mentioned in the sources under consideration, and they are not a matter of a scholar's interpretation. However, the way in which Leone Ebreo has been presented reflects a Christian understanding of the event related to Adam. Eliade claims that Ebreo "tried to connect Plato's myth of the androgyne with the biblical tradition of the Fall."[71] Also, his statement later in his variant, that the dissolution of the androgyne union is a fall, reiterates this misunderstanding.[72]

However, in the Hebrew Bible, and in Ebreo's *Dialoghi d'Amore*, there is no fall that is connected to Adam as an androgyne, an understanding that is an invention of John Scotus Erigena and of Christian Kabbalists, and Eliade read the latter.[73] In doing so, he followed a view he formulated early in his youth, when he claimed that Ebreo left his Jewish-Spanish tradition in order to drink from the "Athene of Medici."[74] However, a perusal of Ebreo's views shows that there is no sign for the two claims of Eliade.[75] On the contrary, the Platonic version is described as different from the two biblical accounts on a crucial issue: Whereas the Bible views the separation between the two sexual aspects of the androgyne as intended to help man, the Platonic version emphasizes this separation as a punishment inflicted by Zeus.[76] Though Ebreo did indeed adopt strong Neoplatonic influences, insofar as the concept of androgyny is concerned, he was more influenced by Maimonides' Aristotelian interpretation of the biblical version, just as his father, Isaac Abravanel, was. Thus, in this version of his discussion of the androgyne, Eliade offers only one single example as to the pertinence of his claims in Jewish sources, namely a Midrashic discussion whose presentation and understanding are problematic. Even in this case, a study that he mentioned in the second Romanian version, by A. H. Krappe, has been eliminated.[77] However, in this later version, Eliade mentions, correctly in my opinion, that Gnosticism is grounded in earlier "Jewish gnosis."[78]

It may be said that in all the main versions of the androgyne as perfection that Eliade presented over the 16 years of repeating his theory, he refers to the Midrash as one of his sources. Almost always, he offers a precise source for his claim, *Bereshit Rabba'* I, 4 fol. 6 col. 2, followed by the translation in English: "man on the right side and woman and on the left side, but God has cloven him into two halves."[79] Sometimes the quote is more expansive, but the last part of it adduced here, dealing with the two halves, does not exist in any Midrashic version of *Bereshit Rabba'* I am acquainted with.[80] That unknown version of the Midrash, assuming the existence of two halves and thus of some form of equality between male and female, does not mean that Eliade attempted to invent or actually invented a Midrashic text. What happened is much simpler: Eliade has simply mistaken the view about the Midrash, expressed by Krappe as his own understanding, as if it were a Hebrew source found in the Midrash. This is, in fact, what the American scholar notes as expressing his own opinion: "Others[81] are of a different opinion: the first man was man on the right side and female on his left: then God separated the two halves."[82] This is not a matter of a scholar rendering into his own words, in a correct manner, the view of earlier Midrashic thinkers, but Krappe's mistake. In my opinion, the concept of two halves does not exist, neither in the specific rabbinic references as adduced by Krappe, nor, to my best knowledge, in the late antiquity rabbinic sources, though it did appear in a totally different type of texts written much later, namely in the mystical sources in the Middle Ages. Krappe's view is not just a paraphrase, but a scholarly opinion that turns out to be erroneous, which Eliade has transformed into a primary text and then quoted as such in a series of his writings.

However, those philological errors are minor issues in comparison to the much broader problem, which consists in the fact that the major claim of Eliade regarding the androgyne as an ideal does not appear in the Midrash, and in fact it contradicts it. Though Eliade never expressly said that the androgyne is, according to the Midrash, an ideal figure, this is the significance of his several citations of the "Midrashic" passage. The Eranos lecture includes therefore a misrepresentation of the Midrashic view that continues what may be found already in the Romanian versions: the implicit assumption that the androgynous status of Adam, which Eliade took so much pain to demonstrate as pertinent, is regarded by the Midrashic authors as ideal. The Midrashic texts, following the Hebrew Bible, conceived of the status of Adam after the bisection of Eve from his body as better than beforehand. Eliade, perhaps following Krappe, applied a Platonic reading of the ideal spherical body in the manner Plato described the androgyne, as being an ideal, to the Midrash, whose conceptual framework is different. However, following Dumezil, Eliade is concerned with the more ancient theories that he translate in terms of androgyny, conceived of as a prephilosophical form of reflection.[83] Thus, Eliade simplifies complexities found in cultures that developed through millennia to one vision that is imposed from another culture, convinced as he was that one basic pattern underlies "religion."

Thus, Jewish material that played a major role in the 1940/1942 versions of his studies, and even earlier, was marginalized in the 1958 lecture at the Eranos conference in Ascona, and what remained is rather closer to a caricature of a more variegated and rich picture of the concepts of androgyne and *du-partzufim* found in Judaism.[84] If the correctness of the thesis of the ideal androgyne depends in a significant manner on the two Jewish sources that lingered in the postwar variants of his discussions, this thesis is groundless. What should be stressed in this context is that the "Midrashic" text is one of the few quotes Eliade adduced verbatim in his essay. I do not know whether the situation I described here is symptomatic of the manner in which Eliade adduced other sources in the context of the ideal androgyne. For the time being, I do not see any serious scholarly attempt to check the preciseness of his quotations and evaluate the correctness of the interpretations he offered, but rather some repetitions of his views, by scholars including those who are acquainted with Hebrew sources.

To summarize: The various variants of the discussions of androgyny represent an extension of some ideas and the acts of re-editing and making changes that are far from a linear development. Eliade added and subtracted material from earlier versions, changed the titles of the variants, and sometimes updated the bibliographies. This dynamic approach does not enrich the earlier discussions by analyses of texts or detailed topics, but by the integration of additional topics into the myth of reintegration. Conceptually speaking, Eliade's views on the topic did not change after they were articulated in 1940 in a newspaper feuilleton.

In the archaic figurines or "texts" there is hardly an account that contains philosophical explanation. Thus, their meaning is universal only if we adopt a certain interpretation of the Platonic myth that explains the manner in which the philosopher envisioned androgyne, a meaning that is projected onto innumerable other pictures, sculptures, and literary compositions, which are much less reflective, creating a consensus that has not been proven by a sustained effort to interrogate the various expressions related to androgyny, in themselves. This transfer of one mode of thought, the philosophical reflective one, onto the variety of archaic examples of what one may call androgyne is quite problematic. Is Plato indeed emphasizing perfection, as both Eliade and Jung claim? Both isolate one of the three categories of humans, the androgynous one, relegating the much more complex distinction between the three forms of primeval humans—males, females, and androgynous—to the last one. Moreover, perfection is not so obvious as assumed, since the splitting was the result of Zeus's revenge because of the humans being insolent. It is the relationship with Zeus that matters more in Alcibiades' discourse than the emphasis on the perfection. Neither does the theory of androgynous perfection fit the biblical Judaism, since the splitting of the original androgyne was done for the benefit of man, and the task of the couple is, according to the Hebrew Bible, to procreate and not revert to a situation which implies sterility. Eliade dealt with the appearance of similarity between two myths that have quite different meanings in the two contexts in which they appear. As Cioran once characterized Eliade: "Mircea has immense qualities and many gifts....He is too much of a writer, namely he adheres too much to appearances."[85]

Like psychoanalysis in its various forms, the science of religion à la Eliade would like to turn into a science, which means to extrapolate from the validity of some findings—doubtful as they are, as seen above—for a much greater spectrum of data, what we referred to above as stability. This uniformity of the meaning of the androgyne is achieved by the decontextualization of most of the topics from their cultural, linguistic, and historical backgrounds, and their interpretation in the context of one basic and more explicit treatment, conceived of as hegemonic, or what may be described as a matrix. From this point of view, the androgyne myth understood Platonically is similar to S. Freud's famous "Oedipus myth." In both cases we face some form of mythical imperialism: The meaning of a certain occurrence of a myth is conceived of as known even before the new data is analyzed, and this meaning is imported or imposed on a variety of different expressions.

In his conversation with Claude-Henri Rocquet, translated as *Ordeal by Labyrinth*, Eliade speaks about a very early experience of watching a lizard, what he designates also as dragon, which left a very strong impression on him. When asked why he said: "Because it was perfect. It was everything: grace and terror, ferocity and smile, everything was there."[86] He argues that he always distinguished between on the one hand, androgynous, conceived of as perfect because the two sexes fuse, and on the other hand, hermaphrodite, which is a "desperate effort to achieve totalization. But it isn't a fusion, it isn't a unity."[87] Are these descriptions of the androgyne fitting the biblical or the Platonic depictions of the original humans? There is room for more than a doubt as to the fitness of this distinction in order to do justice of the original texts, which are much more hermaphrodite than they are androgynous.

In fact, instead of carefully analyzing the documents related to the androgyne, Eliade repeats his vision. Much closer to the vision of pluralism as represented in the founding sources is Elemire Zolla's wise statement in his treatment of androgyne: "The West is a graft on the ancient tree of Israel, from which it so widely differs."[88] I am confident that Eliade would agree with this view, though for very different reasons.

The Earlier Emergence of Totality and Coincidentia Oppositorum: Literaria

In the following pages, I shall examine the conceptual structure that preceded and informed the interpretation of the androgyne in Eliade's essays described above. Conspicuous in this context are the concepts of *coincidentia oppositorum* and reintegration, or totalization. The role played by the concept of *coincidentia oppositorum* in the studies of some of the participants at the Eranos conferences, including Eliade, has been investigated by Steven M. Wasserstrom.[89] Eliade's own use of this concept has also been analyzed by a series of scholars, of whom I would like to mention here only a few: Brian S. Rennie,[90] Wilhelm Dancă,[91] Douglas Allen,[92] and Wasserstrom.[93] However, despite the importance of this concept in the circle of Eranos scholars, there can be no doubt that it is not the Eranos intellectual environment that influenced Eliade's first uses of it. Indeed, in his 1958 lecture he explicitly mentioned C. G. Jung in this context; this is in addition to his earlier discussions.[94] It is not just the minor references to *coincidentia oppositorum* in the second Romanian version that show Eliade's independent use of this concept, but much more the fact that Eliade taught a whole course on Nicholaus Cusanus at the University of Bucharest in 1934/1935.[95] The German theologian is indubitably one of the major sources for the dissemination of this concept. Thus, there is no reason to connect Eliade's acquaintance with this concept or its elaboration to his acquaintance with the circle of the Eranos scholars, who were familiar with the concept from independent sources. My claim is therefore that the centrality of the concept of totality, understood sometimes as even more important than perfection, predates in the thought of

Eliade the essays on the androgyne, and from the beginning, it inspired his interpretation of the concept of totality more than the concept of *coincidentia oppositorum*.[96] Only later, the coincidence of the opposites was moved to the center of the explication of the return to the primordial totality. However, what seems to be important from our point of view is not just the ascent of the centrality of *coincidentia oppositorum*, but also its connection to the concept of the androgyne that is evident in the two versions of the essay on Adam.

The argument that the primordial totality is the ultimate aim of the reintegration is found in almost all the versions of the androgyne theme mentioned above. Formulated in quite an articulated manner in 1939, the theme of totality is, however, not new to Eliade in that period.[97] The "thirst for the all" is a theme that had emerged already in a rather confused short piece entitled *The Apology of Virility*, written and published in its first edition in late 1927, when Eliade was 20, and reprinted in 1928.[98] To summarize the content in the manner in which the author himself did much later,

> The essay was an attempt to make "virility'—a *cliché* I had borrowed from Papini's *Maschilità*[99]—a mode of being in the world and also an instrument of knowledge and, therefore, of mastery of the world. I understood "virility" to be that which (as I was to discover later in India) Buddhist Tantra symbolizes in the *vajra*, literally "thunderbolt," which also represents the phallus, or more precisely, the "spiritual" potentialities inherent in and specific to the organ. I believed, therefore, that virility in its absolute form was equivalent to pure spirit.[100] I accepted Eros only as totally subservient to "virility": otherwise, the absolute unity of the spirit risked being shattered. Love, in all its modes, I saw only as an instrument for the reintegration of the Spirit. This mixture of asceticism, metaphysical exultation, and sexuality (a mixture that again recalls India)…[101]

Later he says about this essay that it was about the wish to experience "*everything at one and the same time*."[102] It is hard to decide whether, and to what extent, the later Hindu experiences or his studies of religion colored the manner in which Eliade interpreted his essay so many years later. In any case, in the original Romanian we find the following passage, whose graphic structure is present in the English translation:

> The torture of all is a virile suffering. A male who reaches the conscience of himself always begins by craving much, even much more, even much more [things].[103] And he sheds blood for each defeat. How could I give glory otherwise to the craving for flesh, and the masculine spirit, but be A Canticle for the Thirst for ALL?
>
> I do not want your body, I do not want your eyes—but all the bodies. And again, if a mystery remains alien—I throw away the body.
>
> …
>
> I long because I wish all…why I cannot live for one hour in all.[104]

However, in this poetic essay he also extols the phallus, writing "Glory to the eternal phallus"[105] in a content in which the later "spiritualization" is hardly evident. No doubt totality is strongly connected to masculinity, but nothing about androgyny is transpiring from this essay.

The claims formulated in this essay reverberated in a novel he wrote over the years 1931–1933, *The Return from Paradise*, published early in 1934. In the novel, Eliade depicts the double love affair of the main protagonist, Pavel Anicet, with two women, Una and Ghighi. While the former stands for One, the latter represents, presumably, Two, as the repetition of the form Ghi in her name shows. While the former is described as the "unity of the spirit,"[106] the latter woman stands for mediocrity.[107] Trying to escape the tension created by this situation, Pavel decides to commit suicide, and in one of the last pages of the novel we find the following reflection before he shoots himself to death: "Death, ecstasy. Death, an instrument of cognition. Death, a means of embracing the unity, the all."[108, 109] The novel finishes by describing the feeling Pavel has after he shoots himself: "In that moment he wished all the things, as in a fall without end, a vertiginous slide toward a bottom unknown to anyone."[110] Again, the form *toate lucrurile*, namely all the things, includes the Romanian term that is also related, etymologically, to totality. I wonder whether this description does not contain the concept of reintegration in addition to the rather clear reference to totality.

The flirtation with more than one women at the same time is also a main theme in the follow-up to *The Return from Paradise*, a novel entitled *The Hooligans*, published late in 1935, where the protagonist, Pavel Anicet's brother, Petru, lives at the same time with both a prostitute, Nora, and his adolescent student and admirer, Anişoara.[111] This time, however, it seems that only his mother is destined to commit suicide. However, nothing metaphysical is involved in this double erotic affair. Dramatically different is Eliade's longest and most important novel, *Noaptea de Sânziene* (in English, *The Forbidden Forest*), where the protagonist Ştefan loves two women at the same time.[112] Much more metaphysical is his short story "The Bridge." This is quite an enigmatic piece of literature that strives to represent some of the concepts that were especially dear to Eliade, such as *coincidentia oppositorum*. One of the main protagonists, perhaps the most important one, is an unnamed beautiful lieutenant who is several times described using the term *coincidentia oppositorum* and negative theology.[113] He is depicted spending his evenings/nights with some twelve or ten young ladies, trying to find out who of them embodies on a certain night the Great Goddess of nature. In my opinion, the implicit orgiastic elements are present even as late as 1963, when this short story was written.

Biographica

The linkage between Eliade's *literaria* and *biographica* is well known and does not need, at least in principle, to be demonstrated. My claim is, however, that to a great extent, this is also the case with his *academica* that results to a significant extent from his *biographica* and *literaria*. I tried to show this above in the context of Eliade's important concept of the camouflage of the sacred in the banal.[114]

Given the importance of the present assertion as to the emergence of Eliade's major claim in understanding religion, from both his *biographica* and *literaria*, I shall dwell now on some details of Eliade's life in 1933, and the manner in which he understood it. Let me return to a seminal passage:

> In a way, I was closer to "magic" than to mysticism. Even in adolescence I had tried to suppress normal behavior, had dreamed of a radical transmutation of my mode of being....I was trying to compensate for my fundamental incapability of becoming a "saint" by resorting to a paradoxical, nonhuman experience, which at least opened for me the way to the mystery of totality.[115]

This confession is an introduction to his description of the affair he had in 1932/1933 with two women concomitantly, Sorana Ţopa and Nina Mareş, which ended in early 1934 with the marriage of Eliade to the latter. While writing *The Return from Paradise* in 1933 he was still beside Sorana, who also read some of the pages in the manuscript, and later on he claims that "I did not understand the profound meaning of this longing."[116] The longing was for this "nonhuman experience" he had mentioned immediately beforehand. He claims that "Only later did I understand that this ordeal had been part of my destiny, which demanded that I live 'paradoxically' in contradiction with myself and my era....Not *les extremes me touchent*—but *coincidentia oppositorum*."[117] The extremes are two ladies: the more spiritual actress Sorana, who corresponds in my opinion to Una in the novel he was writing while she was beside him, and on the other hand the more modest secretary Nina (Nicoleta), who corresponds to Ghighi—notice the repetition found in their names. Eliade decided, unlike his hero Pavel Anicet, who committed suicide, to marry one of the two, an act that he calls in a literary piece he wrote some years earlier, a "spiritual suicide."[118]

Thus, the search for totality, reintegration, and paradoxes were not only some figments of imagination, as in the novel, but at least to a certain extent, the way in which he understood his life, and perhaps even the way in which he felt in the early thirties about what happened to him. Though I am rather suspicious about and accept only cautiously statements that interpret life in rather metaphysical terms, and I suspect that Eliade is anachronistically embellishing his own life, there is no reason to totally deny his testimony as to what he felt when he was engaged in the affair with Sorana and Nina. Indeed, Eliade himself writes that the issues related to *coincidentia oppositorum* "were not part of my thinking at that time."[119] This may mean that at some time between 1928 and 1933, when he wrote the *Return from the Paradise*, they did become part of his thought. In any case, Eliade's confession as to the necessity to "relive" the archaic religions in order to understand them is quite obvious.[120] For that effect he creates a polarity between the two women that—it may well be—does not fit either of them.

In any case, as part of his decision to marry Nina, Eliade articulated, in my opinion for the first time in an explicit manner, the concept of the sacred camouflaged in banality, with Nina becoming the symbol of the banal that hides something precious and unseen by the profane observers.[121]

In 1938 Eliade published another novel, *Wedding in Heaven*, dealing with a problematic that concerns us. When describing the erotic union between Mavrodin, the protagonist of the first part of the novel, and Ileana, another major protagonist, during a salon dance, Eliade describes the feeling of a fusion of bodies, and the awareness that the female body is just his own body. Though he does not use the term "androgyne," it seems that this assumption is underlying the lengthy passage.[122] It is in this context that Eliade uses the term *contopire*.

However, the marriage with Nina was not a spiritual suicide, but a convenient move which allowed Eliade to study and live a rather comfortable life, while Nina was taking care of him and typing his studies. The erotic experiments were not, however, over. As seen above, Eliade conceived of the orgiastic rituals in ancient religions as part of the attempt to realize the reintegration in what he calls the primordial totality. It seems that in 1942, while he was staying in Lisbon and re-editing the brief Romanian essays mentioned above to be reprinted as *The Myth of Reintegration*, he himself strove for some form of personal reintegration by some types of activity. Thus, in January 15 of that year, under the stress of the news related to the victories of the Russians in the war against the German army, he wrote:

> my being is taking refuge in the erotic longing. As if it was taking revenge on the permanent menace under which it lives. The will to love, to embrace, to prolong into being. And there was something else: the urge toward "totalization." My being, without my rational intervention or even without being aware of it, searched for a new equilibrium, even in this tragedy, [by] assimilating that tragedy, by reintegrating the contrary elements in a new, superior unity.[123]

This menace of the "terror of history" that pushed him to retreat into the erotic became, in a while, more than an emotional longing. In June he writes about the cosmic role of the Eros, which is capable of opening creative powers that ensure a spiritual form of posterity.[124] In 1944 he noted that he pointed out in his writings the importance of orgy, which includes the "regression in the primordial amorphous…to the initial redoing of the primitive unity, of the chaos"[125] but involves the war in some form of looking for equilibrium, as orgy may do.[126] The theme of the reintegration in totality recurs later on that year, when he speaks about the only way of safeguarding the individual.[127] However, those reflections that continued earlier theories do not exhaust the attitude to his interest in the topic. On May 1, 1942, he notes:

> Nina and Giza[128] left yesterday for homeland.[129] I am alone[130] and free, for at least three–four months. I was waiting for this break, in order to be able to live freely all my excesses,[131] in order to be able to understand myself, in order to verify whether the crises of neurasthenia of the last months are due to a feeling of inferiority, to the presence of Nina and Giza, or pure and simple to a worsening of my nervous system. I am ready for any experience.[132]

On May 5 of the same year he writes: "An excess in all the things which were forbidden until now, and I hope that my neurasthenia will be healed. I begin this night."[133] Therefore, the neurological problems mentioned here, plausibly some forms of depression and melancholia, predate the departure of his wife, and have nothing to do with his devotion to and love for her. On July 1 he writes: "My struggle with melancholy and orgy. The love that links me—more powerful than any longing for freedom—to Nina."[134] What type of experiences and treatments against the neurasthenia he initiated is not totally clear from the previous discussions, but we may guess something from his later testimony on November 14, 1942:

> Ambivalence and polarity are verified not only in every culture and on every plan…but also in the life of the individual. The effort toward the archetype, toward the clear and creative personality, alternates with the opposite tendency toward degradation, embryonic states, orgy, drunkenness, etc. I reached this theory following attentively myself. Only rarely is polarity verified in a more sensational manner than in my life: askesis and orgy, being a person and the thirst for collective, creation and degradation in erudition.[135,136]

This passage is extremely important for understanding the connection between Eliade's self-perfection and his understanding of archaic religion: What is true on a large scale, or insofar as ancient phenomena are concerned, may be true also for the individual in the present, and this individual here is Eliade himself. His experiences may therefore teach something about religion in general, and vice versa. Let me point out that there is nothing like *coincidentia oppositorum* here. Polarity means that in the same person there are, at different times, different forms of activities, which

Eliade would like to see as opposites. However, even if one accepts them as such, they do not coincide at the same time. In any case, some years later, in 1945 while still living in Portugal, he is much more explicit:

> I feel how my entire being encourages me to throw myself, to consume myself, in what I can designate by a gentle euphemism I learnt long ago to call "life": namely the unlimited erotic experience, permanent adventure, debauchery. Portugal is not the ideal country for such a vocation—but I shall try even here. I shall repeat my well-known technique of liberation by means of excess, of purification by orgy.[137]

The use of the term "technique" is quite revealing: Eliade refers to his decision to behave sexually in one way or another as a technique, a term he uses in other cases in the context of the Yoga exercises or Shamanism, to re-establish equilibrium. His quite profane behavior was assimilated to the specific methods Eliade described in religious cultures. Even more explicit is his even later confession, coming after consulting a neurologist again in Lisbon:

> He told me that there is nothing serious. Melancholies have their spiritual causes, and he cannot do anything. I myself would bear and overcome them would my nervous system be totally healthy. But, unfortunately there are those other crises,[138] which he explains by my unsatisfied supersexuality. The equilibrium cannot come but after the attainment of the erotic equilibrium.[139]

It seems that Eliade did not disagree with the neurologist's diagnosis, and he plausibly tried to find the equilibrium by satisfying his sexuality. How exactly he imagined it happened is not clear.

I adduced those personal testimonies in order to show that between the phallocentric and rather misogynistic approach in the *Apology for Virility* in 1927/1928 and the confessions through years until at least 1945, there is a special preoccupation with sex and orgiastic experiences in Eliade's writings and in the nature of the protagonists of his novels. It is not only his Romanian critics who were shocked by the sexual violence of some of his novels written in the thirties, which include rather obscene scenes in which girls aged 9 and 12 are involved as possessed temptresses;[140] Eliade himself was surprised by this violence when rereading some of those novels in the early forties in Portugal. In 1945, after his rereading of *The Hooligans* a decade after its publication in Romania, he confesses:

> The exasperated and brutal sexuality of this book is pure and simple making me ill. Philip Léon wrote me around 1936 that if indeed the [novel] *Hooligans* reflects my soul and my being, I am miserable, since sexuality turns me impenetrable for a spiritual transfiguration. Then, I thought that he exaggerated. However, today, this fate is depressing me, this

murky and insatiable carnality, which, indubitably, is hindering me to "realize" myself, according to my real stature.[141]

It is hard to find a more sincere and clear-cut recognition of the early erotic exaggerations. Unlike his Romanian critics in the mid-thirties, who condemned his literature as pornography and ultimately were able to suspend his teaching at Bucharest University,[142] I am not concerned with these personal or literary issues in themselves. For my point here, what is more important is to better understand the background of the emergence of the peculiar understanding of the androgyne as related to orgiastic rituals. As we shall see immediately below, both orgies and love or sex became in Eliade's view some forms of what he calls rituals of androgynization, though he never mentions a feeling of androgynization as a personal experience he underwent.

An Early Conceptual Matrix for Later Understanding Androgyny: Eliade as a Strong Reader

The above discussions show that the specific concepts used by Eliade for interpreting many instances where the concept of androgyny is found, according to his views, explicitly or not, can be traced to developments in his writings during the 12 years before his committing to writing his first reflections on the topic in 1938. Never in those early contexts was the term "androgyne" mentioned, though the concepts used by Eliade in order to explicate its religious message had nevertheless been aired in a variety of contexts, personal and literary. It is as if the novels and the earlier essays before 1938 prepared the way for the later proclamation that is connected to the special significance of the androgyne. It was, so to speak, a symbol or an archetype that brought together, according to Eliade, some of the concepts with which he was well acquainted before. This description may account for why the material adduced by Eliade in the first Romanian essay on the topic is relatively poor and hardly convincing, and why some of it was abandoned by him in the later variants of these essays. Even the text "adduced" from the Midrash *Bereshit Rabba* that reappears in the first to the last of these essays is hardly related to the message he would like to illustrate. What in fact happened is that the content from a youthful flirtation with some ideas like totality, paradox, and reintegration, expressed initially without any sustained connection to the history of religion, but rather to the status of the new generation in Romania in the thirties, whose manifesto was sometimes considered to be the *Apology for Virility*, was imposed on a religious concept, androgyny, which has a variety of meanings, and thus it was transformed as part of a sort of perennial theology.

This concept has been applied also to Eliade's understanding of major aspects of Yoga, and then to Shamanism,[143] thus generating a theory that may be considered a vertebral column of his phenomenology of religion, at least for a certain phase in his thought. All this was done out of a sense that the authentic religion is basically one, and that also his own life is but one manifestation of this larger phenomenon that is basically atemporal. This confidence in the homogeneity of the real, in the past and in the present, allowed Eliade to collect from a variety of unrelated sources, ideas, concepts, and impressions, based mainly on secondary discussions, and present them as all pointing, *mutatis mutandis*, in the same direction. He is not adopting a diffusionist approach, but one closer to perennial philosophy.[144]

One of the problems that haunts the scholarly aspects of the above enterprise is their academic genealogy: Eliade started his reflections on the androgyne by publishing them in a nonacademic periodical, without footnotes, and then he elaborated on them later on and added some notes, while he was in Portugal and for a short time in the summer of 1942 in Bucharest.[145] What mattered for him were the more general ideas or intuitions, less so the primary materials he relied on when expressing his ideas. The analysis of the material is very poor for the grand claims he made. Indeed, those claims contributed much to his fame, whereas some of his more mature and important contributions, namely the books on Yoga and Shamanism, ground-breaking and much more solid monographs as they are, have contributed much less to his celebrity in popular circles.

What is the basic problem that daunted the Eliadian interpretation of the androgyne, in the manner in which I understand it? It has to do basically with the assumption of an idealized primordial totality, or state of chaos, from which everything, especially the archaic persons and the mystics, emerges and strives to reintegrate by overcoming the opposites. This is reminiscent of the threefold distinction mentioned above in the variant [C]. Though speaking about reintegration into totality, the assumption is that the techniques are generating a process of disintegration of personality. This view has been conceived of as representing a certain privileged form of religion that was never described as such in any single religious source. The concept was the invention of Eliade, and was used by him to interpret the fragments he discerned of this totality, in the various manifestations in the records that survived—written texts, rituals, or any other form of documentation. It is Eliade alone who possessed this form of total understanding, since, according to him, the original ancient religions were shattered under the impact of the Judeo-Christian tradition, and later by the impact of modernity, and he understood it to be his task as a scholar of the history of religion to restore it in order to heal the alleged wounds inflicted by secularity, positivism, or historicism. With this general picture in mind, he approached a variety of religious documents and chose from them tiny segments in order to reconstruct what he conceived of as the pristine and, for the modern man, the lost picture.

It is this deep conviction that guided him in his interpretation of the religious documents as if they reflect, at least in many cases, the lost primordial totality and the will to regain it, at least in part. This starting point created a hermeneutical propensity that transformed Eliade into a strong reader of texts. This is the manner in which he approached the concept of the androgyne in the texts he produced: The various documents are understood as reflecting a picture that is rarely sustained in its entirety by one single narrative. This is the reason why he reconstructs the total from what he considers a fragment, or in more explicit terms, he assumes that a certain modest discussion encapsulates the much more comprehensive "total," and thus reflects the meaning related to this total, even when many of the elements of the totality are not mentioned in a certain specific context. In other words, Eliade uses an exegetical technique that I call "oblique" analysis: The belief in the existence of a universal totality allows the importing of many elements from one religious context to a quite different one, since both are believed to represent the same theory or type of experience. Religious documents as a whole—another sort of totality—become a hypertext, which allows the believer in a certain theory representing not specific religions or idiosyncratic experiences but a universal phenomenon to bring together different topics from one corpus of writings to another. The need to demonstrate the existence of the whole theory in each of the specific documents is a complex enterprise based upon allowing the imaginative function to play with preconceived assumptions that fill in too many important gaps.

However, the result was an overreading of the documents chosen for interpretation. I checked the above few instances in which Eliade referred to Jewish texts, without attempting to extrapolate to other religious texts. Nevertheless, this "obliqueness" is also evident in other cases that deal with the material with which I am better acquainted. So, for example, Eliade explains the meaning of the Lurianic complex of Tikkun: "as for the *Tikkun*, the 'restitution' of the ideal order, the reintegration of the primordial All, as the secret goal of human existence, or in other words, the Redemption."[146] Though the understanding of Tikkun as restitution is quite an adequate understanding, the interpretation offered by the following phrase "as the reintegration of the primordial All" is an insertion of an Eliadian *topos* in a context that is not related to it. When Eliade uses this phrase he means by it the personal experience of reintegration of man, following his "fall," into the pristine origin. However, Lurianic Kabbalah deals with the reparation of an anthropomorphic supernal structure, whose particles fell within the domain of evil and should be returned by performing the rituals in order to reconstitute the shattered divine

Anthropos. The line between the Lurianic ideas he read in Scholem's *Major Trends in Jewish Mysticism* and his own interpretation is a fine one, given the fact that Scholem himself used the term "reintegration" elsewhere in his studies.[147] Nevertheless, Eliade's formulation here is much closer to the famous Christian formula of *restitution rerum ad integrum*, some form of *apokatastasis*, than to the logic of Lurianic Kabbalah.[148] In any case, in Lurianism the Tikkun is basically a cosmic event triggered by daily human ritualistic activities, and not a final reintegration of the human in totality. The fallen divine spark is not losing its identity when it is caused to ascend back to its pristine place, but instead completing the supernal anthropomorphic structure, which is not undetermined or chaotic, but rather quite structured. It is perhaps not superfluous to remind the careful readers of Eliade that he applied, in quite a vague manner, the formula *restitutio ad integrum* to the manner in which he imagined he would deal with his wife Nina, perhaps expressing his feeling that he was responsible for her 1933 abortion, which he had requested.[149]

A similar case of misinterpretation is related to Eliade's view of a certain ancient custom during the Jewish Day of Atonement, Yom Kippur, as possible evidence for an orgy on this day, when in fact it was forbidden to have sexual relations.[150] Indeed, the original mistake may not be attributed to Eliade, but to Raffaele Pettazzoni,[151] a revered scholar of religion who had influenced Eliade since his youth. However, the result is the same: By assembling material from secondary sources according to a certain preconceived hermeneutical grid, without being aware of the cultural milieus and conceptual contexts, a less than convincing theory is suggested, with no attempt to enter into details. A strong conviction, combined with exegetical ingenuity of descriptions found in the writings of other scholars, conspired in a selective reading that created a totalizing understanding of religion based on Eliade's personal belief in totality, on the possibility of an experience of totalization and reintegration. In many cases, what should be demonstrated by a careful analysis is assumed as already self-evident. This loose approach to texts and their "messages" is quintessential for construing a more comprehensive vision of religion as unified despite its innumerable variants through history.

In this context, it is worthwhile to reflect on the extent to which a statement regarding the yogian experience is more than an imposition of the more general attitude to religion onto a topic that may be understood without those assumptions. In his book on Yoga, in a discussion where the androgynic interpretation of this practice started, we read:

> It is the coincidence of time and eternity, of *bhava* and *nirvana*: on the purely "human" place,
> it is the reintegration of the primordial androgyne, the conjunction, in one's being, of male
> and female—in a word, the reconquest of the completeness that precedes all creation. In

short, this nostalgia for the primordial completeness and bliss is what animates and informs all the techniques that lead to the *coincidentia oppositorum* in one's own being.[152]

Nota bene: the use of the totalizing phrase "all the techniques," which points to much more than the Yoga practice. This time, the "all" that refers to the technique assumes a homogenous effect attained by different techniques. Also, the mention of "tantric orgy" in this context is interesting.[153] This shows that even when dealing with an example of one male and one female, Eliade uses the term "orgy." Again, the concept of reintegration and primordial completeness, and now *coincidentia oppositorum*, too, is projected onto a religious structure of thought, which has not been described previously in such a manner even by Eliade himself. I say this because I did not find the concepts in the expositions Eliade made about Yoga and its psychology and philosophy, which were published in Romanian during the year 1930.[154] So, what happens here is reminiscent of the somewhat biased interpretation of the concept of Tikkun, as discussed above: In both cases there are no technical terms in the interpreted material that reflect the concepts introduced by Eliade. This is a case of strong interpretation of the deep significance of terms and practices, according to a leading assumption not explicitly found in the interpreted material. Such a hermeneutical practice assumes that the scholar knows something that is not explicit in the interpreted text, and yet he is considered to be capable of explicating it by referring to this knowledge.

A reading of Eliade's writings in the Portugal period shows that his thought was dominated by the concept of totality, as we may see especially in one of his essays on Mihail Eminescu and in Eliade's short story "A Big Man," where the protagonist, a rapidly growing man who becomes a giant, a macranthropos,[155] is asked what he sees in the new state, and he exclaims, "*Totul este*" ("All is").[156] This totalizing tendency that characterizes Eliade's understanding of religion may be exemplified by a passage from the very end of the 1942 version of his essay on androgyny in *The Myth of Reintegration*: "Finally, in order to underscore the fact that every individual, with his will or without it, bears in his soul the nostalgia of perfection, it is incumbent to say that even the essential act of love brings about an experience—naturally very pale—of androgyny."[157]

This generalization, based on the assumption that the state of androgyny is indeed fascinating to every individual, and that love—in Romanian, *dragoste*; here, probably meaning also sex—turns into a technique to attain it, does indeed reflect a rather simplistic premise of Eliade's writings: the conviction that what he says is correct in general for many other religious phenomena, which he does not even mention, even if sometimes it applies more weakly. He believes in some form of "nostalgia for androgyny" that is inherent in love.[158] However, this is just an impression that is hardly plausible for such a widespread and variegated feeling. The alleged "absolute reality" encountered in the so-called paradisiacal state, related to an experience of androgyny, is deemed by Eliade to be supportable, but only for a very short time, since one is found still in the human condition.[159] Thus, the ideal of androgyny, and rituals of androgynization, became symbols for a more complex longing for origins, perfections of the beginnings, and nostalgias for Paradise,[160] all part of a re-evaluation of archaism that became an alternative to the Hegelian, developmental, much more philosophical propensities of modern European thought.[161] Such a state or feeling is conceived, therefore, less as a stable achievement, or a permanent state, than as an aspiration or an ideal, both in the past and in the present.

Following the lead of the European occultists or esoterists, who in turn were influenced at least to a certain extent by Kabbalah, both Jewish and Christian, Eliade turned his gaze to beginnings rather than to ends, in a period of lost but, according to him, retrievable type of perfection, with an experience of spiritual androgyny being one of its most important features. Thus different, and in my opinion, diverging religious phenomena like Yoga, Shamanism, Zurvanism,[162] archaic orgies, and even love in general all have been enlisted in what Eliade considers to constitute techniques of reintegration, sometimes called techniques of "going back,"[163] which have a strong erotic component and are interpreted to be related to the reconstitution of androgyny. Sometimes these techniques are related to, or sometimes even identified with, experiences of initiation.

These scholarly preconceptions, gravitating around the centrality of a homogenous vision of religion, represented by the quite frequent uses of the terms "all" and "primordial totality," started relatively early in his career. They are based to a great extent on some even earlier personal propensities as to his human ideals, in his *biographica*, and they are obvious also in his *literaria* in a manner reminiscent of the case of the camouflage of the sacred, discussed in the previous chapter. I am skeptical about the explanatory contribution of these terms, or of the assumption that people were striving to reach an undifferentiated state of being or consciousness by reintegration. The move that may be discerned is as follows: It is in Eliade's biography that we find the first clear examples of the manner in which he spent his youth, first in Romania, then in India, then back in Romania, and then in Portugal; and the life with more than one woman at the same time, the confessions about orgies, real or imaginary, and earlier still, the phallocentric and strongly masculine-oriented approach in the two versions of the *Apology for Virility*. Then, this strong sexually oriented approach to the experience of the totality was formulated in his *literaria*, and only later, after 1938, it was imported and elaborated in his *academica* concerning religion.[164] After it was formulated academically, the search for the ontological totality and an experience of totalization was applied, again, in literary writings like the short stories "The Bridge" and "A Big Man," and sometimes to the manner in which he understands his biography in times of historical or nervous crises since the forties. This circular move between Eliade's various literary corpora, which nourish each other alongside Eliade's life, is in my opinion characteristic of his *oeuvre* in general, more so than for any other scholar of religion I am acquainted with, including those who employed the concept of androgyny as representing an important type of perfection, like Henry Corbin and Elliot R. Wolfson, for example.

Let me point out that the claim made above, about Eliade's acquaintance early in his youth with the books of Paul Vulliaud and some other occultists, does not suggest that these authors were the main source of his religious thought. Romantic literature is certainly another major source of Eliade's thought on the topic of the androgyne. Nevertheless, the examination of the details related to the figures of the occultists and the manner in which Eliade appropriated them contributes to a better understanding of the topic in Eliade's formation while he was in high school, and in the manner in which his vision of androgyny as reintegration emerged later in his career. Undoubtedly, many other sources stemming from other religions have contributed substantially to Eliade's conviction as to the centrality of androgyny as perfection in archaic religion.

A careful re-examination of the evidence found in other channels of religious information, especially Hinduism, which was intimately known to Eliade as a scholar, and the Romantic traditions,[165] where the theme is central and discussed by many scholars mentioned by Eliade,[166] should await the work of other scholars who are competent in those fields. However, beyond the more European sources contained in the literatures of both occultism and Romanticism, the early Eliade added some references to Kabbalah as well as Hinduism and many other non-European traditions in his discussions of his conception of the androgyne and ritual of androgynization.

The more conceptual problem related to Eliade's discussions of the androgyne and the terms used in order to explicate it is the ambiguity of the status of central concepts like totality and reintegration, from the ontological point of view. This means that it is not clear whether Eliade assumes that beyond the different expressions of what he called totality there is an agreement that points to an ontology that is accepted as objective by him, or he is speaking about similarities between forms of thought, which belong to a common type of *imaginaire* rather than to a shared ontology. I am inclined to the view that the ontological approach much better reflects Eliade's position, at least in the first decades of his academic career. Such an assumption implies also the belief in the efficacy of the techniques to reach reintegration, and in the case of Eliade, the use of Yoga while in India and orgies while in Portugal should be understood as part of such an attitude that attributes objective rather than subjective status to the attainment of the individuals. However, it should be pointed out that while Eliade sees in the orgiastic experiences an attempt at reaching some form of inner equilibrium, he does not explicitly claim that he was looking for, or attained inadvertently, a state of androgyny.

In fact, there is a tension between the claims he expressed early in his life as to the priority of masculinity as distinct from femininity, and the contentions he made in the somewhat later period, starting in 1940, about the imperative to absorb the feminine element in the experience of the male in order to attain some form of androgyny, and thus perfection.[167] In any case, I was not able to find either a literary piece of writing by Eliade that revolves around the ideal of androgyny, or a self-perception of Eliade himself as having experienced something similar to androgyny. Despite the methodological claim made at the very beginning of the present study as to the affinities between Eliade's *academica, biografica,* and *literaria,* which holds many of the details dealt with above, especially totality and integration, androgyny is not such a unifying concept, despite its centrality for Eliade's *academica* in most of its stages, even if we interpret it in a metaphorical manner. At least in this case, he did not interpret details of his life in accordance with categories that emerged later on in his scholarship of religion.

In my opinion, we may regard the discovery of the relevance of androgyny as the result of finding a concrete symbol for his more vague pursuits, which were formulated in terms that are not found in archaic religion. In a way, the category of the androgyne, especially as discussed in the small study by Krappe published in 1938, helped Eliade to organize some of his more general inclinations in a more specific manner. This shift, from the many cases in which he insistently references the concepts of totality, primordiality, and reintegration, without mentioning the androgyne, to an identification of these concepts, took place some time in 1938, as we learn from Eliade's review written in 1937 about the voluminous monograph of Paul Mus on the temple of Barabudur, where these terms (except "androgyne") occur many times.[168] Also, in an essay written in 1974, when all the early categories appear together, androgyny is not mentioned.[169] The more elaborate introduction in 1940 of the androgyne as reflecting a particular form of integration into the totality is, in my opinion, less the result of analyzing religious texts and specific examples and much more the insight that there is here an opportunity to exemplify his more comprehensive trend toward totalization, which was already central to his earlier views, by means of the androgyne.[170]

A relative latecomer in comparison to the concepts of "all," "totality," and reintegration, Eliade's concept of androgyny was dramatically informed by the centrality he attributed to these earlier concepts, while it informed them much less, and it does not appear in Eliade's self-perception in his memoirs or in his literary writings. In his academic writings, however, Eliade strove to persuade his readers as to the centrality of the myth of reintegration, and later on, also of the myth of androgyny, and some scholars have been convinced by his approach. In my opinion, his discussions are often quite impressionistic; rarely has a convincing argument been advanced based on detailed and sustained analyses. The reliance on the validity and the relevance of his personal experiences diminishes the importance of the detailed analyses of specific texts and cultures first in themselves, and allows the combination of personal experiences in the present with the archaic prephilosophical speculations of the past as if all are reflecting the same underlying form of religious experience or concept. Thus, sometimes Eliade reinterpreted episodes in his own life as constituting some form of experiencing a more "authentic" religion and a partaking in a search for perfection. Nevertheless, he did not consider himself to be an androgyne. He was too much, as seen above, on the side of virility.

Last but not least: The obscurity of generic terms like "totality," "reintegration," and "androgyne," without distinguishing between different categories, and the imposition of one "archetype" on the vast and variegated spectrum of religious material, is confusing rather than advancing a more precise understanding. Synthesis without a preliminary analysis is too facile, and this is the case with the widespread concept of *coincidentia oppositorum*, which is a central part of his discussions of reintegration. Are male and female indeed opposites? Are they not just parts of the same species, with infinitely more similarities than differences? Are they more opposite or more complementary? The application of concepts stemming from one system, that of Nicholaus Cusanus, to a variety of other conceptual structures is a loose type of analysis.

Eliade's discussions about virility and his views on women[171] show that Eliade not only analyzed ancient texts and archaic mentalities, but also refracted his own axiology. It is here that I see the main methodological fallacy in Eliade's approach: He believes he experiences some sort of archaic experiences, and he presents his convictions as if they constitute, uniformly, the profound structure of reality in the hoary past as well as in the present. The union of the opposites is not the only method of reaching totality. In a passage written in 1931, he proposes a quite different path, and sees askesis, understood as restraining contact with women, and the return of the man to "virginity" as a way of "restoration of the primordial union."[172]

Concluding Remarks

The meaning of a certain archetype or a symbol depends on both their generator and their consumer. Archetypes do not function when isolated but, in my opinion, only when conjugated within a broader and specific sequence of symbols, rituals, and myths. By extracting the symbol or the archetype from this scheme and conjugating it with meanings as formulated in other macro-phenomena, it is easy to create the illusion of a universal archetype always conveying the same message. However, this assumption cannot stand up to a close examination of the meaning attributed to either the symbol or the archetype when examined contextually. What may be learned from the above exercise is that the same archetype can be adopted in order to convey opposite meanings, when functioning in different religious macro-phenomena.[173] This means that even when a certain theme recurs in many cultures, and one may refer to it as an archetype, it is rarely understood in the same manner by the inhabitants of those cultural and religious macro-phenomena. This observation should not prevent comparative research or the study of influences of one culture on another; on the contrary, one may better understand the context of the micro-phenomenon by carefully discerning the different meanings attached to a common theme than by blurring the differences, which is part of the hermeneutics of indistinction.

Moreover, I would say that the same micro-phenomena may be understood differently in the various components of the same religious macro-phenomenon. The manner in which the concept of *androgynos* has been understood by different Kabbalists—they used, in fact, a different term, *du-partzufim*—can point in this direction: Schools of Kabbalah have enchained the same theme in more comprehensive systems that point in directions that dramatically differ from each other. The system of theosophical-theurgical Kabbalah, in most of its early manifestations, though it emerged in Europe, reflects another form of thought that can be described as preaxial, as it is concerned with the nation and body, and an anthropomorphic deity, a view that differs from the theologies dominant in the Christian Middle Ages. The proximity in time and space is not a sufficient reason for reducing Kabbalistic thought to what was *en vogue* in their immediate vicinity, religious or intellectual. This can be demonstrated also in another case, that of the theme of the great chain of being, which has been treated differently by Christian thinkers and theosophical-theurgical Kabbalists.[174] From this point of view, Elemire Zolla's remark adduced above about "Israel," which "widely differs" from the West, and as "patriarchal"—I would rather say, "preaxial"—deserves much greater attention than it attracted for a better understanding of both Judaism and European culture. Needless to say, the manner in which the androgyne has been understood in some recent studies of Kabbalah, under the direct impact of the speculations of both Jung and Eliade, as referring to a divine male-androgyne as a symbol of perfection, reflects the same problems of reductionism as evinced by the two generalist scholars,[175] especially because of the avoidance of attributing due place to the centrality of procreation, for the mainstream of Kabbalists, as the main purpose of androgyny, separation, and then union, both in the divine and in the human spheres.[176]

Eliade's and Jung's approaches to religion, significantly different as they are—the former being cosmically oriented, the latter interiorizing—are deeply influenced by a series of occultist sources, especially alchemical and Hermetic ones, as shown by their use of terms such as *unio oppositorum, coincidentia oppositorum,* "integration" or "reintegration," and *coniunctio.* They served as the background for the reception and mode of understanding the Kabbalistic material. From this point of view, their approach is reminiscent of the Renaissance homogenizing concept of *prisca theologia:* Just as in the case of the Renaissance figures, Jung and Eliade also started with assumptions widespread in Christian thought, which were enriched and modified by additional sources that were not conceived of as being canonical in the theologies of the Middle Ages.[177] The occultist penchant in ascent in Western Europe, especially since the 17th century, continued the approach opened in Florentine Renaissance, and it found its expression in the two 20th-century thinkers discussed above.[178] They constituted strong filters that shaped the manner in which Kabbalistic and other materials have been selected and interpreted. The paramount importance of the psychic, emotional, and intellectual as the main scene of human development, rather than the corporeal, the social, or communal, reflects the impact of the Platonic and the Paulinian bias.

The use of the same theme, or archetype, in many traditions, though filling it with different contents or significance, can serve as a testimony for the psychological importance of the theme of androgyne. This observation may help in formulating another approach to what an archetype may be: a constellation not of one but of different meanings attached by various authors, artists, thinkers to the same verbal or visual expression, with each of those meanings drawing from another spiritual universe. Stability of the psychological complex or of the cosmic worldview is part of the effort by scholars of religion to transcend fluidity in their search for a scientific approach, reminiscent of exact sciences, when dealing with different cultures.

Eliade, like Jung, was concerned with shaping comprehensive approaches to man and universe shared, in their opinion, by all persons as humans, and attempting to create a form of "science." Their views of totality, integration or reintegration, and perfection, without entering into reflections on the variants between cultures or even within the same culture, are part of the emergence of new, modern forms of religion created by these scholars and imposed on materials they surveyed by applying strong forms of hermeneutics that strive to subordinate the physical behavior to the archetype.[179] Without a critical inquiry into the material adduced in order to support the existence of what I call the two "new" religions, Jung's and Eliade's, we are condemned to repetitions of generalizations conceived as scientific findings.

Notes

1. See, e.g., Luc Brisson, *Sexual Ambivalence, Androgyny and Hermaphroditism in Graeco-Roman Antiquity*, tr. J. Lloyd (Berkeley, 2002), pp. 73–84; id., "Neutrum utrumque, La bisexualité dans l'antiquité greco-romaine," in Libis, *L'Androgyne*, pp. 31–61; Jean-Pierre Vernant, "One...Two...Eros," in *Before Sexuality, The Construction of Erotic Experience in the Ancient Greek World*, ed. D. M. Halperin–J. J. Winkler–F. I. Zeitlin (Princeton, 1990), pp. 469–472; Maurice de Gandillac, "Approches platonniciens et platonisantes du myth de l'androgyne originel," in Monneyron, *L'Androgyne dans la littérature*, pp. 13–23.

2. See, especially, Curtis D. Smith, *Jung's Quest for Wholeness, A Religious and Historical Perspective* (Albany, 1990).

3. See Jung's *The Archetypes and the Collective Unconscious*, tr. R. F. C. Hull (Princeton, 1959), pp. 67–68, 173–176, 191–192; *Aion, Researches into the Phenomenology of the Self*, tr. R. F. C. Hull, (Princeton, 1959), pp. 195, 204; and especially his late *Mysterium Coniunctionis*, tr. R. F. C. Hull (Princeton, 1970).

4. See, e.g., *Mysterium Coniunctionis*, pp. 390, 411–414, 429–430, 440, 443–447, 450.

5. Ibid., pp. 438–456.

6. *The Practice of Psychotherapy*, tr. R. F. C. Hull (Princeton, 1966), pp. 308, 313–314 and n. 17.

7. Ibid., p. 250.

8. Jung, *The Integration of the Personality*, tr. S. M. Dell (New York, 1939), p. 38.

9. *Memories, Dreams, Reflections by C .G. Jung*, ed. Aniela Jaffe, tr. R. Winston–C. Winston (New York, 1965), p. 199.

10. *Myths, Dreams and Mysteries* pp. 174–175. On *coincidentia oppositorum*, see also his *The Two and the One*, pp. 78–124, and *Images and Symbols*, p. 14.

11. For a divergence between the two thinkers on this topic, see Ursache's introduction to *Master Manole*, pp. xlii–xliii.

12. See, e.g., his *Access to Western Esotericism*, passim; his "Sensuous Relations with Sophia in Christian Theosophy," in *Hidden Intercourses: Eros and Sexuality in the History of Western Esotericism*, ed. Wouter J. Hanegraaf–Jeffrey J. Kripal (Leiden–Boston, 2009), pp. 281–308; and his "From Prelapsarian Androgyny to Multipolar Constructs of "Love" (Aspects of Christian Theosophy in German Naturphilosophie)," in *Eranos Yearbook (2009–2010–2011)*, vol. 70, ed. Fagio Merlini–Lawrence E. Sullivan–Riccardo Bernardini–Kate Olson (Einsiedeln, 2012), pp. 274–295. See also Rosemary Radford Ruether, *Goddess and the Divine Feminine, A Western Religious History*, (Berkeley, 2005), pp. 228–229, 236–239; Andrew Weeks, *Boehme: An Intellectual Biography of the Seventeenth-Century Philosopher and Mystic* (Albany, 1991), pp. 114–121; and Pierre Degaye, "L'homme virginal selon Jakob Boehme," in Libis, *L'Androgyne*, pp. 155–195.

13. Zolla, *The Androgyne*, p. 6.

14. See the important contribution to the analyses of this topic in Wasserstrom, *Religion after Religion*, pp. 203–214.

15. See, e.g., Zolla, *The Androgyne*; Wendy Doniger O'Flaherty, *Women, Androgynes, and Other Mythical Beasts* (Chicago, 1982), pp. 290–291, 296–297, 314; and more recently, Marcel Tolcea, *Ezoterism și comunicare simbolică* (Timisoara, 2004), pp. 150–151; Wolfson, *Language, Eros, Being*, pp. 261–262; and for the impact on Henry Corbin, see Wasserstrom, ibid., p. 209.

16. Printed in *Revista Fundaţiilor Regale*, V, 3 (martie 1938), pp. 616–632. I reference its reprint in the collection of Eliade's essays, *Secret Things*, pp. 100–117.

17. Ibid., p. 103.

18. (Paris, 1925), p. 202. Vulliaud's French translation of a passage from Zohar I, fol. 90b, is "Il convient a l'homme de se sanctifier au moment de l'union conjugale, enseigne le Zohar, pour que l'enfant qui va naître ait sa figure complète et de manière convenable…La forme de l'homme correspond a la forme celeste." On Vulliaud and the Zohar, see the stark critique by Gershom Scholem, "Vulliaud's Uebersetzung des *Sifra Di-Zeniutha* aus dem Sohar und andere neuere Literatur zur Geschichte der Kabbala," *Monatsschrift fur die Wissenschaft des Judentums*, 75 (1931), pp. 347–362, 444–455. Later on in his life, Eliade mentions Scholem's critique. See his "Cosmic Religion," p. 96. For more on Eliade and Kabbalah, see below in ch. 5. Without being aware of the earlier Romanian discussions of Eliade adduced here, Culianu, *Romanian Studies*, I, p. 250, intuited the possible Zoharic source of Eliade's approach to the androgyne and *hieros gamos*. See also ibid., p. 268.

19. See *Religion after Religion*, pp. 269–270 n. 19.

20. The most comprehensive study of Eliade and esotericism is related to Eliade's acquaintance with R. Guènon and revolves around Eliade's literaria. See Tolcea, *Eliade, the Esotericist*. He mentions some traces of Julius Evola's influence on Eliade's view of androgyne. See ibid., pp. 231–232. On the more scholarly aspects of Eliade and occultism, see Antoine Faivre, "Modern Western Esoteric Currents in the Works of Mircea Eliade, the Extent and the Limits of their Presence," in *Hermeneutics, Politics and the History of Religions*, ed. Wedemeyer–Doniger, pp. 147–157, and Spineto, "Mircea Eliade and Traditionalism," pp. 62–86, and some significant instances in Wasserstrom, *Religion after Religion*.

21. Or complete.

22. See Vulliaud, *La Cantique des Cantique*, p. 201 n. 3.

23. *De l'Unité spirituelle ou de la société et de son but au-delà du temps* (Paris, 1841), p. 1441, quoted in Vulliaud, ibid., p. 201.

24. Most probably an allusion to Galatians 3:28.

25. *De l'Unité spirituelle*, p. 1441.

26. See Wasserstrom, *Religion after Religion*, p. 38.

27. On other instances of the impact of de Saint-Bonnet on Vulliaud, see ibid., p. 154.

28. Ibid., p. 201.

29. This form means, in another context, totalization. See Eliade, *Portugal Journal*, I, p. 102. For more on this Romanian term, see the end of this chapter.

30. *Religion after Religion*, p. 38.

31. *Occultism*, p. 50. See also Eliade, "Occultism and Freemasonry in Eighteenth-Century France," *History of Religions*, 13 (1973), pp. 89–91. For Eliade's awareness of forms of *philosophia perennis*, see his "Some Notes on *Theosophia perennis*: Ananda K. Coomaraswamy and Henry Corbin," *History of Religions*, 19 (1979), pp. 167–176.

32. "Allegory or 'Secret Language,'" p. 102.

33. As we shall see in more detail in ch. 5 below, Eliade had been acquainted with Kabbalah since his adolescence.

34. See *Universul Literar*, IL, 3 (13 Ianuarie 1940), pp. 1, 8. The text has been reprinted in *The Morphology of Religions*, pp. 236–239. The quotations in the following will refer to this later reprint.

35. (Vremea, Bucharest, 1942), reprinted in the collection of his essays in Romanian entitled *The Way to the Center*, pp. 328–386. I shall quote below from this more recent reprint. There is an Italian translation, *Il mito della integrazione* (Milano, 1989).
36. *Portugal Journal*, I, p. 473.
37. *Eranos Jahrbuch*, 27 (1958), pp. 195–236.
38. *Méphistophélès et l'androgyne* (Paris, 1962).
39. pp. 78–124.
40. (London–New York, 1986), vol. 1, pp. 276–281.
41. Cf. *Women, Androgynes, and Other Mythical Beasts*.
42. See, e.g., *Encyclopedia of Religion*, p. 279.
43. Ibid., p. 277. He refers to his *The Two and the One*, pp. 114, 119, 122. Compare to Wasserstrom, *Religion after Religion*, p. 204.
44. *Encyclopedia of Religion*, p. 277.
45. *Patterns in Comparative Religion*, pp. 419–425, and *Myths, Dreams and Mysteries*, pp. 174–175.
46. This theory of the first man as a unity that is also a totality is found also later in his *History of Religious Ideas*, I, p. 165, and see also n. 7 there. It should be mentioned that Eliade's discussions on totality predate the views on totality formulated by Martin Heidegger.
47. *The Way to the Center*, p. 368.
48. Ibid., pp. 374–375.
49. Ibid., p. 375. Compare also the manner in which he describes himself in his *Autobiography*, p. 256: "Perhaps my yearning to love two women at the same time was none other than an episode in a long secret history that even I did not understand very well. I was trying to compensate for my fundamental incapability of becoming a 'saint' by resorting to a paradoxical, nonhuman experience, which at least opened to me the way to the mystery of totality."
50. Already in 1926, in a piece that deals exclusively with the Song of Songs, Eliade put into relief the Kabbalistic interpretations of the Song of Songs. The piece was reprinted in *The Morphology of Religions*, pp. 54–59. Already, at the age of 19, he refers to Vulliaud's book on the mystical interpretation of the Song of Songs. He had earlier in his life become acquainted with themes found in the Zohar, as seen above.
51. *The Morphology of Religions*, pp. 236–237. In version [C], described immediately below, the text is reproduced exactly, but Eliade adds a footnote wherein he refers to Paul Vulliaud's *La Kabbale Juive* (Paris, 1932), 2 volumes, and his *La Cantique des Cantiques d'après la tradition juive*. The question may be asked, how is human marriage consonant with the loss within the divinity or the attainment of indifference? See *The Way to the Center*, p. 371 n. 1.
52. *Universul literar*, IL, 5 (ianuarie 27, 1940), pp. 1, 8, enlarged in *The Way to the Center*, pp. 376–382. It should be mentioned that many years before, Eliade published in a newspaper a small piece entitled "Adam, Eve and Cain" (*Cuvântul*, 1928), and it was reprinted in *The Morphology of Religions*, pp. 239–241; it has nothing to do with the later piece "Adam and Eve."
53. See Krappe, "The Birth of Eve."
54. *The Way to the Center*, p. 378.
55. See the theories exposed in Krappe, "The Birth of Eve," pp. 312–313.
56. *The Way to the Center*, p. 377.
57. See above, Introduction.

58. See, e.g., *Patterns in Comparative Religion*, pp. 356–359; on the connection between orgy and reintegration, see especially pp. 358–359. See also his *Occultism*, pp. 88–92.

59. See e.g., *Solilocvii*, p. 28–29.

60. *The Way to the Center*, pp. 379–380; and compare to the later formulation in *Patterns in Comparative Religion*, p. 424, *A History of Religious Ideas*, I, p. 165 n. 7, and *The Two and the One*, p. 115. See also below, ch. 7.

In June 1941 in his *Portugal Journal*, I, p. 102, when starting to work on the third part of the trilogy *The Return from Paradise*, he writes in a manner reminiscent of the *coincidentia oppositorum* that "time totalizes, [and] melts the extremes. This is the great sense of my novel: that a person cannot accomplish himself if he does not 'totalize' in himself all the extremes, if he does not succeed in loving his enemies, if he does not surpass his political passions not by means of an Indian askesis or a skeptic Olympic placidity—but by living by the Christian message: Love your neighbor." The shift from loving the neighbor to loving and thus melting with the enemy is a rather radical understanding of Christianity. One cannot but regret that this Christian message did not convince the many Christians who, in the same year it was written, started the most brutal war in the history of mankind. Even more bizarre is the coincidence that just before Eliade wrote this passage, on June 30, 1941, a bestial pogrom was carried out by the army of the government that Eliade served as a diplomat, on June 28–29 in Iaşi, when more than 13,000 Jews were killed. See also above, the passage quoted from ibid., p. 170, and my discussion of a passage from October 1945 translated in ch. 7.

61. *The Way to the Center*, p. 381.

62. Ibid., pp. 381–382. See also ibid., p. 387.

63. Ibid., p. 382.

64. Ibid., pp. 379–381.

65. Ibid., pp. 379, 382.

66. Printed as an appendix to *Portugal Journal*, I, p. 475.

67. This move is already evident in his French 1949 work *Traité*, translated into English as *Pattern in Comparative Religion*, pp. 423–425, though he mentions quite succinctly Kabbalah; see p. 425. In *A History of Religious Ideas* (I, p. 165), a text written in 1975 and published in 1978, Adam is still androgyne, though I think that this discussion reflects Eliade's older attitude, as exposed, as he himself mentions in the Introduction, p. xvi, views he lectured in Bucharest and in Paris.

68. See *Eranos Jahrbuch* (1958), p. 220; *The Two and the One*, p. 104.

69. See Wasserstrom, *Religion after Religion*, p. 38.

70. See *Eranos Jahrbuch*, 1953; translated as "Mother Earth" and printed in *Myths, Dreams, and Mysteries*, p. 175.

71. See *Eranos Jahrbuch*, 1958, p. 220, *The Two and the One*, p. 104, and *A History of Religious Ideas*, I, p. 170.

72. See Eliade, *The Two and the One*, p. 122.

73. See ibid., p. 104. On Erigena and androgyny, see Francis Bertin, "Corps spirituel et androgynie chez Jean Scot Érigène," in Libis, *L'Androgyne*, pp. 63–128.

74. Cf. Eliade, *Contributions à la philosophie de la Renaissance*, p. 47.

75. See M. Idel, "The Myth of the Androgyne in Leone Ebreo and Its Cultural Implications," *Kabbalah*, 15 (2006), pp. 77–102; id., *Kabbalah & Eros*, pp. 88–92; Naomi Yavneh, "The Spiritual Esotericism of Leone's Hermaphrodite," in *Playing with Gender: A Renaissance Pursuit*,

ed. J. R. Brink–M. C. Horowitz–A. P. Coudert (Urbana–Chicago, 1991), pp. 85–98; T. Anthony Perry, *Erotic Spirituality, The Integrative Tradition from Leone Ebreo to John Donne* (Tuscaloosa, 1980), pp. 15, 22; Bernard McGinn, "Cosmic and Sexual Love in Renaissance Thought: Reflections on Marsilio Ficino, Giovanni Pico della Mirandola, and Leone Ebreo," in *The Devil, Heresy and Witchcraft in the Middle Ages, Essays in Honor of Jeffrey B. Russell*, ed. Alberto Ferreiro (Leiden, 1998), pp. 191–209; and Sergius Kodera, "The Idea of Beauty in Leone Ebreo (Judah Abravanel)," in *The Jewish Body, Corporeality, Society, and Identity in the Renaissance and Early Modern Period*, ed. M. Diemling–G. Veltri (Leiden, 2009), pp. 301–329, especially pp. 307–310, 318, 326.

76. *Dialogues of Love*, Leone Ebreo, ed. Rossella Pescatori, tr. Damian Bacich–Rossella Pescatori (Toronto, 2009), pp. 279–290.

77. "The Birth of Eve," p. 314.

78. See *The Two and the One*, p. 107.

79. *The Way to the Center*, p. 376; id., *Patterns in Comparative Religion*, p. 423; id., *Myth, Dreams, and Mysteries*, p. 175; *Eranos Jahrbuch*, 1958, p. 220; and id., *The Two and the One*, p. 104.

80. See the translation and the analysis of this Midrashic tradition in Daniel Boyarin, *Carnal Israel, Reading Sex in Talmudic Culture* (Berkeley, 1993), pp. 42–46.

81. Other early rabbinic scholars.

82. "The Birth of Eve," p. 314.

83. See *Eranos Jahrbuch*, 1958, p. 198.

84. See Idel, *Kabbalah & Eros*, pp. 53–103. For another approach to the androgyne and *du-partzufim*, much closer to Eliade's but emphasizing the concept of the masculine androgyne, see Wolfson, *Language, Eros, Being*. Moreover, the phallocentrism in early Eliade, which was unknown to Wolfson, is reminiscent of the emphasis of Wolfson's interpretation of Kabbalah. Given the suppression of the references to the Zohar in the later variants of his essay, neither Wasserstrom nor Wolfson could be acquainted with Eliade's early discussions.

85. See his letter to Acterian, *Cioran, Eliade, Ionesco*, p. 133.

86. *Ordeal by Labyrinth*, p. 9.

87. Ibid. The claim that he always distinguishes carefully between androgyne and hermaphrodite is not accurate. See, e.g., Eliade's *Patterns in Comparative Religion*, pp. 422, 424.

88. *The Androgyne*, p. 20.

89. *Religion after Religion*, pp. 37–39, 203–214.

90. *Reconstructing Eliade*, pp. 32–40.

91. *Definitio Sacri*, pp. 145, 249–254, 255–256, 259, 330–332.

92. *Myth and Religion*, pp. 157–158.

93. *Religion after Religion*, pp. 213–214.

94. *Eranos Jahrbuch*, 1958, pp. 218–219.

95. It should be pointed out that one of Eliade's friends from youth, Marcel Avramescu, a Jew who converted to Christianity as Mihail Avramescu, and was interested in Kabbalah, spiritualism, and occultism, wrote an M.A. thesis on Cusanus at the University of Bucharest. For more on this figure, see below, ch. 5.

96. On totality in Eliade, see, especially, Marino, *The Hermeneutics of Mircea Eliade*, pp. 131–141, and Shafique Keshavjee, "Totalité, paradoxe et liberté dans l'oeuvre de Mircea Eliade," in *Homo religious*, ed. Arcade–Manea–Stamatescu, pp. 262–263.

97. See his essay "The Hindu Pantheon," published first in 1939, and reprinted more recently in *Secret Things*, pp.133–135. The existence of discussions about "total" and "totality" in the earlier Eliade complicates the attribution of the role that the Iron Guard ideology, a totalitarian one, could play in shaping Eliade's scholarship. See Elaine Fisher, "Fascists Scholars, Fascist Scholarship: The Quest of Ur-Fascism and the Study of Religion," in ed. Wedemeyer–Doniger, *Hermeneutics, Politics and the History of Religions*, pp. 261–283. However, concern with integration in totality in this generation predates the rapprochement to the Iron Guard. See, e.g., Eliade's older contemporary, the philosopher Vasile Băncilă, "Spiritualitate," in *Tiparnița literară*, 1, 3 (1929), p. 3. See also ibid., p. 2. It should be pointed out that the "late Culianu," namely the last writings of Ioan P. Couliano, display a certain effort to explain "all" by his *mathesis universalis*, a combinatory explanation of the emergence of cultural creations in many fields.

98. See "The Apology for Virility," *Gândirea* (1928), pp. 8–9. On this piece, see Țurcanu, *Mircea Eliade*, p. 95.

99. The impact of this essay about masculinity on Eliade is evident already in 1925. See his essay published in this year, reprinted in *How I Found the Philosopher's Stone*, p. 232.

100. See the accusation he levels against the Moldavians, that they are melancholic and do not have virility, which Eliade formulated in 1928 in his critique of the Moldavian spirit, in "Against Moldavia," reprinted in the collection of essays by Eliade, *Romanian Prophetism*, I, pp. 97–98. For equilibrium and sensuality, see also *Portugal Journal*, I, p. 336.

101. *Autobiography*, p. 134. For the nexus between masculinity and asceticism, see *Gaudeamus*, written in 1928, p. 129. For an emphasis on virility, see ibid., pp. 136–137. For the use of the term "instrument of knowledge," see also below, the passage from the end of *The Return from Paradise*.

102. *Autobiography*, p. 134. Emphases in the original.

103. In Romanian the form *toate* is feminine and may be understood as pointing to all women. See also the continuation of this passage.

104. See *Maddalena*, pp. 19–20.

105. *Eliadiana*, p. 11. This sentence, which is part of an earlier version published in Botoşani at the end of 1927, does not appear in the version printed later in 1928, in *Gândirea*, where it was probably substituted by the phrase "Glory to the pure masculine." See the reprint in the collection of his short stories *Maddalena*, p. 17, and in Eliade, *Virility and Askesis*, p. 234. Some months later, Eliade published in the newspaper *Cuvântul* two short essays in which he attempts to qualify his early stances, hinting at the first printed version in 1927; they are reprinted in ibid., pp. 272–278. For the praise of Bucharest as a virile city, see also his 1935 short piece "Bucharest, a Virile Center," reprinted in *Secret Things*, pp. 336–338.

106. *The Return from Paradise*, p. 150.

107. Ibid., p. 69.

108. In Romanian the term is *totul*, all. The two terms "unity" and "all," or totality, occur later on in Eliade's studies of religion. See, e.g., *Eranos Jahrbuch* (1958), p. 221, and *The Two and the One*, p. 115. Compare also the phrase found in *Ştefania*, on the last past of the unfinished trilogy of which *The Return from Paradise* is the first part. See *The New Life*, p. 59, where the protagonist says: "Sometimes I would like to seize all."

109. *The Return from Paradise*, p. 299. For the expression "instrument of cognition," see ch. 3. For another discussion of death as an instrument of action, see the view that Eliade attributes to Ion Moța, a major figure in the Iron Guard pantheon, in the fragment of the last part of the

unfinished trilogy. See *The Return from Paradise*, p. 116: "Whoever knows how to die, will never be a slave," upon which he comments, "death understood as a perfect instrument action and insurrection." For the important role that Eliade intended to allow to the Iron Guard, according to his initial notes concerning the novel, see ibid., p. 203.

110. *The Return from the Paradise*, p. 301.

111. In the context of his sexual relationship with her, Eliade mentions a phrase that reflects Plato's androgyny, "the third sex." See *The Hooligans*, p. 174.

112. See Eliade, *Ordeal by Labyrinth*, pp. 175–177.

113. See above, ch. 1.

114. See above, Introduction.

115. *Autobiography*, p. 256. Note the occurrence of the term "nostalgia," attributed to his approach in his youth. For more on this passage, see above, Introduction.

116. Ibid.

117. Ibid.

118. *Gaudeamus*, p. 93, and Turcanu, *Mircea Eliade*, p. 98.

119. *Autobiography*, p. 257.

120. See Eliade, *Ordeal by Labyrinth*, pp. 120–121.

121. See above, ch. 1.

122. *Wedding in Heaven*, pp. 188–189. This description is reminiscent of another novel, entitled Şantier, written in India, p. 282.

123. *Portugal Journal*, I, p. 170. On equilibrium, see also ibid., pp. 150, 235, which I quote in the next chapter. See also below, at the end of this chapter, the passage translated from ibid., p. 102. The concept of equilibrium that recurs in Eliade, including in some of the quotes cited immediately below, may reflect the impact of Lucian Blaga, Eliade's contemporary and a philosopher of culture whom Eliade respected very much, as to the cosmic equilibrium. For more on their relationship, see below, ch. 3.

124. Ibid., pp. 200–201. See also ibid., p. 202: "The Eros has for me a metaphysical function....Love is for me first and foremost an experience with a metaphysical sense."

125. Ibid., p. 235. On the affinity between Chaos and androgyny, see the design of Henricus Kunrath, reproduced in Elemire Zolla, "L'androgyne alchemique," in Libis, *L'androgyne*, p. 145 n. xvii.

126. *Portugal Journal*, I, p. 235.

127. Ibid., I, p. 271.

128. Aldagiza Ionescu, the daughter of his wife Nina.

129. Namely, for Romania. They left for two months.

130. See also *Portugal Journal*, I, p. 210: "Loneliness for me is a constant invitation to vice, foolishness, adventure."

131. In Romanian, *deslanzuiri*, which means also "outbreaks."

132. *Portugal Journal*, I, p. 118. This passage, and the one from November 14, had been adduced in the context of the claims in *The Myth of Reintegration*, conceived of as representing a work written in 1942, in Ţurcanu, *Mircea Eliade*, pp. 320–321.

133. Ibid., p. 119. See also again on the same page, on May 6.

134. Ibid., p. 126.

135. For Eliade's negative attitude to erudition, see ibid., p. 188, and also the Introduction.

136. *Portugal Journal*, I, p. 151. On archetypes in Eliade, see Reschika, *Mircea Eliade*, pp. 52–61.

137. *Portugal Journal*, I, pp. 338–339. See also his Indian behavior, described as "nocturnal debauches" in Ricketts, *Romanian Roots*, I, p. 346.

138. For crises beforehand and later, sometimes described as melancholies, see ibid., I, pp. 116, 120, 136, 138, 139, 141, 159–160.

139. Ibid., I, p. 340. See also ibid., I, pp. 287–288, 292. For the possible identity of the Portuguese neurologist, see ibid., II, pp. 453–454. About Eliade's crisis of nerves in this period and his resort to drugs, see Oişteanu, *Narcotics in Romanian culture*, pp. 390–404.

140. See, especially, the two novels *Isabel si apele diavolului* and *Domnişoara Cristina*. In more general terms about the attitude to temptation and women in those novels, see Simion, *Knots and Signs of Prose*, pp. 65–82.

141. See *Portugal Journal*, I, p. 364.

142. On the entire affair, see Ţurcanu, *Mircea Eliade*, pp. 257–260.

143. See *Yoga*, pp. 55, 97, 99, 270, 271, 304, and *Shamanism*, p. 153 n. 37. Those applications are later than the 1940 essay on the androgyne.

144. See Eliade's minimizing—in fact, dismissing—Krappe's theory as to the possibility of the influence of a hypothetical Hindo-European myth of the androgyne on the Semitic myth in his *The Way to the Center*, p. 378. On Eliade and Krappe in general, see Eliade, *Master Manole*, pp. 145, 312, and Ricketts, *Romanian Roots*, II, pp. 867–868.

145. See Ţurcanu, *Mircea Eliade*, p. 325, and *Portugal Journal*, I, pp. 127, 132, 436, 439–440, 442, 473.

146. *A History of Religious Ideas*, III, p. 174. See also Scholem's various uses of the concept of reintegration, adduced by Wasserstrom, *Religion after Religion*, pp. 38–39.

147. See Wasserstrom, ibid., p. 38.

148. Though such a view is found in other contexts in earlier Kabbalah, it is not related to the specific type of Kabbalah committed to writing in the books of Isaac Luria. See Scholem, *Origins of the Kabbalah*, p. 300 n. 201.

149. See *Autobiography*, p. 277, and *Portugal Journal*, I, p. 274.

150. See Eliade, *The Myth of the Eternal Return*, p. 61.

151. See his *La confessione dei peccati*, II (Bologna, 1935), p. 229. However, scholars in the field who had explored this topic in a detailed manner did not find any vestige of an orgiastic dimension of such a practice during Yom Kippur. See, e.g., Pinhas Mandel, "'There Were no Good Days to Israel as 15th of Av and *Yom ha-Kippurim*': On the Last Mishnah of the *Massekhet Ta'anit* and Its Metamorphoses," *Te'udah*, 11, ed. M.B. Lerner–M.A. Friedmann (Tel Aviv, 1986), pp. 147–178, especially the bibliographical material discussed at pp. 148–149 n. 5 (Hebrew). One of the theories regarding the text referred to by Pettazzoni is that it is an error, and instead of *Yom ha-Kippurim* it should read *Yom ha-Bikkurim*.

152. *Yoga, Immortality and Freedom*, pp. 271–272. This form of interpretation is, however, much more substantial in the Eranos lecture. See *Eranos Jahrbuch*, 1958, pp. 231–235. For the view that the practice of mandala strives to reintegrate the personality, see the interpretation of Giuseppe Tucci, *Théorie et pratique du mandala*, tr. H. J. Maxwell (Paris, 1974), pp. 29–53, 110–111, 113. Eliade was well acquainted with Tucci's writings. See also Wasserstrom, *Religion after Religion*, p. 205.

153. See *Yoga*, p. 272, which repeats in a rather precise manner what he wrote in another context in *Patterns in Comparative Religion*, pp. 419–420.

154. See the series of articles printed in Romanian journals in 1930 and collected recently in Mircea Eliade, *Yoga, Problematica filozofiei indiene*, ed. C. Barbu–M. Handoca (Craiova, 1991), especially pp. 85–110.

155. On this term, see *Eranos Jahrbuch* 1958, pp. 228–229, and his commentary on the legend in *Meşterul Manole*, finalized in Lisbon in 1942/1943; cf., the edition of his essays in *Meşterul Manole* published by Petru and Magda Ursache, p. 106. It is plausible that the Great Man is Eliade himself.

156. See *Portugal Journal*, II, p. 448. For additional references to totalization, see ibid., I, pp. 102, 271.

157. *The Myth of Reintegration*, p. 387. I did not find a parallel to this assessment in other versions of the essay.

158. Ibid. This approach is much less visible in the version in *Eranos Jahrbuch*, 1958. It should be pointed out that the Italian edition of Elemire Zolla's book on the visual representations of the androgyne, entitled *Androgyne: The Fusion of the Sexes (Art & Imagination)*, is *L'Androgino, l'umana nostalgia dell'interezza* (Como, 1989), that is, *The Androgyne: The Human Nostalgia for Perfection*, a title that betrays the influence of Eliade.

159. *The Myth of Reintegration*, in *The Way to the Center*, pp. 386–387.

160. See Eliade, *Myth and Reality*, pp. 50–53, and his *Myths, Dreams, and Mysteries*, pp. 59–72. For "Adamic nostalgia," see his *The Quest*, pp. 99–101, 134.

161. On Eliade as archaist versus Hegelianism in scholarship of religion, see Idel, *Enchanted Chains*, pp. 4–6.

162. See, e.g., Eliade, *Zalmoxis*, p. 110: "Zurvan would be preeminently the 'divine totality,' the *coincidentia oppositorum* whose androgynism is but one of its aspects." However, the sources speak about bisexuality that Eliade would call hermaphrodism. See his *Patterns in Comparative Religion*, p. 422, and Robert Zaehner, *Zurvan: A Zoroastrain Dilemma* (Oxford, 1955), p. 63. However, in a parallel discussion found in *The Two and the One*, pp. 83–84, androgyny is not mentioned.

163. See Eliade, *Myth and Reality*, pp. 79–84.

164. For Eliade's view that in religion sexual images and sex activity in general mean much more than they do in a modern profane society understand, namely form of worship of the power of creation and procreation, see his 1934 essay "Sex" printed in *Oceanography*, pp. 93–101. He returns to these ideas as to the significance of the sexual symbolism many times later on. I cannot enter here the question why Eliade did not understood the alchemical practices as androgyny in his earlier essays on the topic, printed in 1935, 1937, and 1938, the first two reprinted in *The Way to the Center*, pp. 464–504, despite the recurring resort to a sexualized vision of alchemy. However since 1942 this claim occurs in Romanian, *The Way to the Center*, pp. 371–372; French, *Eranos Jahrbuch* 1958, p. 198; and the English, *The Two and the One*, p. 103, versions, but not in his later formulations of his views on alchemy in *The Forge and the Crucible*, despite a reproduction of the pictures where the androgyne is found, see pp. 58–59, 138. What seems to me interesting is the fact that despite Eliade's refrain of introducing the category of androgyny in his studies on alchemy, he claims he did so in his studies on androgyny mentioned in this footnote.

165. Especially important is Goethe's impact on Eliade. See Mac Linscott Ricketts, "Eliade and Goethe," *Archaeus*, vol. 6 (2002), pp. 283–331, and Wasserstrom, *Religion after Religion*, pp. 208–211, 337, note 23.

166. See *The Way to the Center*, p. 368.

167. Wasserstrom's claim in *Religion after Religion*, p. 204, that Eliade's ideal was a masculine androgyne "throughout his long career" is not so obvious from the sources as I know them. See the way in which Ioan P. Culianu described Eliade as a seemingly androgyne, in the text published by Bordaș, "Always a Beacon Light in a Nihilistic World," pp. 308, 334.

168. Reprinted in *The Way to the Center*, pp. 185, 195–197.

169. See "Some Observations on European Witchcraft," reprinted in *Occultism*, pp. 87–92.

170. See Eliade's own testimony that he arrived at the vision of the duality and reintegration related to Goethe's *Faust* and Balzac's *Serafita* twenty years earlier, namely after 1937, since he wrote his confession around 1957, in *Eranos Jahrbuch*, 1958, p. 195.

171. See more below, ch. 3.

172. *Şantier*, in *Prose*, p. 422.

173. This is different from the dual function of the archetype according to Jung, who held that the impact of the archetype on one person may be positive and on another person, negative.

174. See, e.g., Idel, *Enchanted Chains*, passim, especially pp. 223–227.

175. See Wolfson, *Language, Eros, Being*, pp. 261–262. For Wolfson's dependence on Eliade, see his "Woman: The Feminine as Other in Theosophic Kabbalah: Some Philosophical Observations on the Divine Androgyne," in *The Other in Jewish Thought and Identity*, ed. L. Silberstein–R. Cohn (New York,1994), p. 187, reiterated in *Language, Eros, Being*, p. 503 n. 168.

176. Let me reiterate that Eliade's claim as to rediscovery of the meaning of forgotten symbols is reminiscent of the claim by Gershom Scholem in the context of Kabbalah, though in the latter, symbols are mainly words, while in Eliade they are objects or processes.

177. See Faivre, "Modern Western Esoteric Currents in the Work of Mircea Eliade: The Extent and Limits of Their Presence," pp. 147–156, and in ch. 1, above. On *prisca theologia*, see Daniel P. Walker, *The Ancient Theology*, (London, 1972); Charles Schmitt, "Perennial Philosophy from Agostino Steuco to Leibniz," *Journal of the History of Ideas*, 27 (1966), pp. 505–532; id., "*Prisca Theologia e Filosofia Perennis*: Due temi del rinascimento italiano e a loro fortuna," *Il pensiero Italiano del rinascimento e il tempo nostro* (Firenze, 1970), pp. 211–236; Paul O. Kristeller, *Renaissance Thought and Its Sources*, ed. Michael Mooney (New York, 1979), pp. 196–210; Charles Trinkaus, *In Our Image and Likeness: Humanity and Dignity in Italian Humanistic Thought* (Notre Dame, 1995), pp. 726–742, 754–756; James Hankins, *Plato in the Italian Renaissance* (Leiden, 1990), pp. 459–463; Chaim Wirszubski, *Pico della Mirandola's Encounter with Jewish Mysticism* (Cambridge–London–Jerusalem, 1989), p. 198 n. 41; Briggite Tambrun, "Marsile Ficin et le Commentaire de Plethon sur les Oracles Chaldaiques," *Accademia*, 1 (1999), pp. 9–48.

178. It should be mentioned that a strong proclivity to occultism is evident in a quite early piece written by Eliade at the end of his high school years: "Şțiință și Ocultism," reprinted in *How I Found the Philosopher's Stone*, pp. 246–247, an essay discussed in the Introduction.

179. See especially, Carl G. Jung–Ch. Kerényi, *Introduction à l'essence de la mythologie* (Paris, 1980), p. 139.

· 3 ·

THANATOLOGIES

Apotheoses and Triumphs of Death

The symbolism of death allows everything: Extinction or regeneration, a true beginning of a new life.

—MIRCEA ELIADE[1]

If you are ready to die, No fear, weakness, shyness can enslave you. Making peace with death is the most total liberty man can receive on this Earth.

—MIRCEA ELIADE[2]

Initiation is a death and every death, when accepted intelligently, may be equivalent to an initiation.

—MIRCEA ELIADE

A Fascination with the Problem of Death

*I*n 1945, when trying to find the linkage between his personality while in India during 1929–1931 and his present one, Eliade wrote: "To rediscover the elements of unity, to see what did I change, on what path did I evaluate. The constants:[3] the problem of death; the alternance: symbolism."[4] This is a seminal confession as to what constant element unifies his personality, namely, a preoccupation with the problem of death throughout a significant part of his more mature years. This is not just a general reflection, since some days later he mentions that he intends to write a book on "death and initiation" that will comprise 250–300 pages, which, however, was never finished.[5] Some few years earlier, he wrote in one of his short stories: "by means of death you will approach the grand revelation of all meaning, rather than just the end of an earthly life, the gradual dying up of flesh and its absorption into the earth. I have always divided people into two categories: those who understand death as the *end* to life and the body, and those who conceive it as the *beginning* of a new, spiritual existence."[6] For Eliade, the attitude toward death is, therefore, a major touchstone. Indeed, more than any other writer I am acquainted with in the history of religion, Eliade offers different approaches to death with different occasions, so we may speak about his theories of death or thanatology. This means that he had a rather wide spectrum of understanding it that is so wide and rich, given his recurrence to the theme, that it is difficult to exhaust it in this framework. In any case, at least in one interview, in 1936, he speaks about death as some form of technique, a fact that inserts some of the following discussions into the framework of his preoccupation with techniques.[7] Given the fact that Eliade did not write a monograph on the topic, though he promised several times to do so, and that no detailed and comprehensive analysis has been written on the topic by scholars on this subject, to my best knowledge, I shall survey the major occurrences of this topic in Eliade and speculate at the end on its sources and implications.[8] I assume that Eliade would regard this preoccupation as a continuation of the attitude that he discerns in the three masters of his generation:

> It is not accidental at all that the three professors that have led generations of young persons since 1900—Nicolae Iorga, Vasile Pârvan, Nae Ionescu—have confessed altogether a tragic consciousness of existence, and they found nevertheless a heroic sense of this existence, which should be accepted and fructified.[9]

As a follower of all these thinkers who advocated the organistic vision of Romanian nationhood, and as the self-proclaimed head of the young generation, Eliade's own preoccupation with death as a spiritual problem is quite natural. However, this is not obvious for many of his contemporaries from his circle, and even Ionesco, who was very much concerned with death, had a different attitude, as an unimportant issue is quite conspicuous, at least in his early *NO*.[10]

Moreover, in addition to the importance of this theme, as I shall show below, one of the major claims in some of the critiques that addressed the structure of Eliade's scholarship concerns the affinities between some of its contents and attitudes prevalent in fascist movements in general and the Iron Guard in particular, especially the extolling of the heroic death, self-sacrifice, and the importance of the birth of the new man. Undeniably, also Eliade's close connections with several thinkers who were

much more openly identified with extreme right positions, both in Romania—Nae
Ionescu being the most famous one—and after the thirties, abroad—for example,
Julius Evola, Georges Dumezil, Ernst Junger,[11] Giuseppe Tucci, and Stig Wikander—
were invoked in support of arguments about the affinities between seminal parts of
his scholarship and his political affiliations. Thus, important aspects of Eliade's scholarship were explained by some scholars as the intrusion of vitalist elements stemming
from political programs of fascist propensities into the very structure of the religion
he presented as an ancient common structure that has almost disappeared in modern times. In some cases, those claims were made by serious scholars, and they sometimes employed more detailed discussions in order to explicate their arguments.[12]

My intention here is not so much to argue against the power of the parallels that
have been pointed out by scholars, whether phenomenological or historical—namely,
their occurrence in, roughly speaking, the same period; instead, the explanation I shall
offer for these parallels differs from the mechanical assumption that politics simply
invaded scholarship, a form of explanation that I call proximism, or some form of historicism. I also employ here my leading methodology as proposed in the Introduction,
to describe Eliade as developing over a longer period of time. This is the best way of
understanding the growth of his thought, with its historical variegated backgrounds,
but in a more complex manner than considering only the impact of some political program in interpretations of so many texts.

In 1922, at the age of 15, Eliade wrote in a journal about the death of a priest,
a description according to his assessment, at length elsewhere, for the sake of writing a novel.[13] One of the earliest short stories written by Eliade, at the age of 16, entitled "How Did Ri, the Sacred Child, Die," was published only recently, but there is
no conceptual discussion of the nature of death.[14] Much more substantial is the
lengthy description of the death and the burial of his aunt in 1923.[15] When react-
ing to the death, Eliade said: "Light out of Light.... She went to heaven, lets Your will
be done." He mentions a discussion he had with his friend Vojen, but no details are
given.[16] It is in that same year that he wrote a short story about a philosopher who
was atheist, but in the moment of his death he has a revelation of God and repents.[17]
Two years later, Eliade mentions in a discussion on "Science and Occultism" Camille
Flammarion's book *La mort et son mystère*.[18] He maintains later in this discussion the
belief in the immortality of the soul on grounds of spiritism.[19]

However, the first sustained discussion of death seems to be a seminar paper for
the class of a professor at the University of Bucharest, P. P. Negulescu, in 1928, published for the first time much later, in 1987. Its title is "The Problem of Natural Death
and Its Ontological Significance." Eliade distinguishes between corporeal death,
which is conceived of as being necessary since this type of existence is only a tempo-

ral participation in life, and spiritual life, which is eternal, like God. The soul is described as existing independently of its vehicle, just as a symphony may exist independently of the instruments used to play it.[20] The importance of this piece is the early formulation of the belief in a life after the corporeal death, a view that is going to preoccupy Eliade for decades. In an interesting short novel written in 1929 in Calcutta, it is claimed that "only the soul that lifts life by itself, without any reason, is a master of it [life], and only someone that dies like a human being, becomes a real god."[21] This apotheosis of suicide adumbrates what Eliade will claim in his trilogy *The Return from Paradise*, as we shall see below. Some few years later, around 1931, while in India, he wrote a now lost play entitled *The Comedy of Death*.[22]

The glorification of death constitutes an articulated starting point for many discussions in Eliade's literature since 1933, that is, several years before his affiliation to the Iron Guard ideology, and even several months before the beginning of Nae Ionescu's slide into the ideology of this movement in late 1933. Presumably in 1933, Eliade wrote a piece published in a newspaper that I could not identify, but it was reprinted in 1934 in the collection of his journalistic stories entitled *Oceanography*. Its title is "On a Certain Feeling of Death," and it deals with the notion that the moment of death is not just the continuation of an ascending move toward perfection, but also a radical turning point for a form of experience that cannot be guessed from the events of a life, even if it is a perfect one.[23] Though different from the 1928 paper, this piece shares the belief in the existence of an afterlife. This is also evident from another piece printed in the same collection.[24] Again in *Oceanography*, he formulates a view that will be developed some years later concerning representation of death in folklore as an instrument of cognition.[25] From the context of this discussion it is obvious that death preoccupied Eliade's thought very much in an early period of his life.[26]

In early 1935, he declares in a radio speech that it would be a superficial understanding of Christianity to see it as the "humiliation of life and the exaltation of death."[27] Rather, he argues that death is no longer understood as definitive or as a process of annihilation, but as a moment of rest before achieving immortality. Death is presented here as a rite of transition, losing its negativity and understood as constituting a bridge to immortality[28] since Jesus penetrated death and conquered it.[29] However, Eliade continues, this conciliated attitude toward death was already well known before Christianity, in the Dacian space, and it still corresponds to it.[30] Such a view reverberates many times also in his later feuilletons. This is the case with two discussions published in 1939 in *Fragmentarium*, in which he came up with the idea that the deep interest in history in 19th-century Europe is part of a phenomenon known from folklore about seeing the entirety of life in a flash before death as containing a premonition of the dark future of Western culture.[31] This approach was elaborated on later by Eliade in an essay published in 1930 in French and translated in *Myth, Dreams, and Mysteries*.[32]

Let me turn now to some passages from one of Eliade's earlier novels, *The Return from Paradise*. Though written in 1933, the novel was conceptualized at least two years beforehand,[33] but the very beginning was formulated even earlier, around 1928, in Calcutta.[34] Nevertheless, many of its details reflect events related to Eliade's life in late 1932 and early 1933, especially the sexual relationship of the protagonist, Pavel Anicet, with two women at the same time, a parallel to Eliade's concomitant erotic affairs with Sorana Ţopa and Nina Mareş, the latter of whom became his wife in 1934. This type of double affair was later understood in terms of his theory of religion as if dealing with *coincidentia oppositorum*.[35] Some mythologization of Eliade's life is part of his more general understanding of reality and religious fact, what I called hermeneutics of indistinction.

Moreover, the affinities between the details of the novels and Eliade's biography are transparent. The Anicet family, whose members are the protagonists of all the three parts of the unfinished trilogy called *The Return from Paradise*—which is the title both of the trilogy and of the first part of it—were originally a rich family who possessed a farm that has been lost, and now they live an impoverished life. The name of the farm was Arvireşti. As Eliade mentions, his own mother's family name was Arvira.[36] Just as the old Francisc, who died before the novel started but whose figure floats over the descendants, was an officer, Eliade's father, too, was an officer in the Romanian army, and both were decorated for their contributions in WWI. And last but not least: Eliade presents his own family as an impoverished one.[37] Those are the reasons why the obsession with death, dominant in the two published parts of the trilogy that are finished, reflects something of the young Eliade's own preoccupation, present also in the three pieces he wrote earlier, mentioned above.

Pavel Anicet, who is the alter ego of Eliade himself, reflects on the nature of death, and is in search of death as a way to escape the tension involved in the relationships with the two women. In one of his reflections, Anicet asserts:

> I ask myself whether someone who reflected one single time on death with pleasure may benefit from the life around him....It is not about the personal death, the suicide, or all these stupidities. But on death as a concrete existence, as another life, a fuller one, more eternal than our ephemeral eternity....Death as a victory, as a wholeness. Not a death out of despair, not out of fear. Someone who dies in a moment of terrible despair, out of pain, he completely failed his life. But in an ecstasy? But in expectation?[38]

Those questions are not just rhetorical. Toward the end, he redefines this different type of death: "Death, ecstasy.[39] Death, an instrument of cognition.[40] Death, a means of embracing unity, of the whole."[41] Earlier in the novel he compares death to suffering, saying that "And then back to chaos, back to the primordial unity, death....Hm, it is true that death has this rare fascination with unity. You are there alone and nevertheless you are all, you are everywhere. Thirty of unity, namely, thirty of death."[42] A similar message is delivered by Pavel later on in the novel:

I believe in death....It seems to me that there we shall meet the primordial unity, we shall be one, one alone, I shall merely be....The experiences have tired me completely, the dualism of every living, the decomposition that makes its place in any ecstasy, in every love. It is terrible.[43]

Elsewhere he asserts that he does not want to be a martyr.[44] The very end of the novel describes the suicide of Anicet, who thinks just before he pulls the trigger of the pistol that: "This death of mine I create it as I like it. I lived my life as it has been given to me, as the events have imparted it to me. But the death belongs to me, just as I confer it on me, so will I penetrate in the beyond."[45] Eliade himself solved the problem of choice in a different manner, but his novel reflects this theoretical or imaginative attraction toward an ecstatic death. This is escape from duality, which involves a tension, into unity, in the middle of a successful life, by means of a death that does not involve an attempt to flee suffering.

Death here has nothing to do with self-sacrifice, with involvement in a political activity; on the contrary, it is a very personal decision that reflects the lack of involvement in life, including his two concomitant and successful affairs with Una—indubitably, a symbol of unity—and Ghighi, who in my opinion stands for duality because of the repetition of the syllable Ghi.

Those discussions show that Eliade's preoccupation with death as a supreme experience is quite different from his later and much stronger assumption of death as an initiation, which he adopted from ancient Greek sources.[46] Though Paul Anicet also assumes an experiential death, ecstatic, gnostic, and cosmic, yet purely personal, having some implied religious overtones, it is an experience that is depicted as totally antisocial, as Anicet does not care enough even to write some kind of farewell to his family or to either of the two women. Here we have a combination of a personal event, which Eliade describes in detail in his *Autobiography*, as to his own relations in 1932/1933 with the two ladies,[47] and a metaphysical interpretation offered by Pavel Anicet of the solution, an escape from plurality into unity, which is considered also to be a totality. Interestingly enough, the single reference to the possibility of suicide in Mihail Sebastian's *Journal* has to do with the pressure of multiple erotic relationships he had.[48]

This pattern, which can be defined by referencing the title of one of Eliade's collections of studies, *The Two and the One*, appears also in two other novels: *The Hooligans*, published in late 1935, and the much later *Forbidden Forest*, in 1949. The former novel is a direct sequel to *The Return from the Paradise*, and tells the story of two other members of the Anicet family: the mother, who commits suicide at the end of the novel, and Pavel's brother, Petru. However, the triangle here is not just Petru's sexual affairs with two ladies, which ultimately triggers the suicide of his mother, but also the affairs of another protagonist, Alexandru Pleşa, the "perfect hooligan," whose former involvement with Viorica Panaitescu triggers her suicide,[49] while he decides to become engaged on the spot to another young woman, Valentina Puşcariu, whom he did not know a moment beforehand—she is just the first lady he met randomly at a party. He does so premeditatedly, as part of a game that is an attempt to show his indifference.[50] Immediately afterwards, he breaks the engagement, indifferent to her suffering.[51] Death, especially suicide, is therefore quite present in this novel, too.[52] Again, it has nothing to do with a political ideal, or a sacrifice, as the two women are described in quite apolitical terms.

More complex is the occurrence of "the two and the one" pattern in Eliade's most important novel, *Forbidden Forest*. There, Ştefan Viziru, the main protagonist, who again reflects something of Eliade's fate and views, is in love with two women, the idealized Ileana, whose image haunted him for 12 years, and Ioana, to whom he is married. When he finally meets the former and he declares his unfulfilled love for her, they perish in a car accident, which, again, occurs the end of the novel. Here, death is not a matter of a suicide, but it has its somewhat ecstatic dimension, some form of flight, which perhaps is reminiscent of what Eliade attributes, in the same period he wrote this novel, to the Shaman. The two protagonists die in the last moment in some form of ecstatic death, which may stand also for a marriage with death. This time, Stefan is indubitably a person of the right, like Eliade, but again, his death is not related to his political convictions. The novel has been aptly described by Marta Petreu as a novel "of death and burying…of his Romanian part."[53] It is indeed an escape from history and its terror, an issue that shall be dealt with in the next chapter. Let me mention that "the two and one" structure was not just the projection of a personal incident onto his literary works, but something deeper, related to a longing Eliade himself recognizes. In his autobiography he wrote:

> Perhaps my yearning to love two women at the same time was none other than an episode in a long secret history that even I did not understand very well. I was trying to compensate for my fundamental incapability of becoming a "saint" by resorting to a paradoxical, nonhuman experience, which at least opened to me the way to the mystery of totality.[54]

The term "totality" is a major clue for understanding the vision of Eliade, as we have seen above.[55] It should be mentioned that the paradoxical experience is related in other discussions of Eliade to the transcendence of dualities, the *concidentia oppositorum*, and death.[56] In 1945 Eliade expresses his wish "that in death all these will be fulfilled, without suffering because I am divided, that I chose, that I lived the fragment and the finite."[57] According to his presentation of the problematic that concerned him in these novels, in the sequel to *The Return from Paradise* and *The Hooligans*, entitled *The New Life*, Eliade planned to present Petru as confronting again a double love: Nora and Stefania, the lower and the higher, but he planned to let Petru choose the former, the "premoral Magna Mater," which means, in his view, the acceptance of history.[58]

Let me draw attention to a seminal passage that discusses another type of death, this time put into the mouth of the above-mentioned "perfect hooligan," the young Alexandru Pleşa. In a conversation with his cousin Petru Anicet, the former contrasts Anicet's feeling of loneliness with what he foresees will happen in the future:

> Perhaps you are right insofar as loneliness is concerned in a certain type of death—said Alexandru, speaking hotly—in the stupid and bourgeoisie death, death out of illness or old age. But our death, my dear Petru, will be totally different. We shall all die, millions of young men, we shall die while embraced with one another, and no one will then feel alone....You do not notice how nicely the youth is preparing, in all the countries, for death? What are the militias and the battalions of shock, the legions and the armies in the entire world today, linked especially by the common fate that waits for them, the death together? The world had never more successfully prepared young people for a collective death. In a war, in a revolution, only young people will die, and so many young people will die at the same time that no one will feel that they actually die....You think that you are alone in death, since you think only about yourself, or yours. This *esprit de corps*[59] that you were deriding earlier suspends this fundamental loneliness of a person in the moment of death. In the old times, the believers were dying with the priest beside them. Now the young people who grow together, who are close to each other by their suffering as well as by their common fate, will no more need the assistance in the moment of their death: many will die, so many that just one single death will exist: the collective death. On a camp of fight...[60]

Published in late 1935, this is quite an apocalyptic prophesy as to what was going to happen not so long afterwards in Europe. However, what is interesting here is the apocalyptic tone related to the death of many young people together. This experience of togetherness is conceived of explicitly as an antidote for the haunting loneliness that permeates the lives of Eliade's characters in the two novels, especially the lonely death of Pavel. What should be noticed is that no political position is implied here, right or left, though the reference to the military organizations is so obvious. Alexandru describes an international situation, at least implicitly rejecting the national one, and an atheistic death, which is explicitly an antipode of the Christian one. From this point of view, namely the nonnationalistic and the non-Christian aspects of death, he comes close to the death of his cousin Pavel. Alexandru's view is rejected immediately afterwards by the cynical Petru, who declares that "I do not feel the need to lose myself in a million of people, as I do not feel the desire to die together with a million of people."[61] I assume that this is also the view of Eliade at the end of 1935. In 1938 he expressed his feeling of relief after being freed from the detention camp of the legionnaires in Miercurea Ciuc, thinking that "I escaped from the collective death."[62]

In 1936 Eliade published another novel, entitled *Miss Christina*, where themes related to Eros and Thanatos play a central role, though in quite a different manner. Christina was a young girl who was engaging in wild sex with peasants and was killed out of jealousy, and she returns after her death as a vampiric ghost in order to tempt one of the male protagonists, Egor, to make love with her.[63] This quite morbid novel belongs to the fantastic genre in Eliade's writings, and is less concerned with abstract theories we have seen earlier. However, it contains an implicit case of change of gender, when the dead mademoiselle addresses the male Egor using verses of Mihail Eminescu's most famous poem, "Luceafărul," which in the original had the protagonist, Hyperion, address Cătălina: "I would like you to be my bride." The dead Christina is Eliade's counterpart to Eminescu's protagonist Hyperion, the eternal evening star, though he was nevertheless described by Cătălina as a dead figure, in love with a living young woman; here, the dead female figure is in love with a living young man. This reversal is now cast in a context in which death is related to an attempt to fulfill, even postmortem, a missing love. Not surprisingly, also traces of Eminescu's poem "Strigoii" (The Vampires) may be discerned in the novel, and we shall return to the theme of the vampire in ch. 7 below.

Though unrelated to the above-mentioned two novels that were published almost parallel with *Miss Christina*—neither the family nor the place are the same—there is nevertheless a common denominator: the decline of, in fact, the disappearance of a wealthy family—in the first two novels, the Anicet family, in *Miss Christina*, the Moscu family. There is quite a Chekhovian tone that dominates the 1934/1935 novels, reminiscent of the way Eliade understood his own family's fate, as some form of economic decline.

Before turning to the 1937 developments, let me mention also Eliade's assessment in an interview in 1936, where he proclaims that "The problem of death, of redemption, of mystical technique—are valuable especially in this spiritual modern moment."[64] However, in the third part of the trilogy, Eliade puts into the mouth of one of the characters the view that "but in death you recapture your autonomy,"[65] a statement that seems to reflect legionnaire views.

A New Death? Iron Guard
Sacrificial Thanatology

In December 25, 1926, Nae Ionescu wrote in the context of Jesus's death and the killing of several thousand infants, according to the New Testament, that "Every joy is built on a sacrifice."[66] This is understood as quite an actual approach, as he writes immediately afterwards: "We should remember now, on this great day, as a consciousness of the sacrifices that we are indebted—in order to ransom our redemption. All the joys without recollection—do not resist the teeth of time."[67] Three years later, on the same day, the concept of the restraint of Jesus, who accepts flight to Egypt and thus humiliation, is highlighted.[68] Marta Petreu interprets this sermon as dealing with King Carol II in exile, and that Ionescu argued, allegorically, for his return.[69] Interestingly enough, a discourse similar to that of 1926 is repeated by Ionescu on December 25, 1933, in the context of what he sees as the sacrifices of the Iron Guard related to their persecutions by Carol II, which will culminate some days later in the assassination of Prime Minister I.G Duca by the Iron Guard, the suspension of *Cuvântul,* and the imprisonment of Ionescu.[70] The nexus between the two stories printed on the same day seven years apart is inconvertible, and it shows how exactly the same motif, namely, the need of sacrifice, has been adapted to the new political situation and to Ionescu's new affiliation to the Iron Guard. This time, however, the "children" are the members of the Iron Guard in the Romanian prison, to whom Ionescu himself will soon be added.[71] After his release from prison, Ionescu speaks about what he regards as the core of Jesus's redemptive act: not his incarnation, but his self-sacrifice.[72] It is not necessary to dwell upon the huge impact of Ionescu's thought on Eliade's vision of religion, as it was highlighted duly insofar as other topics are concerned in Dancă's study.[73] However, the manner in which Eliade described Ionescu many decades after the latter's death is revealing for our topic here: "Man's mode of being is completely fulfilled only through death, death is above all transcendent."[74] It is hard to understand exactly what Eliade's intention is, but it is fascinating to see that he conceived Ionescu's thought as related to death, which means that he could be one of the sources of Eliade's thanatology. Also in Eliade's eulogy of Ionescu, death plays a central role.[75]

It should be mentioned that Eliade himself was already using the phrase "the creative sacrifice," *jertfa creatore,* in the early thirties, when describing the divine status of the Hindu women as mothers.[76] However, around the end of 1935, Eliade became fascinated by what he called the ascetic and the sacrificial aspects of the members of the Iron Guard, and soon became one of its public exponents. He was especially fascinated by the fate of two leaders of the Iron Guard who volunteered to fight on the side of the Franco regime in Spain and were killed on January 13, 1937, in Majadahonda near Madrid. Their corpses were brought to be commemorated by the SS in Berlin, and then some solemn ceremonies were held in various places in Romania.[77] On January 24, 1937, Eliade wrote in the journal *Vremea* about the deaths of the two leaders of this movement in Spain:

> Rarely in the history of a nation one encounters a death that is so significant as the deaths of those two legionnaire leaders, fallen on the Spanish front. The departure of these seven commanders of Romanian legionnaires to Spain, where they fought as volunteers in shock troops, was symbolic.[78]…Both Ion Moţa and Vasile Marin have given proofs of their spirit of sacrifice: prisons, suffering, moral discrimination, youth lived in a heroic manner. The significance of their deaths surpasses, therefore, the values of the virile heroism.[79] The voluntary death of Ion Moţa and Vasile Marin has a mystical sense: a sacrifice for [the sake of] Christianity.[80]

Eliade seems to be unaware of the reasons for those "prisons, suffering, moral discrimination." The theory of the voluntary death is an invention, based on what Ionescu thought and wrote a little bit later. The two indubitably volunteered, but they could have returned as other legionnaires who joined them did—alive. Eliade's eulogy for the heads of the legionnaires revolves around the sublime significance of their deaths, and is totally consonant with the Iron Guard ideals as formulated by General Gheorghe Cantacuzino-Grănicerul, a high-ranking officer who converted to the Iron Guard. This is a vision of death as a sacrifice, as a form of martyrdom, but not as ecstatic experience. Unlike Alexandru Pleşa's vision in *The Hooligans*, as discussed above, which assumes that in the future youths will die together with one another, but not for one another, the two legionnaires died, intentionally or not, for a cause. It should be pointed out that the more extreme the required sacrifice is, the more violent a movement may become.[81]

As Eliade recognized much later in his memoirs, death was a favorite topic among the legionnaires, but he does not mention, as Laignel-Lavastine correctly noted, that he also contributed to this cult with his own writings.[82]

Death and Yoga

Eliade's most solidly scholarly book, that on Yoga, concerns the techniques leading to immortality, as found in the very title of the book as well as its various discussions. So, for example, we read that

> at a particular moment Yoga came to represent for the Indian mind not only the ideal instrument of liberation but also the "secret" that would conquer death. There is but one explanation for this.…Yoga was identified not only with the way of sanctity and liberation but also with magic, particularly with the magical means of vanquishing death. In other

words, the mythology of the jivan-mukta satisfied not only the thirst for freedom but also the longing for immortality.[83]

In fact, it is an inversion of normal activities that is ensuring immortality, as we read in another seminal passage in the same book:

> The archaism of Yoga is confirmed once again by its initiatory structure. We have called attention to the yogic symbolism of death and rebirth, death to the profane human condition, rebirth to a transcendent modality. The yogin undertakes to "reverse" normal behavior completely. He subjects himself to a petrified immobility of body (asana), rhythmical breathing and arrest of breath (pranayama), fixation of the psychomental flux (ekagrata), immobility of thought, the "arrest" and even the "return" of semen. On every level of human experience, he does the opposite of what life demands that he do. Now, the symbolism of the "opposite" indicates both the postmortem condition and the condition of divinity (we know that "left" on earth corresponds to "right" in the beyond, a vessel broken here below is equivalent to an unbroken vessel in the world of the afterlife and the gods, etc.). The "reversal" of normal behavior sets the yogin outside of life. But he does not stop halfway, death is followed by an initiatory rebirth. The yogin makes for himself a "new body," just as the neophyte in archaic societies is thought to obtain a new body through initiation. At first sight, the rejection of life demanded by Yoga might appear terrifying, for it implies more than a funerary symbolism; it entails experiences that are so many anticipations of death. Does not the arduous and complicated process by which the yogin detaches himself from and finally eliminates all the contents that belong to the psychophysiological levels of human experience recall the process of death? For, in the Indian view, death represents a brutal separation of the Spirit from all psychophysiological experiences. And, looking more closely, we see that the mystery of liberation, the return of the elements (tattva) to prakriti, also signifies an anticipation of death.…[C]ertain yogico-tantric exercises are only an "anticipatory visualization" of the decomposition and return of elements in the circuit of nature, a process normally set in motion by death.[84] Many of the experiences of the world beyond death that are described in the Bardo Thödol, the Tibetan Book of the Dead, are in strange correspondence with yogico-tantric exercises in meditation.…[T]his anticipatory death is an initiatory death that is necessarily followed by a rebirth. It is for the sake of this rebirth to another mode of being that the yogin sacrifices everything that, on the level of profane existence, seems important. It is a sacrifice not only of his "life," but also of his "personality."[85]

Eliade perceives therefore a much more comprehensive process, in which death is just one of the steps necessary for a renewal. Human death is described as part of a cycle, probably influenced by watching the natural world.[86] What remains after the sacrifice of the personality and the building of a new body that is explained in the Hindu texts, according to Eliade's own vision of reality, is quite vague. This vagueness problematizes the possibility of reversibility, a topic essential for Eliade's approach to death and reality in general, since it is not clear what part of the human is returning, according to Eliade's own thought.

Folklore as an Instrument
of Cognition about Death

In 1937 Eliade published an article entitled "Folklore as an Instrument of Cognition" in which he proposes to turn to the evidence found in folkloristic documents about vestiges of mental phases that now have been surpassed.[87] In this context he claims that extraordinary evidence regarding the incombustibility of the human body, which he accepts as based on reliable testimonies, may point to exceptional experiences that refer to modes of existence that he refracts also onto archaic experiences related to death.

> It is a thing known by everyone—he says—that the folklore of all the people, primitive and civilized, abounds in data about death. All those dates are preserved in the popular memory for thousands and thousands of years. Nothing prevents us from presupposing that due to the mental evolution of the human species, knowledge of the reality of death is today impossible or extremely rare for a modern man. We may therefore address the problem of death starting from the folkloristic beliefs that we are entitled to believe have an experimental basis. The folkloristic documents about death may have the same validity as geological documents for the understanding of phenomena that in the present human condition we cannot control experimentally.[88]

Following this methodological passage, Eliade proposes a distinction between the immortality of the soul and the postmortem survival of human consciousness.[89] He is concerned with the latter, and he assumes that only in folklore are there testimonies for this type of survival. The refusal to discuss the issue of survival betrays, according to Eliade, a laziness of thought or a great cowardice.[90]

In August 1937 Eliade interviewed his old friend, the famous Romanian thinker and writer Lucian Blaga (1895–1961).[91] Among the questions he asked is that of the philosopher's need to confront great issues, especially death. According to Eliade's question, philosophers had addressed the issue of immortality of the soul but eschewed that of postmortem survival. The former issue presupposes

> salvation, beatitude, autonomy; survival, however, is linked to drama, to a destiny, and in a certain manner, even to the human condition....As far as I am concerned, I believe that in all religions, just as in the superstitions of all the people, the traces of certain old experiences are found, which in the mental condition of people today are, in their majority, no longer accessible. If my thesis is right—continues Eliade—then we are justified in searching in the history of religions, in folklore, and in ethnography—for documents, traces of concrete experiences, with whose help we may approach from another point of view the problem of death, namely, the survival of the soul, leaving open the question of immortality.[92]

Blaga, who himself was concerned a lot with death in his poetry and thought, recognizes however that he had not yet thought on the question of death, since he meditates on problems one after the other. However, he assesses that he agrees with Eliade's thesis as it was articulated in the *Folklore as an Instrument of Cognition*, discussed above, which he admits he read beforehand, saying that he understands him very well since he lived in his childhood in the village.

> The death in the village has—Blaga argues—a significance that is quite different from that in the city. The soul departs in order to encounter brothers, relatives, friends, in the other world. Therefore, we speak about a new community of the "departed." This is the reason why the pain in the face of death is not so tragic in the village. I remember the crying of my mother for the death of a son that she loved very much: It was indeed a calm, reconciled cry.[93]

In response to this observation of Blaga's, Eliade wrote there:

> In an organic community, pain is manifested almost always by [means of] rituals....In the village and sometimes even in the neighborhoods of Bucharest, the grieving is more a ritual lamentation than the manifestation of the despaired pain of someone who is separated from the beloved being. The ritual lamentation is done, as it is known, by alien persons, the weepers....In fact, the entire life of a person who participates in an organic community is lived with a trans-individual significance, a symbolic one....A person is never alone in such an organic society. This is the reason why death is not so terrible.

The question of the rural life as constituting an organic society is a key issue in Eliade's thought in this period, and we shall address it in ch. 8 on the basis of other texts written at the same time.[94] Several months later, Eliade wrote about the survival of the memory of dead persons, assessing that the folklore or the popular memory cannot retain the specific details of the deeds of a certan hero except to the extent that they are integrated within a preceding spiritual type.[95] This view is reiterated a year later in a feuilleton published again in *Cuvântul*.[96]

In any case, in 1937 Eliade described Bogdan Petriceicu-Haşdeu, whose main impact on Eliade's worldview has been mentioned in the Introduction, as someone who contributed to the "valorification of death, understood as the threshold from which start an endless number of 'forms' that conduce, one after the other, to the ultimate perfection: God—this magic conception of existence and man that was not fulfilled by any Romanian in the 19th century."[97]

It is in the same year, in a major essay entitled "Cosmology and Babylonian Alchemy," that Eliade sees in death a general principle of transformation in ancient and medieval alchemy that is relevant also for the metals: "there can be no eternal life without suffering and death."[98] In an earlier treatment of alchemy, written in 1934, called *Asian Alchemy*, he describes alchemy as a search for immortality.[99] In 1939 Eliade wrote a play entitled *Iphigenia*, in which the ancient Greek heroine is ready to sacrifice herself for the conquest of Troy. It seems plausible, as Mihail Sebastian pointed out, that this type of self-sacrifice has Iron Guard overtones, and it could fairly be entitled *Iphigenia, or the Legionnaire Sacrifice*.[100] Again, as Eliade had to recognize in 1943, the huge Romanian sacrifices during the war, when its army cooperated with the Germans, were futile, and they were prone to trigger more losses with the occupation of Romania by the Russians, who decimated the representatives of what he calls the "Romanian phenomenon."[101]

The Master Manole: Sacrificial Death as Creative

The more general reflections mentioned in the previous section regarding folklore and death were put into academic practice in the same academic year, 1936–1937, when Eliade lectured at the University of Bucharest in a class on the widespread legend of Master Manole.[102] This legend deals with the necessity of human sacrifice for maintaining a building; Master Manole is building a monastery that is destroyed night after night, and he is ready to sacrifice his beloved wife by building her alive into the walls, for this effect. Though Eliade refers to his working on a written version of his commentaries on the widespread legend for years, it is only later on, in the summer of 1943 while he was in Portugal, that his booklet on this topic is printed in Romania.[103] The vaster and annotated version of this study, which he promised in the introduction to the Romanian version, was never published;[104] a shorter version of the Romanian original was translated in 1955 and printed in his collection of studies in English, *Zalmoxis*,[105] and a full version was translated into Italian in 1990.[106] It is hard to ascertain what his views were in 1936–1937 in the class in Bucharest and what was added afterwards, but we may well assume that they were similar to what we have seen in the previous section, based on the content of a much earlier short treatment, "Folklore and Literature," found in a 1932 story printed in *Cuvântul*. Dealing with the legend, he says:

> it belongs to a mode with very ancient roots…it alone produces that fantastic, irrational presence…it introduces us to a folkloric universe, in which the inorganic world possesses an ensouled life and similar laws: where the houses and the churches are living entities, and they cannot subsist if a human life is not sacrificed for them, so that they can live forever from its[107] blood and soul.[108]

This vision seems to be influenced, at least in part, by a theory published by his teacher Nicodim Locusteanu in Eliade's high school's journal in 1927 under the title "Occultist Teachings," to the effect that "everything is alive in nature, even the minerals, even the atoms, like the individual beings. Death does not exist."[109] This sharp defiance of death is found also in Eliade's 1934 *Oceanography*, where he claims that "Death exists only for those who believe in it."[110] This commentary is the most important document comprising Eliade's vision of death in Romanian culture, and it did not attract the attention of scholars dealing with human sacrifice as creative death, and Eliade's connections to the ideology of the Iron Guard. According to his own view in this period, he attempted to describe the "folkloristic mentality"[111] and to depict the "mental universe" of the archaic man.[112]

After accomplishing and printing his study *Master Manole*, Eliade published in Portuguese a short piece called "A Romanian Myth of Death," describing the rites of peasants who waited for the convoys of the souls of the dead in WW1.[113] His interpretation of the rite is that it is not just paying a civic tribute to those who died for the motherland, it also has a deep religious value: "In the popular consciousness— he speculates—death on the field of war has the religious value of a sacrifice and, like any religious sacrifice, death puts the collective in contact with God, a fact that justifies and redeems the collectivity in the face of divinity."[114] In a manner reminiscent of what he wrote about the two legionnaire leaders, as quoted above, he claims that

> those poor souls that were returning home, whom the peasants were waiting for in order to pay them homage for the first and last time, sacrificed their youth not just in order to defend a territory, but in order to justify the people in the face of God. Their death had, for them and for the surviving comrades, a mystical sense beyond the national one. The peasants that were paying them homage, on knees and with candles in their hands, did not give civic honors to the brave patriots but rather participated, in [its] religious sense, in the reintegration of the death in their spiritual environments (family, village, province) before their definitive departure from the world of those alive....We may find their concept of death, implicitly, in all the people of Europe or of European extraction.[115]

It is in a passage between these two quotes that he makes the connection between that custom he had heard about from his father, who was an officer, and *Master Manole*, mentioning the value of the "sacrificial death."[116] However, beyond the interpretation Eliade offers for the rituals, he was interested in much more; at the end of the above piece he wishes that the

> popular elements will be called tomorrow to play a greater role in the organization and the governing of the human society. This, because those people who kneeled, with candles in their hands, in the front of the souls that returned home from the fields of war understand better than us what indeed life means and what justice signifies.[117]

It is obvious from this passage that Eliade himself believes somehow in the efficacy of the ritual he describes as part of what he calls some lines earlier "the organic function in the popular life." In any case, he desires a society that will be grounded in a greater acceptance of those perceptions, even if he does not overtly advocate there what he calls the metaphysical,[118] namely, the ontological status of the events he depicted. Moreover, he claims that the absence of a justification, a rationale, namely, an explanation of catastrophes, generates nihilism and despair.[119] Here we may see the more "mystagogish" turn in Eliade.

In the same period, Eliade wrote in Portuguese an exposition of Romania, its history, and culture, entitled "The Romanians: The Latins of the Orient," where the attitude to death was put into relief in quite an emphatic manner, mentioning the belief in immortality and the hatred of death among the Geto-Dacians, the legend of Master Manole, and the ballade *Miorița*.[120] These three sources, the traditions related to Zalmoxis and the two legends, will recur many times later on in his writings as constituting a reconciled approach to death, which is considered to be representative of the Romanian spirit.

Miori a (The Ewe-Lamb): The Reconciled Death and "Death as Marriage"

There are few specific texts that so embody the importance of the theory of death that represent, according to Eliade, the Romanian ancient tradition, as *Miorița*. Eliade repeatedly refers to this ballade as the quintessential representation of an attitude to death that can be described as "reconciled death" on the one hand, and death as a marriage on the other.[121] This apotheosis of the beautiful ballade was quite *en vogue* in the thirties, as we learn from Lucian Blaga's vision of Romanian space as the "mioritic space"[122] and from references to it in the legionnaire literature. So, for example, in one of his most legionnaire feuilletons Eliade claims that the "The death of the shepherd from *Miorița* is a 'reconciled death.'"[123]

In 1953 Eliade published an important essay entitled "The Fate of Romanian Culture," in which he returns to the above-mentioned custom of waiting for the returning dead souls and adds that he heard that this custom has been practiced in some Moldavian places, not only during WWI but also after the debacle of the Romanian army in the Stalingrad battle in 1942–1943.[124] Afterwards, he declared that "we have reason to believe that the space where Zalmoxis, Orpheus, and the mysteries of *Miorița* and of *Master Manole* were born has not yet exhausted its creative sources: in a land where death is still taken as a marriage, the spiritual springs are still intact."[125] It is only much later, however, in 1963, that he wrote a special essay

dedicated to the ballade, included in *Zalmoxis*, where he surveyed the earlier interpretations and offered his own, which emphasizes the reconciled death of a shepherd
who accepts his death stoically as some form of integration in nature.[126]

The ballade is privileged in his writings, and he refers to it time and again as
representative of the "authentic" Romanian culture since hoary antiquity, because
of both its literary beauty and of its huge number of variants, almost a thousand.
However, Eliade's analysis of its content is a little bit unbalanced. In reference to
the version that was presented first by the poet Vasile Alecsandri as a popular ballade, the shepherd who is killed is not a representative of Romania generally; he
is a Moldavian, that is, he belongs to one specific region in Romania. The story consists of a simple plot: The Moldavian shepherd learns from his ewe-lamb that he
will be assassinated by two fellow shepherds, a Hungarian, but most likely a
Transylvanian—probably considered to be a Romanian too—and a "Vrâncean" one,
which may point to a town in the province of Walachia or Muntenia. Eliade himself refers to the two shepherds who kill the Moldavian one as Walachians.[127] Thus,
the ballade starts with a reference to an internal Romanian affair, the killing of one
Romanian by two others, and only then it turns to the reconciled death as marriage.
Was also this first part of the ballade a representation of the ancient Romanians,
or only the part that deals with "reconciled death"?[128] Moreover, there are great
doubts about its antiquity, and thus its popular extraction, as well as its represen-
tativeness.[129] In this context, let me mention the description of the "ugly," unrec-
onciled death of Sebastian's grandmother, which Eliade presents as representative
of the Jews' attitude to death.[130]

However, even more questionable is Eliade's building on this ballade as a source
for his ancient cosmic Christianity, as he understood it, despite the fact that there is
no imitation of a ritual performed in *illo tempore* by the Moldavian shepherd. Neither
is Eliade's claim to the effect that "The symbolism of the Rumanian folk song *Miorița*
also has—or could have—Christian valences. *Marriage assimilated to death* is therefore not a pagan motif, superficially Christianized."[131] Eliade's emphasis on some
forms of death as a special Christian value seems to me an idiosyncratic interpretation of Christianity, based on very few examples of Romanian folklore whose affinity to Christianity is superficial at best. In any case, Eliade's interpretation of the
ballade has been criticized by a leading Romanian ethnographer of Marxist leanings,
Henri H. Stahl, who claimed in the context of this ballade that both Eliade's and
Blaga's reflections on Romanian rural life were done without a proper acquaintance
with what happened in the field.[132]

Moreover, Eliade's assumption that the ballade reflects a very early mentality is
not so straightforward since according to some scholars, it may well be an invention

of Vasile Alecsandri and thus, as Sorin Antohi informed me, a possible example of an "invention of tradition." In his *literaria*, Eliade uses the ballade in a crucial moment in his novel *Forbidden Forest*, where one of the protagonists, Biris, recites it to his torturers before his death in some identification with the dying shepherd,[133] and in a personal letter he portrays himself as continuing the attitude of the shepherd.[134] Eliade continued to be interested in the question of immortality, as we learn from the remark in his journal in 1957 about Jung's dream of his dead wife, which convinced him of the immortality of the soul.[135]

Heidegger's "Camouflage"

In a note in his journal of 1963, Eliade mentions Heidegger's interest in the concepts of being and nonbeing as part of human experience.[136] In fact, despite Heidegger's atheism, he was one of the favorites of Nae Ionescu, who asked for copies of his books in 1934 to peruse during the few months he was in prison. As part of an attempt to denigrate Eliade, Communist critics claimed that he was impacted by Heidegger, who was sometimes portrayed in this context as the ideologue of Nazism.[137] In 1973 Eliade delivered a lecture at the American Academy of Religion in Chicago entitled "Mythologies of Death." This seems to be the last and quite an interesting statement about our topic here. Here he mentions in a footnote that he is working on a monograph on the mythologies of death, which he had mentioned already in 1943, 1953, 1955,[138] 1959,[139] and 1964,[140] which presumably he never finished, or at least did not publish.[141] The new point he makes is the Eliadian reading of Heidegger's man as "Sein zum Tode," a being towards death. He highlights the philosopher's turn toward the centrality of death, though in a secularized manner, and he offers his specific reading of Heidegger's view that "death, as an altar of nonbeing, hides within itself the essence of being." For Eliade, the intention is the presence of the being camouflaged within nonbeing, drawing the Heideggerian speculations into the horizon of his specific religiously oriented worldview, as he often does. In other words, while Heidegger conceives death as a terminal point, Eliade sees it, in direct continuation of his earlier theories, as a possible starting point for a superior form of a postmortem existence. Again, the existential dimension we have seen in *The Return from Paradise* was retained, while the religious/political one has been suppressed or excluded. This means that when he used the genres of scholarly and literary discourse, Eliade did not retain the political propaganda rhetorics, and it is difficult to discern the reverberation in his articles in *Vremea* and in *Buna Vestire* later on.

A Tentative Typology of Eliade's Thanatology

In fact, we may offer a tentative typology of the approaches to death found in Eliade's writings: The more general approach, dealing with man as a generic term, assumes the ideal of generating a sense of death as a potential experience of plenitude, which has to do with the life of a person, and this sense can be achieved even by suicide. However, when describing man as part of a social/political structure, it is the idea of sacrificial death for a collective religious cause that may attribute to death its sublimity. In other words, the sense is created not by freedom and fulfillment of a certain specific life, unrelated to history, but on the contrary, by entering history and its terrors and then overcoming it. This latter type of death, as self-sacrifice, depends to a great extent on the structure of the collective in which one chooses to live and die, as in the case of the Iron Guard leaders. It is less a chosen death than a planned suicide. After all, only in the latter type may one experience "the act of death" that Eliade attributes to Heidegger. The glorification of those volunteers for a cause that was more than questionable, democratically speaking, and the cooperation of the Iron Guard group with the troops of Franco in Spain did not disturb Eliade at all, given his strong anticommunist penchant on the one hand and strong Christian-oriented vision on the other. However, the manner in which he depicted their sacrifice is much more religious than political: They were imagined to have fought and died for the sake of Christianity, not for Spain or even for Romania.

It seems that the hooligans of 1934–1935 escaped the void of meaningless life by adhering to the Iron Guard, which supplied not only a form of significant life, but also an outlet for criminal activities in Romania by killing many of their opponents, including distinguished figures in Romanian life and even more Jews. The international expansion by participation in the Spanish civil war is one more example of violent and—in my opinion—immoral forms of activity by the Iron Guard, which surpasses by far the amorality of the hooligans as portrayed in Eliade's two novels. Let me point out an important reflection in 1944 as to the significance Eliade sees in the terrible events of WWII. In his *Journal* he wrote:

> The destructions of the war have a sense; they fulfill a role in a universal equilibrium. War—like death in the individual condition—corresponds to that cosmic act that is ignored by man or feared by him: regression to the primordial amorphous, where all is lost within each other, melted in a unity. War fulfills the same role—understandably, on another level—like orgy....I believe that I am one of the few moderns[142] that understand the value and necessity of orgy.[143] War is resembling it...*mahapralaya*;[144] the redoing of the primitive unity, of the chaos.[145]

Though obviously an attempt to overcome the anxiety produced by WWII, that is, to offer a meaning for a historical event, the passage is reminiscent of what he wrote about the need to destroy Bucharest in order to rebuild it, more than 10 years earlier.[146] However, it is far from clear what the equilibrium is that he speaks about, or how the death of someone serves the attainment of such a "universal equilibrium."[147] Thus, the violent destruction of the old is praised, but what is supposed to replace it is more than vague. In any case, we have here a rather positive view of death, like that of war and orgy. In all those cases, dissolution is conceived of as a solution that precedes the emergence of a higher form of existence. In any case, natural processes are identified with human forms of behavior, bestowing upon the latter the amorality of the former.

In the same period, Eliade confesses that he was scared by how much and how deeply he understands the "realities of postmortem," claiming that he has neither the courage nor the lexical means to communicate his insights. "What happens after death"—he confesses—"is known, in a way, to me. I am obsessed especially with an image, which I cannot describe, as to what I guessed about how the souls of the dead long ago are 'resting,' melting in forefathers, in archetypes."[148] A cryptic statement that no doubt was hard to communicate to others, and even harder to work with as a scholar of religion.

On Thanatology and Romanian Culture

Concepts of death and immortality are indubitably a universal theme, found everywhere in religious and secular literatures. However, it seems that Eliade was concerned with those topics more than any other scholar in the history of religion in the 20th century, though this special interest did not generate a monograph or a systematic analysis, but rather a long series of fragmented discussions dealing with different aspects of these themes. Multiple discussions and various conceptual aspects are part of an approach I would like to call the grapefruit approach, a characteristic of traditional cultures, which are concerned less with systematic visions than with the preservation of different traditions that emerged over ages. Eliade had an existential approach, and he attempted to build a picture of a porous universe that allows reversibility and thus immortality, that is, the transition from one type of existence to another, denying the finality of human existence, an approach found in several religious cultures.

There are differences between cultures, nevertheless, as to the relative place some treatments of death hold in the general economy of a certain culture, and the various *imaginaires* related to them. In order to understand Eliade, it is not sufficient to deal with Eliade's views in some books dealing with scholarship of religion; it is necessary to see what is actually found in the sources he analyzed, and what was a general attitude he developed from living in a certain cultural environment. In other words, we may ask whether his Romanian background had something to do with his special emphasis on death in his scholarly thought and the literature he wrote. A reading of several important pieces of Romanian literature, such as Mihail Eminescu's poems "I Have a Single Desire" in all its various variants, his "Memento Mori," "Mortua Est," and "Strigoii," but especially his "The Prayer of a Dacian," as well as some of the poetry of George Coşbuc, especially what I would consider his best poem, "The Death of Fulger," or, later, the poetry of Ion Minulescu, George Bacovia, and Lucian Blaga, will easily reveal an intense concern with death. This is also the case with Bodgan P. Haşdeu, whose impact on Eliade was, as seen above, quite considerable.[149] In Romanian folklore the situation is similar, and this fact has been emphasized duly by Eliade in his analyses of what he conceived to be the two major folkloristic pieces, as seen above.

Even earlier are traditions related to the religions of the Getae, one of the Thracian tribes that were considered the forefathers of the Romanians, whose cult of Zalmoxis was associated with a fearless attitude to death. This figure became a major topic in the depictions of the ancient Dacians by some Romanian scholars who were the immediate predecessors of Eliade.[150] The name Zalmoxis appears in the titles of two works of Eliade's: the academic journal dealing with the history of religion that he edited in the late thirties, and the collection of articles *Zalmoxis, the Vanishing God*. The detailed examination of the extant testimonies from antiquity about this figure—a god, a demon, or a priest—as done in an exemplary manner in a monograph by Dan Dana, has shown, to reference the subtitle of Dana's Romanian monograph, that this was a "god of pretext," which means that many scholars used the vague and fragmentary testimonies regarding Zalmoxis in order to draw from them their conceptions as to the beginnings of ancient Romanian religiosity.[151] This is also the case, according to Dana, with Eliade's analyses.[152]

Let me emphasize that this analysis of trends in Romanian culture as thanatological is not my general impression or even less my invention. We may learn from, for example, a very important scholar of the thought of interwar Romania, Marta Petreu, who wrote recently:

By contrast,[153] the Romanian philosophy—that of *Miorița*, of *Master Manole*, of resignation in the face of fate and death. The philosophy of "the longing" for death and of the difficulty of existence, which was articulated by Eminescu, Cioran, Eugene Ionesco, all of them emerged and grew up upon a collective graveyard of grieving, of archaic crying, as we are.[154]

This modest list could be easily enhanced by reference to the many writings of the factions of the Iron Guard, to the 19 feuilletons Constantin Noica wrote in 1940 in the main Iron Guard newspaper *Buna Vestire*, and even more so to the views of Eliade. He was concerned, however, with the question of understanding death as a potentially positive event, not only in political contexts. Emil Cioran, though also concerned with death, regarded *Miorița* as "that poetic and national curse."[155] Both Marta Petreu's passage and Cioran's negation show how deep the influence of this "popular" poem was in their eyes.

To return to the question with which we began this chapter: Was the conceptual structure of the Iron Guard ideology that Eliade adhered to after late 1935, and perhaps more formally, somewhat later, impacting the concepts of death in his scholarship, as some scholars have claimed? My answer to this question is complicated, and it differs from the two prevailing answers yes or no. In my opinion, some of the content of his scholarship and literature forged in the late twenties and early thirties in which a preoccupation with death is prominent displays an attitude that brought him, later, closer to the ideology of the Iron Guard's emphasis on the sacrificial death, not vice versa. By continuing some earlier Romanian types of thanatologies, both Eliade and the Iron Guard developed views that later encountered each other, because of the existence of certain selective affinities. Both drew from common sources, though they elaborated them differently. According to Eliade, "Everything that happens today in the Romanian culture and politics, and these preoccupations with 'the historical destiny' of our nation, have their central source in the political writings of Eminescu, and in the continuators of the Eminescian thought: Nicolae Iorga and Nae Ionescu."[156] "Everything," I assume, means also the Iron Guard. This does not mean, let me emphasize, that the early thanatologies found in Romanian literature suffice to understand either Eliade or the Iron Guard: Each thanatology also has other independent sources, but there is some overlapping that can explain both the attraction of a scholar of religion to the ideology of the Iron Guard, and the attraction of the Iron Guard, even today, to Eliade's thought, as we shall see in ch. 7.

On the other hand, let me emphasize that I do not assume, as Eliade does, that Romanian culture should, essentially, be understood in thanatological terms. There are earlier and substantial trends that generated later reverberations and created a common denominator that facilitated the rapprochement of Ionescu and Eliade to the xenophobic and anti-Semite ideology of the Iron Guard. Though I do not subscribe to views found in scholarship and in recent legionnaire literatures that attempt to totally disassociate the Iron Guard from fascist or Nazi types of movement, assuming that it is possible to derive the specific structure of the Iron Guard solely from Romanian sources, those sources are, nevertheless, extremely important.[157]

What is characteristic of its ideology, and this has been made clear in quotes adduced above, is the strong connection between its thanatology and an emphasis on sacrifice found in orthodox Christianity. In any case, it is obvious that there were attempts to draw the inspiration of the Iron Guard from Mihail Eminescu, for example,[158] while Nicolae Iorga was one of the earliest initiators of a leading anti-Semite party that evolved shortly afterwards in a more extreme form in the Iron Guard.

This does not mean, to be sure, that Eliade did not later idealize the sacrificial deaths of the legionnaires who fought on the side of the rightist Franco regime in Spain and died there, in terms that are quite consonant to the Iron Guard terminology, as seen above. However, there are two different forms of death: the ecstatic/cosmic one of the person who fulfills himself individually by death, and the collective/religious one, where the ideals of the group or of the religion are imagined to be fulfilled by the fight for them. The existence of the former in Eliade's writings precedes the latter and in my opinion was not affected by it, which is most probably a later addition to his earlier and constant fascination with the problem of death.

On the other hand, let me emphasize that there were also other types of Romanian culture, much more liberal, which differed from the right wing, and they should also be taken into account.[159] Neither was the Orthodox Church in its entirety necessarily anti-Semitic, as the *Memoirs* of the Romanian priest and intellectual Virgil Gheorghiu show. This holds even more for the situation today, despite the significant reverberations of the Iron Guard ideology, as a critical attitude toward the "cultural heroes" of the thirties has become more influential among some Romanian elites.

Death and Death-Experience

The existence of earlier views on death that also persisted much later in Eliade's life, according to which the meaning attributed to death is a possible personal religious fulfillment, does not obliterate the implications of his later views of death as a self-sacrifice, nor does it attenuate the support Eliade gave to the pernicious repercussions of such a choice made by the legionnaires, of which he certainly was aware. However, at the same time, the existence of ultranationalistic theories on death does not necessarily affect the meaning of the specific interpretations he gave to the personal experience of death and his belief in immortality.[160] Though a linkage between the two could, at least in principle, be contemplated, in fact it is very difficult to prove it in Eliade's extant texts. Both interpretations of the *imaginaire* of death are, in my opinion, dealing with human fantasies attempting to find, or to make, a sense of an end, to paraphrase the title of Frank Kermode's famous book. However, not all the fantasies concerning a certain topic, even when occurring in the writings of the same author, should necessarily be combined by a serious scholar as if they are the same.

Last but not least: In the vein of Eliade's general approach, which follows Nae Ionescu's, as it is hard to understand what one does not himself experience, an experience of death is hardly conceivable, at least as far as we know, as an instrument of cognition. However, some sort of obsession with death seems to be reflected in the following statement from his *Portugal Journal*: "It suffices to close the eyes, to think for a moment on death (as I conceive it or as others do), that everything will appear to be infantile. And something more: I have the feeling that I betray myself, that I flee the duty to know reality and to look at it face to face."[161] Was reality tantamount to death, and all the other things—infantile? Are the many recurrences of death and its transcendence in immortality in the writings of Eliade an attempt to cope with this feeling of futility in comparison to the reality of death? Two years later, in Paris, Eliade attempted to convince Cioran and Ionesco as to the immortality of the soul.[162] While the latter was also obsessed by death and thus more open to Eliade's arguments,[163] Cioran remained as skeptical as he ever was.

Those are some of the numerous discussions of death in Eliade's writings.[164] This is a complex spectrum that shows a precocious attraction to the topic of death, and the later developments are better understood as a continuation of earlier propensities in Eliade himself and in Romanian culture. Whether indeed his own death was a grand gathering in the style of *mahaparinirvana*, as Culianu portrayed it, is a question that, most probably, will be answered.[165]

Notes

1. *Journal*, June 26, 1954.
2. "Libertatea," *Iconar*, March 5, 1937.
3. Plural in the Romanian original.
4. *Portugal Journal*, I, p. 367.
5. See ibid., pp. 367–368.
6. "The Secret of Dr. Honigberger," in *Two Strange Tales*, p. 66. Emphases in the original. See also *Portugal Journal*, I, p. 175: "Perhaps my real poles are not life and death."
7. See the interview mentioned in Țurcanu, *Mircea Eliade*, p. 268.
8. It should be mentioned that the volume *Mircea Eliade, Arta de a muri*—*Mircea Eliade, The Art of Dying*—edited by Magda and Petru Ursache (Iași, 1993), is a collection of texts about death extracted from a variety of sources written by Eliade throughout his life, but it is not a book of Eliade's, despite the fact that he is mentioned as an author.
9. "The Professor Nae Ionescu," in *Vremea*, IX, 463 (15 Noiembrie 1936), p. 7; *Romanian Prophetism*, II, p. 179, reprinted as a postface to the volume of essays by Ionescu, *The Rose of the Winds*, pp. 428–429, which he edited. This tragic feeling of existence is attributed also to the

Iron Guard leader Ion Moța. See Eliade, *Legionnaire Texts*, p. 70. On Moța, see below in this chapter and in ch. 7.

10. *NO*, pp. 205–207.

11. See especially Țurcanu, *Intellectuels*, pp. 261–280.

12. See, e.g., Dubuisson, *Mythologies*, pp. 204, 229–230; Grottanelli, "Fruitful Death"; Dinu, "Sacrifice," pp. 57–68.

13. Printed in *How I Found the Philosopher's Stone*, p. 585.

14. Published for the first time by Liviu Bordaș, "The Nearsighted Adolescent and the Grandson of Brahma," *Viața Românesca*, 5–6 (2010), pp. 39–67.

15. Printed in *How I Found the Philosopher's Stone*, p. 620–627.

16. Ibid., p. 620.

17. Ibid., p. 518–519.

18. Ibid., p. 247. See also ibid., p. 248.

19. Ibid., pp. 252–253.

20. Eliade, *Virility and Askesis*, pp. 389–391.

21. "I, the Saint Devil, and Those Sixteen Puppets," printed in *Maddalena*, p. 146.

22. See also above, at the end of ch. 1.

23. *Oceanography*, pp. 65–68.

24. Ibid., pp. 79–81. See also Culianu, *Mircea Eliade*, pp. 40–41.

25. Ibid., p. 192.

26. Ibid., pp. 190–192.

27. *50 Conferences*, p. 115.

28. Ibid., pp. 115–116.

29. Ibid., p. 116.

30. Ibid., pp. 116–117.

31. See *The Way to the Center*, pp. 124–126, 135–136.

32. See *Myth, Dreams, and Mysteries*, pp. 231–245, and see also ibid., pp. 11–12.

33. See *The Return from Paradise*, p. 301.

34. See Țurcanu, *Mircea Eliade*, pp. 216–217. For a presentation of the different parts of the trilogy in English, see Ricketts, *Romanian Roots*, I, pp. 667–709, II, pp. 1007–1042. For Eliade's own description of the political atmosphere in which *The Return from Paradise* appeared, see *Autobiography*, I, pp. 282–283.

35. See Alexandrescu, *From Portugal*, p. 299.

36. *Autobiography*, I, p. 18.

37. Ibid.

38. *The Return from Paradise*, p. 232.

39. The motif of ecstasy is found several times in this context. See ibid., pp. 298–299.

40. The phrase "an instrument of cognition" is found in many other cases in Eliade, who speaks about folklore and love as tools of cognition. See, e.g., Ricketts, *The Romanian Roots*, II, p. 1161, in Eliade, *Images and Symbols*, p. 60, and here below.

41. *The Return from Paradise*, p. 299. For more on death in this novel, see pp. 104, 142.

42. Ibid., p. 77.

43. Ibid., p. 262.

44. Ibid., p. 177.

45. Ibid., p. 300.

46. See Eliade, *Rites and Symbols of Initiation*, pp. 110–111; id., *Myths, Dreams, and Mysteries*, pp. 236–243; and especially Plutarch, *On the Soul*, quoted in Stobaeus, IV, as translated by George E. Mylonas in his *Eleusis and the Eleusinian Mysteries* (Princeton, 1961), pp. 246–65. See also *Religions Australiennes*, p. 171.

47. *Autobiography*, I, pp. 256–268.

48. *Journal*, p. 194, in January 1939.

49. *The Hooligans*, p. 280.

50. Ibid., pp. 250–251, 280–281.

51. Ibid., pp. 300–303.

52. For additional discussions on death in this novel see, e.g., ibid., pp. 18–19, 25–26, 31, 35, 38, 39, 42, 56, 57, 105–106, 144–146, 152–154, 164–165, 176, 179, 267, 269, 280–281, 285–286, 311, 323, 331–332.

53. "Mircea Eliade, Codul ascuns al *Nopţii de Sânziene*," rpt. in her *From Junimea to Noica*, p. 385.

54. *Autobiography*, p. 256.

55. See ch. 2.

56. *Occultism*, pp. 44–46.

57. *Portugal Journal*, p. 319. On the feeling of totality related to an erotic experience during a dance that may be understood as androgyne, and the wish to die in that moment, see the description of Mavrodin in his novel *Wedding in Heaven*, p. 188.

58. See the 1953 piece, printed in *Memoirs*, p. 231.

59. See also Alexandru's view in *The Hooligans*, p. 59, and the ironic reaction of Petru, ibid., p. 61.

60. *The Hooligans*, p. 286. For a similar view from the same protagonist as to the importance of the collective liberty that he preferred to the individual one, see ibid., p. 163, where he describes it as "a euphoric liberty." On the other hand, already in 1928 Eliade speaks about the loneliness of the dying man; see Eliade *Virility and Askesis*, p. 302.

61. Ibid., pp. 286–287.

62. "Capricorn," p. 201.

63. On the publication of this novel and the reaction to it, see *Autobiography*, I, pp. 316–318, 323–324.

64. Cf. Ţurcanu, *Mircea Eliade*, p. 268.

65. *The New Life*, p. 164.

66. *The Rose of the Winds*, p. 46.

67. Ibid., pp. 46–47.

68. Ibid., pp. 47–50.

69. *The Devil and His Apprentice*, p. 129.

70. Ionescu, "Măcelul," *Cuvântul*, X, discussed in Petreu, ibid., pp. 129–130, and her *From Junimea to Noica*, pp. 246–247.

71. See Petreu, *The Devil and His Apprentice*, p. 130, and see also the important discussion in Gligor, *The Troublous Years*, pp. 147–166.

72. Ornea, *The Thirties*, p. 403, quoting this passage from Ionescu's feuilleton printed in an Iron Guard newspaper in 1936.

73. Dancă, *Definitio Sacri*, pp. 26–58, 65–73, 185–188. See also Ricketts, *Romanian Roots*, I, pp. 91–126.

74. Cf. Manea, "The Incompatibilities," pp. 32–33.

75. Discussed in Ricketts, *Romanian Roots*, II, pp. 1092–1093.

76. See *India*, in *Prose*, p. 160.

77. See, e.g., Laignel-Lavastine, *L'oubli du fascisme*, pp. 185–188; Dinu, "Sacrifice," p. 60.

78. On the context of the Legionnaires volunteering in Spain, see Ornea, *The Thirties*, pp. 307–308.

79. On virility in Eliade, see above, ch. 2.

80. "The Sacrifice," in Romanian, *Jertfa*. Quoted and discussed in Țurcanu, *Mircea Eliade*, p. 267; Dinu, "Sacrifice," pp. 62–63, Ornea; *The Thirties*, pp. 201–202; and Gligor *The Troublous Years*, pp. 118–120. On the context of the legionnaires' volunteering for Spain, see Ornea, ibid., pp. 307–308, and Dana, *Métamorphoses*, pp. 63–68.

81. On the affinity between sacrifice and violence, see Moshe Halbertal, *On Sacrifice* (Princeton, 2012).

82. *L'oubli du fascisme*, p. 188. See also Grotanelli, "Fruitful Death," and Gianluca Nesi, "Mircea Eliade e la mitologia nazista del sacrificio ebraica," *Rivista di Filosofia*, LXXXIX (1998), pp. 271–304.

83. *Yoga*, p. 340.

84. This is one more example of the theory of correspondences we discussed in the Introduction.

85. *Yoga*, pp. 361–363. On inversion of normal processes in Yoga practices, see id., *Aspects du mythe*, p. 110.

86. See Eliade, *Patterns in Comparative Religion*, p. 9.

87. On this piece, see now Țurcanu, "Southeast Europe," pp. 251–252, as well as Ricketts, *Romanian Roots*, pp. 869–872, and briefly in Dancă, *Definitio Sacri*, pp. 135–136 and Bordas, "Time, History and Soteriology," pp. 44–45. For an English translation, see in Brian Rennie, *Mircea Eliade: A Critical Reader* (London, 2006), pp. 24–37.

88. *Master Manole*, p. 179. See also Culianu, *Romanian Studies*, I, pp. 285–286.

89. *Master Manole*, pp. 179–180.

90. Ibid., p. 180.

91. For Blaga's thought and Eliade, see Ricketts, *Romanian Roots*, II, pp. 857–864, and Handoca, "Afinități elective: Mircea Eliade," in Handoca, ed., *Eliade File XIV (1983)*, pp. 175–186.

92. "Dialogues with Lucian Blaga," *Vremea*, X, 501 (22 August 1937), pp. 10–11, rpt. in *Romanian Prophetism*, II, pp. 199–200.

93. Ibid. See also Handoca, "Afinități elective: Mircea Eliade," in Handoca, ed., *Eliade File XIV (1983)*, pp. 182–183.

94. See below, chs. 4 and 8.

95. *Master Manole*, p. 146, printed in *Cuvântul*, March 1938.

96. See the issue March 21, 1939, reprinted by Ursache in *Master Manole*, p. 150.

97. Eliade, *Hasdeu*, p. lxxx. On aspects of Hasdeu's thought according to Eliade, see above in the Introduction.

98. *The Way to the Center*, p. 537. See also ibid., p. 238.

99. Ibid., pp. 571–572, 573, 578, 580, 588.

100. *Journal*, p. 305. See also Oișteanu, "Mircea Eliade Between Political Journalism and Scholarly Work," pp. 331–334. A similar reaction is that of Petru Comarnescu, one of the major animators of the group Criterion. See Oișteanu, *Religion, Politics and Myth*, p. 21.

101. *Portugal Journal*, I, p. 200.

102. *Master Manole*, p. 55, *Portugal Journal*, II, p. 186. One of the most important and insightful

studies relevant to Eliade's analysis, Marcel Mauss–Henri Hubert, "Essai sur la nature et la fonction du sacrifice," printed in Année sociologique, 1899, has not been mentioned.

103. Portugal Journal, II, pp. 182, 186–187, 188, 205–206.
104. Master Manole, p. 55.
105. Zalmoxis, pp. 187–190.
106. See Spineto, The Historian of Religion, pp. 40–41.
107. In the original Romanian it is a plural, which I see as a mistake.
108. Reprinted in Master Manole, p. 332. See also his The Forge and the Crucible, p. 31.
109. Cf. Bordaş, "The Journeys of the Nearsighted Adolescent," II. Death does not exist in an Orthodox Christian view. See the contemporary discussion in Gheorghiu, Memoirs, p. 87.
110. pp. 210–212. See also Culianu, Mircea Eliade, pp. 211–212.
111. Master Manole, p. 68.
112. Ibid., p. 62.
113. Translated in Romanian in Portugal Journal, II, pp. 378–383.
114. Ibid., p. 379.
115. Ibid., p. 380.
116. Ibid., pp. 379–380.
117. Ibid., p. 383.
118. Ibid.
119. Ibid., pp. 382, 383.
120. Ibid., pp. 221–222, 268–271, 273.
121. See, e.g., No Souvenirs, pp. 199–200, 304, 324; id., "The Clairvoyant Lamb," in Zalmoxis, pp. 226–256.
122. See his Spaţiul Mioritic (Bucharest, 1936).
123. See Legionnaire Texts, pp. 70–71. For more on this passage, see below, ch. 7.
124. The Fate of Romanian Culture, pp. 37–39.
125. Ibid., p. 45. For more on the context of this passage, see below in ch. 8.
126. Zalmoxis, pp. 253–256. See also No Souvenirs, pp. 199–200.
127. Zalmoxis, p. 227.
128. On inner-Romanian orientalism, see Antohi, Civitas imaginalis, pp. 304–305 n. 5.
129. It is strange that despite the lengthy survey of the bibliography on the ballade, Eliade skips the important discussion of Gaster, Romanian Popular Literature, pp. 313–315, which proposed to see as a major source the myth of Adonis-Tamuz, "from the semito-Egyptian legends."
130. See his For Two Thousand Years, p. 101.
131. No Souvenirs, p. 304, in the context of a view found in St. Augustine. Emphasis in the original.
132. Reprinted in Handoca, ed., Eliade File XIV (1983), pp. 82–83.
133. Forbidden Forest, pp. 500–501, and Olson, The Theology and Philosophy, pp. 153–154.
134. See below, ch. 8, in the cited passage from the letter to Matei Călinescu.
135. No Souvenirs, pp. 2–3.
136. Ibid., p. 200. For the earlier occurrence of Heidegger's name in Eliade, see Portugal Journal, I, pp. 198, 199, 219, 235. See also Culianu, Mircea Eliade, p. 87, and Dubuisson's important discussion in Mythologies, pp. 235–243, as well as Wilhelm Dancă, "Homo religiosus si ontologia pragmatic in viziunea lui Mircea Eliade," in Orizontul Sacru, ed. Corneliu Mircea–Robert Lazu (Iaşi, 1998), pp. 79–94.

137. Ricketts, *Romanian Roots*, II, pp. 1033–1034.
138. *Memoirs*, pp. 149, 227, 228, which he had started in 1938 and dealt with in Portugal in the forties. See also the foreword page of *Rites and Symbols of Initiation*, and *Master Manole*, p. 119.
139. *No Souvenirs*, p. 52.
140. Ibid., p. 217.
141. See *Occultism*, pp. 32–46, and his preface to *Shamanism*, p. xxi.
142. This megalomaniac boast is found also in other cases in Eliade's self-perception. See, e.g., *Portugal Journal*, I, p. 167. In my opinion, the 1945 short story "A Big Man," has Eliade as its protagonist.
143. On orgy as a means to Eliade's search for equilibrium in the same years, see the previous chapter, where I quote *Portugal Journal*, I, p. 126.
144. Namely, the great dissolution or annihilation of the world by its absorption in God, which follows a series of smaller cosmic dissolutions. This is part of a cosmic cycle, and it has nothing to do with the situation of WWII, as implied by Eliade in this context. See his *Patterns in Comparative Religion*, pp. 407–408. This concept is reminiscent of the concept of cosmic jubilee, according to some Kabbalistic views; see more in ch. 4.
145. *Portugal Journal*, I, p. 235. Compare to an interesting parallel found in a 1933 feuilleton by Sebastian, discussed in Petreu, *From Junimea to Noica*, pp. 357–358.
146. See the passage quoted in the next chapter.
147. See also a similar claim in *Portugal Journal*, I, p. 170.
148. Ibid., p. 166.
149. See Eliade, *On Eminescu and Hașdeu*, pp. 72–73.
150. See Dana, *Zalmoxis*, passim.
151. See ibid.
152. See Dana, *Métamorphoses*.
153. To German philosophy, described earlier as consecrating life.
154. *A Day in My Life*, p. 243. See also her *Cioran*, pp. 74, 114–115. For other protests against the fatalistic approach to death in *Miorița*, see Oișteanu, "Mircea Eliade Between Political Journalism and Scholarly Work," pp. 334–336. It should be pointed out that there are scholars who suggest explaining Iron Guard fascination with death as an impact of a German or Teutonic approach. See Culianu, *Romanian Studies*, I, p. 349, and Șerbu, *The Show Window*, p. 248.
155. Cioran *Schimbarea la față a României* (Bucharest, 1990), p. 44; Antohi, *Civitas Imaginalis*, p. 244; and Acterian, *Cioran, Eliade, Ionesco*, pp. 8–9.
156. "Redemption, History, Politics," *Vremea* (26 Aprilie 1936), reprinted in Eliade, *Romanian Prophetism*, II, p. 153.
157. As we shall see in ch. 7, Ion Moța, the second most important figure in the movement, was closely cooperating with Nazi Germany. Traian Herseni, a sociologist who endorsed a legionnaire state of pure blood, was an admirer of Hitler's racially pure state. See Marius Turda, "Nation as Object: Race, Blood, and Biopolitics in Interwar Romania," *Slavic Review*, 66 (2007), pp. 438–439.
158. See, e.g., Veiga, *The History of the Iron Guard*, pp. 161–164; Dana, *Métamorphoses*, p. 67; Boia, *History and Myth*, p. 259 n. 48. Șerban Suru, the main leader of the Iron Guard in recent years, references Eminescu's thought as a precursor of the Iron Guard.
159. For the need to distinguish between different currents in Romania of that period, see Volovici,

Nationalist Ideology, p. 193; Adrian Marino, "Two Ideological Romanias," printed in Chimet, ed., *Mihail Sebastian File*, pp. 57–59; and Petreu, *The Devil and His Apprentice*, pp. 254–256.

160. On Eliade and immortality in writings from the later part of his life, see also Wasserstrom, "The Dream of Mankind," pp. 193–194.

161. I, p. 138.

162. *Portugal Journal*, I, p. 271.

163. See, in more general terms, Andrei Oişteanu, "Eugène Ionesco, între oroarea de a trăi şi oroarea de a muri," *Revista 22*, 3, 11 (2009). How his play "The King Dies" is related to those discussions may be a matter for another inquiry.

164. See also, e.g., his *Journal of Vacation*, p. 117.

165. See *Mircea Eliade*, pp. 285–292. I would like not to discuss here the claims made by the priest Gheorghe Calciu-Dumitreasa as to Eliade's cremation, and Culianu's piece, since they stem from a deeply religious conviction.

· 4 ·

TIME, HISTORY, AND
ANTITHETIC JUDAISM

What will not be repeated is horrifying me.

—ELIADE, PORTUGAL JOURNAL[1]

A Short History of the "Terror of History"

Important as the themes discussed in the previous three chapters are, they nevertheless are rarely part of the ordinary scholarly expositions of Eliade's thought. All of them privileged, for good reasons, discussions revolving around his vision of myth, time, and history, especially as found in his well-known *The Myth of the Eternal Return*. Published first in French in 1949, it was planned years before, as we learn from some of Eliade's remarks.[2] Much of the discussions in his later books are grounded in both the ideas and the materials found in this booklet. The conceptual basis that informed his views, articulated at some length, has earlier sources. As Ioan P. Culianu has pointed out, there are some modest antecedents to the idea of the fall of history or the sabotage of history in the thought of Nae Ionescu and Lucian Blaga.[3] Let me start with a short survey of the history of Eliade's vision of the process of historicization of religion, which means for Eliade also a process of desacralization, or its banalization, and the emergence of what he called the terror of history. Quite early in his career, immediately after his return from India, he wrote

The Chronological spirit, namely the instinct to count the time that is refracted in history—but not manifested eternally in Creation uniformly, I would say in a static manner—is conditioned in general by two principles:

1) Creation (which is cosmic with the Semites and the Chinese, and worldly with the Romans, "the building of Rome").

2) Revelation.

This is the reason why the Hindus are totally lacking the chronological spirit: because their creation is periodical, rhythmical, infinite, not historical, not a unique and irreversible event; and revelation is permanent, starting with the Vedas and repeated in Avatars, a continuous osmosis between humanity and the divine.[4]

Immediately afterwards, Eliade mentions at length the Arabs, who are portrayed as having adopted the chronological attitude, and no doubt the Arabs too should be counted among the Semites. The implied assumption is that the "continuous osmosis" is the patrimony of the Hindu approaches alone. On the other hand, he mentions in the same booklet that the incarnation of God intends more than regeneration of man and his redemption from sin, which can be achieved also "indirectly, by inspiration—like the prophets, legislators, spiritual leaders and some historical events which have a significance."[5]

These embryonic remarks are the cornerstone of many elaborations that stand at the core of Eliade's phenomenology of religion and also of its history, and it had been articulated already in 1932, after his return from India.

The above distinction reverberates in his descriptions of the history of religion; for example, we find that he wrote 50 years later that "As with the Jews and the Romans, Islam—especially in its initial phase—saw in historic events the episodes of a sacred history."[6] To a great extent, Eliade's efforts were to disenchant the concept of sacred history, which for him was something like an oxymoron, as irrelevant for archaic religiosity. Interestingly enough, it is in the same year, 1932, that Eliade wrote a short piece entitled "The Confessions of a Young Man of the Century," where it is written:

All the comfort and nostalgia of the war[7] in Bucharest—seem to me abject. I love so much my dear city that I would like to erase it from the earth in a single night, and build it up anew the next day—a young Bucharest, a stony one without history, without monuments, without mud. I would like that history would cease—to allow life to start from the beginning, to create freely, without superstitions.[8]

As in his later formulations, Eliade is interested in the possibility of renewal, and to a certain extent, of reversibility. These passages show that Eliade's vision of the terror of history that dominates his later books, especially in the Portugal period,[9] has its much earlier source, and did not start in the second part of the thirties as part of Eliade's involvement in the Iron Guard. It seems that the emergence of the expression of a terror of history in connection to Bucharest has something to do with the concept that Romania suffered from a terror of history, namely the various invasions throughout its history, especially in WWI.[10] However, later Eliade framed it in a much wider religious context, which will be analyzed below.[11]

On Archeology and Hebrew Bible

For Eliade the year 1937 was undoubtedly one of special interest in archeology, buildings, and religion. In this year he delivered some talks on Romanian radio, including "New Research about the Most Ancient Civilizations," which dealt with excavations in Mohenjo-Daro and Ras Amarna,[12] and later in the same year, "Archeological Excavations in the Holy Land."[13] Though related not to archeology but to an exceptional building, Eliade also wrote in the same year a review of Paul Mus's voluminous book *Barabudur*, which was itself a book review.[14]

Let me start with a passage printed early in 1937, part of a feuilleton entitled "Before and After the Biblical Miracle":

> The "biblical miracle" remains a question mark; while in Egypt and Babylonia there were perfect moral and religious ideas, the Jewish people transformed those ideas into a religious experience that was excessively fertile. As Charles Jean has noted, nothing compelled the Jews to be monotheists, prophets, or messianics. An explanation by dint of race, by background, by social circumstances, by external influences is insufficient. Some of the biblical ideas have been discovered. Only the Jewish people lived a religious life of the tenacity and density of biblical life.[15]

This passage is a beginning of a long elaboration that shaped, gradually, Eliade's entire vision of the biblical contribution to religion and the history of religion in general. The biblical "miracle" means not only extraordinary but also unnatural or supernatural development. The three nouns "monotheists, prophets, or messianics," which stem from Charles Jean's book, recur in Eliade's writings in different forms as the quintessence of the religious modalities of some Jewish groups, which revolutionized— in his opinion—the entire history of monotheistic religions.

What is more pertinent to our topic is another review written in the same year about the results of another excavation some decades earlier in southern Egypt. Archeologists discovered Elephantine documents written in Aramaic that contain a series of testimonies about a colony of Israelites who lived on an island in the Nile for several decades during the 5th century BC. In those documents there is evidence of the existence of a temple and worship of gods like Bethel and Anath, which had been eliminated from official worship in Jerusalem. A French scholar, Albert Vincent, dedicated a voluminous study, *La Religion des Judeo-Araméens d'Elephantine*,[16] to this major finding regarding the religious life of the ancient Israelites. Eliade's review, entitled "Between Elephantine and Jerusalem,"[17] was published earlier in the same year. The gist of the review is based on the theory, embraced not by Vincent but by another scholar, Adolphe Lods, that the Elephantine colony's worship reflects a form of religion shared by the population of Israelites in the 7th and 6th centuries BC, and that the émigrés took with them, sometime in the 5th century BC when they left the land, the cult of their Israelite contemporaries.[18] These two views are accepted by Eliade.

His main point was that the dream of Jacob as articulated in Genesis 28:11–13, which took place in Bethel, strongly related to the concept of *axis mundi* on the one hand, and to a cult of the stone, or the column—in Hebrew, *matzevah*—on the other hand. This natural form of religion was then overcome by the propagandistic activity of an elite group in Jerusalem that preserved the monotheism of Moses and imposed its religious ideals by force, destroying the expected natural development of this religion, which would have been similar to the religion of the Elephantine Jews. Let me translate some of Eliade's sentences pertinent to his view on the topic:

> Nothing compelled the people of Israel to become monotheistic. The religious evolution of the Semitic race has nothing exceptional in its structure. An elite revealed monotheism to the Jewish people. The Jews were *converted to* monotheism after a long, hard resistance. If left to "evolve" in a natural fashion, the Jews would have acquired a pantheon as large as that which is displayed to us in the papyri from Elephantine: with a Great Goddess[19] (like all the other people that participate in the Afro-Asiatic protohistorical cults), with a God of vegetation (so "popular" on the Mediterranean shores and in Asia Minor), with some other minor gods.[20]

The first sentence constitutes a precise repetition of Charles Jean's view mentioned some months earlier in the same journal, but without mentioning Jean's name. An analysis of this dense passage, and some to be discussed immediately below, reveals the kernel of Eliade's vision of religion not only in the late thirties, but also later in his career. On the one hand, there are positive dimensions—polytheism, nature, vegetation, stasis, inertia, universality, populace—and on the other hand, the much less positive concepts—monotheism, elites, miracles, and conceptual rupture. A certain religion, therefore, is not a variety of approaches that differ among themselves phenomenologically; instead, it consists of two major forms: the first, primordial one, and the second, which is the result of a deep shift in history, and therefore unnatural and historical.

Who exactly is that elite that converted the population and changed the "natural" course of development? The answer is found some lines later in the same review: "in Jerusalem the 'monotheistic' elites were watching"—they were the keepers of Moses' message,[21] or, according to another formulation, those who dealt with the "Mosaic message." Let us quote Eliade again:

> But the intervention and history of this message belongs to "the miraculous." A firm will for proselytism makes room for the first time in the history of mankind (IX–VIII centuries). When Moses' message was taken over by the Jerusalemite elites, the history of the Orient started to change its face. The natural "evolution" would have brought about a religion similar to that at Elephantine. The violence, the pathos, the genius, and the tears of elite caused an absolute monotheism, prophetism, messianism...[22]

This vision of proselytism in the context of the biblical Judaism, and of Judaism in general, is a very precarious one. It seems that an absence of missionary activities is one of the characteristics of Jewish monotheism that differentiates it from the Christian and Muslim forms. Unlike the more universalistic approach in the latter forms of monotheism, in Judaism religion is much more related to a specific "chosen" nation.[23]

At the end of the above quote from Eliade we find the threefold characterization that emerged in the early 1937 chronicle quoted above, again without mention of Charles Jean as his source. Elsewhere, Eliade describes the "Jerusalem elite" as "intolerant and fanatic."[24] He also uses the phrase "natural evolution" elsewhere in this essay,[25] and refers to the monotheistic elite of Jerusalem.[26] This terminology of organicity and naturality appears in the most essential question Eliade attempts to deal with in this review:

> [T]he fundamental problem of Judaism is this: *Is monotheism a category specific to the Judaic spirit or not?* Did the Jew (or the Semite in general) discover it in a natural fashion, in an *organic* [manner], because he had to discover it, because *he could not do otherwise*, because monotheism alone conformed to his mental structure? Or was monotheism the experience of an elite very restrained in the times that immediately followed Moses, very active during the period of the exile, intolerant and fanatic in the postexilic centuries?[27]

What is the basic difference between the elite and the masses? Eliade is quite explicit:

> While Jacob (namely the tradition of the Mosaic elites, which are monotheistic) receives that primeval symbol with all its metaphysical juice, giving to it a theistic nuance, the Palestinian populations transformed that symbolic formula in a "concrete religious experience," living and personifying it.[28]

This is an interesting piece of speculation as to what the original vision was and how it was transformed by the rather unidentified "Mosaic" elites. Elsewhere, Eliade speculates as follows:

> The example of Bethel seems to us to be significant. Indubitably, the Palestinian *population*[29] were acquainted with a god Bethel, just as we found in the pantheon of the Jews from Elephantine. But the "monotheistic" elites in Jerusalem were watching, who faithfully preserved Moses' message. And in the Ancient Testament there are sufficient indications that there were true religious fights against the sanctuary of Bethel, where tradition made Jacob see the ladder of the angels and the house of God, while the Palestinian peasants were seeing just the god Bethel.[30]

This distinction between the more abstract-oriented elite and the more concrete and experiential life of the population also occurs earlier on the same page[31] and becomes more explicit some lines later: "This tendency for the concrete, for the personal, for the organic is almost 'physiological,' this 'experience' has deep roots in the soil of the whole of Asia, and has as its flowers the popular orgies."[32]

Thus, we may safely assume that, for Eliade, the concreteness of the religious experience of the Israelite population or peasants—the latter term reminiscent of the Romanian peasants[33]—is similar to what has been preserved by the Elephantine Israelites. This emphasis on the population stems, indubitably, from Vincent, whom he quotes quite explicitly to this effect.[34] At the same time, in the land of Israel a major religious revolution took place by force, or as Eliade puts it elsewhere, "the appearance of the Mosaic message means a great rupture of level,[35] which almost changed the mental evolution of mankind."[36]

Let me ponder on the possible identity of the unidentified "Mosaic" or Jerusalemite elite[s] that played such a crucial role. A small town like ancient Jerusalem did not have a plethora of social or political layers. Since messianism was not a pressing issue during the First Temple period, nor was there an elite dedicated to "monotheism" as its function, what remains from Eliade's short list by dint of elimination is what he calls prophetism. In my opinion, the prophets are essentially the elite he had in mind. It was they (I propose that Eliade imagined) who did the repressive job that finally accomplished the victory—according to him, the disaster—of the belief in monotheism. However, there can be no doubt that although some of them indeed criticized the prevailing type of cult, with its concrete elements of worship and sacrifices unaccompanied by a more spiritual approach to religion,[37] their claims about the retreat to polytheism was just one part of their activities.

Indeed, Eliade's vision of the prophets as the Jerusalemite elite is, to put it mildly, highly problematic from the social point of view: The biblical prophets were almost invariably opposed to the highest elites active in Jerusalem—the kings and the priests of the Temple—as much as to popular or any other type of idolatry. The only influential Jerusalemite religious elite that indeed could count was the priestly elite, who were quite immersed in performing rituals in what they considered the center of the world, namely the temple in Jerusalem—which corresponds to the heavenly city, much closer to Eliade's vision of archaic religion. A member of an elite, like the king Menasseh, was an idolater. Therefore, Eliade's theory of rupture between elite and populace, allegedly introduced by the Jerusalemite groups described as elites, which he is so insistent about, is a matter of sheer speculation. He may well be right or wrong, but it is hard to see it as more than conjuncture. I am not going to debate here the complex question of the emergence of monotheism and its dissemination, which has not been settled by scholars of the Hebrew Bible. In any case, to give just one seminal example of the problematic involved in this matter, the view of an outstanding scholar of the Hebrew Bible in Israel, Yehezkel Kauffmann, presumably the most important thinker in this field in the 20th century, is that the monotheistic idea was part and parcel of the spirit of the Israelites as a nation, not an elitist view imposed on the masses.[38] It is not my intention to decide who is more correct here insofar as the biblical approach is concerned, but to point out that what Eliade presents in an apodictic manner is far from obvious to leading scholars of the Bible.

However, what is edifying is the fact that Eliade's presentation of the abstract religion of the Israelite elite conflicts with another of his own theories expressed sometime earlier in the very same year, in his monograph entitled *Babylonian Cosmology and Alchemy*. There he deals with the importance of the geographical center, or *axis mundi*, and homologies between heaven and earth, adducing Jewish material in support of his view.[39] In this book, however, there is no mention of a Mosaic revolution or of Jerusalemite elites at all, or of monotheism. He quotes the Jewish material as supporting central issues in his vision of cosmic religion without any hesitation, and without differentiating the material from the plethora of other evidence from many other religions regarding the concreteness of the religious worldview.

We have, therefore, in the very same year, two different—I would say, even conflicting—views from Eliade about what is found in ancient Judaism. On the one hand, the Mosaic revolution removed the concrete dimensions of religion, the affinity between heaven and earth, the omphalic vision of sacred geography; on the other hand, those religious elements remained for several more centuries embedded in Rabbinic literature and much later Jewish literatures like Kabbalah, and all of them are elite literatures of Judaism. In Eliade's November 1937 review of Vincent's book, he refers to his monograph on Babylonia as already published; I assume that it was delivered for publication late in 1936 or very early in 1937.

Monotheism and the Violent Elites: 1937

What happened in the interval between the writing of these two diverging approaches? The most interesting reference to the change in Eliade's attitude to Jews and Judaism is in a passage in the autobiography of Eliade's friend, the Jewish Romanian writer Mihail Sebastian. On February 25, 1937, he noted in his *Journal* about Eliade's conversion to the Iron Guard: "Mircea Eliade's more recent stories in *Vremea*[40] were more and more 'legionnaire.'"[41] Eliade's more open adherence to the right wing of the Romanian political scene in 1937—though clear sympathies were seen much earlier, in late 1935—undoubtedly left its traces on his attitude to Judaism, and I believe that Sebastian's statement is clear, reliable, and corroborated by Eliade's reference to the violent Israelite elite, as I suggested above.

However, it would be quite simplistic to reduce Eliade's dichotomy between the Jerusalemite elites and the rural population in the land of Israel during the first Temple period to an unfortunate embrace of the extreme right, and even propaganda in its favor. I believe that a much deeper change in Eliade's worldview that began several years before he adhered to the ideology of the Iron Guard should also be taken into serious consideration. In the summer of 1931 he wrote about some thoughts he had while waiting to leave India:

> It was precisely the peasant[42] roots of a good part of our Romanian culture that compelled us to transcend nationalism and cultural provincialism and to aim for "universalism." The common elements of Indian, Balkan, and Mediterranean folk cultures proved to me that it is here that organic universalism exists, that it is the result of a common history (the history of peasant cultures) and not an abstract construct.[43]

This modest *internationale* of peasant religion was conceived of as not just a culture in itself, but in fact the superior and somehow more universal culture, and this stance became a leitmotif in Eliade's academic activity. In many ways, it remained a top priority on the agenda that guided much of what he wrote afterwards. Sometimes it amounted to an attempt to establish, at least obliquely, the superiority of Romanian agrarian culture from the religious point of view. This is corroborated by two feuilletons Eliade published in 1932, after his return from India to Romania, in *Cuvântul*, the Bucharest-based newspaper on which he collaborated. In a dispute about the need of alphabetization of Romanian peasants, Eliade took a very interesting position: He did not oppose it, but he claimed that the peasants have their own cultural style, and assumes that Romania is at a point of no return with this project. However, the tone in which he describes the process is almost elegiaic: "[It does] not matter how much we may regret, we cannot return to the organic rural culture."[44] He repeatedly refers to the "centauric nature" of any important culture, which is rooted in life and earth.[45] He insists that "the rural Romanians, for example, have known a culture of organicity yet unattained by any official 'culture,' leaning to the Occident."[46] He recurrently emphasizes that culture also implies a return to nature. In 1935 Eliade envisions only two main layers of population in Romania, which are indispensable: the peasants and the creative elites.[47] These and other similar views expressed in the first half of the thirties demonstrate that the concept of elite versus popular culture, the latter of which is conceived of as rural *par excellence*, is a problematic that antedates the review of Vincent's book in late 1937.

Let me introduce here a discussion Eliade published in May 1935 in a feuilleton entitled "Romanianism and the Complexes of Inferiority." Here he attributes to Jews a "tragic" inferiority complex provoked by the history of the Christian world, a complex that may be solved only by the creation of a Jewish national state.[48] Together with this complex, he also mentions "intransigence,"[49] and later he writes that the Romanians, unlike the Jews,

> have the right to agitate themselves, since their destiny is to demonstrate [their] existence by the most tragic human efforts. They could consider themselves to be persecuted, since this helps them to survive. We [the Romanians] do not need intransigence and intolerance, vices that are alien to our structure.[50]

One must be moved by this naive apotheosis of the character of the Romanians as a whole, an essentialist approach, especially as it was written in 1935, when the power of the most intransigent movement in the history of Romania, the Iron Guard, began its dramatic political rise less than two years after the assassination of Prime Minister Duca by some legionnaires. Were the persecutions of Jews, including in Romania, imaginary, just a Jewish strategy to survive? We are dealing here with the imaginary vices of the Jews, not the imaginary virtues of the Romanians, as forged by a scholar of religion as a simplificator for the masses in feuilletons.[51] Among his various essays of this period in which Jews are mentioned, this is one of the most positive, and my purpose here is not to debate the accuracy of his statements; they may, after all, reflect the specific experiences Eliade had with some contemporary Jews. Eliade's attitude to these contemporary Jews is that competition with them should be conducted not politically, economically, or socially, but by means of cultural creativity—no doubt a veiled polemic against anti-Semites who feared the Jewish presence in Romania, as we shall see in ch. 7 below. What concerns me here is not the politics but the perception of intolerance and intransigence attributed to contemporary Jews that is reminiscent of his description of the ancient Jewish elites, adduced above. The biblical elites, allegedly "intolerant and fanatic," were understood in 1937 in terms derived from what he assumes is a direct experience one may have of Jews in the present: as "intransigent and intolerant." It is less an analysis of the ancient texts than an appropriation of a widespread cliché regarding a vice of the Jews that generated the specific understanding of the ancient Jewish elites. It is at the end of 1935 that Eliade started his adherence to the most intransigent and intolerant political and religious movement in the history of Romania, the Iron Guard, to which those vices were not alien, but part of what Eliade would call "Romanianism."[52] Romanianism constitutes the preservation of the good ancient natural religion, whose parallel was shattered by the Israelite elite of hoary antiquity.

Eliade projected this type of antithetic distinction upon an ancient society whose social structure was even more obscure than the plight of the Jews in modern Romania in the thirties. In his more famous books published also in English, Eliade reiterated this problematic presentation of Judaism as both changing the course of religious history of mankind and possessing the same ideas that reflect the concrete attitude to sacred places. In fact, the kernel of *The Myth of the Eternal Return* is no more than a representation of those two diverging approaches, with no attempt to solve the tensions between them. Given the seminal role this book played in the dissemination of Eliade's view, let me attempt to substantiate this claim.

Eliade reiterates his views about the possible natural development of ancient Judaism in the direction represented by the Elephantine papyri, referring explicitly to Vincent's book.[53] Here, however, the elites are no more "violent and fanatic," as they were in the Romanian essay, and they are identified as the "prophets,"[54] as they are also elsewhere in the book.[55] This elite is presented as involved in religious education, which is now much more concerned with the introduction of the new value of history rather than with shaping a less concrete type of religion;[56] a fascinating and miraculous transformation had taken place between 1937 and 1946 in Eliade's view of the ancient Jewish elites. Yet, at the same time, Eliade presents much of the same evidence on centers, omphalologies, parallel cities, sacred trees, etc. that he had already adduced in *Babylonian Cosmology and Alchemy*, and he uses roughly the same scholarly bibliography.[57] This means that while the texts he cites from ancient Jewish material correspond to the view of religion as concrete, the general representation of ancient Judaism is uniformly related to an abstract vision of this religion, with an emphasis on history. However, there is no reason to choose between the two, since biblical literature is quite a diversified type of thought that cannot be reduced to one single approach. Different voices are expressed in different parts of this literature.

Was "Judaism" Historically Oriented?

As seen above in chs. 2–3, I propose to understand a profound structure of Eliade's religious thought as related to the importance of the return to origins and the reversibility of processes. This is a metastatic proclivity, some form of protest and an expression of discontent with the present: spiritual, political, or just human. The cyclical aspect of Eliade's vision of archaic religion is part of the more comprehensive opportunity to transcend the uniqueness and finality of processes. The theory is that the revelation in monotheistic religion occurs in mythical time, "at the extratemporal instant of the beginning," "in a limited moment, definitely situated in time," and this is the reason it "becomes precious inasmuch as it is no longer reversible, as it is historical event."[58]

Let me highlight Eliade's claim that in "Judaism" time is irreversible, basically linear, and connected to history. This distinction between linear and cyclical time became a leitmotif in his thought.[59] This stark opposition is, however, problematic, since there is no reason to understand complex religious phenomena as fixed and unable to include other views of time.[60]

In fact, there are scholars whose vision of time in the Hebrew Bible runs counter to Eliade's.[61] Moreover, Eliade's emphasis on the strong connection between a historical outlook and Judaism is incompatible with what Yosef H. Yerushalmi, a modern, leading Jewish historian, described as the lack of interest by Jews in this field, and his feeling that as a Jewish historian, he is alien to a major vector of the Jewish culture. He envisioned traditional Judaism as a homogenous traditional society that seemingly confronts modernity with a negative attitude toward its critical claims of demythologization. Or to put it in the more explicit terms found in Yerushalmi, the importance of ritual in traditional (i.e., Rabbinic) Judaism represents an alternative to history.[62] According to him, faith in history characterizes the "fallen" like himself, an expression that reflects Yerushalmi's ironic understanding of modern interest in history.[63] Like Yerushalmi, I am among those scholars who do not assume that traditional Jews had an especially strong historical sense or interest in immanent explanations. However, we should not see the vast and variegated literatures and forms of experiences known as Judaism as so monolithic, static, and closed that they cannot absorb some historical understanding. Such absorption of a more historical consciousness is visible in the 16th century, but the reasons for this interest are debated by scholars.[64]

Let us turn to another distinguished Jewish historian, Arnaldo Momigliano, who described Judaism thus, with reference to his grandfather, Amadio: "The whole development of Judaism led to something ahistorical, eternal, the Law, the Torah....History had nothing to explain and little to reveal to the man who meditated the Law day and night."[65] This is a seminal statement as to the negligibility of history in Jewish culture, coming from the pen of a Jewish historian. Though I see this understanding Judaism as a Platonic one,[66] it has much to do with the Jewish Rabbinic elite. Last but not least, even Scholem assumed that we cannot discern an effort to find meaning in history among the Kabbalists.[67] Indeed, in some parts of the Hebrew Bible and even more so in Rabbinic literature, the law holds a much higher place than history. However, while the Rabbis suppressed interest in history, Christianity introduced the centrality of a specific historical event: the death of Jesus Christ. The meditation on the passion of the founder of Christianity and the expectation of his return in history, after ordinary history, is a central fact in this religion. In most of the forms of Judaism, the contemplation, the interpretation, and even more, the performance of the law played the central role. The obliteration of most of the biblical commandments in Pauline Christianity reduced dramatically the importance of the rituals, and attributed to the meditation on the life of Jesus and its theological implications a major role, while Rabbinic Judaism, in its different manifestations, remained a much more performative religion.

However, beyond the opinions of scholars, let me adduce two examples of concepts of time in Judaism that differ dramatically from the linear historical time that is thought to characterize Judaism. Given its lengthy and diversified development, Judaism incorporated a variety of views concerning time.[68] Eliade's view that Judaism left behind the notion of the circularity of time is true insofar as some aspects of the biblical phase are involved,[69] but totally incorrect in terms of medieval Judaism, with its various theories of cyclical time, as exposed in Jewish astrology and philosophy and in their Kabbalistic versions. Let me adduce two examples, out of thousands found in Judaism, dealing with circular time. In an anonymous passage written by a 16th-century Kabbalist we read:

> The great purpose of the advent of the king Messiah and of the world to come [was not disclosed, as it is said],[70] "The heart did not disclose to the mouth," neither to the vulgus nor to all of the elite but to the few who merit this [i.e., the knowledge of the secret]. It is forbidden to the recipient of this secret to disclose it even to the elite, except to a friend exceptionally close to him. And in the year of Messiah [MShYH], namely, in the year whose secret is 358 of the sixth millennium, which is the year [Shannah], then the Messiah will arrive. [However,] in an occult manner he has already arrived during the several cycles of the worlds which have already passed before the present one in which we are, since at the time when he has already arrived [in the past], then he will come again also this time. And it was said that "and then he will come" means that the Messiah will come in the future at the same time he comes in our time, namely in our world.[71]

The great mystery revealed here concerns the advent of the Messiah at exactly the same time in every cosmic cycle; just as he came in the prior cycle in the year 358, he will appear in our cycle and so also in future cycles. Therefore, the real secret is not just the computation of the precise date of the arrival of the Messiah, but also the fact that this date is the archetype of all the messianic dates past and future, in each of the cosmic cycles.

First, the term translated as "cycles" is *gilgul*; its primary meaning is "rotation," but it was adopted by many Kabbalists as the primary term for metempsychosis. In this particular context, however, where it is employed together with the word "worlds," I assume that its rendering as "cycle" does justice to the general intention of the text. Second, the coming of the Messiah is indicated in this passage by the verb *ba,'* whose plain meaning is indeed "to come." But in some Kabbalistic texts this verb is used to refer to the soul that undergoes a process of metempsychosis, and in at least one instance this soul is the soul of the Messiah.[72] Therefore, though the plain meaning of the text deals with the recurring coming of the Messiah at the same date in each cosmic cycle, a more careful reading may reveal an additional aspect of the subject: The Messiah who returns from time to time is preserving his existence in the interregnum by metempsychosis. What is interesting about this particular date is not the fact that consonants of *mashiyah* amount numerically to 358, but the general conception of history exhibited in the text. This Kabbalist posits that the Messiah will arrive in the Jewish year 5358 and in all the other years of 5358 of the other cosmic cycles. Thus, once in every 7,000 years the messianic advent is to be repeated, *mutatis mutandis*, in each and every cosmic cycle. A linear view of history, found in each cycle, is combined with a much vaster cyclical theory of time. The linear view posits a straight historical line, with developmental progress until history reaches the endpoint of redemption. The circular theory of time presents not only the end of a cosmic cycle but also the beginning of the next one. The view of this Kabbalist does not differ from what Eliade describes in his discussion of cyclical time.[73] His assumption that "Hebrews" assume that the world is lasting only 7,000 years[74] is just one of the many speculations on time in the literature of Judaism.

Another outstanding example in Kabbalah of a more complex type of cyclical time connected to rituals is found in a mid-16th-century commentary on liturgy by a leading Kabbalist, R. Moses Cordovero:

> [T]he matter of the changes of the times [*shinnuiei ha-zemanim*] depends upon the supernal *sefirot* and the directive[75] that reaches us from them. We are the people of God, [therefore] all our behavior and the revolutions of our times[76] are counted by us exactly in accordance to the spheres of the *sefirot*, since the secret of our souls, spirits, and higher souls is that we are sparks hewn from the light of the *sefirot* and all our intention is to imitate the supernal [entities] as far as possible, to link ourselves to the supernal roots, to cleave

to our Creator, as much as possible…and He arranged the periods of the year and the motions of the stars in such a way as to enable us to know, out of their signs,[77] the supernal directives just as they are in the Land of Israel.[78]

This is quite a remarkable passage from the point of view of the religious categories that Eliade attributes to the archaic mentality: We have here an explicit combination of *imitatio dei,* of the center of the world, of a cosmization of religion, and of transcendence of the normal condition by adhering to God by means of the ritual—"our behavior." The entire context has to do with the performance of the rituals related to the Sabbath, which is certainly a cyclical rite. The existence of such a text, which is not exceptional, shows that any attempt to offer a simple picture of the view of time in Judaism as a whole is a dramatic reduction, amounting to a distortion of a complex religion. After all, there are in Judaism, and in Cordovero himself, also views of linear time, related to redemption.[79] So, what is interesting in this quote is not the simple phenomenological perception of the ancient Jews and consequently of Judaism juxtaposed against the different, the archaic, but rather the combination of what Eliade would call archaic elements and the historical ones.[80]

The challenge in describing religions is, in my opinion, in discerning their diversity and the coexistence of variegated concepts dealing with the same topic, not reducing a complex type of religion to just one basic view with small variants. The sharp distinction between the Jewish unilinear vision of history and the archaic cyclical one is far from neat, not only in a long series of available Jewish sources, but also from a careful reading of the material Eliade himself adduced in this context.[81]

Let me point out the possible influence of Eliade's view on Judaism and history on Yosef Yerushalmi's view on these matters. Eliade wrote that "It may, then, be said in truth that the Hebrews were the first to discover the meaning of history as the epiphany of God, and this conception, as we should expect, was taken up and amplified by Christianity."[82] In quite a similar manner Yerushalmi formulated the contribution of the Jews to history: "If Herodotus was the father of history, the fathers of meaning in history were the Jews."[83] Despite the similarity between the two authors in terms of the "meaning of history" and the Jews, there is a significant difference: History is found, according to Yerushalmi, also among the Greeks, not only Jews. The latter added what is perhaps missing with Greeks: meaning. If understood in such a way, history in ancient Judaism is a hierophany, but its importance had already been discovered by the Greeks, as they discovered also science, and both impacted the development of the West much more than the Judeo-Christian tradition, as Eliade wants us to believe. One more time, Eliade selected rather carelessly from the various types of evidence that were easily available in order to construe his theory and create the antithetic Judaism.

This does not mean that Eliade was not ready to acknowledge in some cases the potential created by Judaism to preserve its culture during the vicissitude of history by cultural creativity, invoking the approach of Rabbi Yohanan ben Zakkai.[84] His emphasis, however, is on the success of the Jews in transmitting their values, not on creative aspects of Rabbinic Judaism, which is actually the case.

Exit from Time in Hasidism

As part of his vision of a fluid universe, Eliade claims that it is possible to escape pro-fane time in experiences that are felt as atemporal, thus breaking homogenous time.[85] This is a major argument in his reconstruction of the archaic religiosity, which has been allegedly destroyed by the invasion of an approach to time as historical and lin-ear, based on Jewish sources enhanced in Christianity. However, experiences of tran-scending time are found in a variety of mystical accounts that were articulated in the historical monotheistic religions. Their substantial presence problematizes Eliade's distinction between the archaic and the historical religions. Let me adduce just one such example of many, from a major 18th-century Hasidic leader, R. Dov Be'er of Medzeritch (1700–1772), known as the Great Maggid. He is reported to have said:

> Elijah is alive forever, despite the fact that he is compounded of four elements and they are [immersed] within temporality, though their root is in the unity. And when he draws down the unity[86] within them, they are aggrandized and come higher than temporality and arrive to the simple unity. And [so] he can live forever....And when someone wants to walk a distance of five hundred years,[87] he must walk very much. But in a dream he can walk them in one moment because they are above temporality, and the delight that he enjoys there in the one moment that is above temporality, he cannot enjoy in this world, because he is [immersed] in time, and time had been obliterated [*Batel mi-metzi'ut*], as time is [part of] creation and it cannot receive what is higher than time.[88]

The Hebrew phrase for "higher than time," *le-ma'alah me-ha-zeman*, which points to a sort of human experience and not to a metaphysical layer, occurs hundreds of times in Hasidic literature, though some pre-Hasidic sources for it also may be detected. This ascent to a realm higher than time is tantamount to the soul's going, or returning, to the source and thus transcending creation, which is determined by time.

The Western immersion in time and history was one of the objects of Eliade's critique of the desacralized world, and the transcendence of time was considered a high achievement characteristic of the archaic man. The Hasidic master combines the two moments of transcendence and return in quite an explicit manner. This is not an exceptional passage, and I could cite hundreds of others to the same effect.[89]

However, one of them requires attention in the context of Eliade's views: In another collection of the Great Maggid there is a teaching arguing that

> one should think that he is as nothing, and he will totally abnegate himself and will think in his prayer only on the *Shekhinah*, and then he will come higher than time, namely in the World of Thought,[90] there everything is equal, life and death, sea and land…in order to come to the world of that, there everything is equal…and how shall he come higher than temporality, that there is the absolute union.[91]

Here the ascent over time and temporality is related to some form of *coincidentia oppositorum* on the one hand, and to some form of totality referred to as "absolute union" on the other. In this case, it is not a scholar's interpretation projected on a text but rather explicit phrases.

Hasidism became one of the most active powers in the history of Judaism since 1780, and their views permeated parts of different provinces in the north of Greater Romania. Hasidism was not a sect remote from Eliade, either in time or place. It actually flowered during Eliade's lifetime in the immediate vicinity of places well known to him, namely in the Carpathians, and in three other Romanian new territories— Transylvania, Bukovina, and Maramoresh.

Judaism as Eliade's "Significant Other"

The manner in which the theory of time and history in Judaism was presented in Eliade's brief discussions of Judaism is quite fragmentary, and to a very great extent, nonrepresentative. He hardly hints at major developments, variants, divergences between different views, or similarities between what he chose to represent as an archaic approach to time and Jewish mysticism. This fragmentary and selective approach has to do with a basic methodological assumption as to the compact structure of Judaism versus the compact vision of the archaic. This is a sheer misunderstanding, as it can be seen in the case of Eliade's portrayal of the attitude of the "prophets" toward blood sacrifices, especially in Isaiah 1:11–17, as a total rejection of this Temple ritual,[92] while what is said in Isaiah is that sacrifice (or any other ritual) alone does not suffice except when accompanied by a proper intention. Just one prophet's approach is generalized for all the prophets and implicitly for biblical Judaism, and then for Judaism in general. The fact that an entire branch of Rabbinism deals with the details of sacrifices, and that the circulation of energy as one explanation of the biblical sacrifices is found in innumerable discussions in Kabbalah, as part of a wider phenomenon I call theurgy,[93] is totally ignored by Eliade. Though it differs on other forms of sacrifices known in the Middle East, such as human sacrifices for example, the Hebrew Bible did not oppose other forms of sacrifice. However, reading the cosmic understanding of religion *à la Eliade*, it is easy to imagine Judaism as a whole as standing at the pole opposite to the archaic view of circulation of energy, or locative religion.[94] Though the purpose[s] of the sacrifices in the Bible are not clear—unlike in later forms of Judaism, which offered various rationales—they were eradicated not because of principle, but because of historical-political circumstances, namely the destruction of the Second Temple, and what Eliade presents as Jewish is in fact a Pauline opposition to the validity of commandments that colors the way he portrays the ancient Israelites.

By throwing into relief just one aspect of a complex phenomenon and ignoring or neglecting many others, Eliade constructs stark polarities and supposes a historical development of religion that has very little to do with facts. He reiterates this representation with no attempt to update his understanding of Judaism as an evolving religion that enriched itself over centuries, and ignoring aspects of living Judaism that could affect his analyses.

This is quite a selective approach, which I attribute not so much to an anti-Judaic propensity, namely as rejecting the opposite pole of his preferred religion, but to Eliade's stopping quite early on to update this religion. Judaism remained antithetic to the sort of religion he forged and disseminated. Eliade could easily have had access to many of Gershom Scholem's studies, which were published together with his own studies in the various tomes of the *Eranos Jahrbuch*, as we shall see in the next chapter. For him, Judaism remained practically the same as he imagined it was in the Hebrew Bible, at least implicitly, from the phenomenological point of view, just as the Romanian peasant was understood as an ahistorical being, perpetuating a form of spirituality from hoary antiquity to the present, as we shall see in ch. 8.[95]

Eliade adopted the approach formulated by Nae Ionescu as to the existence of "immutable" religious essences,[96] which distinguishes sharply, for example, even between Orthodox Romanian Christianity and the Russian form, or between Catholicism and Orthodoxy, not to mention between Judaism and Christianity, as discussed in ch. 6. Those are examples of what Sorin Antohi called "ethnic ontologies," whose sources are found in 19th-century German Romanticism.[97] Uninterested in history as Eliade intellectually was, he also assumed that the religious phenomena he analyzed did not change in history. In fact, Eliade built too much on scant material that is rather difficult to understand, while ignoring religious material that is found in abundance, and could apply to a different type of history of religion, even using his own distinctions.

In other words, just as, during the thirties, significant segments of the Romanian elites,[98] political, religious, and cultural, were obsessed with Jews and Judaism, as we shall see in some detail in chs. 6 and 7, so, too, was Eliade's phenomenology of religion shaped *vis-à-vis* what he envisioned to be Judaism. His vision or stereotype of contemporary Romanian Jews contributed something to the manner in which he understood ancient Judaism, and he construed the history of religion as a struggle between the ahistorical-cosmic archaic mentality, which was basically Romanian, as we shall see in more detail in ch. 8, and the historically oriented Judeo-Christian tradition and its modern avatars.

Notes

1. I, p. 138.
2. See, e.g., ibid., I, pp. 283–284, from early 1945. For the evolution of the text of *The Myth of the Eternal Return*, see Mac Linscott Ricketts, "Mircea Eliade and the *Terror of History*," in Gligor, ed., *Mircea Eliade*, pp. 35–65; Bordaş, "Time, History and Soteriology," pp. 41–51; and Ginzburg, "Mircea Eliade's Ambivalent Legacy." For a review of the book by a scholar of Jewish studies, see R. J. Z. Werblowsjy in *Journal of Jewish Studies*, VI (1955), pp. 175–177.
3. See his *Mircea Eliade*, p. 211; id., *Romanian Studies*, I, p. 339. On the pre–World War sources of Eliade's escape from history, see also Balázs Trencsényi, *The Politics of "National Character": A Study in Interwar East European Thought* (London–New York, 2011), pp. 1–2.
4. *Solilocvii*, pp. 77–78. On the stark opposition between the "Judaic" and the Hindu as two reified approaches, see also Robert C. Zaehner, *At Sundry Times: An Essay on the Comparison of Religions* (London, 1958), pp. 14–16, 171–173.
5. *Solilocvii*, p. 60.
6. *History of Religious Ideas*, III, p. 80.
7. WWI.
8. *Unedited Short Stories*, p. 192. See also the passage from *Portugal Journal*, I, p. 235, quoted in the previous chapter.
9. *Portugal Journal*, pp. 221, 223, 228.
10. See Allen, *Myth and Religion*, pp. 305, 328 n. 27, 28.
11. See the critique by Raffaele Pettazzoni of Eliade's escape from history, as related to Hindu sources and personal vicissitudes, in Spineto, *Eliade-Pettazzoni*, p. 70, and Olender, *Race sans histoire*, p. 172.
12. See Eliade, *50 Conferences*, pp. 248–252.
13. Ibid., pp. 263–267.
14. (Paris, 1935) reprinted in *The Way to the Center*, pp. 184–197.
15. *Revista Fundaţiilor Regale*, IV, 3, 1937, Bucharest, pp. 657–661. The quote is on p. 661.
16. (Geuthner, Paris, 1937).
17. Printed originally in *Revista Fundaţiilor Regale*, IV (Noiembrie 1937), pp. 421–426 and reprinted in *The Way to the Center*, pp. 225–231. See also his *The Myth of the Eternal Return*, p. 108 n. 5.
18. *The Way to the Center*, p. 228.
19. He probably refers to the goddess Anat, mentioned in the Elephantine papyri.
20. *The Way to the Center*, p. 229. Emphases in the original.

21. Ibid., p. 229. For the context of these phrases, see immediately below.
22. Ibid., p. 231.
23. Interestingly enough, in the same year, 1937, Nae Ionescu published an essay entitled "Nationalism and Orthodoxy" in which he mentions that "a nation as an historical reality is the consequence of the original sin by which history started, by means of which we have fallen in history." *The Suffering of the White Race*, p. 255. Interestingly enough, national existence is conceived of as a fallen type of existence.
24. *The Way to the Center*, p. 229.
25. See ibid., p. 228.
26. Ibid.
27. Ibid., p. 229. Emphases in the original.
28. Ibid., p. 230. Emphases in the original.
29. Italics in the original. See also below in this passage the occurrence of the peasants.
30. Ibid., p. 229.
31. Ibid.
32. Ibid., p. 230. For more on orgies, see below, Final Remarks.
33. On this issue, see more below and in ch. 8.
34. *The Way to the Center*, p. 229.
35. *Rupere de nivel*. Elsewhere in this essay, at p. 230, Eliade uses this phrase in a positive manner to describe the revelation of God. See also his commentary on *Master Manole*, pp. 103–104.
36. *The Way to the Center*, p. 231. The Romanian formulations in this passage are a little bit obscure.
37. See also Eliade, *Patterns in Comparative Religion*, pp. 4, 74.
38. See his Hebrew monumental *Toledot ha-'Emunah ha-Yisraelit* (Jerusalem–Tel Aviv, 1960), 6 vols.
39. *The Way to the Center*, pp. 495–496, 500–503, 505–507.
40. This is a right-wing newspaper, and the stories published there constitute the most anti-Jewish texts by Eliade, who later claimed that they do not represent his own opinion, but rather a response to questions he was asked.
41. Sebastian, *Journal*, p. 114.
42. On peasants, see more above and below in this chapter, and in ch. 8, below.
43. Eliade, *Autobiography*, p. 204: In its original French it sounds a little bit different. See *Mircea Eliade, Memoire I, 1907–1937* (Paris, 1980), p. 288. See also ibid., pp. 202–204. See also below, ch. 8.
44. "Between Culture and Alphabet," reprinted in *Master Manole*, p. 201.
45. See "Culture," ibid., pp. 198–199, and "Between Culture and Alphabet," ibid., p. 202. I assume that the emergence of this epitheton has to do with Georges Dumezil, who published in 1929 an essay on centaurs at Geuthner in Paris, and was the editor who was sending to Eliade the books on Orientalism he reviewed.
46. "Culture," ibid., p. 199. On organicity, see below, ch. 8.
47. "Romanian Realities," ibid., pp. 272–273.
48. *Romanian Prophetism*, II, p. 84.
49. Ibid.
50. Ibid., p. 86. On this passage see also Volovici, *Nationalist Ideology*, p. 122; Oișteanu, *Inventing the Jew*, p. 16; and Mutti, *Les plumes de l'archange*, pp. 84–85. Eliade does not remember what

he himself wrote about the Romanians who expelled Gaster, and his generous bequest of the most important collection of Romanian culture to the Romanian academy. See his piece reprinted in Eliade, *Master Manole*, pp. 306–307.

51. For Eliade as constantly collapsing a major distinction, see Smith, *To Take Place*, pp. 15–16.

52. On Romanianism, see Ricketts, *Romanian Roots*, II, pp. 903–912. For more on these issues, see below chs. 7–8.

53. *The Myth of the Eternal Return*, p. 108 note 5.

54. Ibid. See also *Aspects du mythe*, p. 209, and Dubuisson, *Mythologies*, p. 206.

55. *The Myth of the Eternal Return*, pp. 103–104. On the violence of prophets see Dubuisson, *Mythologies*, p. 292 notes 83, 95.

56. *The Myth of the Eternal Return*, p. 107.

57. See ibid., passim. The question is not so much the repetition of the same ideas and bibliography, but the lack of updating and rethinking that are so obvious in those instances.

58. *The Myth of Eternal Return*, p. 105. See also his *Myths, Dreams, and Mysteries*, pp. 141–143, 149–150.

59. See, e.g., *The Myth of the Eternal Return*, p. 95; id., *Images and Symbols*, pp. 168–170; id., *History of Religious Ideas*, I, pp. 355–356.

60. See, e.g., Vulcănescu, *Mitologie Romăna*, pp. 19–20. Let me point out that an interesting take on Eliade's view in *The Myth of the Eternal Return*, which is much less dichotomic, was proposed by Ionesco, *Present Past*, p. 140. For a nexus between anti-historicism and anti-Judaism, see Berger, "Mircea Eliade: Romanian Fascism," pp. 68–69.

61. On the cyclical view of history in the Bible, see G. W. Trompf, *The Idea of Recurrence in Western Thought: From Antiquity to the Renaissance* (Berkeley, 1979), pp. 138–139, 156ff; and John Briggs Curtis, "A Suggested Interpretation of the Biblical Philosophy of History," *Hebrew Union College Annual*, XXXIV (1963), pp. 117–123, in which the author, notwithstanding his interesting point, exaggerates when he attempts to over-emphasize the cyclical concept of history by relegating the linear concept to the margin. See also Yerushalmi, *Zakhor*, pp. 120–121 n. 7. On the circular nature of the Jewish festivals in the context of the Eliadean narrative, see Moshe Greenberg, *On the Bible and Judaism* (Tel Aviv, 1984), pp. 161–167 (Hebrew), and Benjamin Uffenheimer, "Myth and Reality in Ancient Israel" in *The Origins and Diversity of Axial Age Civilization*, ed. S. N. Eisenstadt (Albany, 1986), pp. 152–156.

62. Id., *Zakhor*, pp. 6–7, 52. See also p. 92, where he explicitly rejects an essentialist vision of Judaism.

63. Ibid., pp. 86, 98.

64. For a general assessment of the reasons for the emergence of Jewish historical writings in the 16th century, see Reuven Bonfil, "The Historian's Perception of the Jews in the Italian Renaissance," *Revue des études juives*, 143 (1984), pp. 59–82; id., "How Golden Was the Age of the Renaissance in Jewish Historiography," *Essential Papers on Jewish Culture in Renaissance and Baroque Italy*, ed. David Ruderman (New York, 1992), pp. 219–250.

65. Arnaldo Momigliano, "Persian Historiography, Greek Historiography, and Jewish Historiography," *The Classical Foundations of Modern Historiography* (Berkeley, 1990), p. 23, and the remarks by Robert Chazan from "The Timebound and the Timeless: Medieval Jewish Narration of Events," *History & Memory*, 6, 1 (1994), pp. 31–32.

66. See Idel, *Old Worlds, New Mirrors*, pp. 19–20.

67. See *Major Trends*, p. 20, in a passage quoted in the next chapter.

68. On different understandings of time in various forms of Judaism, see Sylvie-Anne Goldberg, *La Clepsydre, Essai sur la pluralité des temps dans le judaisme* (Paris, 2001), and her *La Clepsydre, Temps des Jerusalem, Temps de Babylone* (Paris, 2004). See my "Sabbath: On Concepts of Time in Jewish Mysticism," in *Sabbath: Idea, History, Reality*, ed. Gerald Blidstein, (Beer Sheva, 2004), pp. 57–93, and "Some Concepts of Time."

69. See his *The Myth of the Eternal Return*, pp. 104, 117; id., *The Sacred and the Profane*, pp. 110–111.

70. Cf., e.g., the Midrash *Ecclesiastes Rabba* 12:10.

71. See Idel, "Some Concepts of Time," pp. 168–169, and id., *Messianic Mystics*, pp. 159–160.

72. This is the case of the *Book of Bahir* and in Nahmanidean Kabbalah.

73. See *The Myth of the Eternal Return*, p. 89 n. 59.

74. Ibid., p. 127.

75. The Hebrew term is *Hanhagah*.

76. *Gilgulei zemanenu*. This is a pun on the term *galgalei*, spheres, which appears immediately below.

77. Note the explicit astral reference: The celestial world serves as a visible map that enables one to read, symbolically, its invisible counterpart.

78. *Sefer Tefillah le-Moshe* (Premislany, 1892), fol. 190a, discussed also in Idel, "Some Concepts of Time," pp. 162–165.

79. See Bracha Sack, *The Kabbalah of Rabbi Moshe Cordovero* (Beer Sheva, 1995), pp. 267–278 (Hebrew).

80. See Smith, *Map Is Not Territory*, pp. 104–128, where a description of Judaism as both locative and utopian is found.

81. *Patterns in Comparative Religion*, p. 402.

82. *The Myth of Eternal Return*, p. 104.

83. *Zakhor*, p. 8.

84. See "Capricorn," p. 211. He referred to this in a different formulation in a lecture on exile he gave in Paris in 1948. See Mezdrea, ed., *Nae Ionescu and His Disciples*, p. 56.

85. See, e.g., *The Myth of the Eternal Return*, pp. 79, 150; id., *Images and Symbols*, pp. 22, 57, 60; id., *The Sacred and the Profane*, p. 109 n. 15; Olson, *The Theology and Philosophy*, pp. 150–152. See Eliade's interesting reflections on Platonic anamnesis and the archaic man in *Aspects du mythe*, pp. 147–155. See *Phaidon*, 75e, *Phaedrus*, 249b–250b, and *Menon*, 81cd. On the reverberation of Platonic anamnesis in Neoplatonism and then in the Middle Ages, see Gregory Shaw, *Theurgy and the Soul: The Platonism of Iamblichus* (University Park, 1995), pp. 24, 164, 175, 194, 201. To judge from a perusal of Mary Carruthers's books on memory, anamnesis was not a widespread vision in the Latin Middle Ages. The ascent or return to the source by anamnesis is found in several Kabbalistic sources since the early 14th century. See, for the time being, M. Idel, "Remembering and Forgetting as Redemption and Exile in Early Hasidism," in *Arbeit am Gedächtnis für Aleida Assmann*, ed. Michael C. Frank–Gabriele Rippl (München, 2007), pp. 111–129.

86. Basically, a term for divinity.

87. This is a standard Rabbinic unit of measure used to describe gigantic beings.

88. *Sefer 'Or ha-'Emmet*, rpt. (Benei Beraq, 1967), fol. 7d.

89. See, e.g., the Great Maggid's collection of sermons *Maggid Devarav le-Ya'aqov*, ed. R. Shatz-Uffenheimer, 2nd ed. (Jerusalem, 1990), pp. 116, 123, 149, 234.

90. This is a supernal layer of reality identical with the *sefirah Hokhmah* and with the supernal *hyle*.

91. *Maggid Devarav le-Ya'aqov*, p. 186.

92. *Myths, Dreams, and Mysteries*, pp. 141–142. See also *The Sacred and the Profane*, p. 103.

93. See Idel, *Kabbalah: New Perspectives*, pp. 173–199; id., "From Structure to Performance: On the Divine Body and Human Action in the Kabbalah," *Mishqafayim*, 32 (1998), pp. 3–6 (Hebrew); id., *Absorbing Perfections*, pp. 3, 13, 31, 60, 67, 73–74, etc.; id., *Ascensions on High*, pp. 7, 11, 16–18, 68, 114–115, 120–121, etc.; id., *Enchanted Chains: Techniques and Rituals in Jewish Mysticism* (Los Angeles, 2005), pp. 33–34, 47; as well as Charles Mopsik, *Les Grands textes de la Cabale, Les rites qui font Dieu* (Lagrasse, 1993); Yair Lorberbaum, *Image of God, Halakhah and Aggada* (Tel Aviv, 2004) (Hebrew); Jonathan Garb, *Manifestations of Power in Jewish Mysticism* (Jerusalem, 2005) (Hebrew); Elliot Wolfson, "Mystical-Theurgical Dimensions of Prayer in *Sefer ha-Rimmon*," *Approaches to Judaism in Medieval Times*, III (1988), pp. 41–80. Compare to the understanding of the sacred as created by the ritual, including sacrifice, in Smith, *To Take Place*, pp. 104–105.

94. See also his discussion of the sacrifice of Isaac, which Eliade presents as if it abolished sacrifice, when in fact the sacrifice in itself was not rejected, but substituted by another sacrifice, that of an animal. Cf. *The Myth of the Eternal Return*, pp. 100–111.

95. Though Eliade writes the opposite in "Cosmic Religion," p. 98, namely that Judaism was not fossilized because of Kabbalah; the question is, was it fossilized before the emergence of Kabbalah in the late 12th century?

96. *Lectures on the Philosophy of Religion*, pp. 30, 209. On the static nature of Ionescu's approach, see Dancă, *Definitio Sacri*, p. 64 n. 96. The immutability of the nation was also accepted by Ionescu's disciple Mircea Vulcănescu, and it had an impact on Ionescu's *Preface* to Sebastian's novel, discussed in ch. 6, below.

97. Sorin Antohi, "Romania and the Balkans: From Geocultural Bovarism to Ethnic Ontology," *Tr@nsit online* (*Europaische Revue*), 21 (2002).

98. See Volovici, *Nationalist Ideology*, p. 75: "the Jew as an antithetic term."

· 5 ·

ELIADE AND KABBALAH

Kabbalah in Interwar Bucharest

A survey of the main analyses of Eliade's religious outlook would hardly discern the possibility that the young Eliade had some knowledge of Kabbalah, and even less that it might have had some formative impact on his thought. In fact, the very decision to address the topic may easily be seen as tainted by the professional specialization of the present writer, rather than by the any significance this topic held for Eliade. After all, what can be the significance of the content of this esoteric lore for a Romanian nationalist, or a Christian Orthodox believer, or a pagan, as he defined himself in various places, flowering in frivolous interwar Bucharest? Neither do his memoirs from Portugal, Paris, or Chicago mention any sustained interest in this lore. Though in the third volume of his *History of Religious Ideas* there are several paragraphs on Kabbalah, this is at quite a late stage of his activity, and it is almost totally dependent on the historiography and phenomenology as articulated in Gershom Scholem's books: that is, just derivative repetitions of what any intelligent reader can find in published studies by the master of this field. Also, the theory that spending months in the company of Scholem at the Eranos conferences in Ascona, listening to his lectures and reading his studies and those of others published in several volumes of *Eranos Jahrbuch* over almost two decades, imparted in

Eliade a certain acquaintance with Kabbalah is implausible, given the almost total absence of references to Scholem's lectures. In fact, the few references in Eliade's discussions to Kabbalah, found solely in writings from late in his career, were adduced by Steven Wasserstrom, the only scholar who dealt with Eliade using the same framework for Scholem's thought, and they are rather scant.[1] In the case of many of Eliade's other studies from the second phase of his activities, this lore was not mentioned at all. It seems, therefore, that Kabbalah was such a tiny topic among the thousands of discussions dealing with so many other forms of religiosity that it would hardly help understanding his views.

However, in my opinion, this is quite a superficial understanding of Eliade's background and thought. What seems to have been a more secure moment in his life to have some form of knowledge, the Eranos encounters, hardly yields even a secondary association. When a closer examination of his earlier writings, mostly in Romanian, is undertaken, the picture changes significantly. *Prima facie* this is a paradoxical situation: In interwar Bucharest, during a relatively secular period of his life in one of the most frivolous cities in Europe, a scholar who adhered for important and formative years to the ideology of the anti-Semitic Iron Guard can hardly be considered a plausible candidate for reading Kabbalistic material.[2] However, there is quite explicit evidence that several individuals from Eliade's immediate circle in Romania had an acquaintance with Kabbalah: Nae Ionescu, in his public lectures; one of Eliade's high school friends, Marcel/Mihail Avramescu; an older good friend of Eliade, Vasile Voiculescu, in his earlier studies; and perhaps even in Eugène Ionesco, while in Romania.[3]

As is well known, in the first decades of the 20th century Romania became more and more under the influence of French culture. Romanian intellectuals studied in France, including some important figures in Eliade's circle. In the generation preceding Eliade, this was true of Alexandru Bogdan-Piteşti (d. 1922), an avantgarde, very picturesque and controversial figure who was associated with the esotericist Joséphin Péladan, whom he brought for some lectures to Bucharest. The later was the founder, together with Gérard Encausse, better known as Papus, of the Kabbalistic Rosicrucian Freemason Order in Paris at the end of the 19th century. At least one conspicuous case is evident, that of Benjamin Fondane, who was acquainted with Kabbalah while in Romania, as the series of articles on the history of Kabbalah printed in a Romanian newspaper in 1919 testifies.[4] All this happened when Eliade was in high school. This flux of visits created a strong cultural exchange between France and Bucharest—in both directions—which influenced quite significantly Eliade and his generation. Kabbalah became *en vogue* in France as a result of the books of Adolphe Franck, Eliphas Levi, Papus, Jean de Pauly, and Paul Vulliaud, which most probably made their way to some layers of Romanian elite,[5] as I learned from the oral testimonies of persons living today about what they know concerning their parents' reading, and this reading was not limited to Jews. In my opinion, it is possible to show that Eliade was one of those who read books on Kabbalah in translation, around 1923–1925, and was influenced by their content. He was well aware and sometimes critical of this import of theosophy from France.[6]

Our short detour, which could easily become the subject matter of a full-fledged book, shows that Eliade's interest was not an exceptional case in the cultural landscape of the Bucharest of his lifetime, though the precocity of such an interest should be highlighted as unusual. It also shows that we should not assume that political attitudes, and even religious ones, are actually deterring some intellectuals from attempting to learn something about Kabbalah. This is even more pertinent in the case of the early Eliade, whose attitude to Jews was much less tainted with anti-Semitism than many of his contemporaries.

Early Eliade and Kabbalah

Let us turn to references to Kabbalah in Eliade's own writings. In his last year of high school he was encouraged by his teacher of Latin, Nicodim or Nedelea Locusteanu, a renowned classicist, to study ancient languages. He recommended that the young student start with Hebrew, and Eliade indidates that he indeed tried seriously to do so.[7] At least one page of Eliade's exercises in Hebrew characters, which should be dated sometime soon after January 1922, is extant.[8] The context of the teacher's recommendation was related to the ability to study Kabbalah: "Locusteanu assured me that that there were Cabalistic texts of considerable importance."[9] Eliade confesses that he indeed did read Kabbalistic books in "translation," but he did not find them interesting.[10] Such an early preoccupation with Kabbalah is mentioned also by one of his acquaintances, Barbu Brezianu.[11] I do not want to contradict what Eliade had to say about his attitude to the texts of Kabbalah decades after he read them in translation, but it is exactly in the same period, in 1925, namely the end of the high school, that Eliade became involved in a small disagreement with a Jewish colleague called Solomon Israelovici, who was very skeptical about the value of mysticism or esotericism as a reliable source for scientific cognition.[12] In his response Eliade displays a wide acquaintance with a variety of sources dealing with magic and parapsychology, but for our purposes it is pertinent to emphasize that Eliade answered his colleague by referencing a passage from the book of the *Zohar*, which he believes to be a very ancient text, which contains the heliocentric theory of Copernicus. Let me translate what may be the first direct reference to Kabbalah, and a quite positive one, in Eliade's own writings:

And in the Hebrew magical[13] book Zohar, pericope Vayikra, the discovery of Copernicus is found, anticipated by some twelve centuries. Behold what is written in the Zohar: "And in the book of Rabbi Hamnuna the Old it is explained at large that the entire earth is turning around itself as in a wheel . . ."[14] And it is known that the Zohar is of Assyrian origin and that the Assyrian science has been inherited from the Summer-Akkadians, which precedes Jesus-Christ by forty centuries.[15]

This passage is written in quite a serious tone, by a very curious adolescent who appears to be convinced of the scientific validity of a certain cosmology found in the main book of Kabbalah, and he accepted its antiquity. In fact, the alleged consonance between the Zohar, the Assyrians, and the Summer-Akkadians brings the young Eliade to the verge of Western esotericism, which assumes the correctness of traditions of hoary antiquity, perhaps under the influence of Locusteanu's esotericism or the books he gave to his students. Thus, despite his later reticence about Kabbalah as it was formulated in his Autobiography, we may discern the existence of at least one significant instance according to which Kabbalah may contribute quite a significant piece of information.

What those books of Kabbalah read in "translation" were is hard to find out from Eliade's Autobiography, but we may very plausibly deduce it from some discussions later in his life that were analyzed above in ch. 2. However, let me survey a more general development that possibly inspired Eliade's reading of books of Kabbalah in "translation." With this term Eliade does not refer, in my opinion, to books of Kabbalah translated into Romanian, since to my best knowledge there were none, but to books translated into French.

In sharp contradiction to the above assessment that he did not find an interest in Kabbalah, he wrote elsewhere that his reading of the two voluminous tomes of Paul Vulliaud's La Kabbalah Juive marked his adolescence in a powerful manner.[16] Interestingly enough, a certain Dr. King, who demonstrated his miraculous powers in a session that took place in 1922 in Eliade's high school, wrote an astrological booklet entitled "The Hindu Kabbalah."[17]

In a piece describing King's demonstration written when he was 18, Eliade refers also to a series of occultists, some of whom were related to Kabbalah, such as Eliphas Levi and Madame Blavatsky.[18] A year later, he published a short survey on the Song of Songs, some form of Urzelle of the essay he published later in 1938 which I discussed in ch. 2, where he already refers succinctly to two books of Paul Vulliaud on Kabbalah.[19]

In 1925, in an important piece on Giovanni Papini, one of his most important heroes, Eliade claims that "there is no one who can stop us believing that the practices of Kabbalah of inverting the letters of the words has not been applied on a large scale in the alchemical writings. Even more so since there are texts that recommend fathoming the true meaning of the sacred deeds."[20] In 1928 Eliade twice mentions Kabbalah in discussions of the magic of names, together with other forms of mysticism.[21] Nota bene: the magical nature of Kabbalah in Eliade's eyes, which is consonant with the magical penchant in his earlier phase.

In 1927 Eliade describes the "theosophy of the illumination as coming close to Kabbalah, especially the cosmic visions and the correspondences between man and the universe."[22] This issue of correspondence is strongly related to the magical vision of the universe embraced by Eliade, as seen in the Introduction. In 1928 he mentions the magical power of works in the Bible and in Kabbalah, together with the occurrence of such an approach in a variety of other traditions.[23]

Much more important is Eliade's masters thesis submitted in the same year, entitled *Contributions to the Philosophy of the Renaissance*, where he several times mentions Kabbalah,[24] including in reference to a book in Italian by Umberto Cassuto on the Jews in Renaissance Florence, where Kabbalah is mentioned many times.[25] He describes also the thought of the 16th-century Jewish thinker Yehudah Abrabanel—alias Leone Ebreo—which he considers mystical under the influence of what he calls Alexandrian thought.[26] No intimate acquaintance with Kabbalistic thought is displayed in those brief references, though Eliade claims that the number of the Jewish learned people in Florence was impressive,[27] and that he will not dwell upon the "Jewish Kabbalists who contributed no small amount to the creation of the atmosphere of tenebrous mysticism and fantastic mysticism of the Renaissance."[28] Interestingly enough, following James Frazer, Eliade also claims, in a manner adumbrating Frances A. Yates's famous thesis, that premodern technology emerges out of Renaissance magic, in a context where Kabbalah is also mentioned.[29] What Eliade admired especially is Giovanni Pico della Mirandola's synthesis of occult philosophy.[30] Eliade quotes *De auditu Kabbalistico*, a widespread spurious treatise composed in the Renaissance and attributed to Ramon Lull, as if it were an authentic book of the Catalan thinker.[31] Interestingly enough, Eliade's general vision of the Renaissance is influenced by Nae Ionescu's emphasis on the anthropocentrism of the period.[32] Just as in his later writings, in Eliade's earlier writings the term "Kabbalah" is used without its negative connotations of intrigue or machination, especially as related to Freemasonry, as it is found in many European sources and in Romanian anti-Semitic literature.[33] In 1937 he refers to a view of the Kabbalist R. Bahya ben Asher dealing with the principle of the existence of sexual polarities in the different realms of reality.[34]

In general, it should be pointed out that Eliade was more favorably inclined to Kabbalah than to most of the other forms of Judaism.[35] This survey shows that Eliade was acquainted with Christian Kabbalah, as Wasserstrom claimed and Natale Spineto denied.[36]

Kabbalah as a "Cosmic" Religion

More than reflecting a new theological innovation, Eliade emphasized a new relationship to nature. This is why he invented a new phrase, "the cosmic Christianity." To a
certain extent, Eliade continues a trend found in 18th- and 19th-century Western
Esotericism. The cosmicity of his vision of the sacred and the call for a cosmization
of religious life are characteristic of Eliade's terminology and way of thought, by means
of which he understood a variety of religious phenomena, including Kabbalah. In
1965 a collection of five of Scholem's studies in English translation was printed by
Schocken books in New York. Four out of the five were originally delivered as lectures at the Eranos conferences in Ascona. Eliade wrote a review entitled "Cosmic
Religion" that was printed in the New York Jewish conservative journal *Commentary*
in 1966. While reading the book in the summer of 1965, he made the following commentaries in his *Journal*:

> I'm doing the review of Scholem's book on the Kabbalah. As usual, when I'm in a hurry,
> I'm stating, without developing them, a good number of ideas and comments. Some days
> I must return to this theme: in Kabbalah we have to do with a new, real creation of the
> Judaic religious genius, due to the need to recover a part of the cosmic religiosity smoth-
> ered and persecuted as much by the prophets as by the later Talmudic rigorists.[37]

Let us compare the conception inherent in this issue to a characterization of the
Rabbinic ritual in Scholem's book: "What in Rabbinical Judaism separated the Law
from myth? The answer is clear: the dissociation of the Law from cosmic events."[38]
This dissociation of Rabbinism from cosmic life, unlike Kabbalah, helped Eliade in
his cosmic reading of Kabbalah. In fact, his perusal of Scholem did resuscitate the
view of Kabbalah as "cosmic visions," as he formulated it early in his life in his 1927
piece "Spiritual Itinerary," mentioned above. The addition of the rigorist Talmudists
to the ancient repressive Jewish elites has much to do with Scholem's theory about
the repression of myths in Rabbinic thought, expressed in the most stark manner in
this book of Scholem's.[39] The violence of the ancient Jewish elite mentioned in
1937, as discussed in ch. 4, has indeed been eliminated here, but still the Jewish elites
are described as persecutors who suffocate the true natural religion. However, late
in their history, the Jews who invented and accepted Kabbalah returned to "normal-
ity." The medieval rehabilitation of the repressed elements, Eliade claims, restored the
forgotten and forlorn cosmicity.[40] Finally, the Jews returned to the common denominator. Indeed, when reading Scholem's book, Eliade reacted positively to Kabbalah
because "it will be interesting to compare cosmic Christianity that is the belief of the
rural populations of southeastern Europe and of the Mediterranean, with these
medieval and postmedieval Judaic religious creations."[41]

It is, therefore, not the specificity of Kabbalah or its complex theosophical structure that attracted his attention, but, on the contrary, its alleged conformity with the ubiquitous cosmic religion he argued he had discovered. Those statements are part of an effort not to understand the phenomenon, but to insert one more religious phenomenon into the general scheme of the cosmic religiosity that nourishes his rhetorics. The description of Kabbalah as starkly distinct from Rabbinism is reiterated later in the review he published in *Commentary*, as well as in the third volume of the *History of Religious Ideas*;[42] like Johannes Reuchlin, Nae Ionescu, and to a certain extent also Scholem, Eliade regarded Kabbalah as a religion distinct from Rabbinic Judaism.

However, this cosmic understanding of Kabbalah is hardly documented in Eliade's discussions by references to specific Kabbalistic material that would support his claims. What he attributes to Scholem, namely the interpretation of Kabbalah as a whole as a cosmic religion, is a rather problematic sort of exegesis, if we understand the term in the manner Eliade understood it. According to his view, cosmic religion is related to a life in nature, following its changes and cycles, namely a rural type of religiosity, a basically illiterate type of society, living in a world that is rather pantheistic. Kabbalah in all of its forms I am acquainted with has nothing to do with such a view. It is a highly literate religious phenomenon, a view Eliade could easily have gleaned from perusing the major and certainly the longest essay in the book he reviewed, "The Meaning of the Torah in Jewish Mysticism."[43] In other instances Scholem indeed speaks about cosmic cycles, what the Kabbalists call the cyclical units of thousands of years, which I discussed in the previous chapter. However, these units are much more related to the seven or eight divine powers, the *sefirot*, each of which is conceived of as presiding over each of the cycles.[44] Thus, the natural aspects of those relatively few Kabbalists who adopted them were living a type of life that was far from the concept of Eliade's cosmic religion.

A brief but revealing passage dealing with Scholem's studies is found in a lecture Eliade delivered in 1974 and reprinted in his book *Occultism*. When referring to esoteric doctrines and contemporary scholarship, he mentions "the splendid monographs of Gershom Scholem on Kabbalah and Jewish Gnosticism and mystical systems. Scholem's erudition and insight disclosed a very coherent and profound world of meaning in texts that had been generally dismissed as magical and superstition."[45]

The use of the words "magical" and "superstition" should be better understood in terms of Eliade's understanding of these words, which assumes that they contain some form of valid information from the past, obscured by the changes in human mentality, in the manner discussed in the Introduction and in ch. 3. Once again, Kabbalah was judged in accordance with categories found in Eliade's intellectual apparatus. Whether indeed there was one "very coherent[46] and profound world of meaning in the texts," which we may suspect were very close to other cosmic religiosities, is in my opinion a conjecture that is hardly sustained by the way I understand Kabbalah as containing various schools that differ substantially from each other, and coherence is not a characteristic of these vast corpora. Had he read attentively Scholem's influential book *Major Trends*, he could extrapolate, however, that "The cosmic and eschatological trends in Kabbalistic speculation...are in the last resort ways of escaping from history rather than instruments of historical understanding; that is to say, they do not help us to gauge the intrinsic meaning of history."[47]

To be sure, as in quite numerous other occasions, Eliade judges complex types of religious phenomena only on the basis of secondary literature, embracing views which are not always a matter of scholarly consensus. This is done in a hurry, as he confessed in the passage adduced above, and more elaborate conclusions of his own are postponed to a later, in many cases never realized, occasion. Eliade's oeuvre consists, in its vast majority, in his interpretation of the interpretations of other scholars, a reading of mostly secondary literature. This reading is guided by essentialist presuppositions, which are highly selective. His belief in some form of primordial universalism that embraces all the archaic religions was crucial. This is, at the same time, the true alternative to the fallen later religions of modern man as a modern form of *prisca theologia*, or a *philosophia perennis*, as we shall see below. The paradisiacal state in which the first couple was safely living beside the shadow of the two trees in the bliss of nature was halted by a sin that caused the fall, and this nostalgia of paradise is recurrent in Eliade's approach to religion.

Eliade was certainly influenced by the manner in which Scholem described Rabbis as "rigorists" in the book Eliade reviewed:

> hypertrophy of ritual, which became all-pervading...accompanied by no magical action. The rites of remembrance produce no effect...and what they conjure up without the slightest gesture of conjuration is the memory, the community of generations, and the identification of the pious with the experience of the founding generation which received the Revelation. The ritual of Rabbinical Judaism makes nothing happen and transforms nothing...there is something strangely sober and dry about the rites of remembrance with which the Jew calls to mind his unique historical identity.[48]

Both Eliade and Scholem were towering figures in the modern study of religion. Nevertheless, their areas of research were very different. Eliade, an admirer of the Hindu religiosity and archaic mentality, was focusing his academic studies on the mythical side of religion in general, whereas the mystical ones were dealt with only rarely and tangentially. Scholem focused his academic writings on the mysticism of Judaism, and the problem of the myth *per se*, important as it was, was nevertheless only a secondary issue in his dominantly historically oriented description of Jewish mysticism. Though he often used this term in his writings, Scholem did not attempt to construct an independent theory of myth, or a typology of Jewish mythical thought. His assumption was that we all understand what the nature of the mythical phenomenon is, especially if someone is acquainted with Romantic German philosophy as understood by Schelling.

The first time Scholem directly and elaborately addressed the question of myth was as the result of an invitation to Ascona, where the chosen theme was Myth. When dealing with myth in his essay on "Kabbalah and Myth," the issue of mythical rituals was not addressed; that happened only later, in 1950. It seems that this was the first time Scholem introduced the distinction between Rabbinic ritual on the one hand, and the mythical, or Kabbalistic vision of ritual on the other hand. The introduction of the criterion of orgiastic elements in the definition of the real mythical ritual is strange and superfluous in this specific context of Jewish tradition. It is reasonable to suggest that Scholem attempted to adopt categories proposed by Eliade in order to better formulate the difference between the two versions of Judaism. Eliade, for reasons of his own, embraced views connected to the Hindu and Balkan ancient religions.

The conspicuously negative attitude to Rabbinism is especially evident in Scholem's article read at Ascona, and not so much in earlier or even later discussions of these issues. This is the reason why it seems that he adopted Eliade's criterion for the "authentic" religion in order to apply them to Kabbalism, or in order to define Rabbinism in a negative way. To what extent the reticent attitude of Eliade to the Judeo-Christian tradition did influence Scholem's presentation of Rabbinism—which, to be sure, also has many other sources—is a psychological matter which I cannot enter into here. However, it seems to be noteworthy that the two scholars did indeed, separately, revolt against the common version of the religions within which they were born. If for Eliade real Christianity, unlike what he watched in the West, is a cosmic religion to be found in his generation in India, it seems that for Scholem "the heart of Judaism," as he described Kabbalah from time to time, is deeply structured by Gnosticism. In the two cases, the attempt to revolutionize the understanding of religions in general and the understanding of specific religions in particular was motivated by an initial alienation from the form of religions these scholars encountered as their institutionalized religion. Eliade was fascinated by the archaic peasant religions of the Balkans, much more than with the official Orthodox Christianity. The peasant religiosity was reminiscent, in his opinion, of the Hindu cosmic and mythical religion. On the other hand, Scholem was attracted by the anarchic elements of Gnostic extraction, which allegedly served as the main fountain whence the "dry" Rabbinic religion drank in order to become a fertile religiosity. Though these two scholars considered themselves as expressing, in their academic work, the religious genius of their specific religions and cultures, they imported conceptions from outside in order to elucidate the essence of the respective religions.

A certain revolt or antagonism to the modern type of religiosity motivated the iconoclastic approach of both scholars. Though academics, these two scholars not only were concerned with the analysis of the past, but also had some implicit agenda as to the implications of their scholarly activity for the future: Eliade was concerned with what he considered to be the universals of the archaic religion as they surface in tens of religions; nevertheless, his main enthrallment was, constantly, the mythical archaic religiosity. Scholem directed his efforts only toward describing one type of mysticism, constituted of mostly medieval and postmedieval Jewish schools, but he repeated time and again the Gnostic, namely the mythical, substratum of the later developments. It seems that the ambiance of Ascona, both because of the issues discussed there and because of the spiritual concerns of the participants, had contributed in a way to Scholem's decision to discuss the issue of myth and mythical ritual in a phenomenological manner. The attempt to re-evaluate the archaic in order to restore to the modern man the "lost" soul was an implicit though an integral part of the agenda of the group meeting at Ascona; Eliade integrated into this endeavor, Scholem much less so. The revisionist approach of the two scholars was even more radical in comparison to most of the other participants. Though these scholars cannot be defined as followers of Jung in the strict sense of the word, their activity fell under the orbit of the Jungian agenda of the need for a re-evaluation of the role of the irrational as an essential task of the modern approaches.

Eliade and "Universalistic" Syntheses

Scant and brief as these references are, they are important for the manner in which Eliade conceived his intellectual enterprise later on. In his review of Gershom Scholem's book he wrote: "Pico della Mirandola was not only a great scholar, but he was also a good and sincere Christian; surely he knows what he was looking for in learning Hebrew and trying to decipher and master *Magia et Cabbala*."[49] Unfortunately, Eliade decided not to go into too many details about what Pico knew when he studied Hebrew and Kabbalah. In 1964 he similarly wrote of "Renaissance man's longing for a 'primordial revelation' which could include not only Moses and *Cabbala* but also Plato, and first and foremost, the mysterious religions of Egypt and Persia...a longing for a universalistic, transhistorical, mythical' religion."[50] Moreover, in an interview in 1978, the historian of religions once again articulated his excitement at the idea of Christian Kabbalah: "I was equally excited by the fact that Pico knew Ficino's translations of those texts and that he had learned Hebrew, not just in order to understand the Old Testament better, but, above all, in order to understand the Kabbala."[51] Finally, in the last interview he granted, just months before his death in 1986, Eliade reiterated this view of his past nostalgically: "I wanted to add to the understanding of Western culture, to do what [Giovanni] Pico della Mirandola did in the Renaissance, when he learned Hebrew and studied the Cabala...and I thought that one could go even farther down, not stopping at the Cabala and Zarathustra."[52]

Let me turn to Eliade's source in Pico's thought. In his *Theses* he wrote: "Nulla est scientia, que nos magis certificet de diuinitate Cristi, quam magia et cabala."[53] In my opinion, Eliade interprets the intentions of the first Christian Kabbalist in a rather biased manner. Pico was not concerned with a universal revelation or religion, but with strengthening the validity of Christianity by demonstrating that Christian tenets had been advanced already by pre-Christian figures, including, in his opinion, also Kabbalah. His intention was not to transcend the specific limitations of the Christian messages, but to show that it is prefigured in earlier texts, just as Christian theologians imagined that Christianity is prefigured in the Hebrew Bible. Pico was, in my opinion, a special case of missionary thinker, operating with new tools put at his disposal by new corpora made available by translations by Ficino and Flavius Mithridates.[54]

Pico's intention is to point out that the two sorts of lore, Magic and Kabbalah, are not only consonant with Christianity, but also the best way to prove Christ's divinity. Thus, the relation between the two sciences is significant only insofar as they are in concert with the Christian tenet.[55] The correspondence between the two sorts of lore is meaningless in itself if it does not demonstrate the claim of the Christian theologians. If my interpretation is correct, then Pico did not intend to conjugate the two, but rather to subjugate them to Christianity. In other words, in lieu of the horizontal concordance between the two forms of lore recently introduced in Florence, we should better understand Pico's thesis as allowing two vertical forms of correspondences: between Christianity and Kabbalah on the one hand, and between Christianity and Magic on the other. What counts is less the consonance between Cabala and Magia than their independent confirmation of Christianity. In order to strengthen my claim, let me adduce a passage from Pico's *Heptaplus*:

> But because what is said by the Hebrews is new to the Latins, it could not be easily understood by our people unless, hatched from a twin egg, as they say, I explained a great part, or almost the totality of the ancient teachings of the Hebrew dogmas. I decided to post-

pone this until somewhere else I had written about Hebrew dogmas in greater detail and
had made known to my contemporaries these ideas, showing how much these ideas agree
with the Egyptian wisdom, how much with the Platonic philosophy, and how much with
Catholic truth. And, therefore, if I find the Hebrew agree with us in something, I shall order
them to stand by the ancient traditions of their fathers; if I find a place where they disagree,
then drawn up in Catholic legions, I shall make an attack against them. Finally, whatever
I find foreign to the evangelic truth, I shall refute in keeping with my power; while any
principle which is sacred and true, as from a wrongful possessor, I shall transfer from the
Synagogue to us, the legitimate Israelites.[56]

I assume that the dogmas of the ancient Jews that are new for the "Latins" are
the Kabbalistic views, which preoccupied Pico in other writings, too, written earlier in his short career, to which he indeed alludes. From this passage we learn that,
according to Pico, Kabbalah has affinities to a variety of speculative bodies of literature. This view, which indeed has some historical substance to it, may imply that
for Pico this lore had a much more comprehensive spectrum of concepts than others, though this point is not made in an explicit manner. Unlike the view presented
in Pico's thesis mentioned above, it is not magic that invoked as consonant to
those dogmas, but rather Platonism, Egyptian lore, and Christianity. Thus, I
would caution against presenting Pico's main innovation as the yoking of Kabbalah
and magic, and recommend seeing this link as one of many others, which should
not be given special place in the general economy of Pico's thought. The fact that
it was emphasized later on has more to do with the issue of reception, and has to
be dealt with within the domain of questions related to a theory of reception. What
is obvious in the passage from the *Heptaplus* is the reason for Pico's particular concern with Kabbalah: It may confirm Christianity, and in this case the contemporary Jews should be called to adhere to the views of their ancient masters, that is,
to think or behave in a manner more appropriate to Christianity. However, if
Kabbalah disagrees with Christianity, Pico declares that he will attack it. Even In
the third alternative, namely, what he will do in the case where Kabbalah preserves
something sacred that is not found in Christianity, his view is that it should be
taken by force and transferred to Christianity. Jewish Kabbalah is, at least implicitly, usurpation by the Christians of their real heritage: their being the true
Israelites. These, therefore, are the three types of relationship to Kabbalah: critique
if it does not correspond to Christianity; exploitation as a missionary tool if it does
agree with Christianity; and dispossession if it is found to possess something
valuable that is missing in Christianity. Thus, as in the thesis quoted above, the
main criterion of judging a certain speculative corpus is its correspondence not with
other sorts of lore, but with Christian theology.

Let me address now another thesis that will illumine the missionary aspect of Pico's intellectual enterprise. In his fifth Kabbalistic thesis he declares that

> Any Hebrew Kabbalist is compelled, according to the principles of the wisdom of Kabbalah and its dicta, to inevitably acknowledge the Trinity and each of its divine persona: the Father, the Son, and the Holy Spirit, namely what the Catholic faith of the Christians declares precisely, no more and no less, and without any change.[57]

Therefore, Kabbalah is conceived to be the best tool to convince Jews of the correctness of Christian theology. The intransigent tone of the passage is quite explicit. No dialogue with Kabbalah; no change to be expected in Christianity. Eliade, however, operated with another type of Christianity, and with another methodological assumption, namely that there is a basic difference between East and West, which meant that the West should learn something new from a dialogue with the East. Despite his implicit identification with Pico as someone who studied Hebrew in order to know Kabbalah, as he attempted to do in his childhood, their projects are quite different.

However, it seems that Eliade's perspective on Pico was also filtered by later developments. As we have seen above in this chapter and in ch. 2, Eliade was acquainted with Paul Vulliaud's book *La Kabbale juive*, which was a major source for his vision of androgyny and integration. It should be mentioned that this book had an impact on an early figure whose influence on Eliade was considerable, and still needs more elaboration: René Guènon. Indeed, in his unfinished novel *The New Life*, one of the main figures, Tuliu, who reflects to a great extent Eliade himself,[58] mentions *La Kabbale juive* as having been found in his library together with the books of Guènon and Evola.[59] This presence of Vulliaud's book in the work of the two representatives of esotericism is part of the reception of Christian Kabbalah in France and also in Romania. In one way or another, Eliade, like Pico, attempts to dislocate the Jews, regarded as the "significant other." In a way, Pico's Kabbalah—which misunderstood *more Christiano* without even knowing it—represents the positive aspect of the antithetic Judaism of Eliade. The latter was more concerned with Pico's extension of horizon than with the specific contexts of this extension.

The Neglect of Hasidism

A perusal of Eliade's works reveals a rather strange situation: He was unaware of the existence of the most widespread religious phenomenon in Judaism in Romania during his lifetime and some few generations beforehand: Hasidism. Adherents to Hasidism were present in the Romanian territories in at least tens of thousands, and we may assume that Eliade even saw Hasidim when he visited Czernovitz in his school years, and wondered about the scripts in Hebrew and Yiddish on the shops there.[60] His contemporary in Bucharest, the writer Ury Benador, originally from Bukovina, published from 1934 novels and short stories in Romanian in which Sadigura Hasidism and its leaders are mentioned more than once, based on some quite interesting insights. His other contemporary, Eugène Ionesco, made an effort to read Martin Buber's versions of Hasidic tales.[61] Eliade, however, never mentions Hasidism in his writings, except once when quoting one of Buber's Hasidic tales, which he read in a book by Heinrich Zimmer on India.[62] As far as I could check, he never refers directly to the content of Martin Buber's own books, which popularized the concepts of Hasidism and were available in European languages,[63] some of which were known by Fondane/Fundoianu, who wrote about them in a Romanian newspaper.[64] Neither does he refer to Gershom Scholem's chapter on Hasidism in *Major Trends in Jewish Mysticism* except very late in his life (1985), nor does he refer to the views of Joseph Weiss, an eminent scholar of Hasidism who lectured together with Eliade at the Eranos encounter in 1963.

More specifically, I wonder whether Eliade was acquainted with Hasidism as a phenomenon widespread also in some provinces in northern Romania, including some places in the Carpathians, as a mystical revivalist movement that re-enchanted the natural world[65] by spreading some form of pantheistic ways of thought that hallowed also human behavior, inter alia acts of eating and sex, in a manner reminiscent of Eliade's archaic mentality.[66] He could have drawn an interesting parallel between what he considered the most important religious experience of transcending time, as he understood it, and the Hasidic discussions of attaining an experience of "higher than time," as we have seen in the previous chapter.

Moreover, in one of the most important early Hasidic documents there is a description of the founder of Hasidism as climbing a pillar in a rather Shamanic manner, and Shamanism was found in the Carpathians.[67] I am confident that Eliade, whose contribution to the study of Shamanism was outstanding,[68] would have welcomed such a comparative approach, but it is fascinating to see his ignorance of what happened among some of the Jews living in the Carpathians. Thus, what he missed is an awareness of not just one more specific form of Judaism flowering in contemporary Romania, but a spiritual phenomenon that he described as found in ancient times, a paradigmatic approach closer to what he called archaic religion. I do not know whether the Romanian peasants indeed represent a type that is close to what Eliade imagined constituted cosmic Christianity, given the absence of pertinent documentation. However, about the Hasidic leaders, some of whom acted also as wonder-makers in the 18th and 19th centuries, there are hundreds of tales, and in them some of the leaders, *Tzaddiqim*, were described not only as exiting time, as discussed in the previous chapter, but also as performing miracles.[69] In fact, the only religion that can be understood as displaying some of the most interesting characteristics attributed to cosmic Christianity can be discerned in the bosom of a religion that Eliade saw as its opposite phenomenological pole. Though late in his life he became aware of the conjunction between magic and mysticism in Hasidic leaders from Scholem's chapter on Hasidism in *Major Trends*, he was not aware that such a type of leadership was found during his lifetime in, for example, Moldavia and Bukovina, two provinces of Romania, though not only there.[70]

Although he preached so many times about the necessity of Western cultures and religions being open to Eastern religions,[71] Eliade totally ignored what happened in his vicinity in other types of religious communities living in Romanian provinces. Would it not be more edifying to show first a more concrete example of promoting a mutual understanding of the various religious communities in Romania, instead of subscribing to an extremely xenophobic movement like the Iron Guard? As in the tale about a Hasidic Rabbi of Cracow who looked for the treasury hidden in Prague only to learn there that it is actually found in his own house—the only Hasidic story Eliade summarized from a secondhand source, mentioned above—Eliade, too, looked for inspiration in geographically remote India, and in the Carpathian mountains in the archaic times, when he could have learned something about a cosmic Judaism by being open to other religious communities in his own lifetime.

Very often, scholars offering too general and abstract observations or proposals fail to see the most potentially relevant material found in their immediate vicinity, material that in fact invalidates, or at least dramatically qualifies, their more comprehensive theories. Generalizations issued by Eliade are sometimes as simplistic as those formulated by others about Eliade himself, and we shall turn our gaze in the next chapters to the latter.

Notes

1. See *Religion after Religion*, pp. 37–43, 47–51.
2. For a first tentative survey of Kabbalah in Romania in general, see M. Idel, "The Kabbalah in Romania—a Possible Introduction," *Trivium*, IV, 2 (11), (2012), pp. 216–222 (R).
3. These testimonies will be discussed in a separate study.
4. See the reprint in Fundoianu, *Iudaism și Elenism*, pp. 96–122.
5. Tolcea, "From Marcel Avramescu to Father Mihail Avramescu," p. 695.
6. See the piece he wrote in 1928, reprinted in Eliade, *Virility and Askesis*, p. 50.
7. *Autobiography*, p. 85; *Ordeal by Labyrinth*, p. 5; Ricketts, *Romanian Roots*, I, pp. 84–85; Țurcanu, *Mircea Eliade*, pp. 45–46; Tolcea, "From Marcel Avramescu to Father Mihail Avramescu," p. 274.
8. *How I Found the Philosopher's Stone*, p. 647.

9. *Autobiography*, p. 85. This is one more piece of evidence of some acquaintance with Kabbalah in Bucharest in some Romanian circles.

10. Ibid.

11. Handoca, ed., *Interviews with and about Mircea Eliade*, p. 98.

12. For another instance of a discussion between them, when Eliade was much more positive, see Bordaş, "Between the Devil's Waters and the Fall into History," pp. 61–62.

13. The meaning of magical is certainly positive. See above, in the Introduction.

14. This is a rather precise rendition of a passage from *Zohar*, III, fol. 10a.

15. "Science and Occultism," printed in *Vlăstaru*, II, 8–10 (Mai 1925), pp. 29–30, reprinted in *How I Found the Philosopher's Stone*, p. 246. The historical mistakes found in this passage are immaterial for our purpose here, to show that he did relate to Kabbalah positively. On this essay in general, see also Tolcea, *Eliade, the Esotericist*, p. 108, and our discussions in the Introduction.

16. Ţurcanu, *Mircea Eliade*, p. 41.

17. Bordaş, "The Journeys of the Nearsighted Adolescent," II.

18. Compare also to his discussion of cultist authors in his *Occultism*, pp. 49–50.

19. "Cântarea Cântărilor," *Adevărul literar şi artistic*, VII, 24 (Octombrie 1926), p. 4, reprinted in *The Morphology of Religions*, pp. 54–59.

20. Reprinted in *How I Found the Philosopher's Stone*, p. 237.

21. See Eliade, *Virility and Askesis*, pp. 196, 197.

22. See his collection of small pieces published under the title "The Spiritual Itinerary," in *Secret Things*, p. 60.

23. See Eliade, *Virility and Askesis*, pp. 196–197.

24. Printed in ibid., pp. 410, 411, 413, 414, 417, 426.

25. Ibid., p. 410 n. 45, 413 n. 59.

26. Ibid., pp. 426, 430–432.

27. Ibid., p. 411.

28. Ibid., p. 410.

29. Ibid., p. 411. See her *Giordano Bruno and the Hermetic Mysticism*. He refers later to this book in *The Quest*, pp. 38–39.

30. *Virility and Askesis*, p. 417. For more on this, see below.

31. Ibid., p. 426.

32. See Dancă, *Definitio Sacri*, p. 53.

33. See, e.g., the passage adduced by Oişteanu, *Inventing the Jew*, p. 320.

34. *Cosmology and Babylonian Alchemy*, pp. 534–535.

35. See Dubuisson, *Mythologies*, p. 292 n. 88.

36. See "Mircea Eliade and Traditionalism," pp. 81–83.

37. *No Souvenirs*, p. 266.

38. *On the Kabbalah*, p. 94.

39. See, especially, ibid., pp. 98, 121.

40. See, e.g., his reference to the Zohar in *The Forge and the Crucible*, p. 39.

41. *No Souvenirs*, p. 267. Compare also ibid., p. 189.

42. "A Cosmic Religion," p. 96; id., *History of Religious Ideas*, III, pp. 167, 171.

43. *On the Kabbalah*, pp. 32–86. See also in other parts of the collection of studies, e.g., p. 95.

44. On the theory of cosmic cycles in Kabbalah, see Scholem, *Origins of the Kabbalah*, pp. 460–474;

Idel, *Messianic Mystics*, 115–118; Haviva Pedaya, *Nahmanides: Cyclical Time and Holy Text* (Tel-Aviv, 2003) (Hebrew).

45. *Occultism*, pp. 54–55.
46. On coherence in the context of archaic religion, see Eliade, *Images and Symbols*, p. 176.
47. *Major Trends*, p. 20.
48. *On the Kabbalah*, pp. 120–121. On the paradoxical character of this passage in its context, see Harold Bloom, "Scholem: Unhistorical or Jewish Gnosticism," in Harold Bloom, ed., *Gershom Scholem* (New York–New Haven–Philadelphia, 1987), pp. 212–213.
49. "Cosmic Religion," p. 98, and see already Wasserstrom, *Religion after Religion*, p. 43.
50. *The Quest*, p. 38.
51. *Ordeal by Labyrinth*, p. 20.
52. Interview with Delia O'Hara, *Chicago*, 35, 6 (June 1986), pp. 147–151,177–180; quote by Wasserstrom, *Religion after Religion*, p. 43.
53. *Conclusiones Magice*, 9, p. 79; Compare also *Apologia, Opera Omnia*, pp. 167–168; Wirszubski, *Pico della Mirandola*, pp. 123–124. See Yates, *Giordano Bruno*, p. 105. See also Antonella Ansani, "Giovanni Pico della Mirandola's Language of Magic" in *L'Hebreu au Temps de la Renaissance*, ed. I. Zinguer (Leiden, 1992), pp. 89–114.
54. See Wirszubski, *Pico della Mirandola*. On *prisca theologia*, see above, ch. 2.
55. See Yates, *Giordano Bruno*, p. 94.
56. Introduction to Part III, *Heptaplus, or Discourse on the Seven Days of Creation*, tr. J. Brewer McGawn (New York, 1977), pp. 51–52.
57. *Conclusiones*, p. 83.
58. *The New Life*, p. 212.
59. *The New Life*, p. 155, and see Tolcea, *Eliade, the Esotericist*, pp. 207–208, as well as the description of the alleged library of Zerlendi in his novel "The Secret of Dr. Honigberger," in *Two Strange Tales*, pp. 75–76.
60. See Bordaş, "Between the Devil's Waters," p. 52.
61. See below, ch. 7.
62. *Myth, Dreams, and Mysteries*, pp. 244–245. The story is summarized by Eliade from Zimmer. *Myths and Symbols in Indian Art and Civilization*, ed. Joseph Campbell (Princeton, 1974), pp. 219–221, who copied it from Martin Buber.
63. He mentions en passant Buber, but not Hasidism, in *Aspects du Mythe*, p. 121.
64. Fundoianu, *Iudaism si Elenism*, pp. 96–101.
65. On re-enchantment in Hasidism, see Idel, *Hasidism*, pp. 220–221.
66. See *Patterns in Comparative Religion*, p. 32.
67. On early Hasidism as displaying some Shamanic features, see my *Hasidism*, pp. 214, 218, and id., *Ascensions on High*, pp. 143–166, especially pp. 148–150, and id., "Israel Ba'al Shem Tov in the State of Wallachia: Widening the Besht's Cultural Panorama," in *Holy Dissent: Jewish and Christian Mystics in Eastern Europe*, ed. Glenn Dynner (Detroit, 2011), pp. 69–103, for a comparison between a Hasidic passage and an instance of Shamanism in the Carpathian mountains. Compare to Eliade, *Zalmoxis*, pp. 191–203. Interestingly enough, this specific Shamanic phenomenon in the Carpathians is not mentioned in Eliade's earlier and extensive monograph *Shamanism*. For similarities between many Hasidic discussions on trance and Shamanism, see Jonathan Garb, *Shamanic Trance in Modern Kabbalah* (Chicago, 2011).

68. See Leonardo Sacco, "Neo-Sciamenismo & New Age. Il 'Contributo' di Mircea Eliade," *Archaeus*, XI–XII (2007/2008), pp. 249–304.

69. For the use of Eliade's category of *axis mundi* to describe Hasidic leaders, see Arthur Green, "Zaddik as Axis Mundi in Later Judaism," *JAAJR*, 45 (1977), pp. 327–347.

70. See his summary of Scholem in *History of Religious Ideas*, III, pp. 178–180. Neither was Eliade aware of the Hasidic background of Chagall's paintings, which he discussed. See *No Souvenirs*, pp. 187, 218.

71. See, e.g., *Waiting for the Dawn*, pp. 11–12.

A "SHADOW" AMONG RHINOCEROSES

Mihail Sebastian between Ionescu and Eliade

The years of our brotherly friendship,—and then the years of confusion, of breaking—up, up to rupture, to enmity, up to oblivion.
—SEBASTIAN, JOURNAL, DECEMBER 1944

Shifting Currents in Romania of the Thirties of the 20th Century

*T*he first part of the thirties, when Eliade became one of the most prominent Romanian young intellectuals, also witnessed an unprecedented rise in the participation of Jews in Romanian culture, especially in literature written in Romanian. One of them, Mihail Sebastian—the pseudonym of Joseph Hechter—was especially close to the two leading Romanian intellectuals: Nae Ionescu and Mircea Eliade. The publication in mid-1934 of Sebastian's Jewish novel *For Two Thousand Years*, with a very controversial preface of his protector Nae Ionescu, provoked a bitter scandal that was a great surprise for many contemporaries. Ionescu deeply influenced Eliade[1] and Sebastian, and his "Preface" to Sebastian's novel came as a shock first to Sebastian himself, and then to a long series of authors. Eliade was one of the few who took Sebastian's side, at least to a certain extent.

The sharp reactions from the whole gamut of reviewers were unparalleled in Romanian culture, in terms of both the number and the prominence of the participants, and because of the broadly negative, even violent tone in which these reviews were formulated. Though the novel describes unpleasant moments in the anti-Semitic environment in the University of Bucharest during the late twenties, this fact is certainly not the main issue that ignited the bitter controversy. With the exception of Leon Volovici's and Mihai Iovănel's important remarks,[2] the details of the numerous exchanges and the significance of this controversy for understanding the cultural vectors active in Romanian culture have not yet attracted due attention in scholarship. I would say that because of the intellectual status in Romanian society of the participants in the debates, and its amplitude, the literary corpus of this controversy throws light on a microcosm of Romanian culture in the mid-thirties, reflecting some of its major vectors that for several years coexisted and even cooperated fruitfully, and then separated. To be more explicit: Though this controversy changed rather little in the historical or social scenes—despite its quite great prominence in the press— it reflects much of the intellectual and social tensions that were latent and became gradually conspicuous during the period of the controversy.

The main reason for the explosion of the controversy is the fact that in this novel, Sebastian addressed a topic that was then rather sensitive: the issue of a possible new cultural and social identity, one that involved an attachment to Romanian culture without, however, renouncing or rejecting adherence to Judaism. During the five years before the publication of his novel, Sebastian was successful in securing a rather prominent position in the intellectual world of Bucharest, which was almost exclusively male, as well as in the hearts of some of the city's prominent ladies. As a novelist, a literary critic, a political commentator, and a participant in the intellectual life of the Romanian capital (and only later a gifted playwright and translator), the young Sebastian had no parallel among the Jewish intellectuals, even more so since Benjamin Fundoianu had already left Romania. This is the reason why his proposal for a hyphenate identity—and its contemptuous and sharp rejection by his mentor Nae Ionescu—attracted so much attention.

The Religious Moment in Nae Ionescu's "Preface"

Indubitably, without Nae Ionescu's antagonistic "Preface" to Sebastian's novel, there would have been no large-scale scandal; the specific content of the novel would not have created, for example, the theological debate that we shall survey below. It is Ionescu's singular reading of the novel as a futile instant of escaping the Jewish condition—one that is damned forever—and as a potentially open entity that is realized differently by the individuals, which opened the gates of the bitter controversy. A totally secular novel, as Sebastian's indubitably is, was used by Ionescu as a pretext for formulating some new views regarding the nature of the Jews from a strictly Christian religious viewpoint. It is not my purpose here to analyze Nae Ionescu's shift from an earlier relatively more open approach, which included a lecture to the Jewish Women's Organization in Bucharest at Baraşeum and the promotion of some young Jews, including Sebastian himself, in his journal, *Cuvântul*, to the evidently anti-Semitic tenor of the 1934 "Preface."[3] Nor will I address the reasons for such a shift. As Sebastian himself remarked when asked why he had published an anti-Semitic preface, Ionescu had written some clear critiques of Romanian anti-Semitism in the late twenties.[4] Below, I am concerned only with the religious dimension of the "Preface," which represents an abuse of the content of the novel for the sake of promoting Ionescu's religious-nationalist agenda, and then I shall turn to some of the reactions to it.[5]

The considerable use of a dogmatic approach to Judaism is a common denominator of Ionescu's "Preface" and of the arguments of his disciples who argue with him and with each other. They highjacked the problematic of the novel, a Jewish-Gidean approach, in order to clarify or debate an issue that does not occur in the novel itself. The hyphenate identity of the author as a Jew and a Romanian, the main topic of the novel, has been dramatically marginalized and substituted in the "Preface" by a stark contrast between Jews and Christians. An ethnic issue was transformed into a religious one. While Sebastian actually neutralized religion in his proposal for a new identity, most of the disputants strongly identified Christianity with Romanian ethnic identity, creating a position that prevents a Jew from being or becoming Romanian.

From the very beginning let me note that neither Sebastian nor Ionescu are, in my opinion, coherent writers when dealing with the nature of the Jewish people. This is not just a matter of their having developed and changed their positions over several years, but also of inconsistency in their writings from the very same period.[6] However, without recognizing the inner tensions between their respective views, it would be difficult to understand the conflict between their respective positions. I say this as someone who does not expect coherence either from the professor of logic that Ionescu was, or from the more concretely oriented inclination of Sebastian's thought. That Ionescu was disinclined to any systematization of his thought is a commonplace. In the case of the preface, it contradicts one major issue, his earlier view, as Sebastian skillfully pointed out.[7] Sebastian himself was even less interested in a systematic message. His book was intended, as he put it, to be just a call.[8] This claim that one should not insist on a consistent attitude when quite complex issues are dealt with has nothing to do with another claim, found in Sebastian, as to the lack of incompatibility among the Romanians, a negative feature that is tantamount to the lack of a character among some of his colleagues.[9] This lack of incompatibility may be extended to Sebastian himself, as we shall see below. Last but not least, we shall deal with some ideas formulated in a period of swift and fateful changes and the polarization of camps, in which the transition or conversion from one position to another was notorious as some of the members of the group Criterion were converted from communism to the fascist Iron Guard. In these circumstances, consistency and clarity of position are rare product, and scholarship should consider the three types of circumstances in a serious manner.

In a way, both Ionescu and Sebastian were inclined to a form of mythical thought, at least when dealing with the fate of the Jews as a nation. In what does their myth consist? The myth of the ahistorical Jew who does not change, at least since the rejection of Jesus as the redeemer, informs the two authors and some of the participants in the theological debate we shall survey below. When coupled with an ignorance of basics in Judaism, the use of this generalization reflects a superficial intellectual approach, an abstraction to which we shall return below.

Sebastian's effort to secularize the Jewish condition by emphasizing the role of nature in their identity, as seen in the last passage from *For Two Thousand Years*, was flatly rejected by his mentor. Ionescu correctly understood the message of the novel, but he saw it as, practically speaking, impossible. The attempt at evading suffering by a normalization of the status of the Jews, in this case by assuming also a Romanian identity, was seen by Ionescu as a revolt against the divine decision to punish the Jews forever for their denial of the divinity and redemptive role of Jesus Christ. To summarize the main claim of the "Preface," Ionescu insists that the Jews must suffer; this is a theological statement backed, according to him, by the views of the Eastern Christian Church, and it is a situation that will never change. Ionescu adopts an essentialist vision of the Jewish people, as he does with the Romanian people, and both are part of his vision of the "political collective."[10] According to this approach, it is practically impossible to change or to pass from one collective to another, since each individual is defined by the collective to which he belongs, in a natural and final manner. This view, which he had articulated in more general terms around 1928 (Vulcănescu, who took a course with him at that time, described Ionescu's thought as "static naturalism"[11]), namely some years before writing the preface to Sebastian's novel, constitutes one of the main frameworks for his argument in the "Preface."

Also the view that one is what he is and cannot change just because he strives to become something else, a view fundamental to the "Preface," had been formulated no later than 1932.[12] At that time Ionescu spoke about a "categorical incompatibility" between Christians and Jews, which will disappear only when one of the two religions disappears.[13] This is an antithetic approach that was adopted also by Eliade, though in a more moderate version. According to it, Jews stopped being the "chosen people" the moment they refused to recognize Christ as Messiah.[14]

Nevertheless, it should be pointed out that there are two major affinities between the views of the two authors regarding the manner in which they understood the nature of the Jewish people. The novelist writes, "The Jews are a tragic people,"[15] and this tragic character eludes, according to his view, any explanation.[16] It transcends the social or economical persecutions, which are viewed as nourishing the Jewish tragedy, though not explaining it sufficiently.[17] He adopts neither the Zionist vision of a solution to the exile situation in the Palestinian colonies nor a Marxist one,[18] such as the view of Tudor Teodorescu-Branişte, a socialist journalist and novelist to whom we shall return immediately below. Neither was assimilation an option for him.

Yet, what is even more crucial for the affinities between the two writers is the statement found in the novel regarding the Jewish obligation to suffer.[19] Ionescu claims that on this point he agrees with Sebastian,[20] and the latter recognizes that this phrase was the starting point for Ionescu's main thesis in the "Preface" that "Judah must suffer."[21] However, Ionescu criticizes Sebastian because he does not explain the reason of that suffering, and it is that alleged reason to which he dedicated his "Preface." It is hard to know whether Sebastian or Ionescu, when writing what they wrote, were aware of the line Shakespeare gave to Shylock, "For sufferance is the badge of all our tribe," which Sebastian later quotes in a pertinent context in his *Journal* in 1943.[22] In a way, the entire affair, starting with Sebastian's book, is a comment on Shylock's verse.

In summary, in Ionescu's argument in the "Preface" he does not introduce a new approach in his thought, as some of the concepts he discusses were adumbrated earlier in his writings. Nevertheless, not being so systematic a thinker, Sebastian could not discern the strong divergence between his direction in the novel and Ionescu's way of thought, which is based on premises quite different from his. What is new in the "Preface" is the arrangement of some of the motifs in a way that represents a counterpoint to the pursuit of a double identity in Sebastian's novel, which created a challenge and a focus prompted by his divergent view.

Eliade and Theological Dimensions of the Controversy Over the "Preface"

Ionescu's "Preface" was the main trigger for the controversy over the book, yet its literary aspects were by and large ignored. The book and the preface crystallized interests and tendencies that did not find the proper form of expression elsewhere.

However, it should be pointed out that there was a part of the controversy that was less concerned with the novel than with the theological claims of Ionescu. In this smaller controversy, which did not focus on Sebastian's own views, though he was always mentioned, participants included—inter alia—Mircea Eliade, Gheorghe Racoveanu, Tudor Teodorescu-Braniște, Constantin Noica, Mircea Vulcănescu, and finally also Sebastian himself, in his short response that formed part of *How I Became a Hooligan*.[23] Each of them, with the exception of Noica and Sebastian himself, wrote more than one piece on the topic, and we may therefore speak about a modest polemical literature that was produced in the second part of 1934 and during 1935. The basic point of this theological debate was the verdict pronounced by Ionescu that the Jews' suffering will never end because this curse is an irrevocable divine decree, which probably was part of his theory of immutable forms in religion that he formulated as early as 1924–1925.

This stark judgment concerning eternal damnation of the Jews first drew a reaction from Teodorescu-Braniște, and then, in a different manner, from Mircea Eliade. The first expressed a rather Marxist approach that criticized the theological sentence as formulated by Ionescu for not differentiating between the Christian and Jewish proletarians, or between the rich Jews and the Christian ones. For him, it is the sociological distinction, not the theological one, that should be the main criterion for understanding the Jewish problem.[24] This rather sarcastic approach to Ionescu's view attracted the response of Mircea Eliade, whom Teodorescu-Braniște had criticized some years beforehand, just before Eliade left for India.[25] Eliade's response had a threefold intention: to defend Ionescu from Teodorescu-Braniște's Marxist critique and. in general, against the anti-Semitic label that had been attached to the "Preface"; then to defend Sebastian from Ionescu's critique and to praise Sebastian's courage in putting on the table the problematic he had chosen; and, finally, to offend Teodorescu-Braniște without ever mentioning his name.

The gist of Eliade's theological position is that God is a free agent, and one should not preclude the possibility that He may change his will and pardon the Jews sometime in the future. More specifically, Eliade opted for the freedom of the divine grace, a view that rules out the total exclusion of anyone from the possibility of redemption. Courageous as Eliade's defense of Sebastian is, especially if we remember that he served as Ionescu's assistant at the University of Bucharest, the future historian of religions nevertheless did not see the Jews of his day in a light that is dramatically different from Ionescu's approach. They are regarded as damned, though for Eliade there is still some possible hope for them as a nation in the indefinite future, either because a prophetic wave will generate their general conversion to Christianity, or because the divine grace will decide to pardon them arbitrarily. As to their status in the present, Eliade adopts Ionescu's view, though only implicitly. It is an attempt to defend his two acquaintances as much as it is a critique of Ionescu's totally intransigent eschatology concerning the Jews.[26] Eliade takes issue with Ionescu, claiming that he mixed the phenomenological and historical level of discussion with the theological one. The professor of logic is accused of erring by confusing two forms of discourse: the observation that Jews suffer as a historical fact, and the claim that they will suffer forever, which is a theological statement. None of them, including Sebastian, simply states the right diagnosis: Jews suffer because of Christian anti-Semitism.

It is also possible to understand Eliade's dissension from his "Professor" from a point of view other than the theological or deriving from his friendship with Sebastian. At that stage in his life, Eliade himself was not confident that redemption necessarily belongs only to Christianity. In his important letter to the Italian scholar of religion Vittorio Macchioro, written in 1931 while in India, Eliade confesses his religious plight:

> What I however miss is *a sincere and total religious life, a religious experience*. Sometimes I feel that I am "a good Christian," even *an Orthodox one*, but almost my entire life *passes beyond* Christianity....Nevertheless, a thing linked me to the Church—the participation. The participation together with the sacral community, or in the Holy Spirit, or in tradition, I still do not know. However, I feel that without that *collective experience* and miracle, I shall be a *traviato*.[27] My recent dilemma is this: if we can we reach a "neutral equilibrium"[28] in our religious life and hope for redemption only by participation in a spiritual body, then what can we say about the admirable religious will of the nonbelievers? I cannot believe that, because they are not baptized, they are beyond Christ, beyond the true religion. And if everyone can reach this amazing standard without the help of the Christian Church and the Christian teaching, then my conviction as to the sacral participation is either relative or false.[29]

The actual topic of this passage is Maitreyi Devi, the daughter of Eliade's teacher of Sanskrit and Hindu philosophy, S. Dasgupta, whom he describes in the sentence I skipped as more Christian than himself. Eliade was ready to convert to Hinduism in order to marry her.[30] It is obvious that for Eliade, a traditional Hindu woman could be a perfect believer and Christian. Later in this letter he argues that he "started to believe that Christianity *is not the only way*. And if this is so, conversion is useless."[31] Therefore, when defending Sebastian or the Jews, Eliade reiterated a conviction he had about the superiority of the Hindu Maitreyi over himself the Christian.

Eliade's piece was decisive for the emergence of other responses, which turned the discussion away from the Sebastian-Ionescu affair to the Eliade-Ionescu theological dispute. Eliade's approach was criticized immediately by a young Orthodox theologian from Ionescu's circle, Gheorghe (later, George) Racoveanu, who became part of the extreme right group, and he repeatedly derided Eliade's theological competence in matters of Christian Orthodoxy when Eliade observed that the Church does not condemn the Jews for eternity.[32] Racoveanu was, according to Vulcănescu,[33] the closest of Ionescu's disciples, and the sharp critiques he addressed to the other disputants have something to do with the fact that Sebastian depicted him as simpleton Marin Dronțu in *For Two Thousand Years*, but also with his blind and totally uncritical devotion to the Professor.

Another critic of Eliade's article was Tudor Teodorescu-Braniște, who returned to the topic in a sarcastic derision of Eliade's treatment.[34] Eliade responded then to Racoveanu, attempting to provide some textual evidence for his claim about the Patristic literature,[35] and his response was criticized in turn by Racoveanu.[36] Those exchanges revolve around the Christian axiom that Jews suffer because they "are belated on the way of redemption,"[37] and the differences between Eliade's, Vulcănescu's, and Noica's views on one hand, and Ionescu's and Racoveanu's on the other, concern only the question of whether in the future there is hope for the Jews to be redeemed.

Other reactions, quite interesting given their complexities, came from Mircea Vulcanescu, an author with a solid theological background, but he chose not to publish all his reactions in the press, and the most important one remained in manuscript until recently. He reacted on three different occasions to issues related to Sebastian's book, but the most important piece is a lengthy essay written in the form of a letter from the province, and addressed to Mircea Eliade.[38] To a great extent, it constitutes a reaction both to Eliade's critique of Ionescu and to the views of Ionescu himself. Vulcănescu rejects the deterministic vision of Ionescu that denied the possibility of redemption of anyone born Jewish—since they belong irrevocably to a special nation—and assumes that the individual Iosif Hechter may be redeemed by conversion to Christianity.[39] Following Jacques Maritain, Vulcănescu assumes even the possibility of redemption of Satan, a version of Origen's *apokatastasis*.[40]

In a way, the final redemption was postponed in order to allow the possibility of redemption for all.[41] It was Vulcanescu alone among Ionescu's disciples who openly recognized that Ionescu's preface is "neatly anti-Semitic."[42]Let me point out that during the theological debate, it is Vulcănescu alone who argues, paraphrasing a biblical verse,[43] that God punishes the Jews because He loves them.[44] In another piece, Vulcănescu derides Racoveanu's critique of Eliade, pointing out that the claim that there is redemption of the Jews in the Orthodox Church is found in fact in a major analysis of Christian Orthodoxy that Racoveanu had reviewed in quite positive terms.[45]

With the exception of Sebastian and Teodorescu-Branişte, the theological debate was dominated by thinkers who had strong religious, Christian Orthodox allegiances (at least in terms of the way in which the responses were formulated), all participated in right-wing Romanian politics, and all took seriously Ionescu's totalizing theological approach to the Jews as an ahistorical nation. Though some of them— Eliade, Noica, and Vulcănescu—sometimes adopted theological views different than Ionescu's, they nevertheless remained immersed in the problems as formulated by the "Professor," not by Sebastian's novel.

In fact, none of the persons who contributed to the debate took issue with the shocking manner in which Ionescu addressed Sebastian at the very end of the "Preface": "Iosif Hechter, you are sick, you are substantially sick....Iosif Hechter, don't you feel that cold and darkness are seizing you?"[46] The end of the "Preface"—which was quoted again and again in the debates—is indubitably a sarcastic echo of the end of the novel: Whereas in the novel the author qua architect builds for Blidaru—that is, Ionescu—a house that will be replete with light, as seen in the paragraph quoted above, in the "Preface" Ionescu condemns Sebastian to darkness and cold. Just as the beginning of the novel, dealing with the shadow of the Church that splits Sebastian as a boy during the night, is connected to its end by contrast, so is its end connected to the end of the "Preface." The end of the "Preface" intensifies the situation of the beginning of the novel: It is not just a shadow that covers Sebastian, but rather a darkness that will take possession, according to Ionescu, of the Jew Hechter, a darkness that stands for eternal damnation.

Yet, it is not only the complex problem of the novel that was ignored in the "Preface" and the debates around it,[47] but also the feelings of the author, who was part of the circle from which the critiques emanated. It should be pointed out that despite the negative reception of *For Two Thousands Years*, Sebastian considered it the best piece he had written and the one that would endure longest.[48]

The "Preface" demonstrates that the geographic "Greater Romania" did not create a large enough neutral space of discourse where the identities proposed by individuals or minorities—who were, in fact, a numerically significant and rather culturally developed segment of Romania's population, as big as a quarter of the populace—could be discussed seriously. It generated a feeling among some parts of the Romanian elite that I propose to call cultural "megaloromania." Though it is true that there was freedom of expression, that for example Sebastian or the Zionist Jewish press could publish their views freely, this does not mean that their views were of any concern to the Romanian intelligentsia, even when they reflected the condition of an eminent participant in the Romanian cultural activity such as Sebastian. By "neutral space" I do not mean an opportunity for discussion in which the participants might renounce or bracket their religious convictions—the Orthodox convictions of many of the discussants were quite amazing in their naïveté—but there was no openness to any significant diversity in the theological debate. Despite the strong language they used, the actual differences between those who entered the theological debate were quite small. Religiously speaking, most of the intellectuals in Bucharest lived on an ideologically compact planet, developing their views under the aegis of Nae Ionescu, a thinker and spiritual guide who was far from original[49] but cultivated enough to dominate the thought of the younger intellectuals known as the 1927 generation, whose leader was Eliade.

Sebastian's novel represents a significant conceptual departure; its implications for creating a diversified culture ran against the dominant drive to create a homogenized Romanian culture in order to unify Greater Romania, and this is the main reason it was ignored or criticized. In a way, Sebastian's novel was the nemesis of the relative openness of Ionescu during the late twenties and early thirties, when he chose to promote the young Sebastian. Consciously or not, the novel tested the limits of the cultural horizons of the Romanian interwar elites.

Living with Rhinoceros: Sebastian and Nae Ionescu

The publication of Sebastian's *Journal* years ago opened the door for a better and more detailed understanding of Sebastian's attitude toward two of the most important Romanian intellectuals to whom he was especially close: Nae Ionescu and Mircea Eliade. In both cases, Sebastian recognized rather early their affinities to the Iron Guard, and his lucid remarks reflect his understanding of political shifts in their views and of the nefarious role they played in the political scene of the mid-thirties. As mentioned above, he was much less aware of the negative significance of Ionescu's more general essentialist approach to the nation as an organic entity, a view shared by Vulcănescu and Eliade.[50] As Eugène Ionesco pointed out in his letter to Tudor Vianu, Ionescu and Eliade are the two persons mainly responsible for corrupting the younger generation of Romanian intellectuals by drawing them to the side of the Iron Guard after a short period in which some of them adhered to communism.[51] Later, Ionesco described Nae Ionescu in the literary avatar of the logician as the "rhinoceros with a hat."[52] However, in the period until 1936, Ionesco, too, took some university classes with the Professor and spoke of him highly, even when he was well aware of the "Preface."

Undeniable as the fascination with Ionescu was among his disciples, including Sebastian,[53] we should not exaggerate the power of his spell over them. We need, in fact, a much more nuanced picture of the way in which Ionescu's image was transformed in their eyes over time. Though some of them, such as Gheorge Racoveanu, remained totally faithful to the "Professor," others were much less so. To be sure, this suggestion for a more nuanced approach to the image of the Professor does not minimize Ionescu's totally negative influence on the younger generation. His demonization by various people—Vulcănescu, Maruca Cantacuzino, Sebastian, and some others called him the devil, as Georgu Voicu pointed out, while Mariana Şora and Eliade (as Culianu claimed) called him Mephistopheles—or his rhinocerization by Eugène Ionesco[54] should not lead scholars to assume that all his followers had the same impression of him. It does, however, call them to understand the various metamorphoses his image underwent among his followers, and below I shall try to demonstrate the possibility of doing so in the case of Sebastian.

Many of the controversies discussed above display a combination of dogmatism and dilettantism. The fact that the entire controversy is related to a novel, and that it took place almost exclusively in political journals and newspapers, in exchanges that concerned so many and different sides at the same time, also contributed to lowering the level of discussion. In many cases, what counted as much as the content were the style, the sarcasm, and the personal innuendoes. As Sebastian formulated it once, the debates are concerned more with imaginary obsessions than with truth. I wonder whether any of the disputants were made of the stuff of the serious university professor Alexandru Andronic, the protagonist of Sebastian's play *Ultima Oră*. Perhaps it would not be superfluous to read the play as a background on the dispute over his novel.

What I would like to emphasize is that my survey does not concern the matter of the disputants being right or wrong in the specific religious positions they took, but rather of their pretentious speaking in almost complete innocence of basic facts concerning the subject they discuss. This is clear not only in matters of Judaism, but also, at least to a certain extent, in matters of Orthodox Christianity, as Vulcănescu's reaction to Racoveanu's denial of Eliade's theological proposal demonstrated. Though indeed they claim to represent, each in his way, the stance of the Orthodox Christian Church regarding the prospects of the salvation of the Jews, they hardly addressed in the debates issues that relate to Judaism before the emergence of Christianity. In attempting to fathom the possibilities of divine grace for Jews in the eschatological future, the Christian participants do not display much human grace toward them in the present.

Ignorance of many basics in Judaism was also a weakness of Sebastian himself. His knowledge of Jewish history is quite scant, as we learn from his enthusiastic reaction to Simon Dubnow's monumental *History of the Jews*, which he had read by 1939; in 1941 he confessed that he had much to learn from it.[55] In his novel, the vision of the family of the protagonist's mother is, to a great extent, a stereotype of what he believed was Talmudism.[56] The figure of the Jewish bookseller Abraham Sulitzer, though portrayed in warm terms, is nevertheless repeatedly depicted by the cliché of Ahasverus.[57] Thus, as recognized by some of the participants in the debate, Sebastian indeed was an alienated Jew in terms of the access he had to Jewish thought, but he did not want to sever his relation with the suffering minority. According to his own testimony in 1942, after celebrating the Passover Night ritual, he wrote: "Sometimes, it seems to me that our links to Judaism may be redone again."[58] This quite hesitant sentence betrays, though somewhat obliquely, much of Sebastian's self-awareness as, intellectually speaking, an alienated Jew. Unlike statements where he claimed that his Judaism was an irrevocable fact, here it is presented as only a possible option.[59] Sebastian knew little about Judaism, but nevertheless strove to shape a double identity, a utopian and unrealistic ideal in his lifetime.

His major proposal in the novel was to offer a synthesis of Jewish and Romanian values, without however specifying what exactly these respective values were, and even less how the accord between the two may be achieved. The general feeling one gets from reading Sebastian is that his knowledge of Judaism was quite superficial, and that it was meaningful for him as a matter of family nostalgia, and as an identity that a man of honor should not betray under pressure. Judaism in any of its varieties was never described in any detail as a source of specific values, and I am unable to detect in any of his works any reference to values he would like to adopt.

The most I could find in Sebastian's writings is the confession of the author in the novel that he differs from his grandfather in many ways, but he inherited "a melancholy that cannot be healed."[60] This is, however, much more a sensibility than a specific value, and indeed, in his 1935 lecture at the Institute for French Culture in Bucharest, when dealing with the novel he refers in the same context to both national values and sensibilities.[61] If indeed this is all that he confesses he has inherited, it is hard to evaluate how viable a cultural alternative it could become, at least sociologically speaking. Let me point out that melancholy is a theme that recurs in the works of Jewish authors in the interwar period; Franz Kafka is the best-known one. I would say that Sebastian is one in a series of Jewish interwar melancholics, a group I propose to call "the desolates," whose great literary achievements were put into relief in some of George Steiner's studies.[62] Sebastian is spiritually close to them, both because of his strong European affinity from the cultural point of view, and because of his chronic loneliness and desolation.[63]

As to the Romanian values, which may be relevant for him as an individual, Sebastian is also quite vague. Do Marin Dronțu, Mircea Vieru, and Ghiță Blidaru (literary avatars of the author's acquaintances Gheorghe Racoveanu, Camil Petrescu, and Nae Ionescu, respectively) represent specific Romanian values, and if so, what are they exactly? Sebastian's attachment to the landscape of native Brăila or the beauty of the Danube, genuine as it might be,[64] is hardly a cultural value. Most of the Romanians of his generation had hardly seen those landscapes, with the exception of Nae Ionescu, who was born in Braila, and he minimized the component of the geographical landscape in forming one's identity.[65] For him, the landscape is experienced in different ways by a Romanian and by a Jew, as they belong to different "immutable" structures.

Sebastian's novel expresses, therefore, much more an intention than an articulated proposal. It reflects the situation of the combination of persons with weak Jewish identities and the new opportunities that were open to the Jews of the urban elites, and the need to clarify the status of the new Jews. It was part of the search of a new type of identity in Romania, and part of a wider search that also can be discerned in the work of another important and well-known member of his milieu, the famous playwright Eugène Ionesco.[66] Sebastian's rather mild proposal was, nevertheless, sufficient to stir a scandal. The background of the polarization of the political camps in Romania in those years, with their religious overtones, was much more important than the specific contents of the novel.[67] One can only imagine what the reactions might have been had Sebastian offered details of the "accord" he envisioned between Jewish and Romanian values.

The weakened, sometimes superficial identities of some Jewish intellectuals were met by intensified efforts to strengthen the Romanian ethnic identity as part of the effort to consolidate the newly established Greater Romania. This meeting was fateful, especially in a period when nationalism began its triumphal conquest of political power in some of the important countries in Europe, producing the phenomenon of intellectuals undergoing a process of rhinocerization. The discrepancies between the two forms of identity led to inevitable conflicts, and eventually to some shameful compromises by members of minority groups. However, it would be wise to not conflate the intellectual mistakes of a vulnerable minority, seen sometimes anachronistically, with the more deleterious, fateful, and sometimes atrocious deeds of the majority and the persons who sustained them. It is one thing to be an opportunist attempting unsuccessfully to belong to the majority, and quite another to misunderstand, ignore, or perhaps even sustain lethal crimes committed in public by the majority.

Eliade's Theory of Camouflage and Sebastian's "Nameless Star"

Let me turn to what may be the earliest reverberation of Eliade's theory of camouflage of the sacred, discussed in ch. 1, outside his own writings. The warm friendship between Eliade and Sebastian, which lasted for a decade or so between 1927 to early

1938, is well known in Romanian interwar culture.[68] The two authors were discovered and encouraged by the same intellectual protector, Nae Ionescu, both worked at the same newspaper, *Cuvântul*, for several years, both were very successful authors of novels, plays, and short stories, and both were active members of the same cultural association, Criterion. In fact, they shared more than just parallel lives: Sebastian, a very gifted literary critic, wrote very favorable reviews of almost all of Eliade's early novels, and even of some of his studies of religion, such as a French review of Eliade's book on Yoga in French.[69] On the basis of these numerous and penetrating reviews, one may well conclude that he was the most erudite literary critic of Eliade's novels in the thirties. On the other side, as seen above, Eliade—to a certain extent and in a courageous manner—took Sebastian's side rather than Nae Ionescu's in a period when Sebastian was attacked from all sides, by both Christians and Jews, because he published his Jewish novel together with Ionescu's anti-Semitic preface. Their friendship broke up over Eliade's turn to the ideology of the Iron Guard, and dramatically during 1937 when Sebastian started to feel, increasingly, reluctantly, and quite angrily, that despite their friendship they could hardly speak to each other. From the journals of the two men, the strength of their friendship in the earlier period is obvious. But it is only in Sebastian's journal that the most direct and sensitive observations about Eliade's rapid slide toward the extreme right are found.[70]

In a passage quoted in ch. 1, Eliade describes Sebastian as the only person who responded positively to his intention to marry Nina Mareş in 1934. He was, in fact, the person who introduced his good acquaintance and typist, Nina, to Mircea. His approval does not mean, at least not necessarily, that Sebastian approved of Eliade's reasons for marrying her, or that he was even aware of Eliade's reasons, which involved, in my opinion, the concept of camouflage. However, such an awareness of Eliade's theory in general, and of its application in this specific case in particular, cannot be ruled out. In any case, though Sebastian did not review Eliade's *The Snake*, published in 1937 (the first of his literary writings in which the theory of camouflage is found in a substantial manner, as Eliade himself argued in some of the passages quoted in ch. 1, above), I have no doubt that he read it. What is, however, a fact is that in January 1935, Sebastian twice reviewed Eliade's collection of essays *Oceanography*, which included the first dated occurrence of the theory of the unrecognizability of the sacred. In the first of these reviews he wrote, inter alia: "Mircea Eliade believes in a sort of mystery of the banal things,[71] in their special significance."[72]

Years later, in 1943, Sebastian started to write the most famous of his literary works, a short play entitled *Nameless Star*. It was performed in Bucharest in 1944 under the name Victor Mincu, a pseudonym that circumvented the racial laws against the Jews then in force in Romania. The play became an immediate and lasting success. It deals with the extreme banality of existence in a small Romanian town, where a high school teacher of astronomy, Marin Miroiu, discovers an unknown star. While waiting in the rail station for the astronomical atlas that could finally confirm his discovery, Marin meets by chance a beautiful young lady who arrives in the small town from a great city, fleeing from high society and expressing the intention to commit suicide. Attempting to keep her alive overnight, he brings her to his modest house and tells her about his astronomical discovery. The lady, Mona, is surprised, and she has her first meaningful look at the starry heavens. Listening to his passionate description of astronomy, she falls in love with Marin over a few hours, but in the morning she is able to see the modest conditions and the banality of life in the town, and she leaves. During that crucial night, however, Marin describes to her his contemplation of the heavens in quite a poetic passage hardly representative of Sebastian's usually sober style:

> There are evenings when the entire heavens seem to me deserted, with cold and dead stars, in an absurd universe, where only we, in our great loneliness, struggle on a provincial planet, just as in a town in which there is no running water, the light does not shine, and the express trains do not stop.[73]...But there are evenings in which the entire heavens are replete with life...when in the last of the stars, if you listen attentively, you hear how forests and oceans are rustling—fantastic forests and fantastic oceans—there are evenings when the heavens are full of signs and callings, as if beings who did not see each other, from one planet to another, from one star to another, seek, forefeel and call to each other.[74]

This vision of the heavens as replete with signs, and cosmic calls one listens to, may well be described in Eliade's terms as a cosmic hierophany, and it is quite reminiscent of his theory of camouflage and the need to decipher it, or the need to listen to signs[75] as in, for example, the case of Ştefan Viziru in *Forbidden Forest*.[76] The dramatic spiritual transformation that Mona undergoes after listening to Marin's confession is so radical that her boyfriend, the rich Grig who comes in the morning to "rescue" her, wonders about her decision to leave him in favor of a poor professor, and then says about him: "this individual has a mystery...and at his window miracles are taking place during the night."[77] In other words, under the banal existence of the professor, in the remote and forgotten town, one may find something that transcends his own banal existence. He listens to calls from the universe, understood as full of mystery and as miraculous, which change his life.

I am inclined to see an influence of Eliade's theory of the camouflage of the sacred in the banal, as discussed in ch. 1, on Sebastian's play. However, even if I am wrong, and Eliade did not impact Sebastian, there is something important in what I perceive to be the affinity between the two contemporaneous apotheoses of banality, articulated in the same intellectual circle in Bucharest: In both cases there is a similar

attempt to safeguard it by allowing the possibility of the intrusion of a transcendental form of existence, which turns life into a meaningful event, even if someone like
Mona will have only the memory of such a unique encounter once in her life. What
was seen as a banal existence in Romania or in Bucharest of the thirties invited imaginative strategies to transcend it by the possibility of extraordinary experiences
within that banal existence, and this became an important theme in Romanian literature.[78] After all, the main element that Eliade added to the theory of maya that
informed his theory of camouflage is, as seen above, his emphasis on the banal and
the special attention he asked religious persons to pay to it. The feeling of living in
a banal milieu, which permeates some of Sebastian's writings, may explain his fascination with Eliade's personality and writings after his return from exotic India, and
his publication of a novel and feuilletons about his stay there.

Last but not least, in 1935 Ion Călugăru (the pen name of Ştrul Leiba Croitoru),
a somewhat senior colleague of Eliade and Sebastian on the editorial board of
Cuvântul, published his best-known novel, *The Childhood of a Ne'er-do-Well*, in
which he described the life in Dorohoi, his native Jewish shtetl in northern Romania.
There we find the following statement: "God is hidden beyond the things, and if you
search for Him, you will see Him."[79]

Notes

1. See Culianu, *Romanian Studies*, I, pp. 339–340, and Dancă, *Definitio Sacri*, pp. 25–96.
2. Volovici, "Romanian Writers," pp. 101–108, and Iovănel, *An Improbable Jew*, pp. 157–210.
3. On Ionescu and Judaism, see Volovici, *Nationalist Ideology*, pp. 99–102, and his "Mihail Sebastian: A Jewish Writer and His (Antisemitic) Master," in *Insiders, Outsiders, and Modern East European Jewry*, ed. Richard I. Cohen–Stephani Hoffman (Oxford, 2009), pp. 58–69.
4. *How I Became a Hooligan*, pp. 285–290, 331–332.
5. On some aspects of the theological debate, see Volovici, *Nationalist Ideology*, pp. 101–105.
6. See Introduction.
7. *How I Became a Hooligan*, pp. 314–315.
8. Ibid., p. 237.
9. Ibid., pp. 333–335, *Journal*, pp. 37–38. On this issue, see especially Manea, "Romania."
10. See Voicu, *The Myth of Nae Ionescu*, pp. 46–57. See also the manner in which Vulcănescu describes the 1931 class of Ionescu in *From Nae Ionescu to "Criterion,"* p. 61; Nae Ionescu, "Preface," p. 12; Sebastian, *Journal*, p. 23; Volovici, *Nationalist Ideology*, pp. 184–187; and Petreu, *Cioran*, pp. 237–239.
11. *From Nae Ionescu to "Criterion,"* p. 67.
12. See "Vremea teologilor," printed in Ionescu, *The Rose of the Winds*, p. 316.
13. "Preface," p. 21. No doubt this is the answer to Sebastian, *For Two Thousand Years*, pp. 229–230, where he speaks about the accord between the Jewish and Romanian values.
14. "Preface," p. 21. This is a clear version of the view of *verus Israel*.

15. *How I Became a Hooligan*, pp. 257, 261. See his interview with Camil Baltazar in 1934 about his remaining a Jew, and not "converting" to Judaism: "You cannot convert to a tragedy," in *Realitatea Evreiască*, 277, 1077 (1–20 Iunie 2007), p. iii, and *Journal*, p. 444.

16. *How I Became a Hooligan*, p. 261. Compare also to the critique of the French rationalistic spirit, which lacks the "sense of the tragic," in *For Two Thousand Years*, p. 184.

17. *How I Became a Hooligan*, p. 261.

18. Ibid., pp. 256–257.

19. *For Two Thousand Years*, p. 218, and see also p. 215, and *How I Became a Hooligan*, p. 255.

20. "Preface," p. 8.

21. See *How I Became a Hooligan*, p. 255.

22. *The Merchant of Venice*, scene III. See *Journal*, p. 526, where Sebastian mentions the annihilation of the Jews in Denmark, and then quotes the line as "For sufferance is the ludge [sic] of all our tribe." Sebastian's fascination with Shakespeare has been mentioned by several writers. See, e.g., Iordan Chimet, in Chimet, ed., *Mihail Sebastian File*, pp. xxvi–xxx, and Solomon, *Pages of a Journal*, pp. 161–171, but as far as I can see, no one has cited the above Shakespearean verse as relevant for Sebastian's understanding of Judaism in the novel.

23. See *How I Became a Hooligan* pp. 340–342.

24. See Tudor Teodorescu-Branişte, "Dnii Iosif Hechter, Nae Ionescu, Mircea Eliade şi Harul divin," reprinted in Handoca, ed., *Eliade File*, II, pp. 179–186.

25. Ibid., pp. 179–180.

26. On this dispute, see also the reminiscences of Eliade, *Autobiography*, I, pp. 285–287, and Ţurcanu, *Mircea Eliade*, pp. 222–227, Iovănel, *The Improbable Jew*, pp. 160–185, and Oişteanu, *Inventing the Jew*, pp. 288–289, 321–322.

27. Namely, a corrupted man.

28. On equilibrium as an important ideal in Eliade, see ch. 7.

29. *Correspondence* II, p. 176. Emphases in the original. For another seminal passage in this letter dealing with cosmic Christianity see below in ch. 8.

30. On this affair see Eliade, *Autobiography*, I, pp. 184–186.

31. *Correspondence* II, p. 177. Emphasis in the original.

32. "O problemă teologică eronat rezolvată? Sau ce n-a înţeles d. Mircea Eliade," *Credinţa*, II, 195 (20 Iulie 1934). These critiques did not deter Eliade from collaborating with him after the war in editing some essays of Ionescu's, or from writing an enthusiastic preface to one of his sermons.

33. *Nae Ionescu*, pp. 125–126.

34. Teodorescu-Branişte, "Dnii Iosif Hechter, Nae Ionescu, Mircea Eliade şi Harul divin."

35. "Creştinătatea faţă de iudaism," in Handoca, ed., *Eliade File*, II, pp. 100–106.

36. "Creştinism, Iudaism…şi îndrazneala," in ibid., pp. 166–173.

37. A phrase of Ionescu's from a piece written in 1926, during his philo-Semitic period, and quoted by Sebastian in *How I Became a Hooligan*, p. 332. This phrase recurs verbatim in Eliade's short story "A 14-Year-Old Picture," in *In Dionysius's Court*, p. 67, where it is used by an American, Lucio, in order to deride the alleged backwardness of the religious convictions of Dumitru, a Romanian from the Danube. It is the message of the story, however, that Dumitru's faith in a true God is superior.

38. See "O polemică teologică eronat resolvată?" in Handoca, ed., *Eliade File*, II, pp. 175–178. For the material unpublished in the thirties, see Vulcănescu, *From Nae Ionescu to "Criterion,"* pp.

131–159. For a short and rather contemptuous response to Sebastian, see the summary of the theological polemic in id., *Nae Ionescu*, pp. 129–130.

39. Id., *From Nae Ionescu to "Criterion,"* pp. 147, 154–155.

40. Ibid., pp. 147–148.

41. Ibid.

42. Nae Ionescu, p. 130.

43. Proverbs 3:12.

44. Vulcănescu, *From Nae Ionescu to "Criterion,"* p. 154.

45. "O polemică teologică eronat resolvată?"

46. "Preface," p. 24.

47. *How I Became a Hooligan*, p. 303.

48. *Journal*, pp. 59–60. See also p. 201.

49. See Petreu, *Parallel Philosophies*, pp. 137–182.

50. See Volovici, *Nationalist Ideology*, pp. 86–87.

51. See the English translation of the letter in Călinescu, "Ionesco and Rhinoceros," pp. 410–411, and the Romanian text and discussion in Ornea, *The Thirties*, pp. 183–184, Petreu, *Cioran*, p. 102, and Voicu, *The Myth of Nae Ionescu*, pp. 178–179.

52. See Petreu, *Ionesco*, pp. 122–128; id., *From Junimea to Noica*, pp. 222–223.

53. See, e.g., Daniel Cristea-Enache, "Nae Ionescu—Mihail Sebastian: O influență decisivă," printed in Chimet, *Mihail Sebastian File*, pp. 228, and Petreu, *The Devil and Its Apprentice*.

54. See below, ch. 7.

55. *Journal*, p. 299. See also pp. 235, 302, 337.

56. *For Two Thousand Years*, p. 104.

57. Ibid., pp. 65–67.

58. *Journal*, p. 450.

59. The last part of the *Journal* is replete with negative remarks about activists in the Jewish community in Bucharest and other Jewish writers. See, e.g., pp. 443, 444, 559.

60. *For Two Thousand Years*, p. 50, and ibid., pp. 81, 215. See the occurrence of the expression "very ancient melancholy"—*melancolia străveche*—of the Jews, in a piece written in 1927 and quoted by Geo Șerban in "Remember," *Realitatea Evreiască*, 277, 1077 (1–20 Iunie 2007), p. ii. To be sure, there are examples of some connections between melancholy and some perceptions of Judaism and its affinity to Saturn. However, there is no reason to generalize it as an intrinsic Jewish value representative of Judaism.

61. See the Romanian translation of this lecture, dealing with Romanian and Jewish national specificities, printed by Leon Volovici in *Apostrof*, XII, 5 (132), (2001), pp. 1–12.

62. See Idel, *Old Worlds, New Mirrors*, pp. 52–78. Also, in their case, the urban Jews lived in an interregnum: a slightly de-Christianized Europe that they try to enter as only slightly identified Jews.

63. See also Petreu, *The Devil and Its Apprentice*, pp. 247–261.

64. See the several pieces in which Sebastian wrote so warmly about Brăila through the years, collected in *Journal of an Epoch*, pp. 571–596. This does not mean that Sebastian would not have been daunted by a return to the provincial town if he had to leave Bucharest. As we shall see, the fear of the banality of provincial life is quite evident in "Nameless Star."

65. "Preface," pp. 11–12.

66. See Petreu, *Ionesco*, pp. 207–209.

67. *How I Became a Hooligan*, p. 317.

68. See, e.g., Mac Linscott Ricketts, "Mircea Eliade and Mihail Sebastian: The Story of a Friendship," in *Deux explorateurs de la pensée humaine, George Dumézil et Mircea Eliade*, ed. Jules Ries and Natale Spineto (Turnhout, 2003), pp. 229–243. I dare to depart from the harmonistic hypothesis of a possible reconciliation between Sebastian and Eliade, had the former survived and arrived in Paris as the latter did. Unlike Emile Cioran and Eugène Ionesco, who did remain friendly with Eliade after 1945, as Ricketts mentions, as a Jew, Sebastian was persecuted by the Antonescu regime, a regime that in one way or another helped the other three survive the war in relatively comfortable conditions by paying them salaries. See, especially, Laignel-Lavastine, *Cioran, Eliade, Ionesco*. Compare also the immediate rupture between Paul Celan and Cioran, both members of the Romanian exile community in Paris, when the fascist convictions of the latter were disclosed.

69. See the material collected in Handoca, ed., *Eliade File*, II, pp. 41–89.

70. See Sebastian, *Journal*, pp. 114–115.

71. *Lucrurile banale*. In Handoca's edition, *Eliade File*, II, p. 64, the version is *bucuriile banale*, "banal feelings of gladness," but I prefer the version in the edition of the Romanian Academy.

72. Sebastian, *Journal of Epoch*, p. 302. On the same page, Sebastian quotes a passage from *Oceanography* that reflects Eliade's concern with banality. Sebastian's remark shows, once again, that this passage was understood as part of the camouflage complex of ideas discussed in ch. 1, above; all this is in 1935.

73. Those are problems related to the banality of existence in the town, as is clear from earlier dialogues in the play.

74. *The Nameless Star*, in Sebastian, *Selected Works*, I, p. 204.

75. On hierophanies and signs, see the section with this title in Eliade, *The Sacred & the Profane*, pp. 24–29. See also above, the quote from *No Souvenirs*, pp. 84–85; *Aspects du mythe*, pp. 174–175, dealing with nature and camouflage; and Simion, *Knots and Signs of Prose*, p. 204. For "signs" in Corbin, see Wasserstrom, *Religion after Religion*, p. 176, in quite an Eliadean manner.

76. See Simion, ibid., p. 224. In this limited context I cannot address the several interesting descriptions of the camouflage in this rich and voluminous novel.

77. *The Nameless Star*, p. 224.

78. To a certain extent, Sebastian's earlier play, *Jocul de-a vacanța*, finished in 1936, also revolves around the necessity of escaping the banality of normal life by changing the rules of life during a vacation.

79. *Copilaria unui netrebnic* (Bucharest, 1996), p. 130.

· 7 ·

ELIADE, THE IRON GUARD, AND SOME VAMPIRES

We found ourselves today in the epoch of errors.

—Nae Ionescu[1]

Eliade…an indicator of wrong ways.

—Eugène Ionesco[2]

The Iron Guards think they are saints; They are murderers.

—Eugène Ionesco[3]

How Spiritual Was the Iron Guard?

*U*nlike what a reader acquainted with the quandaries of Eliade studies might expect, this chapter is concerned less with the details of his involvement in Romanian politics than with the subject of how a historian of religion judged the only religious movement whose development he was able to watch in detail, knowing its leaders, and being able to read the pertinent material in original. This is, therefore, a scholarly, professional story rather than a political one.

Let me start with some historical data. The affinities between Eliade and the Iron Guard have been known in principle since the late thirties by many persons living in Romania and outside, but they were not documented until the early seventies of the last century.[4] Even then, they were sometimes vehemently denied by him, and even later, the defenders of Eliade's image tried to deny them, and even to attack those who assessed them and to regard them as "detractors," or of not being sensitive enough to the differences.[5] However, since publication of the studies of several scholars, as well as the journals of both Eliade and Sebastian, this is no longer a question that can be answered in the negative, or even without certainty.[6] Most decisive is written evidence related to the elections of 1937, with reference to Eliade's belonging to the Iron Guard, published in the official newspaper of the Guard; this corroborates Sebastian's claim about the propaganda Eliade made, probably in the valley of Prahova.[7] This decisive piece of evidence has been ignored by a long series of defenders of Eliade who are prone to minimize or neglect the depth of Eliade's rapprochement to the Iron Guard. In the past I have expressed in general terms my opinion in favor of a view of Eliade as a cooperator with this Romanian ultranationalistic movement.[8] Given the scholarly literature that has been written on the topic in the last generation, especially the recent and detailed analyses of Mihaela Gligor,[9] I shall not deal again with the basic finding on the topic, but shall attempt to address two issues that did not attract sufficient attention from scholars: the special status of Ion I. Moța in Eliade's eyes, and the lingering of Eliade's prewar views in later years. My purpose in this chapter is to deal not with the integrity of Eliade's denial of historical facts,[10] but much more with another topic, related to Eliade as a scholar of religion, namely, with his recurring claim that the legionnaire movement he adhered to was a purely spiritual one in its initial phases. My approach casts this as a scholarly rather than a personal issue, which means that I am not concerned with establishing whether he was or was not a fascist or an anti-Semite—I believe those labels are both problematic[11]—but with focusing on this question: How did a prominent scholar of religion judge a religious movement that started and finished its political career during his lifetime, in his immediate geographical vicinity, with its leadership active in Bucharest, taking into account that he was acquainted with most of its leaders and that he adhered to the movement intellectually, and so on.

Unlike in other similar cases, such as those of Martin Heidegger, a philosopher, Paul de Man, a literary critic, and Carl G. Jung, a psychoanalyst, all sympathizers of the Nazi regime, Eliade was a scholar of religion. For this reason the subject I discuss below—namely, Eliade's attitude to the movement known inter alia as the Iron Guard, which was described by him insistently as chiefly religious, spiritual, or even mystical, and basically devoid of political aspiration or violence for most of its history—falls under his basic professional concerns. The possible significance of historical linkages between Eliade and the Iron Guard movement from late 1935, obvious as they are, should nevertheless be elaborated upon, especially by addressing the question of whether such a linkage automatically constitutes anti-Semitism too, and whether such a linkage infiltrates specific contents of Eliade's scholarship. There are scholars whose answer was definitively yes, such as Adriana Berger, Daniel Dubuisson, Cristiano Grotanelli, Alexandra Laignel-Lavastine, Mihaela Gligor, Mihai Iovănel, and Dan Dana. Others, such as Mircea Handoca,[12] Sorin Alexandrescu,[13] Matei Călinescu,[14] Andrei Oişteanu,[15] and Brian Rennie,[16] somehow minimized the impact of these associations. My opinion is that simple answers of yes or no are not doing justice to complex situations.

There are some few anti-Semitic statements in his journalistic stories, and there are potentially anti-Judaic implications in his vision of Judaism, as mentioned above in ch. 4. However, in the very same period there are also other quite explicitly positive statements about some individual Jews, that point in the opposite direction; this is the case with his great admiration for Moses Gaster, which he expressed in his two feuilletons dedicated to him.[17] Without attempting to ignore or minimize the former, my position is that it is also a mistake to ignore the latter; simply, both are true. Here, I would like to invoke the principle of incoherence mentioned in the Introduction, which means that unqualified answers are prone to reduce the complexity of the situation to too simple alternatives, based on privileging one of the opinions and relegating the other to the margin or ignoring it. In fact, scholarship should assume the existence of complexity and incoherence and offer qualified answers; this is unlike the academic approach of Eliade himself, which I discuss in the Final Remarks.

The two topics discussed here are Eliade's enduring attachment to the figure of Ion I. Moţa and the theory that what he called the "tragedy of the Iron Guard" should be integrated. These topics are interrelated, and their common denominator is the fact that years after the war, Eliade did not change his mind about what he claimed was the spiritual nature of the Iron Guard, and he continued to entertain a certain cult of its main leader, Ion Moţa, even after the tragedies inflicted by the early activities of the Iron Guard before 1940 could not be denied. Eliade's pretext that the Iron Guard lost its legitimacy in his eyes after the assassinations of Armand Călinescu and Nicolae Iorga in 1940, when it allegedly changed its original, predominantly spiritual approach, is, in my opinion, more than questionable. Indeed, one may ask how spiritual a movement such as the early Iron Guard can be when its three main principles are anti-Communism, anti-Semitism, and Romanian nationalism, it is based on paramilitary education,[18] and it is led by an "obsessive anti-Semite," Corneliu Zelea Codreanu.[19]

Did Eliade's immediate circle see the pre-1938 Iron Guard as solely spiritual? Let me adduce first a conversation from a meeting between Sebastian and the "Professor," Nae Ionescu, in early 1938, as reported by Sebastian in his *Journal* on January 5[20]:

I left[21] from there with mixed feelings: sympathy, irritation, doubt and disgust.... The anti-Semitic measures of Goga[22] revolted him. Those are insulting, unserious, done in a barbarian spirit, done out of mockery! . . ."How, sir, is it possible to drive people to suicide and to strip the citizenship of a million persons without endangering the very basis of the Romanian state?" [23] I attempted to calm him and assure him that the gradual and violent elimination of the Jews does not constitute such a grave problem, especially since the Iron Guard would not behave any differently. "In fact, yes, but in spirit, no"—was the reply of Nae—. "Because, my dear, although you will laugh, there is a great difference between someone who kills you in an insulting manner and another who does exactly the same thing, but with a pain in his soul."[24]

There is much dark irony in Ionescu's distinction: Having protested a minute beforehand about the discrimination against the Jews by the current regime, nevertheless he openly admits that the Iron Guard will kill a million Jews, but that they will do so, in his opinion, with some form of compassion. Weighed up by the chief ideologue of the Iron Guard, this is a declaration as to the intentions of the Guard, and the notion that there will be some sort of regret for doing it in the hearts of the legionnaires—the most anti-Semitic layer of the Romanian population—is either demented or just sarcastic. Indeed, this is a fine example of why he was described by some of his acquaintances, including Sebastian himself, as the devil.[25] Or, to use Ionescu's own phrase, this passage constitutes an outstanding case of an "amoral sincerity that is very common among learned persons dealing with abstractions."[26] What we have here is no less than the wish for a final solution for the Jews in Romania articulated early in 1938, years before the German plan for a final solution. On such a subject we may adduce Eugène Ionesco's reaction to a discussion he had with a legionnaire about anti-Semitism: "I don't know what makes me angrier: their stupidity or their brutality."[27] No wonder anxiety and terror permeate descriptions from the journals of this period by Sebastian, Ionesco, and Emil Dorian.

Also astonishing is Sebastian's own bizarre attitude, with its absence of incompatibility that we mentioned in the Introduction, but this is another matter. The more general situation, as also reflected in the above discussion, was summarized by Norman Manea quite adequately: "give witness to the everyday lives of 'assimilated' Jews awaiting death from the world to which they thought they belonged."[28] To be sure, Ionescu was once on the side of a Zionist solution to what he saw as the Jewish problem in Romania, supporting, implicitly, the option that the Jews would leave the country for Israel;[29] Eliade supported this too.[30] However, it seems that in the second half of the thirties they were closer to the notorious slogan of the Romanian anti-Semites: "Yids [go] to Palestine!"[31]

What matters from my point of view is the agreement of Ionescu and Sebastian about what the Iron Guard was going to do: If they came to power, they would

exterminate all the Jews, just as the other anti-Semite party would do.[32] This was also
the impression of Aristide Blank, a rich Jewish man of affairs close to King Carol II, with
whom Sebastian spoke the next day.[33] Sebastian's report should be compared to
Ionesco's account of a different conversation: "N.[34] is to be named a lecturer in philosophy at the University of Bucharest. He is very nice, very refined, too nice, too refined,
too distinguished. He is Iron Guard. He tells the party militants to be 'frightfully
good'...He thus tells them that they must kill with 'kindness.'"[35] If Ionescu and Sebastian
in early 1938, as well as Ionesco and another good friend of Eliade's, Constantin
Noica,[36] all understood clearly the murderous intentions of the Iron Guard, then I am
convinced that Eliade, who spent time in their company, was also aware of the murderous potential of the movement he persistently described as "spiritual," ignoring the
criminal acts committed by its leaders many years beforehand. It was just a matter of
reading newspapers, including *Cuvântul*, in which he published pieces about the events
in Oradea Mare in 1927, which had been condemned by Nae Ionescu,[37] and the man-
ifestos of the Iron Guard. Eliade himself, in a piece written in February 1934, warns quite
openly about the danger of the Communists on the left and the "green shirts," most probably the Iron Guard, on the right.[38] Nevertheless, in 1940 he writes that

> for several years death was exalted in Romania by the legionnaires as a supreme sacrifice,
> and killings—individual and collective—were common. On October 30, 1933, a group
> of legionnaires assassinated the prime minister I. G. Duca; in November 1938 King Carol
> and Armand Călinescu ordered the execution of Codreanu and those legionnaires who were
> involved in the plot against Duca. On September 14, 1939, a group of legionnaires killed
> another prime minister, Armand Călinescu. In response, Carol ordered their executions and
> those of several hundred other legionnaires.[39]

What Eliade does not say is that assassinations were not just an activity of the
Iron Guard in general, but that Codreanu himself killed a police officer, Constantin
Manciu, and wounded others in Iaşi early in his career in 1924, long before the dates
mentioned here, just as Moţa tried to kill the "traitor" student during the same
period;[40] another example is the 1936 assassination of Stelescu, an Iron Guard
member who dared to criticize Codreanu. Indeed, as Theodor Lavi assessed the Iron
Guard: "They were assassins from the very beginning."[41] However, despite the obvious discrepancy between what scholars of the Iron Guard see as reality and Eliade's
idiosyncratic perception, he continued to embrace the theory of the spiritual nature
of the movement, giving priority to the Christian Orthodox allegiance—replete
with anti-Semitism as it was—over the iron aspects of the Guard's activities. The
inability to see the complex picture in its totality, because of a personal commitment
to only one side of the complex situation, the ultranationalists, does not distinguish
the scholar of religion from an ordinary simpleminded legionnaire.

It is unfortunately true that the above discussion between Sebastian and Ionescu was basically irrelevant for future victims, as it deals with just a very fine distinction between two types of murderous politics. The Iron Guard pogrom in Bucharest in January 1941 killed 138 Jews; the number remained relatively low only because the Antonescu regime ferociously suppressed the legionnaire rebellion. However, it was only a few months before a much wider pogrom took place, on Antonescu's order and under the auspices of the Romanian army and police in Iaşi. In the summer of that year 10,000 to 15,000 Jews were killed in one single day. Though not all the killings of the Jews in 1940–1941 were done by the Iron Guard themselves, their instigations played a role, perhaps indirectly, in the case of those other atrocities.

To be sure, Eliade was not alone and certainly not exceptional in this neglect or tacit complacency with the crimes of the Iron Guard in the twenties and most of the thirties, as has been duly pointed out by Sorin Alexandrescu: That was the weakness of the judicial system in Romania and of the problematic indifference of the Romanian public in general.[42] Nevertheless, there were a few voices in Romania that criticized or even protested against those crimes, but from late 1935, Eliade was not one of them. He condemned the Guard, but not until 1941, after learning about the assassination of Nicolae Iorga, since this act annulled, in his opinion, the religious sense of the early legionnaires, who were assassinated by the order of Carol II. "Since then,"—he writes—"the Guard is considered a terrorist and pro-Nazi movement."[43] This belated and, in my opinion, very partial understanding of the complex nature of the Iron Guard is one of the main topics of our discussion below.

Eliade's Idol—Ion I. Moţa

As seen above, Eliade claimed that he admired only the earlier forms of the Iron Guard because at that time it was, in his opinion, a spiritual movement, and that when he became aware of the atrocities committed in 1940–1941 by the Iron Guard he changed his mind, having considered the assassinations of two major political and cultural figures by members of the Guard a betrayal of what he believed was the original nature of the movement. However, as seen in the previous section, it would have been quite difficult to misunderstand the sharp anti-Semitic nature of the movement he adhered to from the end of 1935, as well as the murderous activities in the past and the somber prospects for the future. Neither could Eliade avoid the sharp anti-Semitic tone of the leaders, whom he knew personally, especially Vasile Marin, with whom he studied at high school, when Marin was already expressing anti-Semitic views.[44] In my opinion, it is possible to show that long before 1940, Eliade could not have avoided knowing the basics of the Iron Guard intentions, both because of the very name of the movement—how spiritual can an iron guard or a legion be?—and because of its well-known paramilitary structure. Hadn't a "death squad" for this movement already been created in 1933, which assassinated Stelescu in 1936?[45] And were other crimes not committed before 1935? Moreover, there is no reason to believe that he did not know much more than that, as he could learn about it from regular newspapers.

It is obvious that Eliade adored Corneliu Zelea Codreanu, the venerated head of the Iron Guard. This is well known and obvious from evidence from Eliade's own pen; as he formulated it while in Portugal, it was Codreanu who transformed him into a "fanatic Romanian," and this could only have been before his death in 1938.[46] In any case, Eliade does not hesitate to describe himself as a legionnaire,[47] though certainly an "atypical" one.[48]

However, what is much less known is Eliade's attitude toward Codreanu's brother-in-law and deputy leader of the movement: the lawyer Ion I. Moţa. As seen above in ch. 3, Eliade's eulogy of Ion Moţa in early 1937 was unqualifiedly positive and replete with superlatives. So, let me elaborate a little bit on the identity of this leading legionnaire and idol of Eliade's Moţa was not just one of the most prominent figures in the Iron Guard, not only the lieutenant of the Guard's founder and chief Corneliu Zelea Codreanu, as well as his brother-in-law; he was also the translator of the *Protocols of the Elders of Zion* from French to Romanian, in his youth in 1923.[49] Together with Codreanu he planned to assassinate some Romanian dignitaries who were thought to be pro-Jewish, as well as leaders of Romanian Jewry. After the plot was divulged, he tried to assassinate the former conspirator who had revealed the plan, whom he considered a traitor.[50] Moreover, Moţa was present at the international anti-Semitic congresses, and was the author of a series of booklets that articulated the extreme nationalistic and anti-Semitic ideology of the Iron Guard.[51] Eliade might have ignored in the thirties the connections Moţa had with the French *Action Française* and the Nazi Welt-Dienst [World Service], though it is hard to believe that all these pieces of bibliographical and historical information could have escaped the erudite Eliade, who probably knew Moţa in his youth from the latter's participation in the classes of Nae Ionescu. In fact, a very reliable witness, Mircea Vulcănescu, who knew very well the circle of Ionescu and Eliade, described the former as the mentor of both Eliade and Moţa: "Nae Ionescu had links with the Iron Guard; that he was the direct guide of some of the guardists in some of their deeds in the agenda of the movement, as well as outside it (I speak of Ion Moţa, of Vasile Marin, of Alexandru Constant, and of Mircea Eliade)...there is no doubt."[52]

Here Eliade is described as a guardist in quite unequivocal terms, together with three other important leaders of the movement: indeed, quite amazing company. Like Ionescu, who was described by scholars as propagating "a fundamentalist anti-

Semitism,"[53] Moṭa could, for example, declare in print that "This state of things today: the Jewish[54] penetration[55]—because of which we are losing our soul,[56] the body of our nation is emasculated, and our hands are tied so that we can no longer be free— is bringing us to doom."[57] Let me explain some of the terms used in this seminal citation. The so-called penetration of the Jews has nothing to do with a sudden large-scale invasion by Jews in Romania, unrecorded in the available history books, but with the fact that Romania received after WWI huge territories that had previously belonged to the Austro-Hungarian Empire, Russia, and Bulgaria: namely, Transylvania, Bucovina, Bessarabia, and part of Dobrogea. Those annexed territories were populated by significant minorities—Hungarians, Germans, Jews, Russians, and Turks. Some of those minorities did not speak Romanian, either because they did not know it or because they refused to do so in principle, a fact that angered the Romanian nationalists. What happened was that the Romanian nationalists wanted the huge territories now constituting Greater Romania to be cleansed of minorities as much as possible; that is, to have the new territories without allowing the rights of the minorities that populated them before they were attached to Romania. It was only in 1923 that Jews became Romanian citizens as a result of external pressure, a fact that only contributed to the emergence of more virulent forms of anti-Semitic movements.

To a great extent, some of the more educated minorities who were added to the provinces of the Old Romanian kingdom constituted by Moldavia and Wallachia were seen as danger to the biggest part of the Romanian populace, a fact that was exploited by the propaganda of the Iron Guard. What could have been a blessing for Romania was transformed, by a blind hatred of the nationalists, into a curse. Moṭa's fantasies in his writings create the feeling that the Romanian universities were occupied by Jews; he claimed, for example, that at the universities in Iaşi and Cluj, Jews constituted 80% of the students at the law school.[58] Such an absurd claim is difficult to imagine from someone like Moṭa, who was a lawyer, had earned a doctorate from the University of Grenoble, and was considered the "intellectual" of the Iron Guard in its early phase.[59] In fact, quite recent and detailed statistics on the presence of Jewish students in law schools in the twenties of the 20th century demonstrate that they made up no more than 20% of the student population in any year or in any Romanian university.[60] Thus, things that Moṭa could see with his own eyes, that he could understand as a professional in the field—like Codreanu, he was a lawyer— are wildly distorted, and driven by a blind hatred. He called not for a *numerus clausus*, namely, representation of minorities in accordance with their proportion of the population, which was indeed instituted in 1933, but for *numerus nullus*![61]

Elsewhere, Moṭa claimed that there was a danger of an additional one million new Jews,[62] another totally absurd claim, since the entire Jewish community in

Greater Romania never numbered more than 800,000, and an extra one million is, in my opinion, as believable as the claim that the law school population was 80% Jewish. In Moța's view, "the fight for a total elimination of the Jews[63] and of their influence in our nation" was the only way to "stop the doom of our nation,"[64] a view not far from that of the "Professor," adduced above. Moța was afraid of the Jewish presence not only in the domain of economics or in social life but also, especially, in the intellectual sphere, claiming that "tomorrow the intellectual class almost in its entirety will become Jewish or Judaized."[65] Elsewhere, he writes in one of his early feuilletons (1924) that "An infernal spirit has penetrated everything: the Judaic spirit."[66] This is the reason why in the same feuilleton he calls for "a fight for total elimination of the Yids and their influence from our nation."[67] In his opinion, "not resolving the problem [posed by] the Yids is equal to death."[68] Those are but a few excerpts from a vast range of anti-Semitic expressions in a rather slim book, and they show how deep anti-Semitism was rooted in the thoughts of the leading intellectual of the Iron Guard since its inception. It is quite pathetic, and at the same time amusing, to see the obsessive fears of a rather cultured figure, a member of a vast majority, who is provoked to hysteria by the presence of Jews who comprised (at most) 4% of the population of Greater Romania, yet he was ready to volunteer to go to his death in the Spanish Civil War. A certain pursuit of purity of the Romanian nation, culture and soil, obsessed him and Codreanu, as well as many sympathizers of the Iron Guard.

However, unlike Codreanu, who preferred not to travel too much, Moța was an active participant at fascist and anti-Semitic congresses abroad. He participated in the Budapest conference in 1925, and in the one held on December 16–17, 1934, in Montreux, Switzerland. At the latter one Moța was very active, and he convinced the participants to formulate the following statement:

> The Congress, seeing that each State, in virtue of the principle of national sovereignty, is alone qualified to decide, over its own territory, the attitude that it must take towards the citizens, groups, races and religions within its borders, and, taking into account both natural law and morality, declares that the Jewish Question must not be seen as a campaign of hatred against Jewry. However, seeing that, in a great many countries, certain Jewish groups exercise, whether openly or covertly, a harmful influence on the moral and material interests of the Nation, and form a kind of State within a State, claiming all sorts of rights but refusing to comply with all the commensurate duties, and working for the destruction of Christian civilization, the Congress denounces the sinister activity of such elements and is prepared to combat them.[69]

The text of this declaration was imposed by Moța, and its details parallel the content of letters he exchanged during that period with the Nazi Welt-Dienst.[70] Faithful to his religious and national beliefs, Moța, together with other legionnaires, volunteered in the struggle against the enemies of the Christian Church in the Spanish Civil War, where he soon met his death. As Nae Ionescu, with whom Moța had a conversation before leaving for Spain, and with whom he left his will, wrote in his preface to Vasile Marin's book a short time after the two died in Spain:

> Ion Moța went [to Spain] in order to die. The belief that the redemption of our nation necessitated the pathetic sacrifice of his corporeal being descended deep within him; and he left by the dint of a transfigured decision: not in order to fight, not in order to be victorious by fighting, but in order that his death will stop our death. [71] Had Moța returned from the war untouched, the humane joy of those who knew him would stand beside the doubt of Moța, who would think that because of his sins, God had refused his sacrifice. No matter how terrible this thought would be, humanely speaking, I am confident that for the redemption of our nation God had to accept Moța's sacrifice, just as He accepted the sacrifice of the Lamb, for the redemption of humankind.[72]

Indubitably, we face a comparison between Jesus and Moța, reminiscent of other texts by Ionescu we have seen in ch. 4, above.[73] It is known that Moța met with Ionescu before he went to Spain, and that he left with Ionescu his will, to be given in the case of his death to Codreanu and to his family. However, whether Ionescu's analysis of Moța's intention is indeed correct is a matter of debate.[74] So, for example, I would opt for the more mundane explanation offered by a real insider of the circle, Mircea Vulcănescu: Moța volunteered to fight in Spain as a form of expiatory ordeal, because of the suspicion that he had striven to replace Codreanu as leader of the Iron Guard.[75]

In any case, Ionescu's recommendation to God to receive Moța's sacrifice, as He he had done in the case of Jesus, is really moving—no doubt a renewed attempt to advise God now, just as he previously advised Carol II. It should be mentioned that ministers of Nazi Germany and Fascist Italy attended attended the funeral of Moța and Marin.

All of this did not prevent Eliade, even later, from depicting Moța as an extremely attractive figure in the third part of his trilogy *The Return from Paradise*, entitled *The New Life*, written after 1937 but never completed. There he adduces two of Moța's declarations about death: "Someone who knows how to die will never be a slave,"[76] which is interpreted directly that death is the supreme liberation and freedom;[77] and the view that the most powerful dynamite is one's own ashes.[78] To mistake Moța— who had tried to kill another Iron Guard student who was considered a traitor and condemned for it—for a spiritual hero, Eliade had to have been not a nearsighted adolescent, but a blind mature one. Those are just some examples of Moța's image based on works published before his death in January 1937.

In 1948 Eliade wrote to his friend and longtime financial supporter Brutus Coste: "I resign. I know that nothing pure remains pure when it reaches me. In 1938 I adhered to the Iron Guard because of the memory of Moța, just to see in 1940 the Guard led by rogues and *semidocts*, compromising even the memory of Moța. This is 'History'— this is the reason why I opt for Metaphysics."[79] Eliade's distinction between the earlier allegedly "pure" Iron Guard and its degeneration into the brutality of 1940–1941 is to a very great extent artificial since the Guard resorted to political assassinations many years before the killing of Codreanu and the other heads of the Guard.[80]

Eliade's own views in the late thirties are not far from those of Moța. First and foremost, let me point out that Eliade was acquainted with Moța's *Skulls of Wood*, which he quotes, approvingly, in 1938.[81] In his piece entitled "The Blind Pilots" he attacked the Romanian leadership for not paying attention to the deleterious shifts in the situation in the new territories, some which are dominated by Jews. Some weeks later, Eliade asserted that the Romanian nation is close to doom because of minorities.[82] Moreover, in 1935 Eliade wrote to Emil Cioran a letter that discusses, inter alia, his view concerning the content of Cioran's quite recently published book *Romania's Transfiguration*. This is one of the most radical books ever written in Romania, displaying a sharp disgust for minorities in Romania, and for Romanians altogether.[83] Cioran's attitude toward Jews was quite anti-Semitic, perhaps because of some sort of attraction toward them, in a manner reminiscent of this tension in Eliade, who was nevertheless much more positive. After reading Cioran's book Eliade wrote to him: "The chapter about the workers and the Jews is admirable."[84] In fact, already in Cioran's youth he had expressed some mildly negative attitudes toward the Jews, especially the "new" ones—see above, Moța's view about the invasion of the Jews—and a much more tolerant attitude toward the "older" Jews, described as having lived in Romania for only the "last forty years."[85]

New Vampires and a Call for Their Integration

In March 1936 Ion Moța wrote a preface to the collection of his propagandistic stories written during the previous 15 years. At the end of that preface he wrote what may be one of the most horrific descriptions of the state of mind of a leading legionnaire:

> Our soul remained linked to another world; it roams today in a life that is not ours. We feel alien to the world of today; in it we do not find any sense but to put an end to it in order to revive hoary times and enhance their beauty, strength, and the right Romanian order.
> It seems in fact that I and my comrades are some sort of weird beings with two lives, a sort of vampires [*strigoi*] aroused from a world that is set to bear the spirit of fright in the world of today. Indeed, so we are. Uprooted souls that, bearing the unrest over a destroyed life, will not have peace in any tomb until that which has been blemished, wasted, and cursed will rise again. The people of this century should pause for a while from comfort and indifference and

listen to the weird noises that worry the incomprehensible depths and shriek with the winds of night. And it should be known: the governance of the vampires [strigoi], the terrible one, comes closer.[86]

This is quite an ominous, menacing passage, hardly bearing a spiritual message. The good old order, when Romania had not been conquered by the Jews, is mentioned just before this passage, and in that context Moța mentions that he combated the Jews and the thieves who occupied that world.[87] The sense of alienation is quite obvious, and it is reiterated elsewhere in the preface.[88] It corroborates what Ionescu predicted in his conversation with Sebastian, cited above.

The vampires are, quite predictably, the Iron Guard adherents, and in the thanatomania of the Iron Guard, as Culianu designated it,[89] the use of the theme of the vampires is not unknown. In fact, the "poet" of the Iron Guard expressed a similar sentiment when he imagined some anonymous persons, who are most probably the legionnaires, as follows:

In the darkness of night we dream ourselves vampires [strigoi][90]
So that we eat from a hot carcass
In the darkness of night we dream ourselves vampires
But only death is severing hunks from us,
It alone consumes tombs.[91]

This morbid approach is part of the thanatology that is so characteristic of the Guard.[92] I assume that these two leading figures of the Iron Guard shared a common thanatology.

To be sure, both Codreanu and Moța claimed the priority of the spiritual life, dedicated to God and the nation, and the spirit of sacrifice and the readiness to die for these causes. Both the virulent anti-Semitism and the spiritual claims are intertwined, sometimes on the same page. This mixture of extreme hatred of the Jews and the declarations of love of Romania and God generates a special type of demagogical rhetoric. A scholar of religion should have known that words may turn into deeds and may harm, and absent this minimal awareness, little remains of one's expertise of religion.[93]

Those types of bloody images were certainly known to Eliade. In the feuilleton entitled "The Vampires," written in 1938, he refers explicitly to Moța's book and quotes the end of the above-cited passage in which the coming governance of the vampires is foretold, and he offers a comment of his own on it.[94] This feuilleton has not been mentioned, as far as I know, in discussions about Eliade's affinities to the Iron Guard, and I would like to elaborate on its significance and impact. Eliade starts with a verbatim quote from the end of Moța's preface, and writes:

What a decisive return to the Romanian norms! Our people have always refused the tragic [mood], and the tragic sense of existence. The death of the shepherd from *Miorița* is a "reconciled death."[95] We[96] have plenty of melancholy, but never an extreme despair, never the tragic considered as a fundamental condition of human condition. . . ."The Vampires" of Ion Moța will govern for a segment of time. Until "a country like the proud sun in heaven" will emerge.[97]

The last sentence is, in fact, an unattributed quote from the popular Iron Guard view that called for Codreanu to create a Romania as proud as the sun is in heaven.[98] Indubitably, the terrible rule of the vampires, an image that Eliade shares with Moța, is that of the Iron Guard. I assume that Moța, like Eliade, knew that vampires live on blood, and that the predicted terrible governance—in Romanian a strong term is used: *cumplit*—means quite a nonspiritual combat with Jews and "thieves" in order to restore the pristine Romanian order. The Iron Guard, like Eliade, mixed Orthodoxy with a peasant attitude.[99]

A scholar in the middle of events could, perhaps, overlook the dangerous connotations of a passage such as Moța's, which serves as the starting point of his article. However, with the passage of time there was opportunity for more mature reflection by the professional scholar of religion about the actual "early" "spirituality" of the Iron Guard, and we have seen that in 1948 Eliade did not reflect on what had happened in the pre-1940 Legion of the Archangel Michael. Indeed, he never did, though he had several occasions to do so.[100] Let us have a look at a passage written in late 1945, after a conversation with Ionesco in Paris; this is part of Eliade's diary from October 4, 1945, found in the Special Collections of the Joseph Regenstein Library at the University of Chicago, which I shall translate below in the fullest version unknown in scholarship:

> When the discussion returned to the Guard I told him that these problems should be surpassed,[101] once and forever. After the death of Codreanu and of the other leaders, the Guard became a vampire [*strigoi*]. We watched a strange case of vampirism [*vampirism*]. There is an attempt to remain alive in the organism that has been assassinated. As any victim of a violent death, the Guard turned into a vampire [*strigoi*].[102] It cannot rest, either in the grave or in history. With the blood of the legionnaires and of those killed by the legionnaires, the vampire [*vampirul*] continued to "live." All these things must be brought to an end;[103] that is, integrated. It would be criminal and it is already very unproductive to continuously conduct a trial of the Guard. It would bring about a psychological trauma to the entire nation. Psychiatry cures asthenias and neuroses by helping the patient to integrate into his personality certain conflicts, traumas, obsessions, etc.[104] that make his life a failure. We must proceed likewise: to integrate the traumas, the injuries, the mistakes, the crimes, the frenzies[105] of the Guard—and move on. It is not an issue of a process that should be closed, but of a creative act of will and understanding.[106]

This passage, translated in its entirety for the first time, is one of the most bizarre texts I am acquainted with, and it needs a detailed analysis. The fascinating comparison of the Iron Guard to a vampire is highly relevant for understanding Eliade's attitude to the movement. It is reminiscent of Moța's understanding of the legionnaires as living in an interval between the deleterious present and the old pure order they strive to restore, a notion that Eliade used in his own feuilleton; in those two cases, the members of the Iron Guard were already vampires in 1927, not only in 1940. In this passage, Eliade does not propose opening a new chapter by forgetting the crimes, but something quite different: The theory of integration of the trauma that is introduced here is interesting because it would also allow the integration of Eliade himself. Eugène Ionesco, with whom Eliade spoke, recognized that Eliade belonged to the Iron Guard in a letter he wrote earlier in the same year to his friend, the professor of literature Tudor Vianu, which has been quoted by many scholars.[107] It is a case of Eliade's *apologia pro vita sua*. Was he part of the vampire that should be integrated? In any case, I cannot see in this passage any evidence for the view that at that point, Eliade "has left the Legionary episode behind," as Călinescu claimed, despite having seen the entire passage.[108]

In a way, this passage should be read in the context of what Eliade wrote in Portugal in 1941, in a passage I translated above at the end of ch. 2, dealing with loving one's enemies as part of melting the opposition. What concerns me most in this passage is not so much Eliade's refusal to clearly recognize the murderous dimensions of the Iron Guard before 1940, but his call for integration of the "old" good Guard as well as the "new" one: Eliade was eager to "move on." Interestingly enough, here he resorts to the concept of integration in its psychological sense rather than the usual ontological sense that is typical in his writings, as seen above in ch. 2. He sees no problem in absorbing the awareness of the criminal aspects of the activity of the Guard into a future national personality, which would be healthier than bringing the criminals to trial. Strangely, Eliade mixes—or "integrates"—rather indiscriminately the blood of the assassins with that of the victims in the imaginary bloody vampire. Are those so different types of blood, that of the criminals and that of the victims, constituting some form of *coincidentia oppositorum*? As we have seen in another passage, quoted in ch. 2 above, Eliade speaks of the "totalization of the good and bad...definitive melting of the contraries, the annihilation of the human condition by a regression toward the nondifferentiated, in the amorphous."[109] This is part of a much more comprehensive approach, discussed above, which is based on understanding by indistinction, or as a hermeneutics of indistinction: between the victim and the killer, or between persons dead and alive. It may well be that we have here some reverberation of the view that the nation is constituted by people both dead and alive.[110]

What became criminal in Eliade's eyes were not the old crimes or criminals, but those persons who would dare to judge them in the present. He was concerned here with a process of assimilation in order to find a new equilibrium for the nation, in a manner reminiscent of a passage we adduced in ch. 2 from his *Portugal Journal,* which dealt with integration.[111] The moral part of it is obviously secondary. In fact, we have another instance of mythical interpretation, when a major religious concept, once maya and *coincidentia oppositorum,* now vampire, is invoked in order to explain personal or general history.

It is hard to avoid comparing the call for integration here with what may be a possible understanding of Eliade's vampire novel *Miss Christina.* There, the she-vampire wants to return to a meaningful relationship with a man, despite the fact that she belongs to another plane of existence. I hope I am not anachronistically interpreting the novel by using Eliade's 1945 conversation dealing with integration, but I assume that this is what the she-vampire desired: to transcend her situation after death.[112] Let me point out that the imagery of blood resonates with that of self-sacrifice, death, and the circuit of energy by means of it, either human or divine.[113]

The above-mentioned conversation about the vampires took place in October 1945 in Paris, and Eugène Ionesco was the person to whom those things were presumably said. Had Ionesco been arguing with Eliade about what should be done to the legionnaires? This may not be necessarily so. However, some months earlier in the same year, Ionesco describes in a journal his own feelings when leaving Romania in 1942 for France:

> I did everything to leave the country. Everything could happen. To die, to be contaminated, that I shall become a dog:[114] to be inhabited by the devil of the legionnaires....I woke from a nightmare; I escaped from hell...from the Captain [Codreanu], from the vampire [*strigoiul*] of the Captain....But my unconscious is filled with nightmares: a holy horror of hell and vampires have not left me yet.[115]

Without being aware of Eliade's view, as it was mentioned in a later conversation with him, he too referred to the Iron Guard–vampire connection. The fear of becoming a dog is reminiscent of what he would write 14 years later, the famous play *The Rhinoceros.* As scholars have pointed out, one of the major backgrounds to the transformation of the normal citizens into rhinoceroses was the adherence of Ionesco's friends to the Iron Guard.[116] The use of the color green, so evident in the play, symbolizes the representative color of the legionnaires. Marta Petreu insightfully proposed to identify the Logician, who in the play is also a professor, as probably none other than the "Professor" *par excellence* in the thirties in Romania, namely Nae Ionescu, whom Ionesco knew well from a class he took with him at the university, and whom he blamed for his role in the conversion of some of the younger thinkers to the Iron Guard ideology.[117]

Culianu formulated the following quite naïve question, which he intended to ask Eliade: "You lived the rhinocerization of Romania in the years 1934–1938. Do you recognize yourself in the figure of Bérenger, the last person who resisted rhinocerization?"[118] It seems, however, that the story can be complemented by an additional "identification" from the same circle. I suggest that it is Jean, another important figure in the play, who is transfigured into a rhinoceros after the Logician, that represents Eliade. At the very moment of his transformation into a rhinoceros, Jean exclaims: "It faut reconstituer les fondements de notre vie. Il faut retourner à l'intégrité primordial."[119] The final phrase, "It is incumbent to return to the primordial integrity," is strongly reminiscent of Eliade's emphasis on integration and the return to primordial totality, as we have seen in several instances in ch. 2, above. Moreover, the reference to reconstitution of the fundamentals of one's life is reminiscent of the propaganda of the Iron Guard, as formulated in one of the quotes from Moţa, as adduced above. I would opt for the theory that it is Ionesco himself who is camouflaged in the figure of Bérenger, as he was afraid of being contaminated by the ghosts of the Iron Guard, as seen above.[120]

In any case, a reaction to the above-mentioned conversation between Eliade and Ionesco in late 1945 is found in a letter Ionesco wrote to Petru Comarnescu, a major figure in the Criterion group, dated January 1946:

> I cannot see Eliade and Cioran. Though they are "no more legionnaires" (as they say)— they cannot break the engagement they made, once and forever, they remained legionnaires without willing it, and I feel that they are of the folk that appear to me to be hyenas (and I certainly am a hyena for them, we are hyenas for each other—and this is more and more clear as long as history will last—and afterward).[121]

Needless to say, the antagonism among them lasted but some few months, when all three again became good friends for many years; just another case of lack of incompatibility.[122] Nevertheless, tensions between them remained, and according to a letter from Virgil Ierunca to Eliade, Ionesco accused him some time before January 1964 of being responsible for Auschwitz.[123]

At the end of 1946 Eliade returned to the topic of the Iron Guard, remarking that he was moved by the faith of its members who were among strangers for seven years, five of which were in German camps. He asked himself what could be done so that their spiritual forces would not become sectarian, or turn "vampirish, since whether we want it or not, the legionnaire moment is surpassed."[124]

Let me turn now to a question that has been debated for the last two decades among scholars: Did Eliade understand the real nature of the Iron Guard as a violent, murderous movement, as illustrated by the conversation between Nae Ionescu and Mihail Sebastian cited above, or in the view of the unidentified professor of philosophy mentioned by Ionesco, and did he accept it as such, or did he believe, "naïvely" or "myopically," in the spiritual dimension of the movement as preponderant, as others argue. The latter answer was given by Sebastian in his journal after a discussion he had with Eliade about his adherence to the Iron Guard; Sebastian uses the phrase "a catastrophic naïveté" to qualify Eliade's attitude.[125] Some serious scholars accepted this explanation after explicitly acknowledging Eliade's affiliation to the extreme right,[126] while others theorized, in principle, a more genuine adherence to the extreme right movement, without resort to an assumption of naïveté.[127] In some other cases, the concept of "political myopia" has been introduced.[128]

However, I see no reason to adopt the "naïveté" or the myopia explanations, since the story about the vampires, cited above, is an explicit comment on Moța's prediction of the terrible or dreadful governance of the vampires, and it seems quite obvious, to me at least, that Eliade already subscribed to it in his feuilleton in 1938.[129] Is it possible to misunderstand the meaning of the "terrible governing" when he copied it from Moța's preface? His prolonged admiration for Moța, whose sharp anti-Semitism is quite obvious in the book Eliade knew and whose preface he commented upon, cannot leave much room for genuine naïveté, and this is also the case with his positive reaction to Cioran's sharply anti-Semitic book insofar as Jews are concerned. Too much naïveté may turn into stupidity, and Eliade was anything but stupid.

Let me address now the more discussed issue of Eliade and the Iron Guard from the conceptual point of view. That he adhered to this movement in a certain period is in my opinion indubitably true, and attempts by some scholars to mitigate the event seem to stem from a questionable approach. However, the matter may be much more complicated than just having been influenced by Iron Guard ideology. Did Eliade undergo a sudden conversion, a genuine one, or did he adhere out of his admiration for Nae Ionescu, as he claimed? Was it the opportunism of someone who understood the ascent of the Iron Guard as a political power? Was it solely due to his wife's influence? Or was it, as I believe, also a matter of what may be called a "conceptual confluence," as we have seen also in ch. 3. The dominant explanation of scholars is that it was some form of attraction, an unexpected one, like some form of sudden illness, which struck Eliade, who did not adhere to the Iron Guard until two years after his master Ionescu did.[130] On the other hand, there is an interesting remark found in a history of the Iron Guard written by Petre Pandrea, Nae Ionescu's former student in high school and university, who changed political allegiances several times in his life,[131] to the effect that the ideology of the Iron Guard stems from Ionescu's lectures.[132] Like many other controversial statements issued by Pandrea in his various books, this one, too, may be simplistic, though certainly it is not without grounds. At least in the case of Ion Moţa, this may indeed be the case, since he took classes with Ionescu, as Eliade himself confirms in his unfinished novel *The New Life*. As we learn from the memoirs of one of the participants in Ionescu's lectures, the class was full of Iron Guard members, even wearing their uniforms.[133] It may be that the truth is more complex than intellectuals' adherence to the Iron Guard, or Iron Guard thought originating from Ionescu: There were indeed mutual influences, but as I proposed in ch. 3, they should be understood as stemming from a common denominator that preceded both Ionescu and the Iron Guard—some form of Orthodox Christianity, coupled with Romanian nationalism.[134] Because of this common denominator, Eliade, whose thought was permeated with Ionescu's views, could find his way to the ideology of the Iron Guard rather naturally and smoothly, and not as the result of a sudden conversion. In the thought of Eliade, as in that of the Iron Guard, and especially that of Moţa, it is possible to see the emphasis on the mission of the Romanian people, namely an effort to offer a special significance to the existence of the Romanian people as a nation.[135] Needless to say, this emphasis on the centrality of nationality was central to the thought of Nae Ionescu.[136] The sources of such a synthesis may be found in the thought of another important professor, the historian Nicolae Iorga, whom I mentioned above in ch. 5, an influential figure for both Ionescu and Eliade[137] whose ideology inspired, at least for a while, the most anti-Semitic party of A. C. Cuza, from which the Legion of the Archangel Michael, the starting point of the Iron Guard, descended.[138]

If this more complex answer, based on the existence of a significant common cultural/religious denominator, is accepted, then it is harder to accept the theory of Eliade's "sliding," as Culianu put it,[139] than of some form of synergy between Eliade's thought and Christian Orthodox-nationalist ideas that became more fashionable after the emergence of Greater Romania, and the encounter with economic, cultural, and social problems that Romanian elites found hard to cope with in a democratic manner. The ideological biases, together with the economic and social crises of the early thirties, encouraged violence by the Iron Guard, and the accomplice role played by many intellectuals, starting with Ionescu, in backing the murderous movement, which it already had before 1940, though the bloody events in 1940–1941 repulsed Eliade. Nevertheless, Eliade's idealization of Moţa even in the second part of the forties, as pointed out above, shows that it was not only blind admiration for Ionescu that brought Eliade to the Iron Guard, but a much deeper conviction, and a continuing admiration for the two leaders, which continued long after the mentor's death.

If we are to believe a report of the Romanian intelligence service, as late as 1971, Eliade continued to admire Codreanu, though he detested Horia Sima, the

later head of the Legion when it came to power for several months in 1940–1941.[140]
Many years after the war, Eliade declared that he does not "know how history will
judge Corneliu Codreanu."[141] Here, quite surprisingly for a thinker such as Eliade
who deconstructed history systematically, history is conceived of as arbitrary, and he
modestly suspends his judgment when a personality he knew well, and whose his
main attitudes he shared, at least in part, was involved. He declines to interpret the
situation, creatively or otherwise. It seems that he still maintained an idealized vision
of Codreanu, who assassinated a police officer and was known in his youth for a hooligan type of behavior.[142]

To summarize the above discussions: In my opinion, as a scholar of religion,
Eliade failed by not discerning the dangerous combination of national fanaticism and
extreme anti-Semitic hatred on the one hand, and the disciplined paramilitary structures that characterized the Iron Guard from its very inception on the other hand. His
emphasis on one aspect of the organization, the spiritual, ascetic claims, was part of a
wider tendency of his to reduce complex phenomena to just one of their manifestation that he privileged. In this case, the extremes of spirituality and military organization melted into a series of murderous events that affected the lives of thousands of
people. There was no transcendence of the opposites in history, if that ever occurs, but
a wild delirium of assassinations that was the result of the subordination of the spiritual to violence. Eliade's blindness as a scholar is related to his own extreme nationalism during that period. However, what is even sadder from the point of view of a
scholar of religion is that even in retrospect he could not admit the mistake, and he covered his own involvement by reiterating only the spiritual aspect of the Iron Guard.

The reluctance to recognize what a more liberal reader would say was a mistake,
a slip, is in my opinion not only a matter of camouflaging his past, but also related to
a deeper conceptual conviction as to the nature of reality and religion as he understood
them. In my opinion, Eliade regarded the crimes of the Guard as a necessary part of a
process of renewal of the Romanian nation, some form of sacrifice that was indispensable for its purification, or regeneration, just as human sacrifices are necessary, according to archaic religiosity, in order to keep the course of nature in its perfect state.[143] The
killing of the old class of rulers in Romania, whom Eliade hated so much, was
interpreted by Liviu Bordaş as necessary for the affirmation of the young generation,
the so-called 1927 generation, whose leader was Eliade.[144] That could not take place
without blood and sacrifice, as Eliade wrote in one of his unedited fragments of a novel:

> The new generation! Blood and flesh and bones purified by the agony of the war; an inte-
> gral life! Alas with the old ones, with the rationalists, with the skeptics; exalt a young life,
> a young spirituality, our own, out of our experiences, out of our wounds!…Blood, ban-
> ners, crosses, sacrificed bisons, the legionnaires of the sun.[145]

This is a rather vague passage, part of a novel, and I am not sure that its details are so transparent. Spirituality is, therefore, not separated from blood and sacrifices, or from the nationalism of the legionnaires.[146] It is a certain vision of archaic religion that informed Eliade's understanding of contemporary events. This vision of spirituality allows another understanding of Eliade's claim: He understood that spirituality and bloodshed are not opposites, and that crimes should be condemned only when connected to another member of the Iron Guard, as was the case of the horrendous assassination of one of their leaders, Mihai Stelescu.[147]

Did Vampires Die? On the Iron Guard in Chicago

The above discussions of Romanian policy in the thirties of the 20th century do not deal with obsolete issues that died out so many decades ago. In my opinion, reverberations are still evident in various centers in the world: Spain, Germany, the United States of America, and Romania today. Insofar as we are concerned, the Iron Guard was well represented especially in Chicago, the city where Eliade spent most of his lifetime in the USA.[148] The major event in this context related to the presence in the city of the archbishop of the Romanian Orthodox Church in America and Canada, Valerian (Viorel) Trifa, an Iron Guard activist in the early forties in Bucharest whose American citizenship was revoked after many judicial deliberations.[149] According to a report of the Communist security service, Trifa was connected to Eliade via his wife Christinel: "Insofar as Prof. Mircea Eliade is concerned, though he does not make any public manifestation, as said above,[150] he has connections especially by his wife with V. Trifa, Emil Bocioacă, and other legionnaire leaders, who try to influence him."[151] Today it is hard to verify the accuracy of those reports. In any case, Christinel was far removed from the legionnaires, and actually Eliade hid from her his legionnaire past.[152]

In 1974, a booklet entitled *Romanian Nationalism: The Legionary Movement* was published by Loyola University Press in Chicago (reprinted in 1995). The author is Alexandru E. Ronnett, a doctor and a dentist whose services were also extended to Mircea Eliade. Ronnett was a well-known legionnaire, one of the "new" ones close to Horia Sima, namely those whom Eliade condemned as having stained the name of Romania. While in Chicago, Ronnett was the president of a legionary organization called "Freedom Front." Ronnett's apology for the legionnaire movement includes a quite minimal recognition of the sharp anti-Semitic nature of the Iron Guard, ignoring much clearer statements such as Codreanu's and Moţa's adduced above,[153] though his own anti-Semitic tone permeates his web site about Eliade. According to the report of Ted Anton, a Chicago journalist who covered Culianu's assassination, Ronnett said that

> "I know the people who murdered Iorga," says Dr. Alexander Ronnett, an elderly dentist and general practitioner who is a self-proclaimed Chicago spokesman for the Iron Guard. "The only thing they did wrong was to be too kind," he says. "They should have skinned him alive in public."[154]

The doctor's cruel wish is reminiscent of the horrendous way in which the ailing Stelescu was murdered in a hospital—ten legionnaires shot him 120 times and then cut him into small pieces.[155]

Ronnett remained in contact with Eliade as his doctor until the latter's death, and his testimony about Eliade as belonging to the Iron Guard is both detailed and explicit, though not everything in it may be reliable: He claims that Eliade was an enlisted member of the Guard,[156] that he was part of the legionnaire club Axa, and, last but not least, that he was the head of a net [cuib], a small unit in the Iron Guard structure. Moreover, Ronnett reported that in January 1978 he prepared and gave to Eliade a golden medal with the symbol of the Iron Guard, as part of a much greater public ceremony of the centenary of the unification of the two principates of Romania, in recognition of his being the most distinguished Romanian scholar in exile, and Eliade, according to Ronnett, accepted it emotionally.[157] Interestingly, according to one of Ronnett's testimonies, Eliade had quite a different view on Romanians than that which I discuss in the next chapter. He reports that Eliade told him, after he revealed the treason of an Iron Guard person: "Doctor, so we are the Romanians, replete with traitors and sellers. Our history is replete with similar villains."[158]

These small details about the existence of a small Iron Guard net in Chicago may point to something more serious. It was in this city that Eliade's follower, Ioan Petre Culianu, was assassinated in May 1991. When we had the first serious discussion on Eliade, late in 1988 in Chicago, Culianu spoke quite apologetically about his early monograph on Eliade, and stated that he had no idea about Eliade's rightist past, a contention about which I am convinced.[159] Nevertheless, in comparison to the more unequivocal stands of Adriana Berger, Norman Manea, and Leon Volovici, his attitude remained much more hesitant and cautious. He openly admitted the connection between Eliade and the Iron Guard, without however accepting the accusation of Eliade's anti-Semitism. This was already clear from an Italian article published in March 1989 in *Abstracta*, and reiterated in the lengthy interview given in December 1990 in Romanian that was published six weeks before his death, and in a review on a book of Eliade's, printed posthumously.[160] Moreover, in one of Culianu's last books the reader is confronted with a curious situation: Eliade was marginalized, though never openly criticized. So, for example, in *Out of this World*, which deals with shamanistic practices, he totally ignores Eliade's voluminous groundbreaking monograph *Shamanism*, which was in fact one of the first comprehensive treatments on the subject.[161] In Culianu's *The Tree of Gnosis*, Eliade is mentioned only once, in a passage that is in fact an extrapolation from his introduction to *The Eliade Guide to World Religions*.

Shortly before Culianu's death in May 1991, some cautious expressions of reservation regarding Eliade found their way into print. That was part of Culianu's turning his attention to the nefarious role played by the Orthodox Church of Romania during WWII, and his sharp critique of the Iron Guard, which he described in 1991 in the journal *Meridian* as an "Orthodox Ku Klux Klan!" whose inspiration stemmed from the Church. Most of these views are found in his last large-scale interview, published in Romanian in Bucharest a month and a half before his death.[162] However, in my opinion, more serious from the perspective of the Iron Guard than his reservations about Eliade was his invitation of King Mihai of Romania to Chicago in early 1991. One should remember the terrible enmity between the Iron Guard and the two last kings of Romania. It was the father of King Mihai, King Carol II, who clamped down on the Iron Guard, ordering the assassinations of many of its leaders, including its head and Eliade's idol, Corneliu Zelea Codreanu. Thus, Culianu, a fervent liberal, could be seen not only as critical of the ideas and role of the Iron Guard, but also as ready to cooperate with the son of the hated king who had signed a pact with the USSR in 1944—this a month or so before his assassination. He received threats by phone, so he told me, as late as two weeks before his assassination.

The violence of the Iron Guard is not obsolete history: The Iron Guard did not completely disappear after the war; remnants of the movement are still active in Europe, publishing books in Spain, Germany, and Italy, for example, and more recently in Romania, but also in Latin America, Canada, and the United States, most prominently in Chicago! Let me adduce here a reaction of a legionnaire, namely a member of the Iron Guard living in Chicago, as published in the Romanian newspaper *Expres* on July 15, 1991, less than two months after Culianu's assassination.[163] A Romanian reporter, Cornel Nistorescu, for a story entitled "A Crime in Political Dispute," interviewed members of several groups that may have been close to the Culianu affair. Under the rubric "What do the legionnaires say?" he claims, and I translate verbatim:

> I spoke with numerous old legionnaires in Chicago. I prefer not to mention their names. One of them, Eugen Vâlsan, who allowed me to mention his name, told me: "Culianu arrived to Chicago due to Mircea Eliade, and Mircea Eliade was a legionnaire, though he 'did not make legionnaire politics.' I have been with Eliade in the same camp,[164] and afterwards he

'did not make legionnaire politics,' but in his essence he remained what he was. From this point of view, *grosso modo*, because he was close to the world of Eliade, Culianu too belongs to our family. The fact that he intended to soon marry a Jewess was his business. We were not happy with this, but we were not preoccupied by it. This[165] is but another absurd assumption....The last time I met Culianu was at Easter, in the Church. Our relations were more than cordial. All the legionnaires that remained called me [by phone] to learn about the news, and were very sorry. We categorically reject any accusation related to us being involved in the death of this Romanian scholar."

The content of this passage may be shocking for some readers less acquainted with the intricacies of the Romanian background, and I cannot explain here all its possible implications. I chose to delve into some aspects of it because of what I consider to be the most shocking of its assessments: that Culianu was in fact part of the Iron Guard family of Chicago. Some preliminary remarks are necessary. Eliade's detention in custody in the late thirties together with the legionnaires is well documented by many sources, including Eliade's own autobiography. The statement that Eliade "remained what he was"—according to Mr. Vâslan, a legionnaire, but one who does not "make legionnaire politics," an expression that is obscure—may be the wishful thinking of an old man who was recruiting famous acquaintances to his old beliefs. If he means that Eliade was not violent and did not participate in the murders of the Iron Guard, he is certainly right. My reading of Eliade over the years did not unearth any written testimony to the contrary. But what remains for a legionnaire who does not make politics is more difficult to understand. In any case, Vâslan's testimony corroborates those of Ronnett's that has been adduced above.

True or not, the above passage tells a story that is worthy of another discussion: How was Eliade perceived by this legionnaire who was acquainted with him for more than 40 years? Vâslan's assumption is that he did not change, a point that I attempted to make earlier in this chapter on the basis of Eliade's writings and Ionesco's testimony. Anyone perusing the plentiful digital sites of the Iron Guard on the Internet today will easily find all of Eliade's pertinent feuilletons written in the late thirties, material that was once barely accessible even to scholars, now reprinted proudly as belonging to Iron Guard ideology.

However, what is deeply disturbing is the incredible inclusion of Culianu in the legionnaire "family" and the suggestion that, as result, he was allegedly immune from any harm from the legionnaires because of his good relations with Eliade, via some form of elective affinities. These are interesting statements in themselves. If Culianu, Eliade's protégé, were to "betray" the "family" after all, one may ask, how would he be treated? And, following the same line of thought: Did he actually do something that could be seen as a betrayal of the "family"? The answer is unequivocal: In a Romanian article dedicated especially to this topic, he described the Iron Guard as

the *orthodox*: that is, the Christian Orthodox Ku Klux Klan. This article was published days after his assassination, and it is the sharpest and most explicit denun-
ciation of the Iron Guard possible.[166] Despite my efforts to find out whether this
was an older article that was reprinted, as happens in some cases after a death, or
a brand new one, I could not resolve the question. This article is quite explicit and
cannot be misinterpreted by even a superficial reading. However, a concerned
member of the Iron Guard could have found alarming statements to this effect
much earlier in Culianu's published stories.

Is there a penalty for such a betrayal of the "family" into which he was "adopted"?
This is a difficult question. Perhaps a group of elderly legionnaires, living in America
for several decades, took efficient steps to deal with their misunderstanding of the
young Culianu and their late, correct understanding of his journalism? A Romanian
physicist at the University of Chicago and a friend of Culianu, Mircea Sabău, was
reported to have said, in a passage immediately preceding the above quote from
Expres, that the legionnaires in Chicago were old and powerless and their ideology
loose. He may well have been right, yet elsewhere, in an interview published in the
Chicago Tribune on June 2, 1991, he was reported to have thought the opposite!
Nonetheless, to what extent a legionnaire group—note the *we* and *us* forms that recur
in the passage, and the term "family"—that belonged, at least in the past, to the most
anti-Semitic movement in the history of Romania, might in 1991 so stoically watch
the planned marriage to a Jewess of someone seen as being in the "family," and relegate it to the status of a private affair, is less than obvious. In any case, if the above
passage is conveying a genuine attitude, Vâlsan is to be praised for his willingness to
speak openly with a reporter, while his friends were quite reluctant to do so. Do they
have something to hide, if they indeed were so saddened by Culianu's assassination?
Would they condemn it? Would they also agree that now in their "family" there is no
racial discrimination, invalidating Culianu's own judgment of the Iron Guard as an
"orthodox Ku Klux Klan"? Again, I fear that a positive answer to these questions is
disputable. I assume that Vâslan would be astonished to read at the end of Culianu's
essay referencing the Ku Klux Klan that

> [Romanian] Orthodoxy has produced in their time an enormous printed material[167] that
> today appears to be crazy. The Iron Guard started from this ideology, into which they
> introduced elements of mysticism and of secret societies. The danger of fundamental-
> ism in the bosom of orthodoxy is not extinguished. On the contrary, today it is more
> powerful than ever.[168]

Was the Iron Guard in 1991 powerful enough to eliminate a scholar who was perceived as a traitor, just as they did in 1940 when they assassinated another eminent
scholar, Nicolae Iorga, who was in fact one of the most anti-Semitic intellectuals in

20th-century Romania? Did legionnaire vampires haunt people in Chicago as late as 1991? It is hard to answer those questions in a definitive manner. Nevertheless, the reasons for the assassination of Culianu, who transgressed some of the Iron Guard sensibilities, should be explained in some way or another.

The attempt to appropriate Culianu into Eliade's former "family" in Chicago is, at the least, a blatant mistake. It distorts one of the most characteristic themes of his late political writings, that of saying NO. Quintessential in this context is Culianu's feuilleton where he praises Ionesco's courage to say NO against his contemporaries.[169] I would like to stress that my descriptions above are not an attempt to idealize him, or to make him into an uncompromising fighter, a fearless protagonist in a bloody drama. Nevertheless, as one well acquainted with both the terrors of the Romanian Securitate and, later in his life, with the crimes of the Iron Guard, Culianu could not have written his public, uncompromising, and sustained critiques over many months without a substantial amount of intentionality and courage. In fact, I think that both morally and personally he grew, perhaps even significantly changed, as he wrote the journalistic material, but in a direction opposite from Eliade's journalism in 1937–1938. It had to do with his gradually becoming aware of the horrors of the past in Romania, and the confidence that his future place would be America, and these prompted a fresh attitude that was not evident, to my best knowledge, while he lived in Europe. The promising American scene, which gradually produced a viable prospect for him as a tenured professor at the Divinity School in the University of Chicago, coincided with the *coup d'état* in Romania at the end of 1989, and these events triggered a more aggressive expression of his thought. A feeling of freedom, which backed his courage, balanced his apprehensions and fears. One whose family was still living in Romania could not ignore the possibility that they, if not he, might pay a price for his activity.

Last but not least: The above discussions refer to, unfortunately, far from obsolete issues that belong solely to the domain of the past. On the contrary, an inspection of Iron Guard sites on the Internet will easily detect most of Eliade's feuilletons and Codreanu's and Moţa's books, as well as a luxuriant anti-Semitic literature and collections of videos dealing with the alleged Jewish "invasion" of Romania today and other similar stereotypes. Where once the anti-Semites in Romania were afraid of the 4% of Jews there, today they are still afraid, but of a mere 0.04%. Obsessions, like vampires, do not change, though the proportion of obsessed persons in Romania has dramatically decreased, which is certainly good. Eliade was perhaps right that people change only slowly. This is the reason why a modest confession by Eliade about his past and a critique of it would, perhaps, have changed something. But he preferred to remain silent: not only about his youthful mistakes, but also about his ongoing relationship with members of the Iron Guard in Chicago. Was he afraid of being exposed by them?[170]

In one way or another, it turns out that the Iron Guard, though much less spiritual than Eliade claimed it was, played nevertheless a much more important role in the history of religion than imagined.

Notes

1. *The Suffering of the White Race*, p. 47.
2. *NO*, p. 133.
3. *Present Past*, p. 123.
4. The first author to do it in print was Theodor Loewenstein/Lavi, an Israeli historian, in the Israeli journal *Toladot*. I hope to dedicate a separate study to the entire correspondence and the impact of this article, based on additional material.
5. Handoca, ed., Preface to *Eliade File*, II, pp. 6–11; Rennie, *Reconstructing Eliade*, p. 160.
6. See, e.g., Volovici, *Nationalist Ideology*; Radu Ioanid, *The Sword of the Archangel: Fascist Ideology in Romania*, tr. Peter Heinegg (New York, 1990); Berger, "Mircea Eliade: Romanian Fascism"; Manea, "Happy Guilt"; Dubuissson, *Mythologies*; Laignel-Lavastine, *L'oubli du fascisme*; Ţurcanu, *Mircea Eliade*; Dana, *Métamorphoses*; and Mutti, *Les plumes de l'archange*.
7. Adduced by Zigu Ornea, *Permanenţa Cărturarului* (Bucharest, 2002), p. 418, citing "The Central Electoral Committee," *Buna Vestire*, I, 234 (December 6, 1937).
8. See, e.g., Idel, *Ascensions on High*, p. 221; Antohi-Idel, *What Unites Us*, p. 150.
9. *Troublous Years*, pp. 147–166.
10. This issue will occupy me elsewhere when I analyze the exchange of letters between Eliade and Scholem in 1972–1973. It should be mentioned that Călinescu's claim in his preface to Culianu, *Interrupted Dialogues*, p. 25, that Eliade did not answer questions related to his past, is not accurate.
11. See also the important caveat of Culianu, *Romanian Studies*, I, p. 346.
12. See his introduction to *Eliade File*, II, pp. 5–11.
13. See his attempt to make a distinction about Eliade's admiration for Codreanu—that it related solely to his personality and not to his ideology (*From Portugal*, pp. 170–172), as if Codreanu was some sort of movie star who had nothing to say about events in Romania and no influence on them.
14. On Călinescu's description of Eliade as "a humanist erring in politics," namely, in his involvement in the Iron Guard, see his *About Culianu and Eliade*, p. 45. See also ibid., p. 49, where Eliade's judgment of the early Iron Guard is described as a case of "auto-înşelare," namely self-deception. See also pp. 23–234 n. 3.
15. "Between Political Journalism and Scholarly Work."
16. Rennie, *Reconstructing Eliade*, pp. 160–161: "While it is undoubtedly true that the Legion eventually became violently antisemitic, antisemitism was not an indispensable part of its earlier development when Eliade was sympathetic of it." See also ibid., p. 177. Indubitably, this is a very original understanding of the Iron Guard, supported only by Eliade's own impressions or those of the adherents, but not by any serious scholarship in the field. In fact, anti-Semitism was part and parcel of the Iron Guard ideology from the very beginning, just as anti-Communism was. It should be said, however, that Eliade was attracted much more to anti-Communism, and much less to the virulent and violent anti-Semitism of the Guard, as the writings of their predecessor, Nicolae Paulescu, written before and after WWI, amply show. See Volovici, *Nationalist Ideology*, pp. 29, 75, and Oişteanu, *Inventing the Jew*, pp. 152–153, 187, 233, 320, 418–419.

17. Written in 1936 and 1939 and reprinted in *Legionnaire Texts*, pp. 144–147, 150–155. See also Volovici, *Nationalist Ideology*, pp. 124–125; Ricketts, *Romanian Roots*, II, p. 1127.

18. See, e.g., Volovici, *Nationalist Ideology*, pp. 95–180, Petreu, *Cioran*, pp. 45–92, or Veiga, *The History of the Iron Guard*, pp. 55–64.

19. The phrase is from Petreu, *Cioran*, p. 58. On Codreanu's anti-Semitism, see Berger, "Mircea Eliade: Romanian Fascism." To be sure, Codreanu and his companions were not the first virulent anti-Semites in the history of 20th-century Romania, as shown by the earlier writings of the most distinguished Romanian philosopher, Vasile Conta, and the most distinguished scientist, Nicolae Paulescu.

20. On the immediate historical background to this conversation, see Carol Iancu, *Evreii în România (1919–1938): De la emanicipare la marginalizare* (Bucharest, 2000), pp. 262–263, and Țurcanu, *Mircea Eliade*, p. 281.

21. Ionescu's house or villa in north Bucharest.

22. The prime minister of Romania, Octavian Goga.

23. This is the end of Ionescu's speech.

24. *Journal*, p. 146. On this passage, see Călinescu, *About Culianu and Eliade*, pp. 43–44.

25. *Journal*, p. 339; for many other examples, see Petreu, *From Junimea to Noica*, pp. 205–249.

26. *The Suffering of the White Race*, p. 130.

27. *Present Past*, p. 121.

28. "Incompatibilities," p. 32.

29. See Vulcănescu, *Nae Ionescu*, p. 131.

30. See above, chs. 5 and 6.

31. See e.g., Petreu, *From Junimea to Noica*, p. 304. Even the most sophisticated of the intellectuals, such as Noica, used such slogans. See Laignel-Lavastine, *Noica*, p. 218.

32. Sebastian stated this opinion also elsewhere in his *Journal*, p. 235, in September 1939.

33. *Journal*, p. 147.

34. I wonder if this is Nae Ionescu.

35. *Present Past*, p. 124.

36. See Oișteanu, *Inventing the Jew*, p. 289.

37. See Ionescu's feuilleton printed as an appendix to Sebastian's *How I Became a Hooligan*, pp. 331–332.

38. *The Legionnaire Texts*, p. 97.

39. Handoca, ed., *Eliade File*, II, p. 150.

40. See, e.g., Veiga, *The History of the Iron Guard*, p. 79.

41. Gligor–Caloianu, eds., *Theodor Lavi*, p. 342.

42. *The Romanian Paradox*.

43. Eliade, *Memoirs*, p. 48; Ornea, *The Thirties*, pp. 208–209. See also Eliade, *Portugal Journal*, I, p. 103, where he speaks about the "killers of the legion."

44. See Bordaș, "Between the Devil's Waters."

45. See Ricketts, *Romanian Roots*, I, p. 662.

46. See *Portugal Journal*, I, p. 156.

47. Ibid., p. 133.

48. Petreu, *The Devil and His Apprentice*, p. 242.

49. He used the *Protocols* in his propaganda since 1923. See *Skulls of Wood*, p. 174.

50. See Veiga, *The History of the Iron Guard*, pp. 76–77, and Heinen, *The Legion of the Archangel Michael*, pp. 113–114.

51. On this figure, see Petreu, *Cioran*, pp. 78–80, and Turcanu, *Intellectuels*, pp. 70–83, in which the correspondence with the extreme right figure Charles Maurras was printed.

52. Vulcănescu, *Nae Ionescu*, p. 78.

53. Ornea, *The Thirties*, p. 407; Petreu, *Cioran*, p. 77.

54. Moța uses the pejorative term for Jews—*jidanească*, namely, kike-ish.

55. The same term is also used earlier on the same page.

56. This is certainly not a matter of an economic threat but a spiritual one, as in other cases in Moța.

57. *Skulls of Wood*, p. 195. This is also the gist of Codreanu's program in 1937: "The historical mission of our generation is to solve the Jewish problem. All our fights for the last 15 years had this scope, and all the efforts of our existence since then have the same scope." Cf. Volovici, *Nationalist Ideology*, p. 65. For Cioran's view of the invasion of the Jews in Romania, see ibid., pp. 115–116. For Iorga's view of the Jewish invasion and colonization of Romania, see Iovănel, *The Improbable Jew*, pp. 196–198. See also Volovici, ibid., pp. 175, 178.

58. *Skulls of Wood*, p. 168.

59. Veiga, *The History of the Iron Guard*, p. 160, and Heinen, *The Legion of the Archangel Michael*, p. 137.

60. See Lucian Nastasă, ed., *Antisemitismul universitar in România (1919–1939)* (Cluj-Napoca, 2011), or Lucian Boia, *Capcanele Istoriei* (Bucharest, 2011), pp. 97–98.

61. See *Skulls of Wood*, p. 62, Volovici, *Nationalist Ideology*, p. 65, and Petreu, *Cioran*, p. 79.

62. *Skulls of Wood*, p. 39. See also Petreu, *From Junimea to Noica*, p. 307.

63. On the call for an elimination of the Jews, see also ibid., p. 21, where Moța quotes A. C. Cuza, one of the founders of the party from which the Iron Guard was derived, and see also ibid., p. 22. See also Petreu, *From Junimea to Noica*, pp. 303–304.

64. *Skulls of Wood*, p. 196. For more on Moța's theory that there are millions of Jews in Romania, see Ricketts, *Romanian Roots*, p. 659.

65. Ibid., p. 169. Moța uses again the pejorative "kike." Attempts to attribute the anti-Semitism of the Iron Guard to solely economic reasons are an oversimplification of the situation. Cf. Culianu, *The Sin against Spirit*, p. 51.

66. *Skulls of Wood*, p. 194.

67. Ibid., p. 196.

68. Ibid., p. 61. On the elimination of the Jews, see also ibid., p. 192.

69. M. A. Ledeen, *L'internazionale fascista* (Bari, 1973), p. 158. On the search for an international solution to the "Jewish problem" according to Codreanu, see "Mircea Eliade: Romanian Fascism," pp. 60–61, 69–70.

70. See Ion I. Moța, *Corespondența cu "Serviciul Mondial": 1934–1936* (Roma, 1954) on the publication of the French original letters, accompanied by an introduction and a Romanian translation, and his *Skulls of Wood*, p. 30.

71. This is the Romanian version of the Troparion of the Matins of the Resurrection, which is repeated several times, and it reads in English: "Christ is raised from the dead! By death He conquered Death, and to those in the graves He granted life."

72. Nae Ionescu, preface to Vasile Marin, *Crez de generație*, ed. a IV–a, (München, 1977), originally printed in Bucharest (February 1937), pp. xii–xiii.

73. On the theory that there was no one after Jesus like Codreanu, see the testimony from the Iron Guard adduced by Boia, *History and Myth*, p. 259 and n. 48.

74. See the other explanations adduced by Vulcănescu, *Nae Ionescu*, pp. 99–100.

75. Vulcănescu, *Nae Ionescu*, pp. 99–100.

76. This is found in *Skulls of Wood*, pp. 93, 137, in which he describes it as the legionnaire slogan taken from Seneca's *Letter to a Stoic*.

77. *The New Life*, p. 116. Moța's quote from Seneca is cited again in Eliade's legionnaire feuilleton "Libertatea," printed in *Iconar*, March 5, 1937.

78. *The New Life*, p. 116.

79. *Correspondence*, III, p. 475. See also Gligor, *The Troublous Years*, p. 198.

80. See e.g., Ornea, *The Thirties*, pp. 208–209.

81. *Legionnaire Texts*, pp. 70–71, discussed in the next section.

82. *Legionnaire Texts*, p. 149.

83. See Petreu, *Cioran*.

84. *Correspondence*, I, p. 156.

85. Bordaş, "Between the Devil's Waters," p. 60.

86. *Skulls of Wood*, pp. 6–7.

87. Ibid., p. 4.

88. See earlier, ibid., p. 6.

89. *Romanian Studies*, I, p. 349.

90. The term *strigoi* appears also elsewhere in his poems. See his "A Rumor from the Jailers," "Convoy," "Fairy Tale" [Basm], and "Zarca." It is hard to determine exactly when Gyr wrote these poems, though some of them may reflect the period of his suffering in a Communist prison. In any case, Eliade was described as part of Gyr's net of legionnaires in 1938. See Țurcanu, *Mircea Eliade*, pp. 264–265.

91. Radu Gyr, *Foamea*—Hunger.

92. See Petreu, *Cioran*, pp. 113–115.

93. Compare to Alexandrescu, *The Romanian Paradox*, p. 223, who claims that "Nae Ionescu, Mircea Eliade and the other intellectuals who wrote for the legionnaires themselves fell into the net in which the legionnaires were struggling, under the illusion that 'deeds' are not linked to 'words,' and only the latter determine the evolution of the movement." There was no objective net, not even an illusion, but a firm conviction that words would turn into facts. Any lucid thinker could easily extrapolate from watching the events that words written in political contexts might become deeds, as it indeed happened.

94. *Legionnaire Texts*, pp. 70–71. On this piece see the remarks of Ricketts, *Romanian Roots*, II, pp. 926, 927–928.

95. For more on this issue, see above, ch. 3.

96. Namely, the Romanians, but basically he refers to the Moldavian region.

97. *Legionnaire Texts*, pp. 70–71.

98. This is well known, and the text is found, inter alia, on the stamp with the portrait of Codreanu issued in 1940, during the "government of the vampires," namely the Iron Guard period in Romania. See Oişteanu, "Mircea Eliade, between Political Journalism and Scholarly Work," p. 325.

99. Ronnett, *Romanian Nationalism*, p. 19. See more in the next chapter.

100. See, e.g., the interview published in *Nouvel Observateur* in 1986, reprinted in Olender, *Race sans histoire*, p. 165.

101. In Romanian, *depășit*. This linguistic form is found also in another discussion of the Guard, adduced below.

102. Compare the view of Eliade in his *Master Manole*, pp. 105–106, 109, 111–112, 117, that a violent death is always creative, and that the soul inhabits a new body. See above ch. 3.

103. In Romanian, *lichidate* (liquidated).

104. For Eliade's own similar problems some few years earlier in Portugal and his contact with a psychiatrist, see *Portugal Journal*, I, pp. 225, 226, 364, cited in Final Remarks.

105. *Extazele*.

106. Part of the passage has been cited by Călinescu, "Eliade and Ionesco," p. 111. For the Romanian original, published in part by Călinescu elsewhere, see his *About Culianu and Eliade*, p. 68 n. 24. Călinescu omitted some phrases. Thanks are due to Prof. Mac Linscott Ricketts, who kindly sent me the full original text, which has been retranslated here, and to David Brent for permission to translate the full version. My interpretation here differs from that of Liviu Bordaș, "Ultimul interviu a lui Mircea Eliade și *felix culpa*," *România literară*, XLIII, 50 (16 decembrie 2011), p. 11, and his "Ultimele interviuri românești ale lui Eliade și *Felix culpa*," *Europa Novi Sad*, 9 (Mai 2012), pp. 42–43. Compare the view of Louis Pauwels, adduced by Steven Wasserstrom, "The True Dream of Mankind," p. 193.

107. See, Ornea, *The Thirties*, p. 183–184. See also above, ch. 6.

108. Călinescu, "Eliade and Ionesco," p. 111.

109. See *The Way to the Center*, pp. 379–380.

110. See Petrescu, "Ioan Petru Eliade and Mircea Eliade," pp. 414–415.

111. p. 111 I, p. 170. Interestingly, orgy and violence are related to integration.

112. I cannot begin here a discussion of the complexity of this novel, whose main heroine is a vampire.

113. See, e.g., *The Forge and the Crucible*, pp. 31–33.

114. Is this some adumbration of becoming a rhinoceros?

115. *The War with the Entire World*, II, p. 274.

116. Călinescu, "Ionesco and *Rhinoceros*," and Petreu, *Ionesco*, pp. 126–128.

117. Petreu, ibid.

118. Printed at the end of his *Mircea Eliade*, p. 271.

119. Eugène Ionesco, *Rhinocéros* (Paris, 1959), p. 159. It should be pointed out that Ionesco entitled his complex presentation "The Identity of the Contraries," (*NO*, pp. 115–138), which demonstrates that he quite early identified Eliade's interest.

120. See also Ionesco, *Present Past*, pp. 79–80.

121. The text has been printed in Ornea, *The Thirties*, p. 210. See also Ionesco, *Present Past*, pp. 113–114, and Laignel-Lavastine, *L'oubli du fascisme*, pp. 15–16. For Ionesco's reference to hyenas in the description of Romanians in Romania later in 1946, see Petreu, *Ionesco*, p. 159, and his *Present Past*, p. 35, where he refers to a leader of the Iron Guard he met in Paris.

122. Earlier he mentioned as dead in spirit other legionnaires, such as Arșavir Acterian, a fact that did not prevent him from corresponding with him afterwards. See Acterian, *Cioran, Eliade, Ionesco*.

123. Cited in Călinescu, "Eliade and Ionesco," p. 112.

124. See in his unpublished journal found in the Regenstein Library, December 19, 1946. Thanks are due to Dr. Liviu Bordaş for making available this text.

125. *Journal*, p. 115.

126. See Culianu, in a review of books related to Eliade in *Journal of Religion*, 72 (1992), p. 161, where he speaks about "political naïveté"; Călinescu, introduction to Culianu, *Interrupted Dialogues*, pp. 23–24; id., "Eliade and Ionesco," pp. 110, 113, 115; id., "The 1927 Generation in Romania: Ideological Options and Personal Relations," tr. in *Sebastian, Under Times*, pp. 27–28; Alexandrescu, *The Romanian Paradox*, p. 217; and Volovici in an interview he gave in 2008 published in Ovidiu Şimonca, *Observator Cultural*, 603 (December 2011). See also Mac Linscott Ricketts, in a letter to Theodor Lavi. Cf. *Theodor Lavi*, ed. Gligor–Caloianu, p. 348. Lavi, however, ibid., p. 350, rejects this explanation.

127. See, e.g., Alexandra Laignel-Lavastine, and Daniel Dubuisson. See, however, even the position of Călinescu, *About Culianu and Eliade*, p. 39, where he mentions cunning in the context of Eliade's strategy regarding his fate in exile.

128. Alexandrescu, *The Romanian Paradox*, p. 230, and following him, Oişteanu, *Religion, Politics and Myth*, pp. 32–33, 34.

129. In Moţa and in some cases in Eliade, the vampires are allegories for the legionnaires, namely the young generation. Compare the view of Bordaş, "The Conflict between Generations," p. 17–18, who pointed out the possible influence of Moţa on Eliade, but who regards the vampires as referring to the older, ruling, generation.

130. Though Eliade certainly imitated Ionescu by adhering to the Iron Guard, the role of Eliade's first wife, Nina, who was a devoted legionnaire, should not be overlooked.

131. On this figure, see Petreu, *The Devil and His Apprentice*, pp. 58–61.

132. *The Iron Guard*, pp. 283–284, 295; Petreu, *From Junimea to Noica*, p. 240. See also Oişteanu, "Mircea Eliade, between Political Journalism and Scholarly Work."

133. See Gheorghiu, *Memoirs*, p. 400.

134. See Culianu, in a passage adduced below in this chapter.

135. See the quote from Moţa in Palaghiţă, *The History of the Legionnaire Movement*, p. 76, and below, Final Remarks.

136. See especially the series of lectures delivered by Ionescu to legionnaires in the camp of Miercurea Ciuc in 1938, printed as an appendix to Palaghita, ibid., pp. 359–361. On Ionescu and nationalism, see Voicu, *The Myth of Nae Ionescu*, pp. 45–62.

137. See Handoca, *The Life of Mircea Eliade*, pp. 208.

138. My theory about the congenital affinity between the thought of Ionescu and Eliade on the one hand, and the Iron Guard on the other, which caused the rapprochement in a certain moment, is similar to what Laignel-Lavastine proposed for Noica's affiliation to the Iron Guard. See her *Noica*.

139. *Aluneca* in *The Sin against Spirit*, p. 52. This is exactly the term used by Sebastian to describe the surprising involvement in the Iron Guard of his friend Mihail Polihondriade, who found his death because of it. See his *Journal*, p. 235.

140. Mezdrea, ed., *Nae Ionescu and His Disciples*, p. 98.

141. *Memoirs*, p. 26, and Volovici, *Nationalist Ideology*, p. 144. Compare also to what he wrote to Culianu, *Interrupted Dialogues*, pp. 125–126.

142. See Pandrea, *The Iron Guard*, pp. 329–332; Gheorghiu, *Memoirs*, p. 451.

143. For more on this issue, see the Final Remarks.

144. See his "The Conflict of Generations," pp. 17–18.

145. Printed from a manuscript by Bordaş, ibid., p. 18.

146. See also his No Souvenirs, p. 212, quoted in Final Remarks.

147. See Eliade, Correspondence, I, p. 154. For the details of the assassination, see Gheorgiu, Memoirs, pp. 320–321.

148. For aspects of the reception of Eliade by the postwar Iron Guard, see Petreu, From Junimea to Noica, pp. 466–471.

149. On Trifa and the Iron Guard, see Palaghiţă, The History of the Legionnaire Movement, pp. 149–150.

150. Mezdrea, ed., Nae Ionescu and His Disciples, p. 87.

151. Ibid., p. 91. The influence has to do with taking a negative attitude toward Communist Romania.

152. See Petreu, From Junimea to Noica, p. 383; Călinescu, "Eliade and Ionesco," pp. 114–115.

153. See pp. 6–7.

154. Ted Anton, "The Killing of Professor Culianu," Lingua Franca, 2, 6 (September/October 1992). and the web site http://miscarea.net/eliade-aronnett.htm.

155. See Gheorghiu, Memoirs, pp. 320–321.

156. See above, Ornea's similar claim.

157. See http://miscarea.net/eliade-aronnett.htm. He testifies as to Christinel's negative attitude toward the Iron Guard members who visited his house, together with Eliade, as well as her surprise about the use of the symbol of the Guard on the medal. It seems that the medal disappeared, since it is not found in the box of medals, as Liviu Bordaş kindly let me know. Such a testimony, if accepted, problematizes Marta Petreu's reading of Eliade as someone who symbolically died to his past in 1955 and was reborn, thus forgetting his legionnaire past. From Junimea to Noica, pp. 383–385, 386.

158. http://miscarea.net/eliade-aronnett.htm.

159. About the relations between the two scholars, see Călinescu, About Culianu and Eliade, and the detailed and important study by Petrescu, "Ioan Petru Eliade and Mircea Eliade," pp. 410–458.

160. Journal of Religion, 72 (1992), pp. 157–161.

161. This point has been made by Oişteanu in his introduction to the Romanian translation of the book, Ioan Petru Culianu, Călătorii în lumea de dincolo, tr. Gabriela şi Andrei Oişteanu (Bucharest, 1994), pp. 16–17.

162. Interview with Gabriela Adameşteanu, Revista, 22 (5 Aprilie 1991), rpt. in The Sin against Spirit, pp. 37–68.

163. Expres, 15 July 1991, pp. 8–9.

164. Namely, in 1938 in Miercurea Ciuc.

165. Namely, the accusation that they were involved in the crime.

166. Rpt. in The Sin against Spirit, pp. 240–242.

167. In Romanian, maculatură is a sarcastic term for useless printed material.

168. In The Sin against Spirit, p. 242. For the Romanian sources of the Iron Guard, see also Gligor, Troublous Years, pp. 116–118.

169. The Sin against Spirit, pp. 197–199.

170. See Calinescu, "Eliade and Ionesco," p. 114.

· 8 ·

ELIADE AS A ROMANIAN THINKER

The Privileged Status of Romania and Its Traditional Culture

*I*n the previous chapter we have seen that Eliade's adherence to the Iron Guard was not just a matter of a few years, since he remained unaware of the basic harm involved in a mystical movement that is both religiously fundamentalist and anti-Semitic, and paramilitary. This failure aside, Eliade remained a committed patriotic Romanian, and his acute anxiety related to the battles of the Romanian army during 1942–1943 on the Russian front is a fine expression of his deep attachment.[1] However, it should be pointed out that Eliade remained attached to the Romanian people, but not so much to the Romanian state under Carol II, which he hated because of its repression of the Iron Guard, though he was nevertheless ready to serve it as a propaganda attaché.[2] This adherence to Romanian ethnic or closed nationalism became, in my opinion, part and parcel of his views long after WWII. In a way, significant parts of his scholarship can be regarded as a sustained attempt to show that Romanian peasant culture is on the same level as European history "through our myths," especially Miorița and Master Manole.[3]

In a lecture delivered at the Group for Social Dialogue in Bucharest in 2002 that dealt with a comparison between Eliade and Culianu, I claimed, inter alia, that Eliade should be described as a Romanian figure, even after he left Romania and became an internationally recognized scholar.[4] Later, in 2006, at another lecture at the New Europe College in Bucharest, I used a pun to illustrate this point: Eliade was "accidentally Occidental."[5] This Romanian characteristic is, in my opinion, a matter related not only to his ethnic extraction, his personal nostalgic allegiance, or the way in which other persons perceived his personality, but also—and what concerns me here especially—to the type of religion he portrayed in many cases as the primeval and authentic one; subsequently, he generated a history of religion that is nourished by his Geto-Dacian assumption. Unlike him, as I argued there, Culianu was a cosmopolitan figure who did not privilege one form of religion over the other, especially in the last phase of his thought about religion.[6] I would like to elaborate here my assessments as to the Romanian nature of Eliade, including the later phases of development of his thought.

Both Eliade and Lucian Blaga understood themselves as universal men. This is the dedication Blaga wrote in one of his books he gave to Eliade in 1937.[7] My remarks below are not intended to minimize this assessment, which is also a widely recognized fact, but to claim that his wide interests were shaped by a very strong privileging of a Romanian perspective, with, in many cases, quite a triumphalist tone.[8] This is true despite his decision in late 1943 not to apply for a position at the University of Bucharest, and to remain in the West in order to be able to address wider audiences with his scholarship.[9]

Eliade saw himself as a writer, even more than a scholar of religion. As he noted in his *Journal* on October 12, 1946, "My real vocation [is] that of a Romanian writer."[10] All he wrote as literature—short stories, novels, and plays—was written in Romanian, and the protagonists in the vast majority of cases are Romanian, and the background for the stories is mostly Romania, either in the interwar period or during the Communist era. This point of my argument is sustained by an essay entitled "Mircea Eliade and the Obsession of Romania," authored by Eliade's good friend living in exile in Paris, Virgil Ierunca,[11] as well as by Ion Negoițescu.[12] Let me elaborate on this point.

Geographically speaking, Romania is described by Eliade as a meeting point of East and West. This view is formulated in his *Autobiography*[13] as if assumed already in 1931, but it is reiterated in a more articulated manner as late as 1981 in a letter addressed to his friend the philosopher Constantin Noica concerning the possibility of creating an institute of Oriental Studies in Romania for teaching and research of Asian topics:

It is important to realize on the one hand the continuity and the unity of the Asian civilizations, and on the other hand, the creativity of the popular cultures in which, among others, South-East Europe and Romania played an important role. As I have repeated many times, Romania is not just a crossroads, but also a bridge between East and West. If we do so much resemble the "Orientals," this is not because we became Turks,[14] but because in Romania, just as in the South-East of Europe and in Asia in its entirety, the *genius*[15] of the Neolithic has been preserved until recently. The issue is not to return to the past, but to better know and understand the elements of unity of the Orient and of Europe.[16]

This "pontifical" role of Romania gives it a special role of mediation, which is in a way best incarnated by Eliade himself. This removal of Romania from Europe is reminiscent of a much stronger formulation, found again in a letter, which he wrote in 1936 to another good friend, Emile Cioran, which will be discussed below.[17]

Eliade envisioned himself as a representative of the spiritual essence of Romania that preserves the authentic religion, and as its teacher in the West. Though he never formulated this self-understanding in such an explicit manner, this seems to be the camouflaged message of his short story "A 14-Year-Old Photograph," written in Chicago in 1963, about a Romanian from the Danube who came to Chicago and preserves some form of Christian religion, based on the occurrence of a miraculous healing, which is alien to the essence of the Americans. The special nature of the Romanian spirituality is described by Eliade in an important essay for the point I want to make here, "The Fate of Romanian Culture," in which he describes Romanian popular creations as follows:

> [T]hey revealed a spiritual horizon now almost forgotten by the West (although part of Europe, to which it offered a great deal): *the spiritual horizon that accommodated*[18] *Orpheus and Zalmoxis, and that later on was to nurture the Roman-Byzantine spirit*[19]....This part of Europe, considered entirely lost after the Ottoman domination was established here, preserves spiritual treasures that were once part of the very centre *of European culture*: fromDionysian Thracia and Orphic Greece, Imperial and Christian Rome all meet in this part of Europe to create major values.[20]

As he mentions in a passage that was quoted above in ch. 3, this coexistence of Orpheus and Zalmoxis has something to do with the perception of death as marriage. In fact, he becomes mystagogish when he declares in this context that Europe "needs the Orphic and Zalmoxian dimension to become complete and to be able to generate new syntheses."[21]

Last but not least: In his memoirs Eliade confesses that he returned in 1959 to studies of Romanian folklore and religions, which would become the collection of articles *Zalmoxis*, "without being aware that the periodical return to the research of Romanian spiritual traditions was, in a way, a means to keep my identity in the melting pot of the United States."[22]

Eliade's Romanians as a Chosen People: Messianism and Prophetism

In some passages adduced in ch. 4 above, Eliade criticized the Jerusalemite elites in antiquity for their allegedly violent imposition of the historical religion of monotheism, messianism, and prophetism, out of intolerance and fanaticism. As mentioned there, this critique was formulated in 1937, a time when his allegiance to the Iron Guard was already more than a year old. However, what is interesting is that earlier, at the end of 1935, Eliade also articulated one of the most interesting visions of the Romanian people. In a piece entitled "A People without a Mission" we read

> Can we create—or nourish—a messianic spirit, which will elevate us in our own eyes, and then in the eyes of our neighbors? A messianic movement cannot start and cannot be justified but by a powerful spiritual effervescence....Romanian messianism cannot proceed but from our conscience as a chosen people, namely a creative people. A creator of forms of civic and statal forms of life—but especially creator of spiritual and cultural values. Emile Cioran said once that the only rescue of Romania consists in that each Romanian should become a megalomaniac. This dictum had a drop of truth. We must create so much and on so many planes—so that each Romanian will have the conscience of a chosen people. We have sufficient proofs that the Romanian people may be such a chosen people, a creating people....Messianism does not start with critiques....Messianism starts—like a revolution—with the creation of new forms of life, with the creation of a new conscience.[23]

The syntagm "chosen people" recurs in another journalistic piece of Eliade's entitled "The Two Romanias,"[24] and elsewhere he connects again the chosen nature of the Romanian people to megalomania,[25] a view that I referred to as "megaloromania." This vision of the Romanians as a chosen nation recurs also in his introduction to the writings of Hașdeu: "*the entire Romanian people is a chosen people.*"[26] To be sure, he does not intend to include in this national unit any of the minorities. Immediately afterward, he speaks again about "Romanian messianism."[27] In the same period he also refers to Nicolae Iorga as a "prophet."[28] Those are expressions of a much wider development in interwar Romania, in which several intellectuals participated, trying to delineate the "national specificity" of the Romanians.[29]

Moreover, in a piece written in 1939 known as *Fragmentarium,* Eliade claims that in Christianity, it is only in Orthodox Christianity that a concept of patriotism, namely an identification with a specific nation, is known, with the notable exception of Joachim da Fiore. There he argues, rather cryptically, that "the justification of Orthodoxy for history cannot be validated but at the level of the concept of the 'chosen people.'"[30] This is quite an obscure statement, but it seems that it can be decoded by the phrase that immediately follows it: "Now is the time for the 'prophets' and the 'philosophers of history' to continue Joachim da Fiore. More exactly, to fructify his teaching, which failed in the West—though it started from our parts, in the East."[31] This claim is related to the Byzantine background of southern Italy, where there were important Orthodox enclaves. However, the claim that it is Christian Orthodoxy that influenced da Fiore's thought is not proven at all, and there is no corroborating evidence I am aware of, except what stems from Eliade's artificial effort to hastily appropriate this thinker for the area of influence he privileged during that period. In my opinion, this means in Eliade's feuilleton that Christian Orthodoxy and patriotism should be combined now, and related to a specific "chosen people," who are the Romanians. In fact, this is not just a call for the future, but a case of *vaticinium ex eventu,* since the Romanian Orthodox Church was involved in politics, especially in the Iron Guard, as, for example, the funeral of Ion Moța and Vasile Marin was officiated by hundreds of Orthodox priests in various Romanian towns.

Indeed, Eliade is not the only one who envisioned the Romanians in terms similar to the self-perception of Jews. The so-called Legion of the Archangel Michael—an early organization that generated the Iron Guard—was, consciously or not, appropriating the image of the archangel Michael, who in Jewish texts was considered to be the angel appointed to the people of Israel, as representing the fighter against the enemies of Christianity, namely Communists and Jews. Moreover, an Iron Guard priest who wrote a history of the Iron Guard describes the Carpathians as Mt. Sinai.[32] Long before the Holocaust, the concept of fighting in order to create a pure Romanian nation and state was connected to some form of substituting Romanians for the Jews as a chosen nation, part of a closed nationalism.

This puristic attitude toward the land and culture of Romania is corroborated by Eliade's contemptuous attitude toward Europe, that is, Western Europe. In his letter to Emile Cioran he wrote:

> My disgust for what belongs to culture and literature is gradually increasing. I fear—and I am glad—that in some years I shall not write one single line concerning these profane issues. I shall contemplate—pure and simple. Or, if I shall write, I shall compose a book—my last book—about the metaphysical "truth," the traditional, the non-European one, the only one I believe in. Everything I have written until now does not express the truth I believe. I did not lie—but I believe I played a game. All I said concerns much more my individual experiences (and they were indeed always authentic), but ultimately they have no importance, no matter how sincerely I would express them. What matters is that Europe is dying.[33] From stupidity, from an unprincipled spirit,[34] from luciferism, from confusion. My disgust for Europe takes forms of high treason. I hope Romania does not belong to this continent that discovered profane sciences, philosophy, and social equality.[35]

This is indubitably the sharpest critique of European culture and some of its most important achievements, unparalleled in its extremity elsewhere in Eliade's writings.[36] However, in a more attenuated manner, he regarded Europe as oblivious to a certain component of its culture that is preserved only in Romanian creations, which he says, in a text whose context has been quoted above, "reveal a spiritual horizon now almost forgotten by the West (except part of Europe, to which it offered a great deal): the spiritual horizon that accommodated Orpheus and Zalmoxis, and later was to nurture the Roman-Byzantine spirit."[37] Later he speaks about the "Thracian-Roman spiritual syntheses" and the "archaic Christianity" that created "major values."[38] This is part of Eliade's tendency to marginalize Central and Western European achievement in favor of what he calls the archaic and the East.

Cosmic Christianity and Romania

However, it seems that Eliade's most interesting contribution to the *imaginaire* of religions is the concept of "cosmic" or "archaic" Christianity.[39] The very phrase contains a tension between the locative aspect—cosmic, and in many cases Romanian—and Christian, which is much less place-oriented. Emphases on the harmony between the cosmos and Romanian religiosity is, to be sure, not Eliade's innovation, as it is found earlier in his contemporaries Vasile Băncilă and the older Lucian Blaga,[40] but it is Eliade who propagated this vision beyond the borders of Romanian culture, as part of the centralization of what conceived of as marginal. From 1931 he kept repeating the importance of such an ancient type of Christianity, found especially in Romania. In a letter to Vittorio Macchioro, he wrote:

> Before everything we are naturally inclined toward a "cosmic Christianity," so to speak. We feel that everything in the world stands under the spell of our Lord, that doves may be Christianized, and the children are our brothers. We have popular songs that are wonderful, dealing with the fraternity between man (Romanian) and hills, woods, animals—and that fraternity does not exist because of our efforts, but because of the charisma of our Lord. It is hard to imagine how great was the role played by this charisma in our popular *Weltanschauung*. We believe that everything is so because that was the way God left it. There is a wonderful Romanian proverb that says: "We are Christians just as the trees are trees and the birds are birds." It is if as you would say that we are Christians *because we are humans*. In Romanian the word for "Christian" is identical with that for "human." A Romanian peasant believes that his single task is to be "righteous" and "good" ("a righteous man," "a good man"), and being so, he is a Christian. For him, Christianity is not a dogma, an external organism of norms and menaces—but the basis of creation, the single sense of this mundane world.[41]

This mission of documenting, describing, and disseminating the importance of cosmic Christianity—basically inferred from a few sources related to Romania and attributed mainly to the Romanian peasants, though sometimes southeastern Europe is mentioned, too—remained a leitmotif in Eliade's thought, though in some cases he mentions that this religion is found also in many other places.[42] So, for example, we read in his note from July 1960 a statement quite reminiscent of what we quoted from his description of his mission while in India: "I think I can count myself among the rare Europeans who have succeeded in revaluing nature, by discovering the dialectics of hierophanies and the structure of the cosmic religiosity.... I arrived at cosmic sacralities by reflecting on the daily experience of Rumanian and Bengali peasants."[43] This emphasis on peasants as the representative of an archaic, authentic, "original"[44] religion is widespread in Eliade's writings. However, this allegedly fundamental type of religiosity, though invoked tens of times, was not documented in a sustained manner, but guessed by an armchair scholar—"by reflecting," as he formulated it—from implications found in three main literary sources: Miorița, Master Manole, and the brief and elusive descriptions of Zalmoxis.[45] The three pieces are totally unrelated to each other except by their shared topic of death; such a limited rapprochement, though important for Eliade's personal concerns, is hardly sufficient to sustain a significant life for centuries. In any case, the limitation of the analyses to those three sources diminishes the much wider spectrum of popular literature widespread among Romanians, some of which were pseudepigraphic—namely, "contaminated" by the Jewish "historical" approach. The contents of collections of Romanian popular literatures compiled by Anton Pann, George Coșbuc, Moses Gaster,[46] Nicolae Cartojan, and Emil Turdeanu—to mention only a few names—show this presence abundantly, and I do not understand why Eliade ignored this simple fact. There is no reason to reduce Romanian folklore to one single attitude to the cosmos when other ones are found,[47] just as it is futile to reduce Jewish views of time to one single type, as seen above. This is one of the reasons I propose to see in Eliade a simplificator of complexities.

Quite telling in this context is the report of a conversation Eliade had toward the end of his life with a famous Orthodox priest, the dissident Gheorghe Calciu Dumitreasa—whom Eliade helped to rescue from Communist Romania—who asked him if his study of oriental religions did not affect his Orthodox beliefs. Eliade, we learn from this priest, "has assured me forcefully that nothing was moved in his soul from his faith, since he built a simple faith, as simple as one of a Romanian peasant, and that this basis within him remained unshaken. He said this thing with simplicity and very convincingly."[48] This episode was related in the context of the protest against the incineration of Eliade's body, a practice that contradicts Christian Orthodoxy. Whether Eliade believed what he said to the priest some months before his death is not a matter that can be resolved. However, I am convinced that the report of the priest is true, and this means that very late in his life, sometime in 1985 or even in 1986, Eliade was ready to articulate in the presence of a priest a view that regards the simple Romanian peasant as the standard for an authentic sort of belief. Such an approach may reflect once again the impact of Nae Ionescu, who was described as making efforts to believe "like a peasant."[49] The peasant became, indeed, the proto-type of the Romanian, especially in the interwar period.[50]

Eliade's formulation of the specifically Romanian spirit is cast in terms of folk-lore: "a deeply Christian spirit, centered on the mystery of self-sacrifice and redeem-ing Death....It is the folk spirit alone that is continuously and inexhaustibly manifest, and that is why we insisted on it so much: it alone may reveal the constant values of Romanian genius."[51] The phrase "constant values of Romanian genius" reflects an entire theory that flourished especially in interwar Romania related to the renewed empha-sis on the Dacian roots of Romanians, or what has been called the revolt of the non-Latin roots, or autochthonous background, related especially to scholars such as Lucian Blaga, Vasile Pârvan, and in a more radical manner, Nicolae Densuşianu, though its earlier sources are related to the writings of Haşdeu.[52] All three wrote before Eliade's journey to India, and their theory of the resistance of the preclassical Roman elements constitutes the blueprint of his understanding of the structure of Yoga, and thus also the affinities between India and Romania. Eliade offered his special version of the continuity in the religious values in the Romanian territories, which is a combination of the Haşdeu-Blaga-Pârvan approach, which is more open to the pre-Christian elements, with Iorga-Ionescu's much more orthodox religious approach. This view found its most illustrious supporter and exponent in Eliade, and it degenerated into so-called *protochronism*, which assumes the priority and the superiority of Romanian creativity in matters of culture and language to other cultural European phenomena.[53] There is a clear connection between what I called Eliade's cultural mega-loromanianism and the later phenomenon of protochronism. Perhaps, from this point of view, Eliade is transferring to Romanianism the Jewish propensity to see more influences of Jewish culture than are historically demonstrable.

Did these "constant values" of the Romanians also constitute the essence of the ideal religion of Eliade himself? According to his introduction to the anthology of Haşdeu's writings, the Dacian space was "a means of ethical and metaphysical valori-fication of existence."[54] Much later, in 1979, in a letter addressed to Matei Călinescu he wrote:

> One day Cioran told me that my "optimism" is the direct result of such a terrible despair, that in comparison to it, his "pessimism" seems to be "water of roses."[55]...But, like all the Romanians that are aware of the destiny of Romania, I too found the model and the

consolation in Miorița: the sole response we can offer to the bad luck (= History) is the answer of the Shepherd. He speaks about the cosmic wedding, [while] we create despite the condemnation to death, and we create with a trust in the future and on a global scale (Hașdeu, Iorga, Blaga, G. Călinescu), as if we were the inheritors of the English Empire.[56]

In general, Eliade assumed that cosmic Christianity still reverberates in the present, thus creating a continuous line of transmission since pre-Christian times.[57] If this is the culture *par excellence* that represents Romania, it is understandable why the cultures of other minorities living and creating in Greater Romanian territories have no place whatsoever in his accounts of the "new Romania." Forgetting about the pitfalls of history that he so deeply deplores in many other instances—an example of sharp incompatibility—he sees in the movements of young Romanians in his lifetime something quite positive:

> The new Romania wants to live under the sign of history, namely of the spiritual destiny. However, the roots of these fundamental orientations are rooted more deeply. They are found in a great thirst for inner "redemption," for a "sense of existence"—and out of great fear of failure and sterility. This thirst and this fear, which meet each other so rarely in the alphabetized Romanian masses—are characteristic of all the classes of young persons since the war. To feel just this—is already a huge step.[58]

Is this surprising turn to history another instance of imitation of what Eliade saw as the achievement of the Jews, namely their innovation of a life in history, negative as it may be in his eyes? Is this an attempt to show that it is now Romania that enters history, as the Jews did in antiquity? In any case, it seems that concepts found in Judaism, Eliade's "significant other," shaped the manner in which Romanianism has been articulated, antithetically.

It seems that Eliade was not content with praising what he conceived to be Romanianism; he also intended to actively spread it. In 1942, after mentioning his "philosophical system"—whose content is not specified—he wrote: "I discovered the formula for the future center of the Romanian mission, which I would like to establish."[59] This is not, to be sure, part of his function as a *presse attaché* in Lisbon, but his philosophy, which he hoped to be able to disseminate. This missionary aspect of Eliade, connected to his own philosophy, is therefore both early and explicit.

Organic Perceptions of Peasant Religion

Let me address some of the points I dealt with in the previous section from a different angle. Despite the discussions about syntheses, and many other discussions on the necessity of syntheses between cultures in Asia and Europe, Eliade embraced quite an organic vision of religion, at least insofar as Orthodox Romanian religion is concerned. In doing so he followed the leads of Bogdan Petriceicu-Haşeu,[60] Alexandru Xenopol,[61] Nicolae Iorga,[62] and Nae Ionescu.[63] In his "Between Culture and Alphabet" Eliade draws a stark dichotomy between the organic culture and the artificial organization related to semiliterates—what he calls *semidocts*—whom he utterly detested. In Romanian this dichotomy was expressed in quite a fascinating alliteration: *organismul (nu organizatia)*,[64] that is, "organism not organization." It is this structural antagonism that differentiates Eliade's approach from that of Ioan P. Culianu,[65] and I would say also from my own approach as discussed in the Introduction. What is characteristic of the organism is its congenital connectiveness: It is not a free combination of components brought together after having already existed separately, an artifact or a synthesis that assembles disparate elements in new manners of conceptual integration. In these feuilletons religion constitutes for Eliade an organic original given, whose evolution is basically conceived of as a negative change. Moreover, he has seen a deep affinity between various religions, and depicted the differences between them as a matter of nuances. So, for example, he confesses that "continuous reading reveals above all the *fundamental unity* of religious phenomena, and at the same time, the inexhaustible newness of their expressions."[66] This is but another formulation of the notion of "organic universalism":

> It was precisely the peasant roots of a good part of our Romanian culture that compelled us to transcend nationalism and cultural provincialism and to aim for "universalism." The common elements of Indian, Balkan, and Mediterranean folk cultures prove to me that it is here that organic universalism exists, that it is the result of a common history (the history of peasant cultures) and not an abstract construct.[67]

Eliade reports this view as if he had already conceived it in 1931. This means that at the age of 24, he formulated the principle that would inform much of his mature thought and writing, before he had done any serious inquiry of his own in either Romanian or Hindu popular culture, not to mention Mediterranean. This is an effort to find an archaic alternative religious structure and a significant population that lived it, by some form of speculation, as part of his discontent with the culture, politics, and religion of the present. Though repeated many times, this intuition has hardly been elaborated in detail. In other words, we may label Eliade's approach basically a rural one, which emerged as part of his encounter with pre-Arian India and with the more general movement of some Romanian intellectuals in the early thirties of the 20th century toward the culture of the village as the quintessence of Romanian culture. This organicity has to do also with the circulation of energy that connects the various parts of the universe, which depends upon human activity. This metabolic vision differs, in my opinion, from Eliade's cosmic understanding of religion. In a way, Eliade plays with the theory of correspondences between levels of existence, discussed in the Introduction, a reverberation of the famous concept of the world as a macro-anthropos, and man as a microcosm.

Let me attempt to offer a certain methodological compromise between organism and organization. Since my assumption is that religion is changing continuously, one may assume that this change follows the law of the growing organism, and changes do not automatically imply the destruction of organicity. On the other hand, organization may start with a more technical bringing together of elements stemming from diverse systems, and thus assume some form of artificial cohesion. With time, the religious imagination may cement the affinities between those diverse elements and create something that is presented as more organic. This elaboration is mainly part of the speculative efforts of elites.

Therefore, the methodological alternatives are not the two extremes of artificial organization versus congenital organicity, but the wide spectrum comprising different compromises, syntheses, and attempts to reduce tensions and create new linkages between disparate conceptual and spiritual modes of thought. Neither the congenital organicity of a system nor the artificiality of the *ars combinatoria*, as Culianu thought, may account for the diversity of the variants found within even one type of religion, or even one of its major phases.[68]

Some Conclusions

To summarize some of the discussions in this chapter and the two preceding ones, Eliade was caught in a comprehensive process: The emergence of Greater Romania as a territory generated a megaloromanianism concerning its privileged role in culture and history, which was formulated by him, and sometimes by some other Romanian authors who inspired him, as diverging from Judaism, and imagined in a strongly Christian-oriented type of thought. These developments were accompanied in the thirties by the surge of a violent spiritual-political movement with a strong anti-Semitic ideology. Eliade, like Ionescu and Noica, was not openly reticent of these violent aspects, which were understood as perhaps negative but nevertheless necessary for the emergence of a new Romania, purified of its Jewish citizens.

Was this right-wing type of violence in interwar Romania perceived by Eliade as some form of belated response to the violent Israelite elites in ancient Jerusalem who allegedly shattered the cosmic religion of the Israelite population? Phenomenologically speaking, I am inclined to say yes. However, historically speaking, Eliade brought together trends that were previously unrelated, such as the revolt of the pre-Latin forms from Lucian Blaga and Vasile Pârvan's school and the *internationale* of peasants, expanding the Romanian return to the village and peasant much further than anyone else did. Also, his elaboration of the specific nature of Judaism, namely of what he called the biblical miracle, as discussed in ch. 4, is an original contribution, though I believe that it vitiated his understanding of the history of religion. By creating an antithetic Judaism, Eliade simplified in an extreme manner neglected archaic elements that survived in various aspects of Judaism, and created an unreliable picture of Romanianism, generating a dramatic account of a confrontation between the two that has no significant correspondence in history.

This exposition corroborates Daniel Dubuisson's thesis, which is much more extreme than mine, about the potentially anti-Semitic nature of Eliade's metaphysics,[69] though I see it as much more an implicit systemic antithetic proclivity, and much less determined by the Iron Guard extremism—though not totally unrelated to it. Eliade was part of a wider common ground of cultural and intellectual developments in Romania in the thirties, such as Vasile Pârvan's theory, Ionescu's early thought, and Lucian Blaga's approaches, for example; the Iron Guard variant was just one of his sources. The concreteness of the new post–WWI Romanian geography as a specific matrix-space was important for that generation of young intellectuals in the form of the myth of Greater Romania, versus the much more abstract nature of history, which Eliade envisioned as an invention of ancient Jews. Those decisive dimensions of his two antithetic models of religion, geography versus history, were conceived of as competing throughout most of history. By promoting the view about the originality and authenticity of a cosmic religion, which can be described, following mainly Jonathan Z. Smith, as locative,[70] Eliade moves its best representative, the Romanian peasant attached to specific places, to the center of the study of religion. The other model proposed by Smith, the utopian, namely a vision that disregards place, is a more time-oriented one.

Notes

1. See *Portugal Journal,* I, p. 102, and Alexandrescu, *From Portugal,* pp. 172–173.
2. See Sebastian, *Journal,* pp. 236, 294.
3. *Portugal Journal,* I, p. 154. On the "peasant" penchant of the Iron Guard, see, e.g., Veiga, *The History of the Iron Guard,* pp. 172–177.
4. This lecture in Romanian was printed in Oişteanu, *Religion, Politics and Myth,* pp. 191–196, 210–211. This point and the different attitudes to my thesis have been discussed by Dan Petrescu on the one hand and Sorin Alexandrescu on the other, and are published at ibid., pp. 203–207, 212–213. In an introductory study to some of Eliade's short stories Alexandrescu described Eliade as a personality that is "specifically Romanian." See *With the Gipsies and Other Tales* (Bucharest, 1969).

5. For the summary of this lecture, see Alexandru Matei, *Observator Cultural*, 310 (March 2006).

6. In Oişteanu, *Religion, Politics and Myth*, pp. 194–195. See also below, Final Remarks.

7. Adduced by Handoca in his introduction to "Capricorn," p. 196. See also the distinction between universal and cosmopolitan that Eliade draws in the context of his admirable eulogy of Moses Gaster. Cf. the passage translated by Rickets, *Romanian Roots*, II, p. 1127.

8. Handoca, *The Life of Mircea Eliade*, p. 150, which appropriately calls the belief in the exceptional fate of Romania one of the "obsessive ideas" in Eliade's journalism.

9. *Portugal Journal*, I, pp. 215–216.

10. *Journal*, October 12, 1946, and see also his preface to *No Souvenirs*, p. xi.

11. Printed in Bădiliţă, ed., *Eliadiana*, pp. 116–121. Especially interesting is what Ierunca wrote on p. 119 about Eliade's use of Romanian language as a sort of exit from history.

12. See his *In cunoştiinţă de cauză* (Cluj, 1990), pp. 103–104.

13. *Autobiography*, I, p. 204, adduced below.

14. See also Eliade's *The Fate of Romanian Culture*, pp. 11–21. In my opinion, Eliade minimizes the Turkish influence on Romanian culture, visible especially in folklore, as the widespread popularity of the stories of the Sufi figure Nastratin Hogea—namely, Nasr a-Din Hogea—shows. It was this figure that became be the Till Oilenspiegel of Romanian folklore.

15. Emphasis in the original.

16. *Correspondence*, II, p. 413. See also Allen, *Myth and Religion*, pp. 301–302.

17. *Correspondence*, I, p. 151, discussed below.

18. The English translation is not so accurate. It should read: "that spiritual horizon in which Orpheus and Zalmoxis moved."

19. Eliade was influenced by Nicolae Iorga's vision of Romania as a Byzantium after Byzantium.

20. P. 43. Emphases in the original.

21. Ibid., p. 43. On Eliade's early acquaintance with the mystery religions, see his *No Souvenirs*, pp. 212–213. There he assumes that the keys to the mysteries were lost and Europeans elaborated freely on their meanings since the Middle Ages.

22. *Memoirs*, p. 186.

23. *Romanian Prophetism*, II, pp. 136–137. See also Ricketts, *Romanian Roots*, II, pp. 912–915.

24. *Romanian Prophetism*, II, pp. 266–267.

25. Ibid., pp. 20–21. See also Eliade, *Hasdeu*, p. xxxvii, where he mentions megalomania and the Romanian people, and ibid., p. xliv, where he mentions the mission of Romania.

26. Ibid., p. xxxviii. Emphasis in the original.

27. Ibid., p. xxxix.

28. See *Romanian Prophetism*, II, pp. 105, 107.

29. See, e.g., the analysis of Sorin Antohi, "Argumentum biologicum, Despre 'stadiul cel mai înalt şi ultim' al specificului naţional," the preface to Marius Turda, *Eugenism şi antropologie rasială în România, 1874–1944* (Bucharest, 2008), pp. 5–12. For the ascent of nationalism in the interwar period in the Balkans, see now the important monograph Balázs Trencsényi, *The Politics of "National Character": A Study in Interwar East European Thought* (London–New York, 2011).

30. Printed in *Master Manole*, p. 197. In another feuilleton from this collection he describes, though implicitly, the Romanians as an "originary rase" that has protohistory and prehistory, in comparison to the historical traditions of Europe. See *The Way to the Center*, p. 100.

31. *Master Manole*, p. 197. The issue of the chosen people in Judaism is addressed in another passage in *Fragmentarium*. This vision of the failed West is part of the propensity to marginalize

what was perceived as center and centralize what was perceived as margin. Compare also Eliade's distinction between West and East in Christianity in *No Souvenirs*, p. 203.

32. Palaghiță, *The History of the Legionnaire Movement*, p. 77.

33. The Romanian verb is a colloquial one: *crapa*. This view is ultimately echoing views of Nietzsche and Spengler, and is in the line of Nae Ionescu.

34. *Lichelism*. This noun is used also by Cioran, in a letter to Petru Comarnescu, a common friend of Cioran and Eliade. See Petreu, *Cioran*, p. 19.

35. Letter from Eliade to Cioran, written in 1935, printed in Eliade, *Correspondence*, I, p. 151. See also Ionesco's insightful diagnosis regarding Eliade's anti-French feelings, formulated in his letter to Vianu in 1944, translated by Dana, *Métamorphoses*, p. 162, as well as another important passage adduced in ibid., p. 246. For Ionesco's somewhat similar view, see his *Present Past*, p. 53. This anti-Western attitude is reminiscent of that of the Iron Guard. See the view of Moța, quoted in Palaghiță, *The History of the Legionnaire Movement*, p. 76, as well as of the movement Sămănătorismul. See Ornea, *Sămănătorismul*, pp. 175–177, 285–288, 299–302.

36. Compare to *Portugal Journal*, I, p. 187: "I would like to die deriding the imbecility of the white race." See also ibid., p. 205.

37. *The Fate of Romanian Culture*, p. 43.

38. Ibid.

39. See Allen, *Myth and Religion*, pp. 112–118.

40. Vulcănescu, *Mitologie Română*, p. 250.

41. *Correspondence*, I, p. 175, in a letter from 1931 to Vittorio Macchioro. Emphasis in the original. On this passage, see Țurcanu, "Southeastern Europe," pp. 243–244; Handoca, "Was Eliade a Believer?"; and Ricketts, "Politics, Etcetera," pp. 291–292.

42. See, e.g., *Autobiography*, I, pp. 202–203; *Aspects du mythe*, pp. 207–211.

43. *No Souvenirs*, p. 101. Compare also to *Aspects du mythe*, pp. 208–209.

44. Ibid., p. 209.

45. For a critique of Eliade's interpretations of all the three elements, see Dana, *Métamorphoses*, pp. 109–110, 116, 158–159.

46. See, especially, his *Romanian Popular Literature*.

47. See, e.g., Vulcănescu, *Mitologie Română*, pp. 250–253, which juxtaposes Eliade's view on cosmic Christianity with Culianu's view dealing with acosmism, influenced by Gnostic/Bogomil ideas. Compare also to Oișteanu, *Religion, Politics and Myth*, pp. 160–162.

48. Gheorghe Calciu, "Mormântul furat," in *Origini*, 9–10 (septembrie–octombrie 2003), p. 34, adduced by Handoca, "Was Eliade a Believer?" n. 17.

49. *Portugal Journal*, I, p. 292.

50. See also ibid., I, p. 102, Kernbach, *The Mythic Universe of the Romanians*, p. 351, and Gligor, *The Troublous Years*, p. 116.

51. *The Fate of Romanian Culture*, p. 41. For the use of the term "genius" in a similar context, see above, the quote from the letter to Noica, *Correspondence*, II, p. 413.

52. This development has been studied in detail, inter alia, in Dana, *Zalmoxis*, especially pp. 304–311, and Florin Țurcanu, "Occident, Orient și fascinația originilor la Vasile Pârvan și Mircea Eliade," *Studia Politica*, 2 (2002), pp. 761–767, and in another larger version in "Entre occident et orient, Vasile Pârvan, Mircea Eliade et la fascination de la proto-histoire dans la Roumanie de l-entre-deux-guerres," *Studia Universitatis Babes-Bolyai, Philosophia*, LI (2006), pp. 41–52.

53. See, e.g., Boia, *History and Myth*, pp. 78–79, 102–104, 110–111; Țurcanu, *Intellectuels*, pp. 296–298; Dana, *Métamorphoses*, pp. 225–236.

54. Introduction, p. lxxvii. On ethics, see more in Final Remarks.

55. Cioran was known for his extreme despair since the Romanian period.

56. *Correspondence*, III, p. 435.

57. *Aspects du mythe*, p. 211. On continuity, see Kernbach, *The Mythic Universe of the Romanians*, pp. 347–350.

58. "Redemption, History, Politics," *Vremea* (26 aprilie 1936), reprinted in *Romanian Prophetism*, II, p. 155.

59. *Portugal Journal*, I, p. 116. See my view as published in Oişteanu, *Religion, Politics and Myth*, p. 192, and see the reservation of Sorin Alexandrescu, ibid., p. 205. See also the view of Matei Călinescu, "O carte despre Cioran, Eliade, Ionesco," *Revista*, 22 (20 mai 2002), who claims that Romania played quite a modest role in Eliade's later career.

60. See Eliade, *Hasdeu*, pp. xlix, lii–liii, lxx.

61. See Norman Simms, "Romantic Collective Identity: Romanian Myth or Historical Reality," in *Identitate, Alteritate în spaţiul cultural român*, ed. Alexandru Zub (Iaşi, 1996), p. 386.

62. See Damian Hurezeanu, *Viziune organică la Nicolae Iorga* (Bucharest, 1997), and the review by Zigu Ornea, "Organic şi organicism la N. Iorga," *România literară* (22–28 octombrie 1997), p. 9. See Ornea's seminal *Sămănătorismul*.

63. Dancă, *Definitio Sacri*, p. 60.

64. *Master Manole*, p. 201.

65. See below, Final Remarks.

66. *A History of Religious Ideas*, I, p. xv, emphasis in the original.

67. *Autobiography*, p. 204.

68. See more in Final Remarks. For a distinction between organic accounts of cosmology versus constructivist, see Smith, *To Take Place*, p. 22.

69. See his *Mythologies*.

70. *Map Is Not Territory*, pp. 100–103.

FINAL REMARKS

Eliade's Shift in Scholarship

What happened in this field of the study of religion with the emergence of Eliade's scholarship in European languages was no less than a paradigm shift, from a field dominated by a monotheistic propensity, coupled by a Hegelian vision, to one that takes much more into consideration Hindu thought and primitive or archaic religion, filtered as they were by Hindu concepts such as *Brahman, atman,* and *maya,* and by Orthodox Christianity. Confronting the developmental understandings of humanity and religion, both the general one in the form taken by Hegel and Hegelians and the one in the scholarship of religion as found in James Frazer's opus, Eliade was more concerned with turning his gaze to the past and to origins rather than to the future or the end. Eliade did so in order to retrieve some allegedly repressed forms of religion, which were presented as resisting the addition of later layers. This is the case with his paying attention to the pre-Arian culture in India that impacted the Yoga techniques, the premonotheistic religion among the Israelites, and the Romanian pre-Latin and pre-Christian Dacian religion, which were integrated in what he called cosmic Christianity. These examples seem to me quite important since they constitute a pattern that tries to illustrate the vitality of neglected cultures among which Eliade finds a common denominator, and that common denominator serves as raw material for building up his archaic pre-Socratic metaphysics, and his claim of its subsistence in a variety of forms much later. His project may be defined as an attempt to provoke a European cultural anamnesis of its archaic sources, and an encounter between it and Oriental types of thought.[1] In other words, Eliade attempted to bring to the attention of modern scholarship, as shaped in Western Europe, some other dimensions, and he believed himself to be the best candidate to expose them. This proposal, sometimes called New Humanism,[2] is a matter of the reconstruction of the forgotten, marginalized, or suppressed material, its presentation to a global audience, and the hope for a shift in the modern religious orientation as the result of an encounter with other religious cultures. This means that Eliade tried to operate as a scholar and as a religious reformer at the same time, and in the latter hypostasis he was trying to return to the pristine origin, just as some medieval Christian figures tried to retrieve the original, or authentic, ancient Christianity.

Important as it was that Eliade was open to other forms of religion as equally important, or even more important, in the general economy of religion, he has nevertheless a clear propensity toward the archaic, which works with a certain rather clear axiology. Eliade believed that the role of the scholar of religion is also to facilitate the possibility of an encounter between the hegemonic European-monotheistic understanding of religion, with the archaic as he conceived it, and Eastern religions—no doubt a very laudable purpose—but this new mission reflects also the intellectual biography of Eliade, especially the Hindu concept of maya, as much as the Judeo-Christian background that colored much of the study of religion in the generation prior to Eliade's. While the monotheistic understandings of religion represented an allegedly advanced stage, yoked with the assumption of a progressive-Hegelian structure, Eliade worked with the very opposite vector: The good times are not anticipated in the future, but have already flowered in the distant past, and true religion is to be sought in the understanding of the role of the cyclical return to primordial times, *in illo tempore.* Instead of the monotheistic vision based on a stark distinction between proper worship and true exclusive faith and false ones, on the revelation of the totally different entity in some privileged places, times, and individuals, Eliade adopted a much more Hindu-oriented view in order to emphasize ambiguity, coincidences of opposites, and the veiled existence of God even in the banality of quotidian life. One sort of privileged theological *imaginaire*—the Western monotheistic one as represented by Rudolph Otto's Christian stand, for example[3]—has been substituted by another one, a combination of Eastern, Hindu theology revolving around maya as camouflage, imagined as intervening in the affairs of this world, including Eliade's career, with a certain Christian vision of Incarnation, presented as a comprehensive vision of religion in Eliade's theory of the sacred. In this context, the vision of the sacred and of religion in general as sociological, from Emile Durkheim and his school (which is, in my opinion, some form of Jewish societal approach), which preceded the two others mentioned previously, should also be recalled. In each of the three cases of major theoreticians of the sacred of the 20th century, there was a biographical starting point that is quite evident, and it gradually becomes a general theory of the nature of the sacred, and it has been at least implicitly extended to more universal proportions.

However, it cannot be said that the two other great theoreticians were not acquainted with Hinduism. This is certainly the case with Rudolph Otto, an accomplished Sanskritist, and also with Emile Durkheim, at least according to the view of Ivan Strenski, who pointed out the impact of the illustrious Indologist Sylvain Levi on Durkheim.[4] However, neither of these scholars invested as much energy as Eliade did in an experiential encounter with Hindu mystical techniques, and the impact of Hinduism on their own visions of the sacred, if it exists at all, is much more veiled than in Eliade's thought.

His comprehensive vision of religion is indubitably a daring and ambitious project. He dealt with more religions than any other scholar before him, but each of those religions is understood as being a closed system, with unchangeable structures, whose basic views can be dealt with *en bloc* as similar or different from each other. This means that religious phenomena that developed over huge periods of time, for millennia, are regarded as basically homogenous from the conceptual point of view. Terms such as "Hindu," "Hebrew," "Judeo-Christian," "Semites," "Arabs," "Romans," and "Oriental" represent in Eliade's writings entire conceptual structures, conceived of as being stable. As seen above, the approaches to time in Judaism, for example, changes from one major phase to another, and a proper understanding requires more refined analyses, such as distinguishing between a variety of views found in biblical, Rabbinic, and Kabbalistic forms of Judaism. There is no plausible reason to impose one single vision of this topic on a huge and diverse literature. This emphasis on the necessity of dwelling upon specific phenomena is quite a modest requirement for understanding that is to be emphasized, especially in the case of a generalist scholar who is not concerned with divergences, tensions, and various developments in a certain religion. Eliade should have more adequately distinguished between different approaches found within each of the above forms of Judaism. After all, the transition that he described, from the popular, archaic religion to the historical one, may not be the last of the substantial shifts that occurred in Judaism. Why should someone distinguish so sharply between Western and Eastern Christianity, as Eliade does, but not between medieval forms of Judaism and ancient ones? The vision of a homogenous West is hardly understandable, and it results from Eliade's strong one-dimensional reading of the Judeo-Christian tradition. In a way, Eliade was an

"Orientalist" and an "Occidentalist" at the same time, as he reduced the wide variety of views found in religions that developed over millennia, both in Western culture and elsewhere, to simple schemes. Although he rhetorically fought against the reductive approaches of Marxism, historicism, or Freudianism, he himself reduced much more, by a simpleminded dichotomy: myth/history or cyclical/linear times, camouflaged sacred/personal theologies. When a scholar excludes in such a complete manner some forms of reductions without attempting at the same time to learn something from them, he or she is likely to offer just another drastic reduction. From this point of view, Eliade's method is not better than Edward Said's approach to what he called Orientalism, which reduces the much more complex attitudes found in the West to a single one, an approach I propose to call Occidentalism. In a way, though an Occidentalist, Eliade was nevertheless also a Hegelian thinker, since he attributes to some historical developments—such as the allegedly Jewish discovery of meaning in history and the exclusive adoption of the linear time, or the Christian Incarnation, or even the impact of Hegel—too great a role in large-scale groups of religious phenomena. In my opinion, those dramatic shifts added new theories to older ones, which continued to have their impact later on, and created complex structures.

Eliade's attempt to operate with a simple assumption, that the stasis of the primordial, strongly locative, should be preferred to the developments introduced by other understandings of religion, ignores the obvious. Changes, for good and for bad, are inevitable. I do not embrace any form of evolutionary assumption regarding progress, nor an apotheosis of the archaic. Nevertheless, Eliade's lamenting tone regarding the deterioration of religion because of changes introduced by one elite or another is, from the scholarly point of view, quite deplorable. Artificiality and organicity are not, by definition, good or bad. Neither are "original religions" or organic ones superior. Those epithets depend on the vantage point of the scholar and his/her predilections, and Eliade obviously had very strong predilections in matters of religion. In my opinion, anything artificial may become, because of routine, part and parcel of a certain way of life after it assumes the aura of canonicity, and organistic forms of religion can become the starting point of chauvinistic and antiliberal approaches, and Eliade's own approach to politics in the second part of the thirties is just one example of this danger *de facto*.

He offered an ahistorical reading of what he considered to be Romania, related to a certain preoccupation with a reconciled death that stemmed from a few often obscure references to Zalmoxis, via the two folkloristic pieces, up to the redemptive sacrificial death of the leaders of the Iron Guard. Such an ahistorical reading obliterates differences between sacrifice and victim, between the fate of the individual and the necessity of the "nation," and it culminated in an apotheosis of persons whose attitudes to other human beings were deplorable, to say the least. The role of the reformer, in Romania or on a global scale, means drastic reductions, anachronisms, and distortions that a serious scholar must learn to avoid. The distance between a scholar and a preacher of an old/new religious situation should be maintained in order to provide a reliable academic account, which may be less interesting than rediscovering one pristine type of religion, more vibrant than the dominant Judeo-Christian religion, which is allegedly necessary for the modern man. As Ithamar Gruenwald remarked in connection to Eliade, "it is always easier to speculate on meaning and symbolism than it is to investigate—and then assess."[5] From this point of view, Eliade's early acquaintance with and continuous interest in occultism and traditionalism à la Guénon left its mark on his ambivalent attitude to scholarship, as we shall see in some detail below.

Eliade's Personal Experiences and His Theory of Religion

We have analyzed above a series of themes found in different type of discourses used by Eliade himself and by some of his acquaintances: Ionescu, Sebastian, Ionesco, and Vulcănescu. My emphasis was on the need to survey as many significant occurrences of these themes as possible in order to point to sources or parallels, and to weigh their statistical density, the changes that may be discerned, and the various relationships between the different literary genres. The main focus was neither Eliade's political positions nor his literary achievements, but the emergence of his thought on religion in general, and also on Jewish topics in particular, as manifested through the years.

In some cases in discussions above, I have pointed out the existence of affinities between experiential moments in Eliade's biography and the structure of some of his discussions of privileged topics in his theory of religion.[6] In one case, he admits that "I reached this theory following attentively myself."[7] Moreover, he admits that by closing eyes and thinking on death, he understood the triviality of existence as some form of maya. This passage may explain why death plays such a great role in his writings, since he attempted to confer upon death a sublime meaning.[8] Also, his insistence on the central role of the myth versus history may stem from the centrality of the folklore in what Eliade perceived as representative of the Romanian spirit, and a transformation of a complex of inferiority—the lack of a glorious history—to one of superiority.[9] And his insistence on the centrality of the camouflage has to do with his need to obscure some aspects of his own life in history, as seen in ch. 7. Though all these motifs may have earlier sources, either Hindu or Romanian, the statistical density in his writings may nevertheless betray his specific propensities.

Some other aspects of his personal biography, such as loving two women at the same time, or his orgiastic behavior in Portugal and perhaps also in India, may also contribute to a better understanding of his references to *coincidentia oppositorum*, orgy, and totality.[10] His taking drugs may explain his insistence on the exit from time as a superior form of experience.[11] In other words, the contribution of the *biographica* to the understanding of the *academica* may be quite substantial. It is hard to determine when and to what extent his scholarship reflects his biography, just as it is difficult to determine when his theories on religion inform the manner in which he narrates and interprets events in his own life. This overlapping is not surprising in a worldview that was described in Romanian as *trăirism*, namely, the need to live out authentically something that you would like to understand, an approach that was characteristic of Nae Ionescu's attitude and adopted by some of his followers. Eliade, following him, mixed his experiences with his literature, and both with his scholarship, as seen, for example, in ch. 1.

However, it would be a mistake to reduce his scholarship to projections of his experiences and fears. He would argue that the affinities are part of the very structure of reality, and that he and other religious persons who preceded him had similar experiences, since they encountered the same reality. This means that by inquiring into the testimony of the *homo religiosus*, one understands not specific and different religious structures, but various reactions to a basically similar cosmic and existential situation. Thus a spiritual path and the techniques that it may involve are conducive not only to personal experiences, but also to a certain type of metaphysics. Experience is therefore not only a matter of transformation of the self, but also an elevated way for understanding, and both goals depend on the academic research that intends to recover what he considered to be the forgotten archaic ontology.

Last but not least in this context: Eliade's insistence on the archaic man's return to the origins, paradise, creation—in one word, to the past as a formative religious experience, is reminiscent of his own propensity to do so. In his *Portugal Journal* he confesses: "It is interesting to observe that in 1925–1928 I was struggling vigorously against the sickly attraction to return to the past."[12] Obviously here it was his own past, but this strong predilection to return in time must have an impact on his emphasis on his most famous contribution to the history of religion. Just as the interwar Romanian returned to the Geto-Dacian past, and Eliade to his biographical past, Eliade's archaic man returns, eternally, to the past. Also his emphasis on reversibility of time in the archaic mentality is paralleled by his fear of things that cannot be repeated.[13] Thus, we may conclude at this point that whether or not there was an archaic man as imagined by Eliade is a question that scholars of the Neolithic should decide. Eliade, however, certainly described himself in this vein.

Between Violence and Amorality

Let me examine now another possible major affinity between Eliade's personal life and his theory of religion. Eliade's intellectual career is commonly understood as revolving around an early, stark, and sustained distinction between myth and history, conceived as the background of both the development and the nature of religion. History as destroying myth is indeed a widespread phenomenon, which can be understood as a critical attitude that dissipates belief or as a reflective attitude that differs from and questions the more experiential attitude to life. Descriptions of religion that privileged the mythical abound in Eliade's writings, and brought him a widespread recognition as the prominent scholar described, ironically enough, as a "historian of religion." Though critical of the historical penchant he attributes to the Judeo-Christian tradition and to modernity, Eliade has nothing critical to say about what he called cosmic Christianity, with its strong rural limitation of horizons and its inherent violence, as seen in each of the three main themes—Zalmoxis, Miorița, and Master Manole—where killings are main components. In all three themes, it is not just an attitude to death that is described but also, let me emphasize, a premeditated killing. In a cosmic religion, morality is subordinated to the natural processes, independent of the well-being of the individual person.

Cosmization of religious life, by widening the scope of religion beyond a human encounter of the sacred, created the concept of a natural religion, and Eliade described cosmos as speaking to man not by words but by signs.[14] It is much less an articulated communication than it is an indication, a symbol that should be interpreted by a religious man. A linguistic type of semantics is therefore much less important in this type of religion than in others. The necessary job of keeping nature working is done less by rituals that are semantically oriented, such as prayer, than by strong acts such as sacrifices and orgies. In both cases, an element of violence is obvious.[15] For Eliade, this was not just a matter of the Neolithic man, but also something that was actual. In 1943 he remarked in his *Portugal Journal*:

> The act of creation,[16] the Eros, is capable of untying primordial powers and visions, of a strength that surpasses by far the contemporary mental horizon; cf. the mystique of the archaic orgies, Dionysos, etc.... If there are certain archaic secrets that are accessible to man as such, to the raw man/animal, then those secrets reveal themselves only to the person who embodies the total Eros, the cosmic one, without problems, without neurasthenia.[17]

No doubt, neurasthenia is a malady that haunted Eliade in exactly this period of his life, an illness he attempted to heal by means of participating in orgies. The contemporary mental horizon to be transcended seems to be the Western concern with "profane philosophy" and science, as he wrote in a letter to Cioran, discussed in the preceding chapter. However, earlier in his book on Yoga published in 1936, he spoke about the ideal of the yogin as a reversal of values:

> This "reversal of all human values" that the yogin pursues is, furthermore, validated by a long Indian tradition; for, in the Vedic perspective, the world of the gods is exactly the opposite of ours (the god's right hand corresponds to man's left hand, an object broken here below remains whole in the beyond, etc.). By the refusal that he opposes to profane life, the yogin imitates a transcendent model—Ishvara.[18]

In fact, Eliade creates a strong opposition between the cosmic values as original ontological valences, and the moral values, which are understood as being later, and conceived of as "banal."[19] Or, according to another formulation, there is a dichotomy between two types of powers: the cosmic ones and the personalized one.[20] Indeed, as Eliade underlined several times, archaic religions should not be judged by the criteria of other religions, especially the Judeo-Christian ethics.[21] So, for example, he writes in 1964: "'Spiritual perfection' does not always imply a moral conception acceptable to the Judeo-Christian tradition or to European humanism. This independence of the Spirit with regard to morality does not necessarily mean cruelty, abnormality, or indifference toward one's fellow men."[22] For Eliade, spirituality is thus not necessarily distinct from violence, as we have seen in ch. 6 above. As a scholar I can certainly understand the need to neutralize one's ethical judgment in order to better comprehend a certain type of religiosity, alien as it may be. However, this attitude changes when the scholar starts to preach a certain religiosity as superior to others, and plays the role of a mystagogue. The "primacy of the spiritual," a phrase which Eliade used many times in the thirties, following Jacques Maritain, is a nice misuse of the thought of the famous Catholic theologian. However, the fact that an act of violence does not necessarily mean a cruel actor does not diminish at all the pain it inflicts on other people, including their ritual killing!

The prominence of the sexual elements in the three successful novels by Eliade mentioned above—to which we should add the earlier and more famous novel *Maitreyi*—drew the attention of the "older generation," especially the powerful figure whom Eliade admired to the very end of his life, the extremely prolific historian (and for a time, also the prime minister) Nicolae Iorga. After a deliberation at the Romanian academy concerning the scandalous novels, a trial began against Eliade for literary pornography. As the result of it, he was denied the role of honorific assistant professor at the University of Bucharest, at the chair of Nae Ionescu. This event was widely covered in the press, and the younger generation openly took Eliade's side.[23] Interestingly, this episode is reminiscent of what happened 80 years beforehand when Bogdan P. Hașdeu, one of the giants of Romanian scholarship and a writer whose material was edited by Eliade, as seen in the Introduction, was excluded from the university for the very same reason, namely the promiscuity in his novels. However, the stark, brutal sexual aspects of *The Hooligans* were emphasized in the review by Ionesco, who was very far from the mentality of the old generation.[24]

Those sorts of brutalities are not connected to the Iron Guard's rather ascetic ideology, or to its deadly deeds, and Eliade was for most of 1935 still resisting adherence to this movement. They hardly fit even the often amoral, lax behavior of some of the members of Eliade circle, the Criterion, or even the admirers of Nae Ionescu, whose views are referred to three times in *The Hooligans*.[25] Nae Ionescu himself was certainly not known as a model for an ascetic attitude insofar as his extramarital affairs with various women were involved. Eliade's protagonists, too, are members of the bohemian elite, relatively educated, somewhat younger persons. Since I am unable to find a corresponding type of elite whose behavior was so brutal, I assume that this is the way Eliade imagined the younger elite to be, disillusioned and living senseless lives, brutalizing not only their own lives, as they pondered death and eventually committed suicide, but also those of all the women with whom they were in contact.

Without entering into psychologisms and attempting to find precise correspondences between those protagonists and Eliade's life[26]—after all, those are fictional figures in works of literature—the image that Eliade projected about the meaningless of life is important for understanding his own avatar a few years later—a supporter of the Iron Guard, which supplied to Romanian youth some ideals that were considered worthy of dying for. Social allegories or just fictional inventions the nihilistic protagonists may be, but they became part of Romanian reality in the mid-thirties because of the success of the books, the scandal of the trial of Eliade, and the support he received from intellectual members of his generation for his freedom to teach at the university. An obsession with death, an apotheosis of suicide, and repeated depictions of sexual rape are violent approaches, which are coupled with indifference toward social[27] and political activity, and they predated by only months Eliade's involvement in the political, or what he would call his fall into history. I assume that Eliade himself was well aware of this nature of his novels when he put into the mouth of one of the characters in *The Hooligans*, the novel writer Balaban, the following self-reflection: "His books are desperate, inhuman,[28] [and] fundamentally sad."[29] A feeling of sterility haunts several figures in the two novels.[30] They are perhaps the subjects of the description, "the young generation that has been sacrificed by life."[31] As one of the older and richer protagonists in this novel, a Jew who converted to Christianity, Mr. Baly, summarized it:

The great energies are today found outside order. The young ones who want to advance…run today wherever the force is found. Someone who wants to have a contact of whatever nature with force, with energy, with power—must be against order. I designate this contemporary social phenomenon, the phenomenon of necessary disorder….No one is happy nowadays about the actual order. Until a new order is realized, we should resign ourselves to a long and sad necessary disorder.[32]

In my opinion, none of the figures in the novels represents a legionnaire, though a Communist—Emilian—and a utopian religious revolutionary—Eleazar—seem to point to some forms of alternatives to the actual order. What the long and sad "necessary disorder" is was not specified. But in reading Eliade, one can discern that violation of women and violence are a common theme in some of the novels written in the mid-thirties such as *The Return to Paradise, The Hooligans*, and, to a certain extent, also *Miss Christina*. In addition to the obsessive preoccupation with death, as seen in ch. 3 above, there is another core element that recurs several times in the first two novels: scenes of brutal rapes of women, described sometimes in quite graphic terms and intended to violently humiliate the women[33] (they are described more than once in the *Hooligans*, where the women are described as demonic[34]); this is in addition to descriptions of many other sexual encounters that are depicted in milder terms. This is not a matter of an ungenerous reading of his novels by persons who are conservative in their ethics. Eliade himself remarked on two occasions about the sheer brutality of his descriptions in *The Hooligans*. On May 22, 1945, he noted that he tried to reread the novel, but after one hour he renounced it:

The exasperating and brutal sexuality of this book is turning me ill, pure and simple. Philip Léon wrote me around 1936, that if *The Hooligans* indeed reflects my soul and being, I am a wretched case; sexuality makes me impenetrable for any spiritual transfiguration. I thought, then, that he exaggerates. Nowadays, however, this destiny, this troublous, insatiable carnality is depressing me.[35]

Ten days later, when he returned to reading the novel, he was again negatively surprised: "How much cruelness. There are chapters that make me ill, pure and simple, because of their wildness. The personages are sometimes inhuman….How did I see life then, that I could be so cruel?"[36] It seems that what happened in the period when he wrote the two novels reflects what he admitted was the "heroic amorality" in which he lived between 1929 and 1933.[37]

Such praise for amorality was also expressed a year earlier when he wrote a rather strong feuilleton claiming the superiority of the violence of the hero, who should not be judged by the ordinary criterion of morality. Let me adduce a passage from this early feuilleton, where the hero that surpassed hatred is described as follows:

Those who are obstacles to him, he measures their powers, their reservoirs, their positions—and [then] he annihilates them. There is no morality, no mercy. Those first steps are beyond ethics, they are inhuman....For one who surpassed hatred, the death of those who are an obstacle to him happens in calm and perfect manner....The person who surpassed hatred comes close, he takes control of him,[38] he strangles him or he shatters his skull. He is not guilty. The first steps are inhuman, blind forces. The strong one succeeds. The weak ones—idealists, the mediocre, the sentimental ones—should not stand in his way. No one should resist the person who surpassed hatred. He is always victorious...a hero is never guilty.[39]

Here we have quite an elitist approach,[40] which does not fit other descriptions of the ideal figure as a peasant, or the international of peasants we discussed in ch. 8.[41] Also his interest in folklore, understood as a matter of a group but incomprehensible on the level of the individual, reflects an antinomy.[42] This is a sort of incompatibility between the various trends of thought embraced by Eliade.

In this context let me mention that the implementation of metaphysical concepts, such as living a life that exemplifies *coincidentia oppositorum*, as Eliade claimed he lived, when the feelings of other persons (in this case, two women) may be affected, is problematic.[43] Transcending the ordinary type of human experience, an objective that Eliade personally pursued, means intrinsically also transcending the ethics of the society in which one lives. What happened in the presentation of violence as a proper means of worship is the vision of a specific dimension of a complex picture, namely the need to trigger the vitality of the cosmic cycle by human sacrifices, which is a strong belief in some archaic societies, including in Zalmoxis' cult. The actual fact of the cultic sacrifices of the lives of many persons in a violent manner is never criticized. In fact, amorality is explicitly described by Eliade in connection with the new beginning that is connected to the *illud tempus*. In a seminal passage, he notes a similarity between his own view of regeneration and time and that of Berdiaev: "...to connect it to my observations about the regeneration of man by the abolition of time, by the return to the amoral moment, of 'that time.' What sense may have *incipit vita nova*: the repetition of Creation. The struggle of man against 'history,' of the irreversible past."[44] The abolition of time is also that of the present creation, and the new creation, starting from the very beginning, has other rules than the earlier form of life. The possibility of an obliteration of the old in the name of the new is quite an optimistic message, though one may wonder about the exact contents of the new life, and the price paid for such a renewal. This issue should be discussed since it is too easy to proclaim that the present is just banal, and the repetition of the same act alone is "creative." Why, one may ask, is the historical approach, with all its unexpected developments and challenges, not more creative than the mimetic repetition of the same rituals in order to return to the old myths? Is not the transcendence of the present related to acts of violence?

The cult of violence was not limited to the ordinary Iron Guard members or its two most important leaders, killed in Spain, as seen in chs. 4 and 7. Even Ionescu in 1933 approved of political violence that includes assassinations,[45] and the intellectual Constantin Noica, a good friend of Eliade's, wrote in 1940: "Violence does not relate always to blindness: sometimes it relates to a thirst for purity. The Captain and Moţa struck. Many of the very good ones struck. But they struck because this gesture had a purifying sense for the soul of this nation. And they did not strike except then."[46] This is the diagnosis of the most "philosophical" member of Ionescu's circle of disciples and an extremely prolific writer for the Iron Guard.[47] Like Eliade, with his early cult of a violent hero, Noica, too, attempted to validate violence, at least in some cases, as some form of necessary evil. It is therefore amazing to see that violence is conceived of by Ionescu and his disciples as necessary and even indispensable only in the cases that serve one's ideology or religiosity, and as negative when allegedly used by an elite that does not subscribe to one's axiology, as was the case with the alleged "violent elite in Jerusalem" described in ch. 4. Selectiveness is indeed a major weakness in the manner in which Eliade deals with what he himself assumes are the religious data, or what he called facts. This is one more example of incompatibility. In fact, the recourse to violence was especially applied to Jews and those seen as being their tools, even if they were part of the Romanian leading class.

However, let me emphasize that in this case, Eliade's own behavior changed in the second part of his life, and from diverse testimonies he emerges as a very generous and welcoming personality, though his conceptual approaches changed less. With time, descriptions of violent behavior dissipated even in his literary works, and some of them have been interpreted metaphorically by a scholar.[48]

"Our Unhappy Studies": Quandaries Concerning the Validity of the History of Religion

Reading Eliade's writings, one is impressed by the certainty with which he presents his ideas, and even more so by his repetition of his main concepts when applied in different contexts, without significant qualifications. However, this sharp confidence is only one dimension of his approach. He was sometimes aware of the problem that his emphasis on the rare and elusive moments of hierophany in the understanding of religion creates for an academic discipline. There are several instances in which Eliade expressed explicit contempt toward scholarship in this field. More curiously, in several instances Eliade derides erudition, and he is even prepared to describe it as a vice:

This vice[49] which I satisfy beside a library full of erudite treatises, beside a table fraught with dictionaries and texts—elevates me in my own eyes. It gives me a weird sense of freedom. I say to myself that not everything is lost.[50]...With this "secular" reading I satisfy all the hatred I have for erudition,[51] and for the honest and inutile work, for these cherished sciences—which, just because they are dear to me, I burn with desire to despise them, to "betray" them, to humiliate them.[52]

The attraction to academic work on the one hand, and the feeling that it is "inutile work" on the other hand, is quite a fascinating situation, which returns, *mutatis mutandis*, like a leitmotif during his life. In two later instances he expresses his vision of the discipline as "unseizable" (elusive). When writing to Raffaelle Pettazzoni, the first scholar of religion whose theories Eliade studied seriously in his youth, he confesses: "vous etiez mon premier maître dans cette passionante mais insaisissable 'science' des religions."[53] There is something of an oxymoron here: a science that is in fact "unseizable." More than 20 years later, in a letter addressed to another scholar of religion and a close friend, the Swedish Orientalist Stig Wikander, he wrote: "in fact, I am more and more attracted to literature—and there are days in which I regret that I have abandoned it for some fascinating, though unseizable[54] disciplines."[55] "Disciplines" here take the place of "science," but this does not diminish the oxymoronic nature of the statement. The two characterizations of the study of religion are interesting: "dear," *passionante* and "fascinating" on the one hand, and *insaisissable* as a possible parallel to "inutile," on the other hand, betray Eliade's profound attraction to the study of religion, but at the same time also his understanding that there is something unreachable in the entire endeavor. In one instance at least, Eliade expresses the feeling that a literary or poetic language, more than a scientific one, is a better tool for expressing his spiritual experiences.[56]

Even more interesting is another passage found in a letter written in January 1953, responding to one from the same Wikander, and to his comments, in a rather reserved manner, on some claims about symbolism made by Eliade's *Images and Symbols*: "I am again assaulted by doubts. I believe that we should study more the Time, in order to reach for something more solid than our unhappy studies."[57] Eliade's feeling about the vanity of research of religion may be reflected in a letter by his friend Cioran, where he confesses to his friend Arşavir Acterian in 1986:

When finally you understand the meaning of the word vanity, nothing in this world may touch you. Shadow and dream. Eugène [Ionesco] understands it all. And Mircea [too] but in a bookish manner. History of religion, what an error![58]

This tone is rather new and quite different from the much more confident attitude we can easily discern in Eliade's writings from the thirties. In one of them he first mentions Lucian Blaga's "regal indifference" toward the "specialists," and then writes:

> Though I have several "discoveries" in my mind, I do not have the courage to edit them and publish before I have checked all the information and consulted all that was written about the problem. I lose thereby five-six years for a scientific book which I could write in just six months. The superstition to verify everything, to read everything, to know everything that was done before you—as if this could improve your own ideas in whatever manner....[59] But perhaps this is not a superstition, the terror of the "method" etc. My passion for erudition means, perhaps, the passion of man for nothingness, for the meaningless, ephemeral, minor aspects of life. Other people spoil their time with talks, with insignificant adventures, with sleep—and I spoil it with erudition. This is the same victory of the useless and ephemeral. The same participation in sleep and the mediocrity of the human condition. When the instincts are no more successful than to cause the person to fall asleep, to cause him to become solidary with becoming insignificant—then the abstract, noble passions intervene.[60]

This is an example of a deep ambiguity toward the profession he chose, scholarship, but at the same time also an exaggeration. His claim to read or know everything on a topic he had decided to address was hardly met in a rather great number of cases, and we have dealt with such examples in chs. 2, 4, and 5, above. Later in his life he even referred to a "degradation in erudition."[61, 62]

Another surprising confession from the early thirties runs as follows: "I published so many mediocrities and lies—but I did not publish anything of what I myself think."[63] This ambiguity toward his academic publications may well be connected to his early affiliation to occultist thought, as seen in ch. 5 above. As Culianu asked himself rhetorically:

> It is possible to count Eliade, besides someone like a Guénon or an Evola, as a champion of "traditionalism"? Perhaps yes, but it should be said that that his influence surpassed that of Guénon and Evola since Eliade knew how to preserve the magical etiquette of the university "science," while being, at the same time, much more permeable to the message of the diverse cultural currents of his epoch (the psychoanalysis of Jung, which was criticized by Evola). The fact that he completely assimilated *'the tools of the doomed West'*[64] ensured a larger audience in circles which, though not traditionalist, still felt the "nostalgia of the origins."[65]

An issue that deserves special investigation is the possibility that in a lost letter addressed by Eliade to Julius Evola, he might have implied that he intends to serve as "a Trojan horse" in academy. However, given the fact that this is an implication from a formulation found in Evola's letter written at the end of 1951, which answers Eliade's lost letter, caution is necessary.[66] Surprisingly, Ionesco saw Eliade in quite a similar manner, as he wrote in a letter to Tudor Vianu about Eliade's attempt to introduce into the academy his special evaluation of protohistory as constituting a Trojan horse.[67]

However, the success of disseminating ahistorical myths started to encounter critical eyes, which also interrogated Eliade's much less successful involvement in real history. The more universal approach that he proposed for the study of religion as a whole became just one phase in his developing vision of religion, which included earlier and much more particularistic approaches, as seen in the previous two chapters. Moreover, a resort to philology, which he used so skillfully in his book on Yoga but which he neglected otherwise, facilitates the understanding of his academic enterprise in a much more critical manner by an analysis of the proof-texts of his theories.

Religion in Eliade Versus Culianu: A Comparison

To examine an additional angle for understanding Eliade, let me compare his approach to religion to Ioan P. Culianu's. Culianu was quite an urbane and much more cosmopolitan type of intellectual.[68] In his later writings the entire realm of religion, and apparently also of human creativity, is a matter of different combinations of some given basic elements that return in various forms of interactions, in systems. Culianu's view can be summarized as *ars combinatoria*, and Eliade's by the phrase *coincidentia oppositorum*. For Culianu, evolution does not consist so much in the manner in which an organism develops over time; instead, the different arrangements of the same elements in new forms of interaction create new forms, in religion or otherwise. Concepts such as natural and organic, which played so central a role in Eliade's romanticized vision of the cosmic religion, lost any role in Culianu from his very earliest academic writings. He was concerned much more with differences, their importance and their histories, than with the common denominators that interested Eliade. The questions that concerned him more were: How did the systems emerge out of the basic elements? Were those specific combinations emerging by the dint of the latent possibility that is actualized systemically? Or, were those combinations the result of the pressure of social, political, or spiritual circumstances, independent of any individual or group? Or, are they the result of human choices, which brought some of the elements together and were projected into history? To my best knowledge, Culianu did not address explicitly the three possibilities; the questions related to the specific reasons for the emergence of one combination or another did not attract too much of his attention. The third possibility is less congruent with Culianu's views, since for him the system is much stronger than the individual. In a manner reminiscent of Foucault and Derrida, Culianu gives priority to the system as a more comprehensive force that determines much of human creativity in a variety of fields. On the other hand, Culianu—like Eliade—is less concerned with the social or the economical or political determinism, though he recurrently asserts that the materialization of one combination or another is found always in history. To a great degree, the circumstances are occasions for the embodiment of spiritual developments much more than major factors in their shaping. We remain, by elimination, therefore with the first alternative, namely with the assumption of some immanent force within the basic elements and their interactions. Since these interactions are rather mathematical, that is, taking into consideration, at least ideally, all the possible kinds of combinations, organicity should hardly be considered as an inherent dimension of those combinations. Conceptually speaking, in his much longer life, Eliade developed much less than Culianu did in his 41 years. The latter's adoption of the cognitive sciences represents an effort to integrate the study of religion in a much larger field of human sciences, unlike Eliade's attempt to differentiate his approach to religion from any other methodology.

Eliade's Three Main Sources

Let me attempt to summarize my discussions above from the point of view of how to understand the thought of Eliade. I propose to see in the two most central factors of his life—the Romanian interwar period, which includes the writings of his teachers and contemporaries such as Lucian Blaga, and the much shorter Hindu experience and his acquaintance with these two cultures—the determinant factors in his thought and literature, as well as in his self-awareness. A third major source of inspiration for Eliade's approach to religion is the Italian Renaissance, a topic to which he dedicated his masters thesis in 1928. As seen in ch. 5, in his writings he returns to the paradigmatic nature of the intercultural encounters of Florentine Renaissance and its reverberations in the European occultist various movements, like Paul Vulliaud, René Guénon, and Julius Evola.[69] In fact, Eliade called for "a second Renaissance," or a New Humanism, which should be much more comprehensive than the Italian one, and this approach is fundamental for him.[70] This call for a new, expanded humanism, which would be inclusive of many cultures unknown to the Italian Renaissance thinkers, is definitely reminiscent of the Italian new concept of humanism.[71]

The implication of the emphasis on these three moments as formative for Eliade's worldview is that two other intellectual factors in Eliade's life, his more formal adherence to the Iron Guard at the end of 1935,[72] and his prolonged participation in the Eranos encounters at Ascona from 1950 to 1967,[73] should be seen as less formative from the intellectual point of view. The latter's impact on Eliade's writings can only rarely be established by use of strict historical and philological tools. The first event was indeed early but relatively short, while the second was a long but relatively late in his intellectual development. In both cases, it is difficult to pinpoint precise sources and ideas that interfered with Eliade's earlier views, formulated before his involvement with the extreme right; the issue of the intervention of Iron Guard ideology and Eliade's writings is quite complex, and some of its aspects have been discussed in chs. 3, 7, and 8. However, in the case of the three other sources, the impacts are quite obvious and profound. This does not mean that these two events should be ignored or neglected in scholarship, but only a careful inspection of the possible impact of more concrete literary sources should determine the relevance or the depth of the impact of those events.[74]

To summarize: in my opinion, Eliade was indubitably a member of the Iron Guard and made legionary propaganda in 1937. However, since I see in the Guard not a fascist movement but an Orthodox ultranationalist one, there is no reason to see in Eliade a fascist in a specifically technical sense of this term. The extreme anti-Semitism of the Guard from its beginning, with which I am convinced Eliade was well acquainted, did not, however, play a significant role in Eliade's writings, unfortunate as some of his few Guardist feuilletons written in 1937–1938 indeed are. These feuilletons added much to the nefarious attraction of young intellectuals to the Iron Guard. As a scholar of religion, more decisive than his sporadic anti-Semitic expressions is, in my opinion, a systemic antithetic Judaism, namely a phenomenological vision he forged concerning Judaism as the opposite pole of what he conceived of as being the archaic religion, which he identified with and regarded as consonant with what he called the character of the Romanian people. It is this stark dichotomy, which constitutes the gist of his phenomenology of religion, that I see as based on substantial scholarly misunderstandings. From this perspective, which relegated the Jews, and also the Judeo-Christian tradition, to a status as the "significant other"[75]— to put it mildly—Eliade parallels the Iron Guard views, without necessarily drawing from its ideology, but from sources common to both Eliade and the Guard, such as Iorga and Ionescu, for example. A comparison of his writings about the Jews to those of the two shows that he was much more moderate and, if labeled anti-Semitic, it is an anti-Semitism that differs from that of his predecessors in both tone and substance. These differences do not make him a great humanist, as scholars like to portray him—his attitude to women, to Sebastian, the above-mentioned combination of violence and amorality, all suffice to invalidate such an attitude—nor someone who was able to understand, as a scholar of religion, the nature of the events in which he participated, nor a courageous person ready to reassess later on his earlier evaluations as mistaken, rather than camouflaging them. It turns out that participation in a religious event does not necessarily contribute, as Eliade claimed, following Ionescu, to its proper understanding: Just another case of incoherence.

Last but not least: An issue that cannot be dealt with here is the reception of Eliade's theory especially in the USA, and to a certain extent in Europe. First and foremost, Eliade started his expositions of religion in feuilletons in Romanian periodicals. The tone of these pieces is much more popular, and this helped in disseminating his views after WWII in the West, when he added footnotes and bibliographies to expositions that conceptually were much earlier. He began as and remained mainly a simplificator. Moreover, some of the positive reviews came from people of quite right-wing political positions such as Noica, Guénon, Evola or Wikander. Eliade's arrival in the USA coincided with the mounting fears of the dangers of Communism during the Cold War, and Eliade was a fierce anti-Communist. His huge popularity in the two first decades of post-Ceauşescu Romania, including in the small contemporary circles of the Iron Guard, also had to do with the reactions to the atrocities of the Communists. It seems that the study of religion has dimensions that are hardly purely academic, and they include not only the scholar's biography, but also the political circumstances that framed his scholarly activity.

Notes

1. See, e.g., his own formulations in *Aspects du mythe*, pp. 142–170.
2. See also ch. 5, above.
3. See Moshe Idel, "*Ganz Andere*—On Rudolph Otto and Concepts of Holiness in Jewish Mysticism," *Daat*, 57–59 (2006), pp. v–xliv.
4. See Ivan Strenski, *Durkheim and the Jews of France* (Chicago–London, 1997).
5. See his *Rituals and Ritual Theory in Ancient Israel* (Leiden, 2003), pp. 81–82 n. 48.
6. *Autobiography*, I, p. 256, cited above in the Introduction. See also Olender, *Race sans histoire*, p. 164.
7. *Portugal Journal*, I, p. 151, quoted in its context in ch. 2, above. See also ibid., p. 170, about his drive to totalization and reintegration and finding a new equilibrium, discussed in ch. 2, above.
8. See above, ch. 3.
9. See chs. 4 and 8.
10. See, especially, Eliade, "Mythes de combat et de repos, dyades and polarités," *Eranos Jahrbuch*, XXXVI (1967), pp. 98–100, and in the next section.
11. Oişteanu, *Narcotics in Romanian Culture*, pp. 374–419, 471–473, 480–484.
12. I, p. 121.
13. Ibid., I, p. 138.
14. On Eliade's assumption that words and deeds, unlike thoughts, diminish a person, see his "A Man Who Wanted to be Silent," in *Maddalena*, p. 123.
15. See the important analysis of Eliade's vision of religion and violence in Dubuisson, *Mythologies*, pp. 228–234.
16. In the context, it is procreation.
17. I, pp. 200–201. On the relation between orgy and neurasthenia in Eliade's life in this period, see ibid., pp. 118 (adduced in ch. 2, above), 126, 199, 235 (quoted in ch. 3). The comparison in the

last passage between death, orgy, and war as a dramatic return to primordial unity shows the importance of violence. See also his view of orgies in *The Myth of the Eternal Return*, p. 58.

18. *Yoga*, p. 96.

19. "Dimensions religieues," pp. 272–273.

20. See his "Puissance et sacralité," pp. 39–44.

21. *Religions Australiennes*, p. 171.

22. *No Souvenirs*, p. 212.

23. *Romanian Roots*, II, pp. 779–788.

24. *War with the Entire World*, I, pp. 255–256.

25. See pp. 171, 247, 308.

26. See, however, *Autobiography*, I, p. 301, which claims that the novels reflect his experiences.

27. See Pavel Anicet's declaration that the social is a dream, in *The Return from the Paradise*, p. 175.

28. Compare to Marcella Streinu's description of her rape as "inhuman," twice, in *The Hooligans*, p. 275, and Petru Anicet's desire to become inhuman, ibid., p. 229. See also above, Final Remarks.

29. *The Hooligans*, p. 248.

30. See again, ibid.

31. Ibid., p. 44. Compare also ibid., p. 39: "The majority of people today are humiliated by society, are annihilated by events.... Almost no one is capable to fulfill his destiny."

32. Ibid., pp. 254–255.

33. See the scene of Emilian's brutal rape of the maidservant in *The Return from Paradise*, pp. 163–167, the rape of Vally, ibid., pp. 212–216, and the rapes of Marcella in *The Hooligans*, pp. 256–258, 274–275, 290–291.

34. Ibid., pp. 38, 40, 259–260. Compare especially to the 1936 novel *Miss Christina*.

35. *Portugal Journal*, I, p. 364. See also his intention to delete the sexual scenes in *The Return from Paradise* for the Portuguese translation, cf. ibid., p. 185.

36. *Portugal Journal*, I, p. 366.

37. Ibid., I, p. 321. See also Eliade's description of the two novels as "strident amoralism," which reflects, according to his view, "my recent experiences," not a Gidean attitude, as his critiques claimed. See *Autobiography*, I, p. 301.

38. The opponent.

39. See Eliade, *Askesis and Virility*, p. 75. On amorality of *homo religiosus*, see Dubuisson, *Mythologies*, pp. 232–233, 284.

40. Compare also to the concept of the "chosen person" in his *Portugal Journal*, I, p. 121.

41. Compare Spineto, "Mircea Eliade and Traditionalism," pp. 80–81.

42. See the texts adduced in Ricketts, *Romanian Roots*, I, p. 614.

43. See above, ch. 3.

44. See *Portugal Journal*, I, p. 383.

45. Valeriu Râpeanu, *Nicolae Iorga, Mircea Eliade, Nae Ionescu* (Bucharest, 1993), p. 175.

46. Constantin Noica, "Sufletul cetății," in Niță, *Noica: o filozofie a individualității*, ed. Adrian Niță (București, 2009), p. 149. For the background of this passage, see Laignel-Lavastine, *Noica*, pp. 217–218.

47. See Sorin Lavric, *Noica și mișcarea legionară*, 2nd ed. (Bucharest, 2008).

48. See Cave, *Mircea Eliade's Vision*, pp. 172–173.

49. Of reading *belles lettres*.

50. See also *Şantier*, printed in *Prose*, p. 301.

51. The same hatred toward erudition is found also in *Portugal Journal*, I, p. 293. See also his auto-biographical fragment of 1953, translated and printed in *Imagination and Meaning*, pp. 114–116.

52. *Şantier*, in *Prose* (1931), p. 364. Compare to the way he describes, on the same page of this book, how he treats one of his girlfriends in India, Ruth. See ibid., pp. 364–365, and again, p. 394. On the dilemma created by his confidence that one needs a few months to write something intelligent based on one's ideas, but several years to document it, because of his propensity, which he calls a "superstition," to read "all that has been written about the problem," see his *Journal of Vacation*, p. 98.

53. *See* Spineto, *Eliade-Pettazzoni*, p. 166 (November 1947). It is known that Pettazzoni's more historical approach was different from Eliade's phenomenological one.

54. The French original is, again, *insaisissables*. See *Correspondence*, III, p. 374.

55. *Always the Orient*, p. 216 (January 1969).

56. *Autobiography*, I, p. 190.

57. *Always the Orient*, p. 152.

58. *Cioran, Eliade, Ionesco*, p. 136.

59. Ellipsis in the original.

60. *The Journal of Vacation*, p. 98.

61. On Eliade's negative attitude to erudition, see ibid., p. 188.

62. *Portugal Journal*, I, p. 151. See also ibid., I, p. 229.

63. *Şantier*, in *Prose*, pp. 389–390.

64. The sentence in italics is in English in the original Romanian text.

65. Culianu, *Romanian Studies*, I, p. 244.

66. See Mincu–Scagno, eds., *Mircea Eliade e l'Italia*, p. 253; Petrescu, "Ioan Petru Culianu and Mircea Eliade," p. 453 n.121. The most comprehensive study of Eliade and esotericism is related basically to Eliade's acquaintance with Guènon, and revolves around Eliade's *literaria*. See Tolcea, *Eliade, the Esotericist*. On the more scholarly aspects of Eliade and occultism, see Antoine Faivre, "Modern Western Esoteric Currents in the Works of Mircea Eliade, the Extent and the Limits of their Presence," in Wedemeyer–Doniger, eds., *Hermeneutics, Politics and the History of Religions*, pp. 147–157; Spineto, "Mircea Eliade and Traditionalism," pp. 62–86; Dubuisson, *Mythologies*, pp. 297–303; Laignel-Lavastine, *Cioran, Eliade, Ionesco*, pp. 324–325; and in some instances, Wasserstrom, *Religion after Religion*. On Eliade's desire for another type of university, see ibid., p. 42.

67. Quoted by Dana, *Métamorphoses*, p. 254, and see also ibid., pp. 161, 162, 169–170, 232, 277. See also Timuş, in her introduction to *Always the Orient*, p. 67 n. 1.

68. On this typology, see Idel in Oişteanu, *History, Politics and Myth*, pp. 194–196.

69. See Eliade, *Contributions à la philosophie de la Renaissance*, pp. 9–59; id., *History of Religious Ideas*, III, pp. 251–255; id., *The Sacred & the Profane*, p. 227; id., *The Quest*, pp. 37–39; id., *Ordeal by Labyrinth*, p. 20; id., *Journal*, III, p. 280. See also Culianu, *Mircea Eliade*, pp. 138–140; Ţurcanu, *Mircea Eliade*, pp. 39–42, 112–115; Dudley, *Religion on Trial*, pp. 43–44; Dancă, *Definitio Sacri*, pp. 47–54; Faivre, *Access to Western Esotericism*, p. 44; Dubuisson, *Mythologies*, pp. 275, 279, 294, 297–299, 310 n. 25; and Wasserstrom, *Religion after Religion*, pp. 42–47. It should be mentioned that a strong proclivity to occultism is evident in a quite early piece written at the end of his high school career, "Science and Occultism," reprinted in *How I Found the Philosopher's*

Stone, pp. 246–247, which is discussed in the Introduction and in chs. 2 and 5.

70. See *The Quest*, pp. 55–57. There were, nevertheless, earlier European calls for integration of India into Europe, such as Schopenhauer's. See also above, ch. 5.

71. See ibid., pp. 1–11, Faivre, *Access to Western Esotericism*, p. 108, and Ţurcanu, *Mircea Eliade*, pp. 443–446.

72. This point was made repeatedly by Dubuisson, *Mythologies*, and see also above, ch. 7.

73. See Wasserstrom, *Religion after Religion*.

74. See my *Ascensions on High*, pp. 216–228, and chs. 3 and 7, above.

75. See above, the end of ch. 4.

KEY TO ABBREVIATED
REFERENCES IN THE NOTES

Mircea Eliade's Texts, Interviews, Journals, and Conferences

50 Conferences—*50 de conferințe radiofonice, 1932–1938* (Bucharest, 2001) (R).

Always the Orient—*Intodeauna Orientul, Corespondentă Mircea Eliade*—*Stig Wikander (1948—1977)*, ed. and tr. Mihaela Timuș (Iași, 2005).

Aspects du mythe—*Aspects du mythe* (Paris, 1963).

Autobiography—*Autobiography, Vol. I: 1907–1937*, tr. Mac Linscott Ricketts (San Francisco, 1981).

"*Capricorn*," "*Memoirs of Mircea Eliade*"—"*Capricorn*," "*Memoriile lui Mircea Eliade*," ed. Mircea Handoca, *Revista de istorie și teorie literară*, XXXV, 1–2 (1987), pp. 187–217.

Contributions à la philosophie de la Renaissance—*Contributions à la philosophie de la Renaissance*, tr. Alain Paruit (Paris, 1992).

Correspondence—*Mircea Eliade, Europa, Asia, America, Corespondentă*, ed. Mircea Handoca (Bucharest, 2004) 3 vols. (R).

"*Cosmic Religion*"—"*Cosmic Religion, On the Kabbalah and Its Symbolism* by Gershom Scholem," *Commentary*, 41/3 (March 1966, New York), pp. 95–98.

"*Dimensions Religieuses*"—"*Dimensions Religieuses du renouvellement cosmique*," *Eranos Jahrbuch*, XXVIII (1959), pp. 241–275.

The Fate of Romanian Culture—*The Fate of Romanian Culture, Destinul Culturii Românești*, tr. Bogdan Ștefănescu (Bucharest, 1995).

Forbidden Forest—*Noapte de Sânziene* (Bucharest, 1999) (R).

The Forge and the Crucible—*The Forge and the Crucible, the Origins and Structure of Alchemy* (New York, Evanston, 1981).

Fragments d'un journal—*Fragments d'un journal* (Paris, 1973).

From Primitives to Zen—*From Primitives to Zen: A Thematic Sourcebook of the History of Religion* (New York, Evanston, 1967).

Gaudeamus—Gaudeamus (Bucharest, n.d.) (R).

Hasdeu—Eliade's Introduction to his edition of "Writings of Bogdan Petriceicu-Hașdeu," *Scrieri Literare, Morale și Politice* (Bucharest, 1937), pp. XXXVII–LXXX.

History of Religious Ideas I—*A History of Religious Ideas*, I, tr. Willard R. Trask (Chicago–London, 1978).

History of Religious Ideas, II—*A History of Religious Ideas*, II, tr. W. R. Trask (Chicago–London, 1982).

History of Religious Ideas, III—*A History of Religious Ideas*, III, tr. Alf Hitlebeitel—Diane Apostolos-Cappadona (Chicago–London, 1985).

The Hooligans—Huliganii, ed. Mircea Handoca (Bucharest, 1991) (R).

How I Found the Philosopher's Stone—Cum am găsit piatra filosofal., Scrieri de tinerețe, 1921–1925, ed. Mircea Handoca (Bucharest, 1996).

Images & Symbols—Images & Symbols, Studies in Religious Symbolism, tr. Ph. Mairet (New York, 1969).

In Dionysius's Court—In curte la Dionis (Galați, 1981) (R).

Journal, III—Journal, III, tr. Teresa Lavender Fagan (Chicago–London, 1989).

Journal of Vacation—Jurnal de vacanță, ed. Mircea Handoca (Bucharest, n.d.) (R).

Legionnaire Texts—Textele "Legionare" și despre "Românism," ed. Mircea Handoca (Cluj-Napoca, 2001) (R).

Maddalena—Maddalena, Nuvele (Bucharest, 1996) (R).

Maitreyi—Maitreyi (Bucharest, 1986) (R).

The Master Manole—Meșterul Manole, together with other essays rpt. Petru Ursache–Magda Ursache (Iași, 1992) (R).

Memoirs—Memorii, II, ed. Mircea Handoca (Bucharest, 1991) (R).

"Methodological Remarks on the Study of Religious Symbolism"—"Methodological Remarks on the Study of Religious Symbolism," *The History of Religions, Essays in Methodology*, ed. M. Eliade–J. M. Kitagawa, (Chicago, 1959), pp. 86–107.

The Morphology of Religions—Morfologia religiilor, Prolegomene, ed. Mircea Handoca, *Jurnalul literar* supp., 2nd ed. (1993).

Myth and Reality—Myth and Reality, tr. Willard R. Trask (New York, 1963).

The Myth of Reintegration—Mitul reintegrări, rpt. in *The Way to the Center*, pp. 328–386 (R).

The Myth of the Eternal Return, tr. W. R. Trask, Harper & Row (New York, 1959).

Myths, Dreams and Mysteries—Myths, Dreams and Mysteries: The Encounter between Contemporary Faiths and Archaic Realities, tr. Philip Mairet (New York, 1975).

The New Life—Viata Nouă, ed. Mircea Handoca (Bucharest, 1999) (R).

No Souvenirs—No Souvenirs, Journal, 1957–1969, tr. F. H. Johnson, Jr. (Cambridge, 1977).

Oceanography—Oceanografie (Bucharest, 1991) (R).

Occultism—Occultism, Witchcraft, and Cultural Fashions, Essays in Comparative Religions (Chicago, 1976).

On Eminescu and Hasdeu—Despre Eminescu și Hașdeu, ed. Mircea Handoca (Iași, 1987) (R).

Ordeal by Labyrinth—Ordeal by Labyrinth: Conversations with Claude Henri-Rocquet, tr. Derek Coltman (Chicago–London, 1982).

Patterns in Comparative Religion—Patterns in Comparative Religion, tr. Rosemary Sheed (New York, 1963).

Portugal Journal—Jurnalul Portughez și alte scrieri, ed. Sorin Alexandrescu, tr. Mihai Zamfir, (Bucharest, 2006), 2 vols. (R).

Prose—Proză: India, Biblioteca Maharajahului, Șantier (Bucharest, 2003) (R).

"Puissance et sacralité"—"Puissance et sacralité dans l'histoire des religions," *Eranos Jahrbuch*, XXVI (1952), pp. 11–44.

The Quest—The Quest, History and Meaning in Religion (Chicago–London, 1971).

Religions Australiennes—Religions Australiennes, tr. L. Jospin (Paris, 1972).

The Return from Paradise—Intoarcerea din Rai, ed. Mircea Handoca (Bucuresti, 1992) (R).

Rites and Symbols of Initiation, tr. W. R. Trask, Harper & Row (New York, 1958).

Romanian Prophetism—Profetism românesc (Bucharest, 1990), 2 vols. (R).

The Sacred & the Profane—The Sacred & the Profane: The Nature of Religion (New York, 1959).

Secret Things—Lucrurile de taină, ed. Emil Manu (Galati, 1996) (R).

Shamanism—Shamanism: Archaic Techniques of Ecstasy, tr. W. Trask (Princeton, 1974).

Solilocvii—Solilocvii (Bucharest, 1991) (R).

The Two and the One—The Two and the One, tr. J. M. Cohen (New York–Evanston, 1965).

Two Strange Tales—Two Strange Tales, tr. W. A. Coates (Boston–London, 1986).

Unedited Short Stories—Nuvele inedite, ed. Mircea Handoca (Bucuresti, 1991) (R).

Virility and Askesis—Mircea Eliade, Virilitate şi asceză. Scrieri de tinereţe, 1928, ed. Mircea Handoca (Bucharest, 2008) (R).

Waiting for the Dawn—Waiting for the Dawn: Mircea Eliade in Perspective, ed. David Carrasco–Jane Marie Law (Boulder, 1991).

The Way to the Center—Drumul spre centru, ed. Gabriel Liiceanu–Andrei Pleşu (Bucharest, 1991) (R).

Wedding in Heaven—Nunta în cer (Bucharest, 1986) (R).

Yoga—Yoga: Immortality and Freedom (Princeton, 1958).

Zalmoxis—Zalmoxis, the Vanishing God: Comparative Studies in the Religions and Folklore of Dacia and Eastern Europe, tr. W. R. Trask (Chicago–London, 1972).

Studies

Acterian, *Cioran, Eliade, Ionesco*—Arşavir Acterian, *Cioran, Eliade, Ionesco*, ed. Fabian Anton, (Cluj-Napoca, 2003) (R).

Alexandrescu, *Mircea Eliade from Portugal*—Sorin Alexandrescu, *Mircea Eliade dinspre Portugalia* (Bucharest, 2006) (R).

Alexandrescu, *The Romanian Paradox*—Sorin Alexandrescu, *Paradoxul român* (Bucharest, 1998) (R).

Al-George, *Archaic and Universal*—Sergiu Al-George, *Arhaic şi universal. India în conştiinţa culturală românească* (Bucharest, 1981) (R).

Allen, *Myth and Religion*—Douglas Allen, *Myth and Religion in Mircea Eliade* (New York–London, 1998).

Allen, *Structure and Creativity*—Douglas Allen, *Structure and Creativity in Religion, Hermeneutics in Mircea Eliade's Phenomenology and New Directions* (The Hague, 1978).

Antohi, *Civitas imaginalis*—Sorin Antohi, *Civitas imaginaris, Istorie şi utopie în cultura română*, 2nd ed. (Iaşi, 1999) (R).

Antohi, ed., *Ioan Petru Culianu*—Sorin Antohi, ed., *Ioan Petru Culianu. Omul şi opera* (Iaşi, 2003) (R).

Antohi–Idel, *What Unites Us*—Sorin Antohi în dialog cu Moshe Idel, *Ceea ce ne uneşte* (Iaşi, 2006) (R).

Arcade–Manea–Stamatescu, eds., *Homo Religiosus*—L. M. Arcade–Ion Manea–Elena Stamatescu, eds., *Homo Religiosus: To Honor Mircea Eliade* (Los Angeles, 1990).

Bădiliţă, ed., *Eliadiana*—Cristian Bădiliţă, ed., *Eliadiana* (Iaşi, 1997) (R).

Berger, "Mircea Eliade: Romanian Fascism"—Adriana Berger, "Mircea Eliade: Romanian Fascism and the History of Religion in the United States," in *Tainted Greatness, Antisemitism and Cultural Heroes*, ed. Nancy A. Harrowitz (Philadelphia, 1944), pp. 51–73.

Boia, *History and Myth*—Lucian Boia, *Istorie și mit în conștiința românească* (Bucharest, 1997) (R).

Bordaș, "Nae Ionescu, India and Mircea Eliade"—Liviu Bordaș, "Nae Ionescu, India și Mircea Eliade. Un triunghi metafizic scalen," *Tabor* IV, 6 (Cluj-Napoca, 2010), pp. 48–57 (R).

Bordaș, "Time, History and Soteriology"—Liviu Bordaș, "Time, History and Soteriology, Some Considerations concerning Eliade's Philosophy of History and the Indian Philosophy of Transcendency," in *Professor Mircea Eliade, Reminiscences*, ed. Mihaela Gligor–Marc Linskott Ricketts (Calcutta, 2008), pp. 41–51.

Bordaș, "Between the Devil's Waters"—Liviu Bordaș, "Between the Devil's Waters and the Fall into History, or an Alternate Account of Mircea Eliade's Diopteries," *International Journal of Humanistic Ideology*, IV, 2 (2011), pp. 43–75.

Bordaș, "The Conflict of Generations"—Liviu Bordaș, "Conflictul generațiilor în România inter-belică. Mircea Eliade și tatăl său,"*Revista de istorie și teorie literară*, XLIV, 1–4, (2007), pp. 1–18 (R).

Bordaș, "The Journeys of the Nearsighted Adolescent" II—Liviu Bordaș, "Călătoriile adolescentului miop prin țara brahmanilor și fachirilor (II)," *Viata Românească* (2011) (R).

Bordaș, "Always a Beacon Light in a Nihilistic World"—Liviu Bordaș, "'Always a Beacon Light in a Nihilistic World.' Mircea Eliade and Ioan Petru Culianu—Documentary Contributions," *Studii de istorie a filosofiei românești*, VIII (Bucharest, 2012), pp. 303–360.

Călinescu, *About Culianu and Eliade*—Matei Călinescu, *Despre Ioan P. Culianu și Mircea Eliade: Amintiri, lecturi, reflecții* (Iași, 2002) (R).

Călinescu, "Eliade and Ionesco"—Matei Călinescu, "Eliade and Ionesco in the Post–World War II Years: Questions of Identity in Exile," in *Hermeneutics, Politics and the History of Religions*, ed. Christian Wedemeyer–Wendy Doniger (Oxford–New York, 2010), pp. 103–131.

Călinescu, "Ionesco and *Rhinoceros*"—Matei Călinescu, "Ionesco and *Rhinoceros*: Personal and Political Backgrounds," *East European Politics and Society*, 9, 3 (1995), pp. 393–432.

Cave, *Mircea Eliade's Vision*—David Cave, *Mircea Eliade's Vision for a New Humanism* (New York–Oxford, 1993).

Chimet, ed., *Mihail Sebastian File*—Iordan Chimet, ed., *Dosar Mihail Sebastian* (Bucharest, 2001) (R).

Culianu, *Interrupted Dialogues*—Ion P. Culianu, *Dialoguri întrerupte. Corespondență Mircea Eliade–Ioan Petru Culianu* (Iași, 2004) (R).

Culianu, *Mircea Eliade*—Ioan P. Culianu, *Mircea Eliade*, tr. Florin Chirițescu și Dan Petrescu, postface Sorin Antohi, 2nd ed. (Bucharest, 1998) (R).

Culianu, *Romanian Studies* I—Ioan Petru Culianu, *Studii românești. I: Fantasmele nihilismului, Secretul doctorului Eliade* (Iași, 2006) (R).

Culianu, *The Sin against Spirit*—Ioan P. Culianu, *Păcatul împotriva spiritului* (Iași, 2005) (R).

Dana, *Métamorphoses*—Dan Dana, *Métamorphoses de Mircea Eliade, à partir de Zalmoxis* (Paris, 2012).

Dana, *Zalmoxis*—Dan Dana, *Zalmoxis, de la Herodot la Mircea Eliade, Istorii despre un zeu al pretextului* (Iași, 2008) (R).

Dancă, *Definitio Sacri*—Wilhelm Dancă, *Mircea Eliade, Definitio Sacri* (Iași, 1998) (R).

Dinu, "Sacrifice"—Radu Harald Dinu, "Sacrifice–Death–Salvation. Some Remarks on Mircea Eliade's Early Religious Thought," *Archaeus*, XIV (2010), pp. 57–68.

Doniger, "Time, Sleep, and Death"—Wendy Doniger, "Time, Sleep, and Death in the Life, Fiction, and Academic Writings of Mircea Eliade," in *Mircea Eliade e le religioni asiatiche*, ed. Gherardo Gnoli (Roma, 1989), pp. 1–21.

Dubuisson, *Mythologies*—Daniel Dubuisson, *Mitologii al secolului XX*, tr. Lucian Dinescu, (Iași, 2003). I use the Romanian enlarged version of *Mythologies du XXe siècle (Dumezil, Levi-Strauss, Eliade)* (Lille, 1993).

Dubuisson, "The Poetical and the Rhetorical Structure"—Daniel Dubuisson, "The Poetical and the Rhetorical Structure of the Eliadean Text: A Contribution to Critical Theory and Discourses on Religions," in *Hermeneutics, Politics and the History of Religions*, ed. Christian Wedemeyer–Wendy Doniger (Oxford–New York, 2010), pp. 133–145.

Dudley, *Religion on Trial*—Guilford Dudley III, *Religion on Trial: Mircea Eliade & His Critics*, (Philadelphia, 1977).

Faivre, *Access to Western Esotericism*—Antoine Faivre, *Access to Western Esotericism* (Albany, 1994).

Gaster, *Romanian Popular Literature*—Moses Gaster, *Literatura populară română*, ed. Mircea Angelescu (Bucharest, 1983) (R).

Gheorghiu, *Memoirs*—Virgil Gheorghiu, *Memorii. Martorul Orei 25*, tr. Sanda Mihăescu-Cârsteanu (Bucharest, 1999).

Ginzburg, "Mircea Eliade's Ambivalent Legacy"—Carlo Ginzburg, "Mircea Eliade's Ambivalent Legacy," in *Hermeneutics, Politics and the History of Religions*, ed. Christian Wedemeyer–Wendy Doniger (Oxford–New York, 2010), pp. 307–323.

Girardot–Ricketts, eds., *Imagination and Meaning*—Norman J. Girardot–Mac Linscott Ricketts, eds., *Imagination and Meaning: The Scholarly and Literary Worlds of Mircea Eliade* (New York, 1982).

Gligor–Ricketts, eds., *Encounters with Mircea Eliade*—Mihaela Gligor şi Mac Linscott Ricketts, eds., *Intâlniri cu Mircea Eliade* (Bucharest, 2007) (R).

Gligor, ed., *Mircea Eliade*—Mihaela Gligor, ed., *Mircea Eliade. Between the History of Religion and the Fall into History* (Cluj-Napoca, 2012).

Gligor, *The Troublous Years*—Mihaela Gligor, *Mircea Eliade, Anii Tulburi: 1932–1938* (Bucharest, 2006) (R).

Gligor–Caloianu, eds., *Theodor Lavi*—Mihaela Gligor–Miriam Caloianu, eds., *Theodor Lavi în corespondenţă* (Cluj-Napoca, 2012) (R).

Glodeanu, *The Coordinates of the Imaginary*—Gheorghe Glodeanu, *Coordonate ale imaginarului în opera lui Mircea Eliade* (Cluj-Napoca, 2001) (R).

Grottanelli, "Fruitful Death"—Cristiano Grottanelli, "Fruitful Death: Mircea Eliade and Ernst Jünger on Human Sacrifice, 1937–1945," *Numen*, 52, 1 (2005), pp. 116–145.

Groza, *The Phenomenologization of Time*—Elvira Groza, *Fenomenalizarea timpului în concepţia lui Mircea Eliade* (Cluj, 2006).

Handoca, ed., *Interviews with and about Mircea Eliade*—Mircea Handoca, ed., *Convorbiri cu şi despre Mircea Eliade* (Bucharest, 1998) (R).

Handoca, ed., *Eliade File, II*—Mircea Handoca, ed., "*Dosarul*" *Eliade*, II (Bucharest, 1999).

Handoca, ed., *Eliade File, XIV (1983)*—Mircea Eliade, ed., "*Dosarul*" *Eliade, XIV (1983)* (Bucharest, 2008) (R).

Handoca, *The Life of Mircea Eliade*—Mircea Handoca, *Viaţa lui Mirca Eliade* (Cluj-Napoca, 2002) (R).

Handoca, "Was Eliade a Believer?"—Mircea Handoca, "Fost-a Eliade necredincios?" *Apostrof*, XII, 3 (2011) (250).

Heinen, *The Legion of the Archangel Michael*—Armin Heinen, *Legiunea "Arhanghelul Mihail." Mişcare socială şi organizaţie politică. O contribuţie la problema fascismului internaţional*, tr. Cornelia şi Delia Eşianu, ed.şt., Florin Ioncioaia, (Bucharest, 1999) (R).

Idel, *Absorbing Perfections*—M. Idel, *Absorbing Perfections, Kabbalah and Interpretation* (New Haven, 2002).

Idel, *Ascensions on High*—M. Idel, *Ascensions on High in Jewish Mysticism: Pillars, Lines and Ladders* (Budapest–New York, 2005).

Idel, *Enchanted Chains*—M. Idel, *Enchanted Chains, Techniques and Rituals in Jewish Mysticism* (Los Angeles, 2005).

Idel, *Eros & Kabbalah*—M. Idel, *Eros & Kabbalah* (New Haven, 2005).

Idel, *Hasidism*—M. Idel, *Hasidism: Between Ecstasy and Magic* (Albany, 1995).

Idel, *Messianic Mystics*—M. Idel, *Messianic Mystics* (New Haven, 1998).

Idel, *Old Worlds, New Mirrors*—M. Idel, *Old Worlds, New Mirrors: On Jewish Mysticism and Twentieth-Century Thought* (Philadelphia, 2010).

Idel, "Some Concepts of Time,"—M. Idel, "Some Concepts of Time and History in Kabbalah," in *Jewish History and Jewish Memory, Essays in Honor of Yosef Hayim Yerushalmi,* ed. E. Carlebach–J. M. Efron–D. N. Myers, (Hanover–London, 1998), pp. 153–188.

Ionesco, *Journal en miettes*—Eugène Ionesco, *Journal en miettes* (Paris, 1967).

Ionesco, *NO*—Eugène Ionescu, *NO* (Bucharest, 1991) (R).

Ionesco, *Present Past*—Eugène Ionesco, *Present Past, Past Present, A Personal Memoir,* tr. Helen R. Lane (New York, 1971).

Ionesco, *War with the Entire World*—Eugène Ionesco, *Război cu toată lumea,* eds. Mariana Vartic–Aurel Sasu (Bucharest, 1992), 2 vols. (R).

Ionescu, *Class on Metaphysics*—Nae Ionescu, *Curs de metafizică,* ed. Marin Diaconu (Bucharest, 1995) (R).

Ionescu, *Lectures on the Philosophy of Religion*—Nae Ionescu, *Prelegeri de filosofia religiei,* ed. Marta Petreu (Cluj, 1993) (R).

Ionescu, "Preface"—Nae Ionescu, "Prefață," published together with Mihail Sebastian, *De două mii de ani* (Bucharest, 2000) (R).

Ionescu, *The Rose of the Winds*—Nae Ionescu, *Roza vânturilor,* ed. Mircea Eliade (Bucharest, 1990) (R).

Ionescu, *The Suffering of the White Race*—Nae Ionescu, *Suferința rasei albe,* ed. Dan Ciachir (Iași, 1994) (R).

Iovănel, *The Improbable Jew*—Mihai Iovănel, *Evreul improbabil: Mihail Sebastian: o monografie ideologică* (Bucharest, 2012) (R).

Kernbach, *The Mythic Universe of the Romanians*—Victor Kernbach, *Universul mitic al românilor* (Bucharest, 1994) (R).

Krappe, "The Birth of Eve"—Alexander Haggerty Krappe, "The Birth of Eve," in *Occident and Orient: Being Studies in Semitic Philology and Literature, Jewish history and philosophy and folklore in the widest sense, in honour of Haham Dr. M. Gaster's 80th birthday: Gaster Anniversary Volume,* ed. Bruno Schindler–Arthur Marmorstein (London, 1936), pp. 312–322.

Laignel-Lavastine, *Noica*—Alexandra Laignel-Lavastine, *Filozofie și naționalism, Paradoxul Noica,* tr. Emanoil Marcu (Bucharest, 1998) (R).

Laignel-Lavastine, *L'oubli du fascisme*—Alexandra Laignel-Lavastine, *Cioran, Eliade, Ionesco, L'oubli du fascisme* (Paris, 2002).

Libis, *L'Androgyne*—Jean Libis, *L'Androgyne* (Paris, 1986).

Manea, "Happy Guilt"—Norman Manea, "Happy Guilt: The Scandal of the Romanian Intellectual Mircea Eliade's Past," *New Republic* (August 5, 1991), pp. 27–33.

Manea, "The Incompatibilities"—Norman Manea, "The Incompatibilities: Romania, the Holocaust, and a Rediscovered Writer," *The New Republic* (April 20, 1998), pp. 32–37.

Marino, *The Hermeneutics of Mircea Eliade*—Adrian Marino, *Hermeneutica lui Mircea Eliade* (Cluj-Napoca, 1980) (R).

Mezdrea, ed., *Nae Ionescu and His Disciples*—Dora Mezdrea, ed., *Nae Ionescu și discipolii lui în arhiva Securității*, vol. II, *Mircea Eliade* (Bucharest, 2008) (R).

Mincu–Scagno, eds., *Mircea Eliade e l'Italia*—Marin Mincu–Roberto Scagno, eds., *Mircea Eliade e l'Italia* (Milan, 1987).

Monneyron, *L'Androgyne dans la littérature*—Frédéric Monneyron, *L'Androgyne dans la littérature* (Paris, 1990).

Moța, *Skulls of Wood*—Ion I. Moța, *Cranii de lemn* (Madrid, 1951) (R).

Mutti, *Les plumes de l'archange*—Claudi Mutti, *Les plumes de l'archange, Quatre intellectuelles roumains face à la Garde de Fer: Nae Ionescu, Mircea Eliade, Emil Cioran, Constantin Noice* tr. Philippe Baillet (Chalon-sur-Saône, 1993).

Oișteanu, "Mircea Eliade Between Political Journalism and Scholarly Work"—Andrei Oișteanu, "Mircea Eliade Between Political Journalism and Scholarly Work," *Archaeus*, VIII (2004), pp. 323–340.

Oișteanu, *Inventing the Jew*—Andrei Oisteanu, *Inventing the Jew, Antisemitic Stereotypes in Romanian & Other Central-East European Cultures*, tr. Mirela Adăscăliței (Lincoln–London, 2009).

Oișteanu, *Narcotics in Romanian Culture*—Andrei Oișteanu, *Narcotice în cultura română, Istorie, religie și literatură*, 2nd ed. (Iași, 2011) (R).

Oișteanu, *Religion, Politics and Myth*—Andrei Oișteanu, *Religie, politică și mit. Texte despre Mircea Eliade și Ioan Petru Culianu* (Iași, 2007) (R).

Olender, *Race sans histoire*—Maurice Olender, *Race sans histoire* (Paris, 2009).

Olson, *The Theology and Philosophy of Eliade*—Carl Olson, *The Theology and Philosophy of Eliade: A Search for the Centre* (New York, 1992).

Ornea, *Sămănătorismul*—Zigu Ornea, *Sămănătorismul*, 3rd ed. (Bucharest, 1998).

Ornea, *The Thirties*—Zigu Ornea, *Anii treizeci. Extrema dreaptă românească* (Bucharest, 1996) (R).

Palaghiță, *The History of the Legionnaire Movement*—Ștefan Palaghiță, *Istoria mișcării legionare* (Bucharest, 1993) (R).

Pandrea, *The Iron Guard*—Petre Pandrea, *Garda de fier. Jurnal de filosofie politică. Memorii penitenciare*, ed. Nadia Marcu-Pandrea (Bucharest, 2001) (R).

Petrescu, "Ioan Petru Eliade and Mircea Eliade"—Dan Petrescu, "Ioan Petru Culianu și Mircea Eliade, prin labirintul unei relații dinamice," in *Ioan Petru Culianu*, ed. Sorin Antohi (Iași, 2003) (R), pp. 410–458.

Petreu, *Cioran*—Marta Petreu, *Cioran sau un trecut deocheat* (Iași, 2011) (R).

Petreu, *A Day from My Life*—Marta Petreu, *O zi din viața mea fără durere* (Iași, 2012) (R).

Petreu, *From Junimea to Noica*—Marta Petreu, *De la Junimea la Noica, Studii de cultură românească* (Iași, 2011) (R).

Petreu, *The Devil and His Apprentice*—Marta Petreu, *Diavolul și ucenicul său: Nae Ionescu–Mihail Sebastian* (Iași, 2011) (R).

Petreu, *Ionesco*—Marta Petreu, *Ionescu în țara tatălui* (Iași, 2012) (R).

Petreu, *Parallel Philosophies*—Marta Petreu, *Filosofii paralele* (Cluj-Napoca, 2005) (R).

Râpeanu, *Polemics, Controversies, Eulogies*—Valeriu Râpeanu, *Nicolae Iorga, Mircea Eliade, Nae Ionescu. Polemici, controverse, elogii*, 2nd ed. (Bucharest, 1999) (R).

Rennie, "The Influence of Eastern Orthodox Christian Theology"—Bryan Rennie, "The Influence of Eastern Orthodox Christian Theology," in *Hermeneutics, Politics and the History of Religions*, ed. Christian Wedemeyer–Wendy Doniger (Oxford–New York, 2010), pp. 197–213.

Rennie, *Reconstructing Eliade*—Bryan S. Rennie, *Reconstructing Eliade, Making Sense of Religion* (Albany, 1996).

Reschika, *Mircea Eliade*—Richard Reschika, *Mircea Eliade zur Einfuerung* (Hamburg, 1997).

Ricketts, "Glimpses into Eliade's Religious Beliefs"—Mac Linscott Ricketts, "Glimpses into Eliade's Religious Beliefs as Shown in the *Portuguese Journal*," *Archaeus*, XIV (2010), pp. 27–40.

Ricketts, "Politics, Etcetera"—Mac Linscott Ricketts, "Politics, Etcetera," *Archaeus*, XIV (2010), pp. 265–304.

Ricketts, *The Romanian Roots*—Mac Linscott Ricketts, *Mircea Eliade, The Romanian Roots, 1907–1945* (Boulder, 1988), 2 vols.

Ronnett, *Romanian Nationalism*—Alexander E. Ronnett, *Romanian Nationalism: The Legionary Movement* (Chicago, 1974).

Scholem, *Major Trends*—Gershom Scholem, *Major Trends in Jewish Mysticism* (New York, 1969).

Scholem, *On the Kabbalah*–Gershom Scholem, *On the Kabbalah and Its Symbolism*, tr. R. Manheim (New York, 1969).

Scholem, *Origins of the Kabbalah*—Gershom Scholem, *Origins of the Kabbalah*, tr. A. Arkush, ed. R. J. Zwi Werblowsky (Princeton–Philadelphia, 1989).

Schwarz, ed., *Dialogues avec le sacré*—Fernand Schwarz, ed., *Mircea Eliade: Dialogues avec le sacré* (Paris, 1987).

Sebastian, *The Accident*—Mihail Sebastian, *Accidentul* (Bucharest, 1962) (R).

Sebastian, *For Two Thousand Years*—Mihail Sebastian, *De două mii de ani* (Bucharest, 2000) (R).

Sebastian, *How I Became a Hooligan*—Mihail Sebastian, *Cum am devenit huligan* (Bucharest, 2000) (R).

Sebastian, *Journal*—Mihail Sebastian, *Jurnal, 1935–1944*, ed. Gabriela Omăt, preface and notes Leon Volovici (Bucharest, 1996) (R).

Sebastian, *Journal of an Epoch*—Mihail Sebastian, *Jurnal de epocă*, ed. Cornelia Ştefănescu (Bucharest, 2002) (R).

Sebastian, *Selected Writings*—Mihail Sebastian, *Opere alese*, I (1956) (R).

Sebastian, *Under Times*—Mihail Sebastian, *Sub vremuri* (Bucharest, n.d.) (R).

Şerbu, *Shop Window of Memories*—Ieronim Şerbu, *Vitrina cu amintiri* (Bucharest, 1973) (R).

Simion, *The Knots and Signs of Prose*—Eugen Simion, *Mircea Eliade, Nodurile şi semnele prozei* (Iaşi, 2006) (R).

Smith, *Map is Not Territory*—Jonathan Smith, *Map is Not Territory: Studies in the History of Religion* (Chicago, 1993).

Smith, *To Take Place*—Jonathan Z. Smith, *To Take Place* (Chicago, 1987).

Solomon, *Pages of a Journal*—Petre Solomon, "*Am să povestesc cândva aceste zile*": *Pagini de jurnal, memorii, însemnăi*, ed. Yvonne Hasan (Bucharest, 2006) (R).

Spineto, *Eliade–Pettazzoni*—Natale Spineto, *Mircea Eliade–Raffaele Pettazzoni, l'histoire des religions a-t-elle un sens? Correspondence 1926–1959* (Paris, 1994).

Spineto, *The Historian of Religion*—Natale Spineto, *Mircea Elidae, storico dele religioni, con la corrispondenza inedita Mircea Eliade–Károly Kerényi* (Brescia, 2006).

Spineto, "Mircea Eliade and Traditionalism"—Natale Spineto, "Mircea Eliade and Traditionalism," *Aries*, 1 (2001), pp. 62–86.

Tolcea, *Eliade, the Esotericist*—Marcel Tolcea, *Eliade, Ezotericul*, rev ed. (Bucharest, 2012) (R).

Tolcea, "From Marcel Avramescu to Father Mihail Avramescu"—Marcel Tolcea, "'I did not Come to Do, but I am Destined to Be'—From Marcel Avramescu to Father Mihail Avramescu: Landmarks to a Spiritual Biography," *Trivium*, IV, 2, 11 (2012), pp. 265–281; 3, 12 (2012), pp. 448–501; 4, 13 (2012), pp. 693–704 (R).

Țurcanu, *Intellectuels*—Florin Țurcanu, *Intellectuels, Histoire et Mémoire en Roumanie de l'entre-deux-guerres à la'apres-communisme* (Bucharest, 2007).

Țurcanu, *Mircea Eliade*—Florin Țurcanu, *Mircea Eliade, Le prisonier de l'histoire* (Paris, 2003).

Țurcanu, "Southeast Europe"—Florin Țurcanu, "Southeast Europe and the Idea of the History of Religions in Mircea Eliade," in *Hermeneutics, Politics and the History of Religions*, ed. Christian Wedemeyer–Wendy Doniger (Oxford–New York, 2010), pp. 241–260.

Veiga, *The History of the Iron Guard*—Francisco Veiga, *Istoria Gărzii de Fier 1919–1941. Mistica ultranaționalismului*, tr. Marian Ștefănescu (Bucharest, 1993) (R).

Voicu, *The Myth of Nae Ionescu*—George Voicu, *Mitul Nae Ionescu* (Bucharest, 2000) (R).

Volovici, *Nationalist Ideology*—Leon Volovici, *Nationalist Ideology & Antisemitism: The Case of Romanian Intellectuals in the 1930s*, tr. Charles Kormos (Oxford, 1991).

Volovici, ed. *The Dilemmas of Identity*—Leon Volovici, ed., *Mihail Sebastian, Dilemele identității* (Cluj-Napoca, 2010) (R).

Vulcănescu, *From Nae Ionescu to "Criterion"*—Mircea Vulcănescu, *De la Nae Ionescu la "Criterion,"* ed. Marin Diaconu (Bucharest, 2003) (R).

Vulcănescu, *The Good, Quotidian God*—Mircea Vulcănescu, *Bunul Dumnezeu cotidian. Studii despre religie*, ed. Marin Diaconu (Bucharest, 2004) (R).

Vulcănescu, *Mitologie Română*—Romulus Vulcănescu, *Mitologie Română* (Bucharest, 1987) (R).

Vulcănescu, *Nae Ionescu*—Mircea Vulcănescu, *Nae Ionescu, așa cum l-am cunoscut* (Bucharest, 1992) (R).

Wasserstrom, *Religion after Religion*—Steven M. Wasserstrom, *Religion after Religion: Gershom Scholem, Mircea Eliade and Henry Corbin at Eranos* (Princeton, 1999).

Wasserstrom, "The True Dream of Mankind"—Steven M. Wasserstrom, "'The True Dream of Mankind': Mircea Eliade's Transhumanist Fiction and the History of Religion," in *Building Better Humans: Refocusing the Debate on Transhumanism*, eds. Hava Tirosh-Samuelson–Kenneth L. Mossman (Frankfurt, 2012), pp. 181–203.

Wedemeyer–Doniger, eds., *Hermeneutics, Politics and the History of Religions*—Christian K. Wedemeyer–Wendy Doniger, eds., *Hermeneutics, Politics and the History of Religions: The Contested Legacies of Joachim Wach & Mircea Eliade* (New York, 2010).

Wirszubski, *Pico della Mirandola*—Chaim Wirszubski, *Pico della Mirandola's Encounter with Jewish Mysticism* (Cambridge, 1988).

Wolfson, *Language, Eros, Being*—Elliot R. Wolfson, *Language, Eros, Being: Kabbalistic Hermeneutics and Poetic Imagination* (New York, 2005).

Yates, *Giordano Bruno and the Hermetic Tradition*—Frances A. Yates, *Giordano Bruno and the Hermetic Tradition* (Chicago, 1979).

Yerushalmi, *Zakhor*—Yoseph H. Yerushalmi, *Zakhor, Jewish History & Jewish Memory*, 2nd ed. (New York, 1989).

Zolla, *The Androgyne*—Elemire Zolla, *The Androgyne: Reconciliation of Male and Female* (New York, 1981).

NAME INDEX

SUBJECT INDEX

Studies in Mystical Traditions

Philip Wexler and Jonathan Garb
General Editors

The role of mysticism is dramatically changing in Western society and culture as well as in the relationship between spiritual traditions throughout the world in the era of globalization. After Spirituality: Studies in Mystical Traditions seeks to develop a wide range of perspectives—anthropological, cultural, hermeneutical, historical, psychological, and sociological—on mystical and spiritual centers, figures, movements, textual and artistic products. The series will appeal to broad audiences, ranging from scholars to students to teachers.

For additional information about this series or for the submission of manuscripts, please contact:

Philip Wexler and Jonathan Garb
philipwexler@mscc.huji.ac.il | jgarb@mscc.huji.ac.il

To order other books in this series, please contact our Customer Service Department:

(800) 770-LANG (within the U.S.)
(212) 647-7706 (outside the U.S.)
(212) 647-7707 FAX

Or browse online by series at www.peterlang.com